Over the Horizon

THIS IS THE FIRST BOOK THAT LINKS LONG TERM
STRATEGY WITH PRODUCT AND SERVICE DESIGN.

In spite of it all, we still got it finished – on time!

Over the Horizon

Planning Products Today for Success Tomorrow

Bill Hollins and Gillian Hollins

Direction Consultants, UK

JOHN WILEY & SONS, LTD

Chichester • New York • Weinheim • Brisbane • Singapore • Toronto

Other Wiley Editorial Offices

John Wiley & Sons, Inc., 605 Third Avenue,
New York, NY 10158-0012, USA

WILEY-VCH Verlag GmbH, Pappelallee 3,
D-69469 Weinheim, Germany

Jacaranda Wiley Ltd, 33 Park Road, Milton,
Queensland 4064, Australia

John Wiley & Sons (Asia) Pte Ltd, 2 Clementi Loop #02-01,
Jin Xing Distripark, Singapore 129809

John Wiley & Sons (Canada) Ltd, 22 Worcester Road,
Rexdale, Ontario M9W 1L1, Canada

Library of Congress Cataloging-in-Publication Data

Hollins, Bill.
    Over the horizon / Bill Hollins, Gillian Hollins.
        p.   cm.
    Includes bibliographical references and index.
    ISBN 0-471-98717-4
    1. Product management—Great Britain. 2. New Products—Great
Britain—Marketing. I. Hollins, Gillian. II. Title.
HF5415.15.H595   1999
658.5—dc21   99–20567
                                                                   CIP

British Library Cataloguing in Publication Data

A catalogue record for this book is available from the British Library

ISBN 0-471-98717-4

Typeset in 10½/13pt Plantin by Mayhew Typesetting, Rhayader, Powys
Printed and bound in Great Britain by Biddles Ltd, Guildford and King's Lynn
This book is printed on acid-free paper responsibly manufactured from sustainable forestry, in which at least two trees are planted for each one used for paper production.

Contents

About the Authors

Bill Hollins

I usually lie about my occupation. Not to you but to the mere mortals that I meet at parties. This started many years ago. Whenever I told anyone that I was an engineer I was always expected to either fix their car or explain in detail the workings of every consumer durable that was giving them trouble. If I failed it was assumed that I wasn't a very good engineer. At that time, I was a hydraulics engineer, so for a quiet life I would say I was a plumber. This worked well and I became quite proficient at fixing jammed loo cisterns, but it never seemed to have the charisma of the occupations of my contemporaries who worked in banks or sold insurance. In other words, it didn't impress the women!

I ended that phase of my 'job description' after I was cornered at one party by an enthusiastic plumber who was thrilled to find a fellow traveller. All he wanted to discuss was the intricacies of his trade of which there are many and none of them bear close inspection. I learned a great deal that night but most of all I learned that I should not say that I was a plumber.

At last I became a designer. A job with a bit of street cred, so I thought. The next few years were spent having to discuss the latest colour, every outfit around me and whether flares were on the way back (I hope so, I still have a wardrobe full of them). If I explained that I was an engineering designer all I got was 'why do they design cars that break down and incidentally, did I know how to fix theirs?' I had almost gone full circle and was still getting my hands dirty at parties.

But I have noticed in the past two or three years that people are beginning to understand about products and services. Not you lot who have known for years but the average man on the Clapham omnibus. He (and she) is now becoming clued up on good and bad products. This is affecting their purchase decisions and they are becoming selective and discriminative about what they buy. Now the majority are able to judge and will only buy what is good wherever it comes from.

As for me, I've moved into Design Management. Unfortunately, people have views on both design and management and I usually take umbrage with all of them. I've stopped going to parties, partly my choice but partly that I stopped being invited. Who wants to invite an argumentative old sod who can't tell the truth and won't even fix your car any more?

Gillian Hollins

Just because Bill wants to write a lot of waffle on himself it doesn't mean that I have to. Somebody in this relationship has to have a cool head and a modicum of sensibility. So here is my pen picture.

Having worked for several years in industry, I decided I needed a change of career and moved into academia and subsequently spent some time undertaking research at Henley Management College. I am now Principal of Direction (Consultants).

We have been running our Consultancy since 1985, specialising on how organisations (especially in the service sector) manage the early stages of their new products. My particular interest is in the 'people side' of the Total Design Process.

◆ ◆ ◆

How This Book Came About

We almost called this book 'Haemorrhage'. 'Haemorrhage', a sanguine tale of how bad product management is leaving companies to bleed to death and the only clots are in the board room. We even offered to write it using simple words, in big writing, using eight simple panaceas, which, if followed, would ensure success. Most top management are still ill educated and like these books. Of course, they don't work, life at work isn't that easy but, by the time they find out, we will be doing a Tom Peters-like world lecturing tour, shouting at our audiences.

Unfortunately, the publishers failed to be as enthusiastic as we were. Perhaps they were right. So you have this, which is aimed at quite a different group of readers. To do the enclosed will be a hard slog but will have a greater chance of actually bringing results than our first idea.

Foreword

In this book, the husband and wife team of Bill and Gillian Hollins continue their onslaught on the weak management of design in the manufacturing and service industries in the United Kingdom. Their analysis of the country's industrial situation is depressingly accurate and they pick out some enlightening cameos from their own experiences, which will strike some chords with many of us. However, they do not let a justifiable misery overwhelm them. Rather, they look to what can be done, and what must be done, to make companies strong.

They take a long term approach, as well as making clear what needs to be done now to ensure that long termism is a real option. Their approach to current problems and an immediate start on their solutions is handled well in Chapter 2 which, inter alia, includes advice on the practice of Benchmarking, a much neglected stimulus to improvement of performance.

They look at how new products and services can be built on a company's present position by a process of improvement and by innovation. Then they think the unthinkable and take their reader over the foreseeable horizon to help them accommodate the future so that they can enjoy a profitable part in it.

Bill and Gillian Hollins take a strong line on marketing. They talk of marketing and designing as inseparable. This must be true, since the sole reasons for product design and service design lie in customers' needs and customers' wishes. It was only in the late 1970s that I asked a series of industrialists how they obtained information about their market. A not infrequent response was that listening too closely to your customers could ruin your company: customers would frequently want things that were difficult to make! Similar sentiments are still heard, though in a different form. Those who run industry are frequently quicker to plead for the subsidy of a weaker pound to boost their sales than to look for ways in which they can be profitable by being competitive at world class levels.

Then and now, many managers who should be managing change spend their best efforts looking for ways to resist it. They will benefit from Bill and Gillian's teachings.

Concerned managers and designers will find much in these pages from which they can benefit. Some of the expected is here: concurrency in decision making, Just in Time production, empowerment. Some sacred cows are dismissed, with sound reasons for doing so. Always there is the upbeat message: 'We **can** do it. We **can** compete and we **can** win at world class levels.'

I recommend this book to all who practise or exercise management in our service, design, and manufacturing industries. I also recommend it to those studying to enter those industries and to those teaching and researching in related areas. It could do a lot of good in political circles, too!

Professor Peter Hills,
President, Institution of Engineering Designers

Preface – Your Products and Services more than Ten Years on

What you do **NOW** to manage products and services more than ten years into the future. So when tomorrow comes it doesn't take you by surprise.

There are quite a few books, standards and papers around that tell one what they should do to make their organisation competitive in the short term through new products and services. There are a few strategy books that take this a step further to suggest how to survive into the medium term. There are even books on foresight planning that focus on the possible direction of the future. This book takes a different direction. It focuses on what you should be doing now to be able to plan for the products and services your organisation will be producing in the future. There are almost none that take a serious look at survival through an organisation's products well into the future – say more than ten years. This is what is attempted here.

Currently, companies are being advised to take a ten year horizon (e.g. UK Government Competitiveness white paper (1994), BS 7000 Part 1 resubmission (1995)) but there is almost nothing written that gives prescriptive ways on how to do it.

◆ Is it possible to look even further ahead so that organisations can position themselves now so that they can develop the generation after the generation after the next generation of their products and services?
◆ Can they predict enough of the future to be able to plan their products and services beyond ten years into the future?

> **The purpose of this book is to suggest that not only can it be done – this is how to do it!**

It sounds like an impossible task. Product life cycles are collapsing, companies are forced to operate in global markets, and changes in technology happen so fast that the world of tomorrow will be a radically different one to the one we experience today.

Well, actually, it is possible to predict a lot of what is likely to happen and, even those areas in which it is not, to those can be given sufficient 'shape' so the future does not come with too much of a surprise. Even in those very vague areas organisations can develop so that they can be adaptable and able to respond. It is also possible to build a system within an organisation that can evolve with these changes and cope with the unexpected.

At the end of the 1980s, Bill was asked by the organisers of an exhibition to write, in two hours, a short article for the exhibition catalogue (for which he was remarkably well paid for such little work). This is reproduced below.

MEETING THE CHALLENGE OF THE '90s

At the start of each decade we are promised that the next ten years will bring forth radical changes in our place of work. And why not? After all, change is happening faster than ever before and there is an exponential rise in technology – but only in certain areas. Many things will not change and, as we move into the next century, our lives will still be dominated by the familiar combustion engine and electric motor.

There will be noticeable change brought about by new technology. However, it often takes in excess of five years for a new innovation to become widely available so the seeds of change being sown today will not have real impact until well into the next decade. These innovations will not be made by your obvious competitors, but by organisations operating in quite a different sphere. It's a lesson from the past that will be applicable in the future – take one step sideways when looking for potential competitors . . .

In the '80s we acquired all kinds of gadgets at the forefront of technology, crammed full of features we don't know how to use and don't really need. In the office, we have word-processors, desk top computers, telephones and calculators with functions we don't need but have paid for. In our factories, we have computerised systems such as MRPII and machine tools which are too complicated to alter to be truly flexible. If you don't need a function, or if it is difficult to use, then it is bad design. I believe the next ten years will bring about a decade of 'hidden technology' where design will be focused to make things operate more easily. We will be able to set our machines (and our videos) without having to consult encyclopaedic training manuals – perhaps through bar codes. We will be able to input our computers without so much typing – perhaps through linking in a fax machine. In short, design will make life a little less complicated and technology will make products and processes ergonomically sound.

This will start in the field of mechatronics as designers interface the advances in electronics with other aspects of engineering. Linking CAD and CAM will integrate design and production and, coupled with the widespread adoption of JIT, it will be possible to make variants specifically to order in a true 'pull' system.

Towards the end of the decade, parallel processing and Very Large Scale Integration will give even greater sophistication in machine control and greater power from desk top computers, making possible the first effective, but basic, voice recognition and control. It will be the next century before the first bio computers will lead the way in design to a truly artificial intelligence expert system, not programmed to select the best of existing concepts but able to generate true new concepts.

The 'leaner, fitter' industry promised in the '80s enters the next decade emaciated, crippled by high interest rates that restrict investment in the capital equipment vital if we are to take up the challenge of 1992. Over the next ten years, British companies will lose ground in the automotive, machine tool, tele-communication and most electronic market sectors. Good designers will continue to be scarce, but they will be better used, through management appreciation that design is a Total Process incorporating the market, product quality and makeability. The sooner we can meet the challenge of the '90s the better.

Well, wrong about bar codes and videos but they are easier to set thanks to 'Video Plus (R)'. And 'speech recognition', that converts speech into text, was reported in 'Strategy' in February 1997. Surprisingly, JIT hasn't advanced as much as anticipated but we still believe that its time has come, to give innovative advances in customer service. We were asked to write another view of the future around the same time, and this is reproduced at the start of Time Frame Four.

Many years ago, Peter Drucker said that the main aim of an organisation is survival. There needs to be profits now but not at the expense of the organisation's survival. What companies do need is direction. But how can they make sufficient profit now to satisfy their shareholders and still be able to continue to compete in an increasingly competitive world? Trade barriers are coming down and consumers now have the choice of the best in the world. The best on offer should be your organisation's products or services now. They should also be the best in the future. Many of the management decisions which see you into the future should also be being made now.

Companies are bombarded with an increasing number of management 'techniques' that are promised to improve the effectiveness of organisations and many of these have been widely implemented. But what effect do these proposals have on the capabilities of our organisations? Are we now 'leaner and fitter' and ready for growth or are our organisations, as said earlier, 'weak and emaciated' and unable to cope with a changing world? It could be suggested that, in the long term, organisations will suffer as a result of these short-term management ideologies. So, this book will avoid the 'fashionable' gimmicks that might bring short term gains, but gain that is unsustainable. Khalil Barsoum, General Manager of IBM UK, supported this viewpoint when he said, at a lunchtime meeting of senior managers at the opening of Manufacturing Week, that the recent waves of downsizing, outsourcing and trendy efficiency ideas from Japan should now be replaced by new products and markets, (Comment, *Eureka*, August 1990). Unfortunately, we believe that short termism has a long term future.

Another important dimension is to realise that there is no Tayloristic 'one best way'. As a result, do not expect a simple set of panaceas that, if applied, guarantee success. Panaceas don't work because life isn't that simple. And things aren't that predictable, if it were, we would all be rich. So there will not be a few simple rules to follow. Instead, there are guidelines which can be pretty precise at the start, but these become more vague the further we project into the future. Beyond ten years, it is more a case of 'fuzzy logic' which shows the general direction that should be taken by top management. If you are, at least, going in the right direction it is easier to change course slightly as circumstances change or the situation becomes clearer rather than if you are flailing about in all directions.

This book also avoids the 'total case study approach' in which successful companies are identified and their reasons for success described. Unfortunately, taking a snap-shot of particular organisations in a particular market environment in a particular time frame and with particular personnel, as well as a specific set of circumstances, often doesn't help (or hold true) when one tries to apply these techniques nearer home. Descriptions and examples will be given and there will be many short case studies drawn from our experiences and some anecdotes, but only to clarify the various range of actions being proposed.

And one final point. This book will not eliminate all product and service failures. It will, though, eliminate many of them. The aim is to give the future a form and thus allow an organisation to avoid the products and services which do not match up to this future.

◆ ◆ ◆

Acknowledgement

Thanks to Jane Minardi for the cartoons in this book.

Introduction

At the start of the next century we live in a cut throat world. Finance is scarce, borrowing expensive and competition fierce. Organisations must develop products and services that customers want, that can be made and supplied, at a price people are prepared to pay and that return a profit for the company. Without fulfilling all these criteria the product can be deemed to be a failure. The solution is clear, do things that people want or don't bother starting. To achieve this aim is obviously far from easy.

Certainly, it is necessary for organisations to be able to move, seamlessly, into the future. This must be done through a constant supply of well designed competitive products. For the actual design of these products the work on design models and processes must continue. To make sure organisations are moving forward in a logical manner there needs to be work on the strategic link with design. There must also be a further dimension that links in with these. There must be a view of the future so that the strategic plan has a target at which it can be aimed: an 'estimation' of what your products and services are to be like more than ten years ahead.

Take a look at the top twelve companies in the United States in 1900 (*Strategy*. April 1996):

American Cotton Oil Company
American Steel Company
American Sugar Refining Company
Continental Tobacco Company
Federal Steel Corporation
General Electric Company
National Lead Corporation
Pacific Mail Company
Peoples Gas Company
Tennessee Coal and Iron Company

United States Leather Company
United States Rubber Company

Only one of these companies has been able to adapt and survive. People still want the products of the General Electric Company, the rest are nowhere. Some shrank and were taken over by the newer larger conglomerates, others just declined as they were unable to adapt to the latest demands in a changing world. It is necessary to change and be prepared for change if one's company is to survive today. Another feature of the above list is that ten of the top twelve were natural resources companies, which linked them to one or a few sites. Nowadays the world's largest companies are not linked to one site. They are global and can move throughout the world.

Research carried out by Shell and reported in *Strategy* (Arie de Geus 1997) reveals 'that the average life span of all firms is around twelve years, while that of identified "large" firms is only fifty'. That is why in this book we have considered it necessary to describe how to survive into the future as well as thrive in that future.

It is possible to survive long term. In Sweden Stora is still thriving 700 years after its formation (McMaster 1996), but in a very different form to when it was founded. They have moved through copper mining, forestry, hydro-electricity, then paper making and chemicals. This required really long term planning They have future plans described for the next fifty years. Some Japanese companies have plans for the next one hundred years and even in the UK McLaren Cars Ltd. have a plan for their future that spans fifty years – so proposing some rules for planning products for a period of ten to fifteen years is not too outlandish.

Henry Ford said 'it is not the employer who pays the wages, he only handles the money, it is the product that pays the wages'. One of the keys is to look at your product and service offerings. Only by focusing on what actually brings in the money can one define a set of parameters which is right for your organisation. The way one manages the development of products and services is quite similar and where they are different these differences will be highlighted. This book will work for you if you operate in manufacturing, services, or, as most companies do, between the two. The best that top management can aim for is to make the environment right for radical change to blossom and then to provide the tools so they know how to make these radical changes.

The research that went into this book has been going on, in earnest, for about three years. It followed the author's involvement with The British Standards Institution in the development of all of their 'Design Management' standards. After the design management standards that covered the manufacturing, service and construction sectors had been published it was decided to produce a standard that would look at the longer term.

'Captains of industry' were invited to state how they would develop products for the long term future and it was found that few had any idea on how to even approach this problem. So far, top managers who have been consulted propose that this new standard should include activities such as market research, benchmarking, and even business process re-engineering. Whilst important, these are things for products being developed now, not for the products of ten years into the future. Progress is now being made in the development of this new standard, following some primary research into some innovative organisations.

On the other hand, feedback shows that there was clearly a need for such a text to offer guidance. So, over this period it was decided to do our own research and develop this book. This goes a lot further than the thirty pages of the proposed British Standard, though it is recommend that you read both.

The Service Sector

Services are products, these special types of products need to be designed, this process must be managed. Nowadays, in industrialised countries, most people are employed in the service sector. The following information was researched by Fahmia Huda (1997).

Figures have shown that whilst the manufacturing base in most countries is shrinking, the service industries are expanding (percentage of GNP in the UK is 63.1%) and now employ 75.5% of the work force (Lewes and Entwistle 1990). More recently (Vaugon 1996) figures have shown that the GDP income from manufacturing was 21.8% in 1995 compared to 66.1% in the services industries. Church (1996) quoted that 'in spring 1995, 25% of employed men worked in the manufacturing industries compared with only 12% of employed women' and Labour Market Trends (CSO 1996) has reinforced this with figures which show that, in September 1995, there were 2.6 million males in full time manufacturing but 5.9 million full time males in the service industries. When figures for all the working population in September 1995 are taken into consideration, then 3.9 million against 16.1 million (a ratio of 1:4) in the service sector represents the significance of the growth.

Figures from other sources, which compared employment in service industries against manufacturing across the European Union, also showed the same trends, with 58% being quoted for the UK. The highest levels of service employment were in Holland (72%) whilst the lowest recorded was in Greece (54%) (Farish 1996).

In the USA, the service sector also contributes over two thirds of the GNP and employs three quarters of the workforce (Mersha and Adlakha 1992). Haynes and DuVall (1992) have figures of '70% of GNP and 85% employment in the service sector and growing,' but more recent figures claim that they account for '72% of GNP and 76% of employment for the USA' (anon. editorial, *Journal of Services Marketing* 1995). Between 55% to 75% of the total workforce is employed across the service sector in industrialised Western economies (Mattsson 1994) whilst world-wide, services account for 58% of the total world-wide GNP (Cronin and Taylor 1992).

This makes improvement to the effectiveness of organisations in the service sector to be of increasing importance. There is even a large service content in manufacturing organisations that has been estimated at up to 25% of those employed in these companies.

The importance of the development of service products is only just being appreciated in the service sector. Many service companies do not even realise that they are involved in design when they consider new service products. They do not have the ethos that industry has so it must be remembered that those in the service sector, in many cases, being unfamiliar with the whole concept of developing new services in a structured manner, need extra and specific guidance. Engineers may know what product development is even though many of them do it badly. Many of those involved in the management of services haven't got that far. Managers and others leading the process have an even more important role in the service sector. They need to take the role of educating as well as co-ordinating the process in many companies.

Also, in the service sector it is often very difficult to identify those at which the work should be aimed. To explain this take the analogy of TQM. To delight the customer one first needs to know who the customer is. Who is the customer for primary school education? The pupil, the parent, school governors, tax payers, local authority, or central government? Or in an X-ray department in a hospital, is the customer the patient, the local GP, other wards in the hospital, the tax payer, or the hospital trust? Until the customer is clearly understood one cannot begin to identify what they want.

The same good practices that apply in the development of manufactured products apply, by and large, to services. Furthermore, good leadership and training are even more important in this sector for services to benefit from the experience that has been developed over the past thirty years in engineering.

For a definition of a service we have taken the definition from the British and International standards BS EN 9000, but added the extra Note 4 from BS 7000 part 3. This definition, given below, is shown in the standard.

Results generated by activities at the interface between the supplier and the customer and by supplier internal activities, to meet customer needs.

NOTE 1.   The supplier or the customer may be represented at the interface by personnel or equipment.

NOTE 2.   Customer activities at the interface with the supplier may be essential to the service delivery.

NOTE 3.   Service is intangible and as such cannot be stored.

NOTE 4.   Delivery or use of tangible product may form part of the service delivery.

NOTE 5.   A service may be linked with the manufacture and supply of tangible product.

Planning and implementing new services is, in most cases, no different from planning and manufacturing products. The reason why customers buy particular services is not that much different from why they buy products and the reasons for products and services failing are the same.

How to Use this Book

From experience, the natural reaction to being confronted with a set of tools and techniques is that 'they may work everywhere else but we are different and they won't work for us'. Usually, after some explanation and consideration, those people agree that their situation is not as exclusive as first thought and that their problems are quite common elsewhere. The solution to these problems also can be common. Read these pages with an open mind and try to read across to your own business or industry sector.

It can be assumed that what we say here can be used in both the manufacturing sector and all the differing service sectors. There are differences and these will be highlighted where they occur. This book will work right across the service sector, for financial institutions such as finance, banks and insurance, transport, public facilities, the health service, tourism, retailing or the not-for-profit sector. Even the smallest organisations operating to service just a local market should be able to benefit if they are planning on introducing a new service.

This book is also aimed at small organisations as well as the large. Small companies have already been identified as having better communication than large and being more amenable to change. With less of a 'stagnant' infrastructure to shift, probably, small companies are in a better position to benefit from what we have put in these pages.

Tomorrow's basic requirements are today's delight features, (Deming 1986), therefore, continuous improvement through new offerings to customers should be a basic strategy of all businesses. This isn't a case of people working harder but of working smarter.

Essentially, organisations must look at the strategic side of product development and also survive the present whilst preparing for the future. For example, Process Models are vital for the present, and fine for, say, three year 'slices' of time, but do not work for planning further into the future. No matter how much iteration is built in, they will be too inflexible and too short term. What is needed is a more systems approach, with built-in flexibility to cope with the unexpected.

The approach that we have taken is to 'slice' the managerial prospective up into four sections called 'Time Frames'. Although these four parts look at certain time frames that make up the future, they are not to be undertaken in sequence, but in parallel. It is necessary to consider and confront the longer term future long before one gets there so that the organisation sets itself going in the right direction. Focus for the future is needed now and the organisation needs to survive now so they can progress efficiently into the future. In effect, the longer term product strategic thinking for any new product range will eventually become the product tactics as the Time Frame reduces. As time passes any particular product or service area will 'move' forward in the sequence – in effect, as one moves forward, into the future. Then there will be a new future and the user will plan different types of products and services being investigated in Time Frame four.

The length of each Time Frame will vary depending on the type of product or service. Also, depending on the Product Status (see Time Frame four), it may be better to move straight into the third Time Frame where it is necessary to consider new concepts.

In the first three Time Frames there will be some of the content with which you are familiar but in Time Frame four these are developed further into new areas to improve the long term prospects through your product offerings.

The First Time Frame looks at what is being undertaken now and how it can be made more effective. Also discussed is what an organisation must do now to prepare for a 'safe passage' into the future. This first Time Frame describes how to improve your competitiveness with your current products and services without damaging your organisation's prospects for the future. After all, it is these that will finance the future.

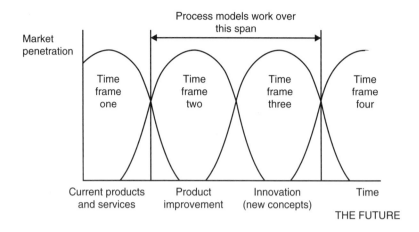

Figure I.1 The four Time Frames that make up this book

The Second Time Frame is about the development of your organisation's next generation of products or services and focuses more on efficient improvement to these products and services. This second Time Frame shows how to choose the new products and services to develop over the next few years. These products will need to be developed now and will complement or replace your current products.

The Third Time Frame is where improvement is no longer sufficient and new concepts, creativity and innovation are required. Of course, in some cases innovation will be required in your next product, so use this section in that situation. This third Time Frame looks at the management of new products and services over the medium term, say, five to ten years. Companies often find these to be the difficult ones, but they need not be.

The Fourth Time Frame looks at what people in an organisation need to do to ensure survival more than 'ten' years ahead. Ten years is chosen as a typical figure. Some industries move more quickly than others and may reach this time spectrum earlier, some later, but all will have to confront it sooner or later if they are to survive. This is the new area for research into product management. Most senior management thinking is locked into how to cope with the immediate competition, what customers want now and whatever current crisis is confronting them.

Each Time Frame is divided into 'Organisational Issues' which tend to relate to the broader issues within a company and 'Tools and Techniques' which propose a series of activities which will improve the development of new and existing products and services.

In each part of the book there is advice interspersed with a series of sectioned off 'case-studies'/anecdotes. In spite of many of these appearing to be somewhat 'tongue in cheek', these are (almost all) true and mainly relate to our experiences in consultancy. The aim of these are to clarify the points being made as well as to, hopefully, amuse.

This book has been written for top managers who are looking at the strategic side of their organisation's products and services and those who have to implement these plans. It will also be useful to those on post-graduate management courses.

Time Frame One

Survival in the Present

1

The Organisation

What to do now to Remain Competitive in the Future

The starting point? 'Where we are is no accident – it is part of the continuum of the past, present and future' (Brown 1996).

It is not suggested that you should be at the forefront of technology and technological change, though it is nice if you can command such a position. Only a few organisations can do that. The majority don't have the expertise to be in that league. Don't worry, there is a great deal of profit to be made by being a follower. Remember, pioneers get the arrows, settlers get the land. There are even greater rich pickings that can be made from being associated with all the products and services that themselves can be associated with, or used with, these advances in technology. You can be well positioned to take advantage of these only if you are in the right place at the right time to benefit from the many niche products and markets that spring up whenever the new breakthroughs appear. For example, increasingly there is a market for home delivery of food from restaurants. If there was a low cost, effective 'box' in which this food could be delivered to the door – and this became the industry standard – there would be a fortune for the company that developed and produced it. There is always a bigger potential profit for the company that actually makes such products, but this also is accompanied by greater risk.

The fashion is to sell rather than make, the richer countries have products made abroad in low wage economies then import back. It sounds like a great idea: no set up costs, no risk, switch on and off supply when required, so no problems with demand variation. It is a great idea until one realises that such companies may be considered as 'empty organisations'. It doesn't take too long before the manufacturers realise that they actually have all the expertise to develop and make the product and that all they need to develop is a marketing arm. Suddenly your badge disappears from the product and their badge is substituted. Many products cannot be easily protected by patents and if yours is one such product beware of giving it away. Never outsource your core skills.

Organisational Issues

What many companies are currently doing

Companies' current myopic management. Many companies in the west are plagued by short term thinking and this is reflected in their short term decision making. To appease shareholders companies like to take on new product developments that give a fast return. Certainly, the companies benefit for the short term but this is at the expense of long term growth and, perhaps, survival.

Companies must learn to think beyond short term profits for company survival and sustained growth in the future. In the UK, the City doesn't like attempts by companies to change. Porter (in Spottiswoode 1996) has argued that diversification usually destroys shareholder value. City investors worldwide must accept a slight reduction on their fast return of investment in order to finance the future, otherwise the companies in which they currently invest will slide further behind their world competitors. Of course, this is far from easy to achieve. Rarely has an investor any interest in the organisation in which they invest beyond the basic one of making as much money as fast as possible in the shortest period of time with very little risk. This flies in the face of being able to take the long term view that is best for the organisation. There has to be a balance between the short term product improvement and the longer term radically new product or service.

Arie de Geus (1997) has argued that in order to survive organisations need to be managed for survival rather than profit. This means financial conservatism but also core values with which their staff identify and this will include tolerance of diversity being one of the keys. Lack of this tolerance makes companies efficient in the short term and in a stable condition but may be ineffective in the long term. The type of mentality and operational characteristics which are useful in a receiver's tool kit to drag a company out of the mire do not keep a healthy company remaining healthy.

As Michael Johnston (1997) has written 'In businesses managed for survival there is a great deal of openness to experiment and the sort of diversity that allows it to act as a complex, adaptive mechanism in a constantly changing environment' whereas 'in businesses managed for profit . . . it is people . . . who are sacrificed to preserve capital assets.'

It is still necessary to appease the shareholders and, therefore, short-termism is going to be with us indefinitely into the future. But companies cannot rely on continuing small design improvements to their existing products. What organisations must learn to do is to speculate on innovation for a proportion of their resources. In Time Frame Four we suggest, that, for many, 0.5% of turnover will be sufficient.

The short term products will provide the capital for these long term, more risky, innovations and the dividend for their shareholders. 3M, perhaps, has the solution, which could be followed by most organisations. 15% of their investment in new products is made on highly speculative ideas and from these comes their exciting new products, which could include Post-It notes. What is often forgotten is that this means that 85% of their investment in new products is made on the less exciting 'cosmetic' improvements and these pay for the far more risky and speculative long term ventures.

A sure fire cure for much short-termism would be to make it illegal for directors' share options to be cashed in within ten years. This would force some long-term planning if they are to make money from these share options, to the good of the company and country. Not much hope of this we fear. Such a proposal will certainly reduce short term profits, but in relative terms it is quite a small price to pay for the survival of the organisation.

> **IT IS NECESSARY TO ACCEPT LOWER PROFITS NOW TO BE ABLE TO INVEST IN SUBSTANTIAL GROWTH IN THE FUTURE.**

City investors must learn to be leeches rather than vampires. They must learn to accept a slight reduction on their fast return of investment in order to finance future products or the companies in which they currently invest will slide further behind their world competitors. Lower profit now for sustained growth in the future.

Take, as a comparison, the Biotechnology industry in Japan. Quite a few years ago the Japanese steel industry proposed that they plan to move into Biotechnology. At that time they had neither the knowledge or even the manpower trained to do it. They stated that there would be no return on investment for twenty-five years and yet they were able to borrow the money to invest in this area. Compare this with the financial problems currently experienced by the financiers of the Channel Tunnel. Around 1987, Bill was questioning a party closely involved in the Channel Tunnel and queried the anticipated low cost of the project, then proposed at

£4.6 billion. In answer to 'they will never do it for that' they said 'we all know that, but if we really tell them how much it is going to cost, nobody will buy any shares!'

IEE President, Dr John Parnaby (1996) has stated that the UK's future success through initiatives such as the Technology Foresight exercise will remain difficult as long as companies are forced to mortgage their long-term prospects in pursuit of short-term profits.

> *Short termism can create a superficial impression of success through the milking of business but ultimately leads to failure. It forces some chief executives to behave in a lemming-like fashion as they rush to cut training, innovation and product development budgets in order to prop up the half year return on sales and return on investment results and prevent the risk of youthful City analysts marking down their share price. The result is the strangulation at birth of any hope of product leadership or market penetration.*

Organisations, especially in the west, tend to design for profitable niches rather than large market share. The reverse is true in Japan. Again, this is a profit driven decision. Take as an example the British motor cycle industry, although the same could be said of many such industries in many parts of the world. The companies in this industry had all the market in the UK and in many others. They then came under pressure in one segment. The Japanese started exporting small bikes to this country. This made life difficult for the British manufacturers, which meant that they had to work a bit harder to compete and perhaps be unprofitable in the short term or take the easy way out and abandon that segment of the market. And why not? The other segments were so much easier and so much more profitable.

The indigenous industry then came under pressure in slightly larger engine bikes. The easy way out of this problem was the same as before, that is to drop out of the market segment which is under pressure and concentrate on profitable market niches. They did this and again became profitable in the smaller market and everybody (including shareholders) were happy.

As the threat from the competition grew, often due to lack of invest-ment in new products, one by one the profitable segments become less profitable and are subsequently dropped from the companies portfolio. Suddenly the British motorcycle industry was small but very profitable, selling big engine bikes to the enthusiast. But, though relatively profitable, they had lost their overall market. The unit profits were high on each bike sold but there were not enough of these sales to support investment in new machines that could compete with the onslaught from abroad.

Furthermore, operating in such a small niche, they had lost economies of scale in manufacture, purchasing, and worse of all, in sales and distribution, so selling costs became much too high as a proportion of total costs. Their apparent short term profitability had turned into inevitable failure. The eventual result of these management policies is that the company was left with no chance of survival.

So, British motorbikes went from the entire market to the market for larger bikes to the market for super-bikes to the market for the enthusiast to market failure. This may seem an obvious example but the same has occurred in the British television, hi-fi, radio, car, machine tool and quite a few other industries.

The problem in this example is that Western industry tends to aim for the unit profit on items sold. The Japanese and companies in South East Asia tend to operate on **marginal productivity**. They consider the additional cost of producing one additional item. In manufacturing or in selling hamburgers, this would be the additional cost to produce one more, with all the overheads being carried by other products in the range. Essentially, this can mean just the materials and actual cost of production. This is a great way to attack export markets if one has a healthy home market which can support this doctrine for a short period. This often leads to accusations of 'dumping' in these foreign markets, when it is, in fact, not the case. It is also a good way to introduce new products and to get them accepted quickly in the market.

Of course, selling a product in this way undermines the home based competition and allows you to get a foothold in their markets. Having damaged or even destroyed the competition your organisation can then start to increase prices. This is sometimes known as **penetration marketing** and usually can only be undertaken by a large organisation that can offset the high start-up costs of a new product or service by spreading them over products which are more established and are already profitable. This is the opposite of the more usual approach called **skimming**. Skimming is where a high price is charged when a new product is introduced. This is more normal for the following reasons:

1   A great deal has usually been spent on developing the product and it is necessary to get this money (often borrowed) back as quickly as possible.

2   There are often high promotion costs at the introduction of a new product or service and the high cost of this needs to be recouped in the higher prices charged.

3   At the start of a new product or service introduction the company is at the start of the learning curve. They may be operating quite

inefficiently and unit costs are quite high. This is a case of 'practice makes perfect'. After a period of time and practice the time taken and costs incurred tend to fall. This 'learning curve' was first measured in the assembly of bombers in America in the 1940s.

4   Often at the start of any new product the item is 'knife and forked' together using few dedicated and efficient methods of production. After a period of time more automation can be introduced and the costs of producing the item falls, usually followed by the selling price.

5   When a new product is introduced there are certain groups of people who must have it because it is the latest style or fashion and they are prepared to pay more for the privilege of being the first on the block to have one. In marketing books these are known as 'innovators' but we prefer to call them 'the Jones's' and they live next door to you.

To summarise, the usual practice in many countries, is to maximise profits as much as possible. This may please shareholders in the short term but can destroy companies. By taking a longer term view and by careful manipulation it is possible to ensure a much healthier future. You will be ensuring long term survival at the cost of short term profits. And shareholders won't like it.

The moral of the above can be summed up as:

> **TO BE COMPETITIVE TEN YEARS FROM NOW IT IS NECESSARY TO REMAIN COMPETITIVE NOW, through maximising market share, within your chosen market.**

Developing products for market share makes an organisation less under pressure, in the long term, from competitive forces. It is always easy to segment a market to find a profitable niche. This does not lead to long term survival. Attack a market head on by developing a full product range and remain competitive in the future.

Other short term things to avoid

Other current management fads also act against being able to plan well into the future. Business Process Re-engineering focuses on the processes currently used and eliminating anything which does not appear to bring in money now. This brings short term gains but the net result of this is an inflexible, rigid organisation incapable of coping with change now, never mind change in the longer term.

As John Thompson said at a conference, 'The Agile Organisation', in 1996:

As organisations strive to compete, new management philosophies of re-engineering, business process redesign and reinvention have meant that:

♦ *too often the ideas have been translated into excuses for mindless cost-cutting, leaving the employees disillusioned;*

♦ *too often the focus on reconstruction has led to an excessive focus on the corporate navel, resulting in exhausted employees devoting more energy to doing business with themselves rather than understanding how they might add value to their customers;*

♦ *too often the well-intentioned moves to become more competitive have left employees feeling betrayed by redundancies and fearful for their own futures.*

Having investigated some of the claims made for BPR, we asked the Central Office of Information to give the names of some organisations who had claimed to have made radical saving through the introduction of Business Process Re-engineering. Some of these companies were then contacted and, amongst other things, were asked the question 'how much of your savings were made through redundancy?'

The rather sad answer from almost all that we asked was that, in fact, almost all the sweeping savings that were promised from BPR had been made through savings in labour costs through redundancy. It was only at Leicester Royal Infirmary that it was reported that there were no redundancies. In this hospital, BPR had been used to provide better focus for an already heavily over-worked staff. They found that BPR achieved this aim.

Another problem with BPR is that it cuts what are old, and believed to be, unprofitable products. Research carried out by Stuart Bush discovered that it was often these outdated products that were most profitable.

The logic is simple. During the declining phase of the product life cycle almost nothing need be spent on these products. R&D ceases, all the production tooling and machinery has been paid off, the product almost sells itself and so no promotion or sales-force time is needed. In many cases, with a declining product the costs are very low and it is almost pure profit. These are the products that get cut in BPR and this can hit the bottom line. Also, BPR can cut new products that take time to become established. This cuts the future health of the organisation.

Downsizing, Rightsizing or other names given to flattening organisations, has had the same effect. It makes an organisation too inflexible to respond to change and, therefore, certainly too inflexible to manage for the long term future. Fortunately, both Business Process Re-engineering

Magnitude of whole life cost areas

Product	Breakdown of whole life cost						Total WLC
Aircraft windscreen	Purchase 39%	Installation 4%	Refurb 56%				pence/flying hour
Public service bus	Purchase 21%	Road tax 1%	Fuel 11%	Maintenance 67%	Disposal -1%		63 pence/mile
Private hire vehicle	Purchase 22%	Financing 7%	Fuel 29%	Maintenance 35%	Insurance 22%	Road tax 1%	30 pence/mile
Saloon car	Purchase 39%	Financing 14%	Fuel 29%	Maintenance 18%	Insurance 14%	Road tax 3%	31.5 pence/mile
Laser printer	Purchase 36%	Service 6%	Electricity 1%	Ink 46%	Paper 12%		2.4 pence/sheet
Central heating system	Purchase 23%	Installation 3%	Gas 59%	Maintenance 14%	Disposal 1%		30 pence/hour

Figure 1.1 Magnitude of whole life cost areas
(by permission of Stuart Bush)

and Downsizing are beginning to get discredited, as both of these management fads result in a reduction in morale and a loss of the company memory. Experience within an organisation is a vital foundation on which activity for the future can build. Long term viewpoints are not considered and there is too much emphasis on what is best for now.

> **AVOID RESTRICTING FLEXIBILITY AND LOSING EXPERIENCED MANPOWER (the company memory)**

Total Quality Management, on the other hand, is an essential prerequisite for survival in the future. Reliability, something performing to specification over a period of time, has been shown to be the most important aspect of a product. This is achieved through quality. Quality starts with design as can be seen later in this section.

Benchmarking is a worthwhile exercise but it will only make an organisation as good as that which is currently around now, not in the future. Use Benchmarking to get 'up-to-speed', now move on from following others to predicting new improvements.

How not to start – mission statements

Mission statements are often too vague to allow them to be implemented. They all include words like 'global', 'be the best', 'increase sales' (easily done by reducing the price), etc. The worst we have seen was 'to grow by ten times in the next three years', which was so horribly vague as to be laughable. Worst of all, these mission statements are usually written by several very well paid members of the organisation who should be spending their time doing something more valuable for the organisation rather than wasting their collective time. Having spent this time on a pointless exercise they then waste everybody else's time as well by announcing the statement with suitable pomp and presentation.

By all means have a mission statement, if you must, but don't fool yourself that it has anything to do with strategy. And if you do have a mission statement at least make it unambiguous, achievable and measurable. A mission statement should indicate the values of the organisation and the direction in which it should be going. This will show to those employed in the company and those who deal with the organisation where it aims to be. This will enable all to share a common cause.

2
Tools and Techniques in this Time Frame

There now follows a series of tools that can improve the overall operation of your existing products and services. These have been chosen for two reasons. Firstly, they do not cost a great deal to implement but can result in a significant improvement to the product performance. Secondly, these are the building blocks which are further developed for the proposed set of activities in the fourth Time Frame section of this book.

Corporate Identity and Corporate Culture

There is always a snigger when . . . the logo designer suggests that she and her agency are managing their customer's self interest. Often such claims are wishful thinking at best, and confusing self-promotion at worst.

(Skinner 1997)

The problem we have with corporate identity is three fold. Firstly, there is no way of deciding when an organisation actually needs a new corporate image. Having decided that one is needed, and the cheque books come out, there is no way of deciding if one is going in the right direction, for the new corporate image. Then, having decided on the new identity, it is difficult to measure whether it is right or not, except after it has been put on the market long enough for some measures to be taken. On the other hand, back in the eighties, and before its take-over by Electrolux, Zanussi convinced many that they were offering us 'the appliance of science' from the worst equipped white goods factory in Europe – so perhaps it works after all.

When BA announced their new identity – painting the tails of planes in different styles – at a cost of £80 million, the *Daily Mail* announced 'BA believes the change of image will allow it to increase the number of passengers it carries each year by 70 per cent to reach 51 million by 2005'

(*Daily Mail* 2 June 1997). As a potential passenger, are you more likely to fly BA because the tailplane is painted differently? How much value do you put on this 'change of image' when you purchase your ticket? Or would you have preferred the old tail paint and a slight reduction in the ticket price.

Corporate identity is only useful if it achieves something. You need to project the type of organisation you plan to be, then put in the processes to get you there. You also need to advertise these processes within the organisation and to train people to know how to use these systems. You also need to explain the benefits to them, as well as the organisation, of aiming for a target and keeping on course to reach that target. In some cases, a corporate identity may be more useful viewed from the inside of an organisation than viewed from outside.

The same could be said of corporate culture. The environment within which new product development takes place, influences both the quality and the success of the process. There is a need to provide an atmosphere in which people are both motivated and are prepared to work together towards common objectives and share a common belief in the project. It is important to ensure that progress is adequately rewarded and that failure is tolerated and seen as an opportunity to learn from mistakes. 'A process that goes on forever is a way of life' (Moorhouse 1997).

In any organisation there needs to be a culture that permeates from top to bottom, that identifies the type of company that they are and aim to be. This needs to be one that tolerates mistakes, and also one that encourages those within the organisation to be involved in change in a proactive manner. For this reason we believe that a corporate culture should be constructed internally in any organisation. This needs then to be demonstrated to the outside world through the corporate identity. The corporate identity can then be the organisational attributes identified in its visual expression:

1   A visual expression of corporate-wide attributes.
2   Company-wide held views of organisational behaviour.
3   That which an organisation uses to distinguish itself.

Alan Topalian (1984) has written that 'At one extreme there are organisations that have succeeded in cultivating distinctive identities that are clearly understood by staff and are conveyed efficiently and unambiguously to interested parties outside. Others, alas, succeed only in conveying amorphous muddles which do little to enhance business prospects.'

This should then result in a corporate image which is defined as 'the perception of an organisation reflected and the associations held in the consumer memory' (Shaw 1993). Now this can be measured and what you can measure you can manage. John Redmond (1995) said that 'you cannot separate the product from the perception of the product'. The company's image is its products and services and 'the designer is the barometer of social change'.

Total Quality Management

TQM was one of those fads that people tried, found it didn't work, so gave up. They were wrong to do this because although TQM involves a lot of time and commitment, it results in enormous benefits and a more competitive organisation. But this does take time and by the time you get there you will have reached Time Frame Four.

Bill visited Rover, not that long ago, to look at various aspects of their design management for an award, which they won. It was said that they were just reaping measurable benefits in a programme that had, by then, been going eight years. TQM is vital and necessary and not a management fad. If you have tried and failed with TQM then start again. If you haven't even started then the sooner you do the sooner you will reap the benefits. The problem is that these benefits only become apparent after some years, by which time the majority of the less brave have given up and moved on to the next trend. The real danger is that if you have not included a TQM programme and your competitors have been beavering away on their initiative, you will be hit hard where it hurts most – in your reputation.

Crosby wrote a good book called *Quality is Free* (first published 1979) and what he was saying was right. Unfortunately, most managers don't read, (present company excepted because you have got this far) and most got no further than the title. Crosby should have added one more word to the title: 'Eventually'. What he was saying was that quality costs run at a certain level and then an investment is made in a quality initiative. After a period of time quality costs reduce to a level much below what they were before. After a further period of time, and this could be years, the total amount spent on this quality initiative is retrieved and so quality is, in fact, 'free'. It does require patience and it does require money, a lot of money.

The short sighted view was experienced when working at a university in London. We were all called together for a meeting and it was announced that we were to become a 'Total Quality Institution' with a campus wide quality initiative. The obvious question was 'what is the budget?' Back came the reply 'There is no budget, quality is free'. There seemed to be little reason to stay at the meeting. The initiative stumbled to a halt a couple of months later.

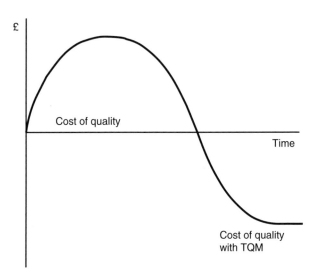

Figure 2.1   Cost of quality to a base of time. EVENTUALLY a quality initiative will pay for itself

CASE STUDY – ANSWER THAT PHONE

Oddly, a good example of the effect of quality happened in the same institution a few months later. This university had a terrible phone system. It was not uncommon to have to wait up to ten minutes to have the phone answered. This was not the fault of the telephone operators because they were working flat out, it was just that there were not enough of them. It was at a time when universities were trying to make significant increases in their student numbers. Eventually, they employed more telephone operators (at, of course, a cost to the institution). At the next intake they were surprised that there was a sudden large rise in student applications.

The explanation could have been as follows. There are lots of universities and colleges in London (all basically connected by the underground train service – the tube) offering a similar range of courses. A prospective student would ring up for details of the courses, wait some time to get through, then give up and try elsewhere. When the phones were improved and they could actually get into the system there was, of course, a greater chance of converting these enquiries into paying students. The whole process that a student would take in applying for a course through getting the brochure, being interviewed, accepted and receiving joining instructions could be blueprinted (see Chapter 10). It was then possible to identify the bottlenecks that needed to be improved.

It is always surprising that companies care so little about their telephone operators. They are often amongst the youngest, poorest qualified and poorest paid of their employees but they are often the first contact a customer has with the organisation. They are trained to pick up the phone within three rings (a quantitative

> *measure) but then are not trained in how they should then act (a qualitative measure). Quantitative measures are easier than qualitative measures but both are important and need to be considered as part of a TQM programme. Probably, in the service sector, where the quality of a service is often the person giving it, the qualitative measures are more important.*

There is no intention here to discuss that which has been covered in so many other books on the topic of TQM. It has been said that about 80% of TQM initiatives fail (Brown 1993, Fisher 1994). Having been involved in several TQM initiatives, including heading up a Teaching Company Scheme, here are some tips on how to avoid failure.

1   Deming focuses on the managerial aspects of TQM and certainly this must be 'driven' from the top of an organisation. Top management must do more than merely support TQM with a nod from the golf course. Initially, there really needs to be management commitment and this means active participation. Management must agree that meetings will be held in the firm's time and must appoint a person whose sole job is the Total Quality initiative, and not keep taking this person off this role whenever there is a crisis in another area. TQM must have a high priority in an organisation and must be part of the organisation's business strategy.

2   Teams must start with an objective and training must be undertaken right at the start. Newsletters and posters are useful but are not a substitute for proper training and a training plan. When those involved are trained then it is possible to empower them – not before.

3   Companies must get away from a 'Piecework Mentality'. If people are paid on the quantity they produce than they will produce quantity. The emphasis must be on quality output and if a bonus is to be paid then it must be based on quality achievement.

4   Those involved in the programme must know what is in it for them.

5   The Quality Manager must be sited at the 'coal face' and not tucked away in an office away from where the quality problems are likely to occur.

6   What you can't measure you can't manage. But there is no point in taking measurements without a preplanned purpose for taking those measurements. Quality Costing highlights the important areas as can be demonstrated with Pareto analysis. This is also known as the 80–20 rule, that is 80% of problems on cost areas emanate from 20% of the company's activities. This gives focus and priority to the work to be done.

7   There cannot be TQM until there is process control and measurement, BS EN ISO 9000 is the world's biggest ever selling standard and it does also help in a TQM programme.

8   Reports must actually state what went wrong and how the problems can be cured, otherwise, they tend to be a waste of time. Quality problem reports should not be an excuse for a witchhunt, but a recipe for improvement.

9   People react better when they can see that barriers are being broken down, change is being accepted and things are being achieved. Although the literature states that one should concentrate on the big issues, morale is often boosted if these are interspersed with smaller problems which are easily cured. This shows those involved clear evidence that things are getting better.

10 Total Quality Management takes longer than you expect – so plan for less.

It is generally accepted that quality should be built into a product at the design stage. Quality initiatives fail mainly through lack of real management commitment, lack of a sizeable budget to see it through and lack of patience in waiting for significant improvements.

CASE STUDY – FIRE FIGHTER

To be effective, a TQM programme is a strategic matter as it may take several years before any significant measurable benefit will accrue. It always needs a manager with foresight and patience.

Some years ago, near the start of an attempt to put a Total Quality Management programme into one site of a fairly large manufacturing organisation, the programme was discussed with the managing director. He opened the discussion with the statement: 'My view is that a manager's job is to deal with problems as they occur.' This sounded as if he reacted to crises as they occurred rather than actually planning the future to avoid most of these crises, as if he spent his life fire fighting. This fear turned out to be accurate. It could also be assumed that unless he could be persuaded to start planning then the TQM initiative was doomed right at the start. Unfortunately, again, he could not and the initiative failed.

If your staff are well trained, well supported (by management), well paid, well motivated, have the right equipment and enough time to do the job, have comfortable working surroundings and don't feel to be under threat, why should they make mistakes? Unfortunately, they will but they won't make so many. If they haven't the right working environment then it's down to you and their errors are your errors.

As Deming said about TQM, 'you don't have to do this, survival isn't compulsory'. Incidentally, Deming gave his last lecture in a wheelchair and in an oxygen tent. If we hadn't got our message over by then, probably we wouldn't have bothered.

CASE STUDY – QUALITY STARTS AT THE START

As consumers, we now expect much more from our purchases than we did only a few years back. We used to tolerate faults that now would cause us to complain. As a result, manufacturers now have to work to levels of quality that were once considered impossible. Anything less than the best can leave your organisation open to expense, loss of customers and even ridicule. To avoid this you need to start quality right at the beginning.

In 1974, we bought our first new car, a Vauxhall Viva. It cost £1208. We drove it around for three years and then sold it for £1210 when we got our first company car. When we bought our Viva it was a time of high inflation so we didn't actually make money on the car but we probably deserved to for the first weekend's work put in on it.

Back in those days, companies tried to eliminate faults by inspection and only the best operatives were considered to be suitable material to become inspectors. As an apprentice, back in the swinging sixties, Bill saw the best of a department getting their white coats and then spending their days checking on the work of those others still in brown overalls. So the best workers were not producing anything and spent their lives checking the work of others. With statistical process control, and a bit of luck, we could get down to 99% good components.

This sounded great until some years later we got our new car. We did what everybody did in those days with such a purchase. The first weekend was spent going over the car tightening screws or fitting all those that were laying on the floor pan under the carpet (note – deluxe model). With spanners, we tightened bits on the engine and made a note of all the bits that needed to be put right. Our list had twenty-five things on it which was given in on the initial 500 mile service and they were put right. This was the normal practice then which we certainly wouldn't tolerate now. Of course, the list contained only the faults that could be found. These parts were probably also made with components that were 99% correct. But a nut and a bolt with that level of accuracy only has a 98.1% chance of fitting and these errors multiply the more parts there are in the finished product.

In the Viva, there must have been about 3000 parts which means that about thirty were faulty – and we only found twenty-five. Goodness knows how many piston rings were missing, or even if the brakes were connected up correctly. Too late to worry now, and we don't have to, because we survived the Viva and now we have TQM. It doesn't take long to realise that the only acceptable level of quality is total.

Recently, Bill was talking to one of his students from the Near East who was unshakable in his belief that 95% quality is good enough in his father's factory. They made light bulbs and he believes that if one in twenty of the bulbs sold doesn't work then the customers are quite content to take them back to the shop and change them. We doubt that this is true even now and as soon as a competitor appears on the scene with more reliable bulbs then this company will be out of business.

Having accepted this level of quality have you ever thought that it could be the case that whenever a bulb goes the customer just returns it saying that it is new but faulty and the bulb gets changed? How can the shop keeper tell if the bulb is new or not? The customer need never buy a new bulb again, just keep recycling new for old. (Thinks; it is a little known fact that in this country light bulbs are guaranteed for 1000 hours; again, how do they know how long it has been used for? We need never buy a new bulb again – as long as we don't keep on returning them to the same shop! On the other hand, the manufacturers here operate TQM so we would soon get found out.)

When on a visit to America, quite a number of years ago, somebody asked why quality cars from Britain were fitted with Lucas bulbs. He referred to them as 'Lucas, prince of darkness' which was both funny and sad. Lucas have got their act together now. If cars were fitted with bulbs as supplied by my student's father, on average and including dashboard lights, every car would have a bulb not working.

Even 99.9% good parts isn't good enough. If the Apollo space craft that went to the moon in 1969 was working to this level of quality, it would have had 560 faults in it. Picture the scene:

Hey Neil, have you managed to fix that thing that converts our urine back into drinking water?

No, but you don't want to drink too much because the space loo has jammed.

That doesn't matter Buzz, there appears to be a leak round the porthole . . .!

We collect all those 'recall notices' you see in newspapers and laugh about them in lectures. When a company gets it wrong they have to let everybody know just how poor they are. They have to make the announcement in every newspaper, which costs a lot. The actual recall and correction costs more and whilst they are doing that the companies are not doing something profitable. And at the end of the day they have lost face and a lot of money.

There was one such notice recently that announced that 'when switched on the lamp holder becomes live', and presumably, the customer dead! There was considerable ridicule handed out when 'vorsprung durch technik' Audi had to recall 98,000 of their cars some years back when they used 'screws of insufficient strength'. Certain Philips/Bauknecht dishwashers no doubt did a splendid job on your dishes but 'a combination of unusual circumstances may occur in the electrical system . . . possibly creating risk of fire in the appliance'. 'Nice clean dishes, mum, shame the house burnt down.' And when did you last buy Austrian wine? The anti freeze may have gone from it but so have the customers. The knock on effect in damaged reputation can be terminal to the company even if the purchaser survives.

It is said that the cost of poor quality rises by a factor of ten at each stage of the process until it is detected. It is easy to appreciate how a faulty 10p electrical resistor costs £1 if it is only discovered after it has been fitted on to a circuit board and how this goes up to £10 if the fault is found on the finished item. The above paragraphs on recall notices demonstrate how this simple fault can eventually end up costing the company £100 (or more) if left for the customer to discover in the final electric appliance.

The biggest ever recall occurred in America where four to five million General Motor trucks were recalled because of the faulty positioning of the fuel tank. In a side on collision the tank can ignite! That is surely evidence enough that quality starts right at the start – with design.

Quality starting at the start is fairly obvious if you are the customer who has purchased the product. You want the product to work, and keep on working – reliably and safely. It must perform well and look good. Increasingly, people also want their products to be easy to use and we will be saying more of this in Time Frames Two and Four.

If you want people to want it, then make it easy – which is down to design and designers. But in TQM there are customers at every stage of the process. We also must realise that if you want to make it, so that people want it, then make it easy to make (if that makes any sense). We must think about how the product will be made and who are the people that are going to manufacture it and implement it. These are customers every bit as much as those outside of your organisation who will queue up to buy the finished products (we hope).

This requires effective communication between the designers, the makers, the suppliers, the users, and everybody else that gets involved. We must end this 'over the wall' communication by breaking down the barriers that often exist between the various departments who are involved in the total process. This is no different from what TQM has been advocating for years.

Figure 2.2   Over the wall communication

When it is realised that there are 4.5 million parts in a Boeing 747, it becomes apparent that it is not possible to operate large scale manufacturing today without TQM.

Adding Value or Adding Cost

Just in Time (JIT) is an effective way of organising your business. JIT is one of those techniques that manufacturing organisations are slowly working towards. We shall see that it actually works even better in the service sector. A lot of people think that JIT is a matter of making suppliers deliver at the time that you require components and that the result of this is to eliminate the need to hold stocks. This is not surprising, as this is the part that is most publicised; it is also the part that should be introduced last.

The simple premise behind JIT is that the company can take an order and can deliver the finished product in a very short time. This means that someone can order a suit, a wedding cake or a car and take delivery twenty-four hours later. Therefore, the whole aspect of JIT is to reduce the time that parts, work in progress and finished goods are held within the organisation, tying up finance. For example, if one looks at a particular bought in item in an organisation, which has been bought in to be fitted to some other part that you make, how long is it that the item is actually in your organisation? By tracing particular components, it can be seen that, for the majority of the time, they are taking up space and tying up money.

The key is, anything within your organisation which is part of the products that you produce, if you are not adding value then you are adding cost. For example, the actual time to produce a finished sweater from the time the sheep is sheared could be only two days. Yet the actual time is often weeks. This means that the company is only adding value for two days and tying up capital for the rest of the time.

Looking first at manufacturing, the aim is to eliminate work in progress (WIP). This means, as parts are delivered they go straight on to production. As they come off the first machine, rather than clutter up the place the component goes straight on to the next machine in the production process and, again, off that machine and straight on to the next machine. At the end of the production cycle the product should go straight out to the customer. Not only is this adding value most of the time, it also means that a customer's order can be completed in a very short time. This, in turn, means that it might be possible for bespoke things to be made to customer requirements. For example, customers go into a car showroom and specify precisely what they require for their new car from a menu. This is then transmitted to the car factory over telephone lines and this becomes the build ticket on production the following day. The car can then be delivered to a customer's requirements the day after that.

This sounds so obvious, why doesn't everybody do it? The answer is that it isn't that easy. Almost no manufacturing organisations have achieved JIT, although many are taking continuous steps towards it. There are several serious drawbacks with JIT. The first being that you are operating on the edge of a precipice. If a machine breaks down or if a component arrives late production stops. If quality falls below that required or a worker is absent or a strike occurs, production stops. In most organisations the WIP acts as a buffer and if, say, a machine has broken the buffer can be used until the machine is fixed. In a complete JIT system there is no margin of error. But every time such a bottleneck occurs and is cured the organisation becomes more efficient and more profitable.

On visiting a factory owned by an American company in the North East of England, there seemed to be a lot of electric motors cluttering up production. The answer to the question 'why don't you operate JIT?' was 'we do, if you count the number of electric motors, there is a two hour buffer stock. We use a quarter of a million electric motors a week. If we didn't operate JIT, just imagine how big our factory would have to be.'

There is a sequence for the introduction of JIT. First, introduce planned maintenance and, of course, this should be done at quiet times or during holidays. In Japan, they operate their machines at only 80% capacity, as they believe that this makes them more reliable. In Europe and America, we tend to be ruled more by accountants, who are trying to write off the cost of the production equipment as quickly as possible. So the practice here is to run the machines flat out. We go along with the western view because if you purchase a machine rated to give a certain performance it should be expected to give you that performance. The next stage is to introduce a total quality management programme. Of course, this takes many years to fully implement. But JIT can only work if there is TQM. There needs to be a 'line of balance', this means that all machines need to operate at about the same speed. If one machine works twice a fast as the machine preceding it in the cycle, there will need to be two feeder machines to give smooth production.

It has been found to be successful in organisations to have smaller single purpose machines rather than large multi-purpose machines. These are easier to maintain and easier to push out of the production line if they break and be replaced by a similar machine. There also needs to be multi-skilling of the workforce and the training that it involves. This will allow cover when other key workers are absent. This also allows the workers to move to alternative products during periods of low demand in other products.

With no WIP the factory space is smaller, the production plant should be arranged so that there is little space between the machines and to get down the movement of material from one machine to the next. It has also been found that the optimum shape for a production line in JIT is a horseshoe shape. This means that work comes in from the road, through the production line and is back where it started again to be loaded on to a lorry for delivery.

Regarding daily deliveries from suppliers, this is only practical for large volume or high value items. Nuts and bolts are not generally part of the JIT system. With these large volume high value components look at the stock turnover per year. If you are turning over stock twice a year try to increase this to five times a year, then ten times a year, then twenty times a year. This is sometimes known as the '5, 10, 20 club'.

Optimising manufacturing, of course, is a good thing, but this should not be done alone. Toyota spent a lot of effort in reducing the time taken to build a car but then found that it took a long time to get the finished car to the customer. The whole process needs to be part of the JIT system. Car companies have learned a lot from next day document delivery companies in this respect. When the full process is reached it is known as a pull system, this means that things are truly made to order. Nearly all the other such systems are push systems, that is, products are made to an anticipated demand and then supplied to customers as they require. Another feature of JIT is that the theory does not require computers, but it can be made faster and more effective with the use of computers.

JIT in the service sector

We have, so far, talked about manufacturing, JIT works even better in the service sector. Where in manufacturing we tend to be talking about lumps of metal, in the service sector we tend to be talking about people and people are part of the process. Lumps of metal take up space and tie up capital, but they don't complain, people do. Effectively, WIP is people queuing or cluttering up the service operation.

Take as an example a hairdresser's shop. The appointment system ensures that customers come when they are 'needed' and this eliminates 'goods inward stock', or people sitting in a waiting area reading magazines. Assume that all get their hair washed and then cut. As washing

takes only half the time of cutting, to get a suitable line of balance you
need one person washing for every two cutting. It is necessary to ensure
that the person comes straight from washing to cutting, so they are not
hanging around with water dripping down the back of their necks. Having
completed their haircut, they should then pay, this takes very little time,
and then leave. If efficiently organised, a hairdresser's shop has very little
waiting area and this need only accommodate those who come early. It is
an effective use of the space that the owners are paying for. A dentist's
surgery is similar. But often in the out-patients department of a hospital
there can be large areas filled with people waiting and this is mainly due
to inefficient organisation of the process.

There is one further advantage to be gained from applying JIT in the
service sector and that is, as said above, when the customer has finished
they go home. In manufacturing, you have finished stock and this is the
worse kind of stock, because you have added all the value to it. A serious
problem with JIT is matching the planned production to the variations in
demand. Almost no companies have achieved total JIT, most still make to
an anticipated demand and if they get that anticipated demand wrong,
they can end up with insufficient stock or finished stock they can't sell. It
is essential to have a clear understanding of the demand in manufacturing
throughout the year and in services throughout the year and throughout
the day.

In manufacturing you can overcome demand variation by holding
stock, this allows you to produce evenly. In services you cannot hold stock
and, therefore, meeting and coping with demand becomes even more
important. To overcome problems of demand variation many organisations have products that have demand peaks at different times of the year.
For example, who makes ice cream and who makes sausages? The main
demand for lawn-mowers is in Spring and, apparently, for DIY electric
drills is in Autumn. And who makes these? This means that companies
can utilise the plant and the people in that plant throughout the year by
moving from one product to the other. This is another reason why staff
have to be multi-skilled. There is another alternative and this is to export
to other parts of the world where their particular national variations in
demand for that product allow a smoothing of production.

Blueprinting

This is a simple but effective way of identifying areas for improving the
way your organisation delivers its products and services. The system has
probably been around for many years, but the earliest reference we have

found was in a paper published by Shostack (1984). The process involves describing, in minute detail, the various stages of the manufacture of a product or the delivery of a service. It is important to remember two things:

1 The entire process needs to be mapped; and
2 It should be mapped in very small steps in order to identify problem areas, for which a cure can be identified.

This takes time and several people to map the process, but once complete the blueprint shows up 'bottlenecks' or areas for possible improvement. It also shows qualitative measure, which can then be put into a (more easily dealt with) qualitative form. For example, London Underground map the entire process that a customer takes from entering the station and purchasing a ticket, right through to having the ticket collected automatically and the passenger leaving the station. They have then identified areas where improvements are possible and have achieved this on impossibly tight budget systems. For example, they have developed signage to guide passengers through a complicated system. Compare this to the (apparently superior) French Metro. In this respect, the London Underground system is far superior.

In another area, Lynn Randall (1993) undertook a study of the operations of the out-patients department of a hospital in Exeter. She did this through Blueprinting and improved the operation of the out-patients department, greatly reducing patient waiting time. As a spin off from this research, it was also found that the car park was now much more empty. The hospital was planning to purchase additional space so that they could enlarge the car park. Having improved the out-patients so that there were less people waiting it was then found that a larger car park was no longer required and the considerable investment was saved.

Other studies have taken the idea further and identified that not all queues in the process have the same value. In Sweden, it was found that people were more concerned about queuing to buy train tickets than they were about waiting on the platform for the train. This was because when one is waiting for a ticket you might miss the train but when you are waiting on the platform you won't. This means that it is possible to rank for importance the various bottlenecks in the blueprint and those problems of higher order should be overcome first. A queue of people waiting to buy tickets may be reduced by the addition of automatic ticket dispensers. Likewise, a queue of people waiting to hand in their ticket to the ticket collector at the end of their journey could be eliminated by automatic ticket collection barriers at the end of the journey. On the other hand, if it is known that everybody has a valid ticket, why bother to collect it?

A good starting point with Blueprinting is to ask a simple question and then, through the blueprint, try and find the answer. For example, why do you have to check in two hours early for a European flight? To answer this five blueprints will need to be produced. One will be for the actual passenger, one for their luggage, one for maintaining and refuelling the plane, one for cleaning and loading the food and one for changing crews and the flight checks. Now, in practice, this blueprinting becomes difficult because a lot of these functions are undertaken by different organisations. But if only one organisation's blueprint is used the identified benefits may not be realised because they are not of the Critical Path.

The five blueprints described above occur in parallel, but they need not nor cannot all start together. For example, the blueprint for the luggage cannot start until the passenger has checked in. Likewise, they need not all end together. For example, passengers cannot be allowed on to the plane until the refuelling has been completed. Having placed all the blueprints in sequence, initially, by looking at the time of each of these, the bottlenecks can be observed. When so displayed, these very much have the appearance of a Critical Path Analysis chart (CPA) also known as Project Evaluation Review Technique (PERT). These were started around the same time in Great Britain by the CEGB to plan power stations and in America by the military to plan rocket projects. In a CPA chart are shown the anticipated time to do and completion dates for each stage of a project. On a blueprint, the actual time taken is shown for each stage and also the activities that occur at each stage is described in more detail. In CPA, the activities that make up the shortest possible time to completion are called the Critical Path. Any activity that can be improved on this Critical Path will reduce the overall time for the whole project. Likewise, any improvement on the blueprint Critical Path will improve the overall operation.

At London Gatwick Airport they expressed concern that the departure lounge was full to capacity between 7.30 and 9.30 with customers flying to America. Does it need to be? If such blueprints existed it should be possible to reduce the time from checking in to flying out to one hour, the result being a less crowded departure lounge. But is it that simple? There are shops in the concourse and these are a vital source of revenue and we must ensure that people spend sufficient time in those shops. This raises the next question, how long do people typically spend shopping? Has the research actually been undertaken to determine how much time people spend shopping and how much time people spend waiting? This should all be part of the blueprint. If people are shopping for twenty minutes and

BLUEPRINT OF THE OPERATION OF PASSENGERS BOARDING AT AN AIRPORT

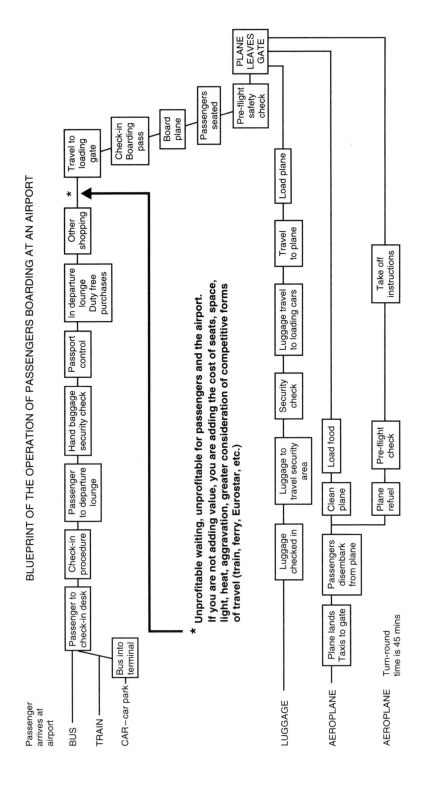

* Unprofitable waiting, unprofitable for passengers and the airport.
If you are not adding value, you are adding the cost of seats, space,
light, heat, aggravation, greater consideration of competitive forms
of travel (train, ferry, Eurostar, etc.)

Figure 2.3   Blueprint of the operation of passengers boarding at an airport

hence bringing in revenue, but then cluttering up the place whilst waiting and not bringing in revenue for another twenty minutes (adding value and adding cost again), that second twenty minutes could perhaps be eliminated. The next comment that usually comes back is that a lot of people turn up much later than the final check-in time. Our answer to that is, of course they do, because they can get away with it. If the final check-in time was adhered to, people would turn up on time. If everybody turned up over a shorter timespan it may be necessary to open more check-in desks, but these would be open for a shorter period of time. People would still turn up to check-in in a normal or Galcian distribution.

Another comment levelled at us, when making a plea for the above, is that if everybody could check-in and board the plane in a short period of time people wouldn't bother to fly Club Class, although they may prefer to pay extra for better on board service and comfortable seats. But also it may only take one airline to realise the improvements that can be made and implement these to leave all the other airlines behind. If you are involved in the airline business this could be yours. So when we are next at a major airport we don't want to be asked to grade the comfort of the seating areas, because we don't want to waste our time being seated at all. Furthermore, do we really need a fifth terminal at Heathrow Airport in London? Blueprints of the above could convince us of its necessity, or otherwise.

As can be seen, blueprinting is an excellent tool by which to improve any process just by 'walking through' it. It also can incorporate some of the techniques of Just in Time. Blueprinting can also be used in an 'enhanced' form to identify how any service can be improved, and this is described in Time Frame Three.

It is also possible to 'stretch' the blueprint, often at the completion end, to include more of the service aspects of the offering. For example, include selling as part of a car production, and servicing and even down to taking responsibility for reclaiming and re-cycling old cars at the end of their life. In a service this could mean a supermarket delivering shopping and then collecting the waste, whilst taking more orders. Look at either ends of a blueprint in order to identify extra potential markets. London Underground have done this when they identified that some passengers would even like transport from the station to their home. A scheme is being introduced at some stations to provide a minicab pick-up service, which has been booked by train customers.

Another 'tip' when doing a blueprint is to do it and then do it again. First, describe all the boxes, then subdivide these into twice as much detail and twice as many boxes. This system works better the more details that are described.

Relationship Marketing

During this decade, this has become one of the important parts of marketing and by introducing relationship marketing various other new processes will be found to be necessary in order to improve your existing services. The aim of relationship marketir ; goes beyond the traditional transaction or a focus on a single sale. As it has been shown that it is easier to retain customers than it is to find new ones, relationship marketing addresses how to keep customers through additional services linked to the original sale and repurchase.

One of the effects of relationship marketing is that it tends to 'stretch' the organisation's involvement with mainly the service side of their offerings. This will be shown up in the blueprint.

Benchmarking

Why does it take five times as long to change an air conditioner in a factory than it does to change an engine on a Boeing 747? Is it to do with the skill of the operators, their training, the ease of fitting, accessibility, correct tools or motivation? The answers to these may be identified through benchmarking. It is widely said that this was first undertaken by Xerox, who looked at why their Japanese factory was more efficient than the ones in America. Having identified where they were better, they copied it.

Florence Nightingale actually benchmarked the performance of her military hospital in the Crimean War against the best military hospitals in London. She compared the number of deaths in her hospital, month by month, with those in London and displayed these as a series of circular histograms that she called 'Cockscombs'. A typical cockscomb is shown below. It is to her credit, and those of her less famous helpers, that within a year she had reduced the death rate to that below the military hospitals in London, which, at that time, were considered the best in the world.

The process of benchmarking has now become widespread and many companies improve their existing processes through benchmarking. The way to undertake this is to first look at what your organisation is doing and, in this respect, the blueprinting described above can assist in this process. When certain areas are found that could be improved, look then to other organisations who probably do that particular aspect better.

There is competitive benchmarking, but the problem here is why should a competitor assist you? Far better is to find an organisation who excels in this area but is not in competition. Benchmarking is usually a

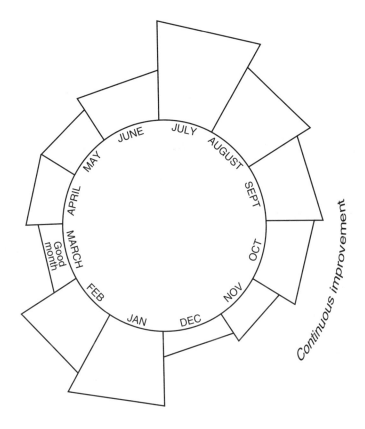

Example: Number of defects

Figure 2.4   A 'Cockscomb' as a way of comparing quality

case of give and take, so if you wish to be shown by one organisation how
to improve one of your processes, you must have something to offer them.
It is possible, therefore, to set up 'benchmarking clubs'. These are companies of similar size and, perhaps, a similar range of skills but which are
not in competition. For example, there was a benchmarking club that
involved Rover, JCB, Black and Decker and Motorola. None were
directly in competition, all had something to contribute to each other and
all could learn from each other. By not being in competition they could
freely discuss various areas for improvement. Car companies have also
learnt from next day package delivery companies and drug delivery to
dispensing chemists, when they came to look at how to reduce the
delivery of finished cars to customers.

Benchmarking clubs are surprisingly easy to set up. Once you have found areas that need improvement and have identified companies you believe to be good at this, contact those organisations. You will then find that they often have areas that they perceive need improvement and if you can assist them your benchmarking club is underway.

Empowerment? Grab It, You Can Only Do Better

One of the buzz-words of recent years has been 'empowerment', in which organisations 'achieve better results through involvement of all employees in continuous improvement of their processes' (European Foundation for Quality Management). We have been introduced to flatter organisations, where typically, the levels of management are reduced from eight to three and, as a result, 'we all have a greater say in decision making' (don't we just!). But have you noticed that these organisational charts are still drawn as 'triangles' and nobody ever dares disturb the position of those persons lucky enough to be at the top?

There is no doubt that empowerment is a good thing but too often it is used as another excuse for making redundancies, and terms like 'flatter' organisations often go with 'leaner' and 'fitter', which usually means emaciated, too understaffed to cope and unable to offer a decent service to their customers. Often it is those developing things for the future who are 'redundeed'. (Great word that. We got it out of a management book, sounds like being moved to the East Scottish coast). Work for a healthy future is often difficult to justify if you only look at the bottom line of the latest balance sheet.

Anyway, you should grab at your empowerment and don't be afraid to use it. You probably won't do any worse than many top bosses.

So Where are you Going?

Some years back, the top managers and thinkers in a large utility spent several days in discussion trying to decide what they needed from their products. After a tortuous amount of discussion they came to the unsurprising conclusion that their customers wanted:

- ◆ the right job;
- ◆ at the right price;
- ◆ at the right time;
- ◆ and of the right quality.

Perhaps they needed to go through all the discussion to realise the obvious, but it is not a bad thing on which to keep your focus.

◆ ◆ ◆

Summary of Time Frame One

In this time frame we have looked at what organisations are doing which is reducing their chances of surviving into the future. Proposals have also been made as to how organisations can improve this situation. A series of fairly well known techniques have been expanded and these can be used to further increase the competitiveness within organisations.

These all concern the existing products and services. These tools and techniques can also be used in the subsequent sections. In the next Time Frame we look at making existing product ranges better but keeping the same basic concept – product and service improvement.

Time Frame Two

New Products and Services

Product Development is an honourable profession, so let's honour it by doing it well.

(Don Clausing 1998)

3

Organisational Issues

Introduction

According to an editorial in *Engineering* (April 1997) only one sixth of manufacturing companies in the UK carry out new product development. Similar research does not seem to have been undertaken elsewhere but it may be assumed that the situation in the majority of the industrialised world is similar. This means that, for example, only 20 000 companies in the UK are actively considering products that will ensure their future. The rest seem destined to depend on other companies for sub-contract work for their survival. If yours is one of these now is the time to break out. There are no figures available for the service sector but the situation there is probably just as bad.

In this section, new products that are an improvement on existing products are considered. This means that the basic concept remains the same. Innovative new products are considered in the next Time Frame in this book.

Some of the most useful recent work in developing new products has been the realisation that Specifications can hold the key to controlling the management process of new products. Not only do they provide a mantle around the process, they can also specify the framework in which new products and services are allowed to develop – those which are right for the organisation. This thinking has been developed further. Specifications can be identified and compiled in a series of steps that describe the stages, in sequence, of the product development.

Also considered in this section are teams and team leadership. Development should always be undertaken in groups because, today, no one person can have all the skills or knowledge to make the best decisions. The process is also a vital aspect that enables new products and services to be effectively developed.

The processes by which you develop new products and services are also of major consideration in this Time Frame. Apart from identifying the sequence in which things should be done, it also allows those managing the project to identify concurrencies, the people who should be involved, the costs and time scale of the project early on in the project. This is good management of any project.

The Background

What constitutes the development of new products has 'grown' over the past twenty years. Design as undertaken by art school designers was once considered to be an end in itself which resulted in products that were for an 'educated elite' (Walker 1989) but were invariably difficult to make, expensive to buy and had limited appeal. This type of design was a throwback to the Arts and Crafts movement but failed to fulfil the needs of those operating in mass markets.

In the mid seventies, as supply began to approach demand in most product areas, companies considered design as starting at the concept stage and also included consideration of ease of manufacture (e.g. Anderson 1975). In the mid eighties pioneers, starting with Stuart Pugh (1982) proposed 'Total Design' in which the market was given prior consideration and a thorough specification was developed all before the concept stage of design. This still widely accepted model ends at the selling stage but the scope of 'Total Design' has been extended to include everything up to, and including, 'disposal' such as servicing, marketing, and redesigns. (Hollins and Pugh 1990, BS 7000 1989, Andreasen 1994).

The application of Total Design has also been widened to include services (Hollins and Hollins 1991) and The British Standards Institution has published sector standards on design management of manufactured products, services, and in the construction industry (BS 7000 parts 2, 3 and 4). The total process has been yet further expanded in recent research and publications to include a strategic viewpoint so that organisations can set themselves in the right direction for future developments. This results in developments of process models accentuating the front end of the process. But these future strategic development models are only applicable up to about three to six years ahead.

The Right Product

On the whole, the committees of the British Standards Institution are manned by fine, upstanding, bespectacled, grey haired gentlemen. At one of their meetings held in September of 1994, one of the committee members, Tony Stevens spoke:

> *THATCHER SAID, WHY ARE THE JAPANESE KICKING THE SHIT OUT OF US?*
> *SHE WAS TOLD — 'QUALITY'*
> *FIVE YEARS LATER SHE SAID WHY ARE THE JAPANESE STILL KICKING THE SHIT OUT OF US?*
>
> *SHE WAS TOLD — 'DESIGN'*
> *FIVE YEARS LATER THE JAPANESE ARE STILL KICKING THE SHIT OUT OF US.*
>
> *THE REASON IS THAT THEY PRODUCE THE RIGHT PRODUCT*
> *— AND WE DON'T!*

What is the Right Product?

Get it right first time – know your customer, your product and your capabilities

Your company must offer products that customers want, that can be made, at a price people are prepared to pay and return a profit for your company. Without fulfilling all these criteria the product can be deemed to be a failure and, in time, so will your organisation.

The focus for the whole of this book is the very early stages of the process. This is where (85%) the main management decisions are made, but only small costs (15% to 20%) are actually incurred. Make these decisions whilst the they are still in a paper, or very simple prototype form. This will allow aspects to be severely modified, or abandoned, without incurring significant expense. This will also significantly reduce the time taken for the product to reach the market. The process, as described, takes a 'top to bottom' approach but will, in practice, be iterative. This means that as new and better information becomes available those involved in the process may need to backtrack to check on, or change, some of the earlier work. This is quite normal in good management as long as this iteration is kept under control and it is realised that there comes a point where further changes are unnecessarily disruptive, time consuming and expensive.

Various people will be responsible for the implementation of each of these early stages and these people should have this responsibility included as part of their job description. This should also indicate areas where additional training must be given to enable those involved to do these tasks.

IT USED TO BE SO MUCH EASIER

In the early days of aviation the aircraft designers were also the test pilots. This had the automatic effect of weeding out the bad designers.

(Igor I. Sikorsky)

The people who used to cast the cannons in the middle ages were also taken to the battle to fire them. This had a similar effect to the above.

Getting the right product is never cheap, it is, therefore, not surprising that many British companies hold back rather than inflict themselves with a financial millstone. But without a constant supply of new designs the company's products soon become outdated, they lose customers and rapidly the company spirals into decline. If you create no new products your organisation will slowly decline and fail. If you develop the wrong product, or even the right product but do it badly, you can go out of business far faster than if you hadn't bothered. The failure rate of new product design is pretty daunting but many failures can be avoided and developing the right products is still probably the best way to keep ahead of the competition.

Increasing Competition

With national barriers being broken down companies must operate in a world market and competition is fierce. As more developing countries and the Eastern Bloc start manufacturing competitive products, their low wage economies will increase the supply of low cost goods. The more successful countries are not trying to compete only on price, but also on 'non price' factors that give added value as perceived by the customer.

The breaking down of these trade barriers is great for consumers. Never before have customers had such choice for practically whatever they wish to purchase. You are also consumers. When you go to buy something you generally decide how much you are prepared to pay, then select the product that gives you the most for your money in that price bracket (see Figure 3.1). You can almost be certain to get 'value for money', because there is nearly always a wide choice.

Now, as producers, the situation is far more difficult. You are up against the very best in the world. It is not good enough to be nearly as good as the competition. The best is now available for customers to buy and unless your product is the best, they won't buy yours.

Why we buy products and services

Reliability	User familiarity	Quality	Finish

Ease of installation   Packaging   Safety

Wider environmental use (temperature, humidity, etc.)   Price

Performance (accuracy, energy use, speed, range)   Conforming to standards

Availability/speed of delivery/effective distribution   Durability

Add on features/added value/perceived value   Less pollution/more green

Maintainability   Compatibility with existing systems   Size

Save time/save labour/save money   Ease of use (ergonomics)

Status/image   Life in service   Comfort   Reputation of manufacturers

Credit policy   Shelf life   Familiarity   Aesthetics/style/fashion

After sales service   Less legislation (tax, insurance)

Figure 3.1   Why we buy products and services

As you see, people buy (what they perceive as) **benefits**. This is also partly affected by **emotions**, which explains why people don't all buy the same item. Look again at Figure 3.1. If this is why customers buy products and services then these factors must be uppermost in your mind when you develop your products. The point is that these benefits are all features that you can identify and build into your products and services.

Most thriving companies tend to change their product and service offerings frequently. It is not uncommon for a company to derive 70% of its profits from products introduced in the last five years. This may be obvious for companies working in the field of electronics but the same applies to many other organisations operating in what were once considered traditional, slow moving, conservative industries. Today, new products are the life blood of any business.

CASE STUDY – CHOICE MEANS COMPETITION

Some years ago we took a holiday in Albania. Don't ask us why but it seemed a good idea at the time. It was certainly interesting with unusual aspects such as no private car ownership, which allowed us to do much of our siteseeing from the centre of the road. But it was not a great place for shopping. There was almost nothing on sale and the shelves were often so bare that sometimes it was difficult to guess what sort of business certain shops were in.

All this meant that whenever there was a delivery of anything new, demand outstripped supply and instantly crowds would gather. Such was this occasion – a delivery of training shoes. To be trendy down the local Tirana disco you had to have a pair of these resplendent footwear and as this shop keeper had them all you had to get them from her.

Albania is pretty close to Greece and they share similar shopping habits so around the counter there was a neatly formed semicircle of men and women 'queuing'. Behind the counter there was this woman, on the counter a large pile of training shoes and a box. The shopping 'experience' followed this pattern; a customer would put some money in the woman's hand and she would put it in the box. No change was given. She would then take a pair of trainers from the top of the pile and hand them to the customer. We went outside and not surprisingly, down the side of the shop there were people swapping and changing these new shoes until they found a pair that fitted.

It is only when one sees such a situation that you realise how easy shopping is in Britain. Providing you have the money you have **choice** *for almost everything that you want to buy. If you want a compact disc player there are shelves of them to choose from. You can take your time and select from the vast selection of products in the high street from wine to wardrobes. Car show rooms are full of special offers to encourage you to purchase. In 1970, there was a four month waiting list for any car, now you can demand 10% off and you will get it. The customer is king (or queen).*

But, as said at the start of this section, choice means **competition***. It's good if you are buying but hell if you are selling. Although many markets are far from 'free' the barriers are certainly coming down and the result is a hard life for producers. Furthermore, there is now over-production for almost anything you care to mention. With these more open markets, over a period of time, the best companies will survive and thrive and the others will decline and fail. The only way to survive is to have the best products.*

But what is the best? Just look at how you make your (larger) purchase decisions. First you decide that you have a need for a particular type of product. Then you see what is available and you buy the one which has the most of what you consider are **benefits***.*

Those who realise this are very important people, the organisations that employ them (and undervalue them) owe their very existence to them and their ideas for these new products and services. Use them well and the company will survive, but use them badly (or not at all) and the company will soon be out of business.

Anyway, back in Albania we saw another similar scene. A delivery of a stock of 42 inch, D cup, salmon pink bras (honestly). Similar semicircle of customers, similar pile of goods, woman serving and box for the money. Of course, Bill went out and looked down the side of the shop – no, they weren't.

Allow Time

Currently, organisations have fewer people working as fast as they can. Fewer are employed full-time but these people are working much harder – a month more per year than they were twenty years ago! This is certainly optimising efficiency, but only in the short term. The result is that there is less time to plan and, subsequently, more time spent 'fire fighting'. All this is not conducive to long term new product management. Unfashionable as it may be, it is advocated that companies:

> **ALLOW SOME SLACK IN THE ORGANISATION'S CURRENT PROCESSES.**

Again, as time equates to money it is necessary to accept an apparently 'inefficient' workforce (one which is not working flat-out all the time) in order to survive in a more healthy state. Empowerment and trust of those involved is needed.

In your organisation allow people thinking time. And if this involves some of them gazing out of the window some of the time with a vacant look on their faces, so be it. If the workforce is motivated they will work hard. The 'vacant gazers' should be judged on their overall contribution to the organisation over a period of months rather than on one or two apparent incidents of laziness.

Time to think is important but this should be focused and channelled into something useful. You must provide this direction and you must provide the right climate for this thinking. Furthermore, when people have thought of something which is worthwhile to the organisation there must be a mechanism in which these ideas are captured and not allowed to drift away. This is more than a suggestion scheme.

What is needed is a forum where people can come to state their ideas without the fear of ridicule. All the rules of Brainstorming need to be applied here. From the company's point of view they need to be sure that the ideas have a focus which is generally in the direction that they want to go. Therefore, people within the organisation need to be given a (written) 'agenda' of the plans and policies of the organisation. This is certainly more than a bland Mission Statement. It should also include a copy of a skills audit which should indicate whether the ideas are more easily achievable using the staff and skills already available.

Skills Audit

It is proposed that a skills audit be carried out to state, in broad terms, the capabilities in your organisation and of your main subcontractors or suppliers. This should take about four man weeks depending on the size of company. The effect of this audit will be to identify the known and available experience or know-how. Activities that are needed for any new product or service that you are developing which do not figure in the skills audit can be thought of as innovative processes which will require more time to organise. The aim is to identify or anticipate problems before they occur so that they can be confronted and eliminated. These processes may be new to the organisation but unless they are truly innovative the increase in risk and cost associated with such processes will generally not be great. From experience, typically, it will cost an additional 10% to subcontract a process that already exists, but is new to the company, than an equivalent subcontracted process of which the organisation is already well experienced – and will already appear in the skills audit.

The skills audit has a lower priority than the other main inputs to the design process for two reasons. Initially, the skills aspects should not, in most cases, restrict the development programme, especially if you are a market led organisation. Secondly, although it would be an advantage to have this skills audit at the outset, there is time to compile it before the later stages of the process, when it will be used.

The skills audit, of course, will be the same for all the products and services that will be developed and it will be expanded with each additional new skill or technique used. When it has been compiled it will provide an additional input into the development process and will show the lower cost directions to take. The skills audit will not necessarily restrict ideas or render some of them unsuitable because, in many cases, it is possible to train or employ people with particular skills or to subcontract this part of the skill to another operation.

Strategy, up to Six Years Ahead

Increasingly, new products have become a strategic issue in organisations. As organisations live or die on their products this **should be the responsibility of the main board**. They should consider what business they are in and focus the new products to meet the corporate objectives of their organisation.

Understand the strategic issues within your organisation. This will include the success factors relating to **political, economic, social, technological and environmental** (PESTE) factors and the **strengths, weaknesses, opportunities and threats** (SWOT) analysis. Understand changing customer requirements, competitors suppliers and substitutes. The strategies to fit the circumstances must meet the needs of the organisation, be feasible and be acceptable to managers, staff and shareholders.

Lauterborn (1993) has stated that Kotler's 4Ps (Product, Price, Place and Promotion) reflect a 1960s mentality and have no place in the 1990s. We think this is somewhat harsh as all ten Ps found in the various marketing books are useful. Lauterborn then went on to state that to succeed now, today's marketeers must consider the customers wants and needs, the cost to satisfy and the convenience to buy. This is what the earlier stages of new product management are all about but we need to think even further ahead than this. Furthermore, they have to have the right competencies to defend their position against emerging competition.

ORGANISATIONS MUST BE PREPARED TO COPE WITH CHANGE AND BE PREPARED TO PLAN FOR IT.

In any company, to plan for the next few years, the top management must specify the broad parameters to which any new product must conform. For example, without such guidelines those involved in new products could spend time developing products for markets that do not meet the overall aims and objectives of the company and could even compete with your existing product range. This means not working in isolation, consideration must be made of the entire environment in which a company operates. Companies need vision and have a strategic framework to achieve this vision. Furthermore, they must have the right competencies to defend their position against emerging competition. Organisations must be prepared to cope with change and be prepared to plan for it.

CASE STUDY – HANDICAPPED DESIGN – DRIFTING INTO NEW PRODUCTS

It is surprising how companies drift into their new products. Some while ago there was a big company in Silicon Valley. It was a multi-billion dollar company that operates worldwide. Their R&D building was crammed full of the latest technology that one would expect to find in a company in Silicon Valley in the 1990s. They had some very successful products but, increasingly, their new developments were failing. Once the decision had been taken to develop a new product or range the work was spectacular. Top people, top equipment and facilities – no expense was spared in getting the product developed. The problem was that they were not developing the right product.

Of course, our interest is in the very early stages of the product development process. How do they choose the projects that feed into the process that are developed in this hi-tech high cost environment? On tracing back through the product development route in order to see where the ideas came from it was found that the error was right at the start. The company had been founded by a very bright man who really had his finger on the pulse. His products were world beaters – but he was now dead and the company was going into rapid decline.

The group that now chose which new products should be developed were drawn from those who had a good record in choosing new products (presumably in the hope that lightning struck twice) and other 'blue eyed boys' in the organisation who, presumably, were good at golf. The second criteria seemed more important than the first.

Apparently, every six months or so this select group would get together for a golfing weekend and between the tees they would decide the products to be developed. The ideas of those who had good ideas before were given more credence. By the time the game was finished the product development programme for the next few months (years) had been settled. The odd thing was that most people spoken to, in this company, knew that this happened, felt that it might not altogether be the best way, but accepted it. The organisation then invested literally millions of dollars on developing products on what was little more than the whim of a few people. Based on the deliberation of these weekend's vague ideas no expense would be spared in developing the product – for them usually to be expensive failures.

The solution was clear. The error was at the very start – product ideas chosen on a whim. What was needed was a structured sifting process through which all new ideas would be put. The sift would ensure the product's suitability with the market and with the company's capabilities.

Our services were offered and it was suggested that they paid one dollar for each one hundred dollars that I saved them. An offer you couldn't refuse? Surprisingly they did. This seemed confusing until a more 'street wise' individual put us right. Suggesting that they replaced personalities with processes was bound to be rejected by the personalities who were likely to lose their cosy status through what we proposed.

Did the company improve? No, they decided against replacing the golfing weekend product selection method by a more structured approach. Perhaps, top management sometimes have their own interests more at heart than those of their organisation.

An extreme example but a true one. It is worth considering the situation in your organisation. How do you choose the products that you put into your design process? That is, right at the very beginning. Get that wrong and whatever you do subsequently must also be wrong. Rubbish in rubbish out, no matter how good is the design process in between. Several organisations now use Quality Function Deployment, which, at least, makes an attempt to replicate the customer requirements in the subsequent design of the product. But, we have noted that these customer requirements are often little more than guesses by managers sitting round a table. If they are going to be guesses they may just as well have a bit of fun and make them on the golf course!

Fashion

Contrary to what many may think, the rag trade or fashion industry is very much rooted in this Time Frame. In most cases, it is a static product and therefore, the static disciplines should be emphasised when involved in any fashion-conscious product. There will be plenty of changes, especially in aesthetics and the use of new materials, but the basic concept generally remains unaltered. In fact, change in men's fashion is very slow and there is no better example than the tie. Originally 'invented' as a glorified bib, it is now considered 'smart' and necessary for job interviews and certain restaurants. And what is it? Just a bit of thin cloth tied in a certain way. Nothing more, nothing less, but it does allow magnificent freedom in aesthetics. Fashion design is easier to predict in the long term than in the short term.

4

Tools and Techniques in this Time Frame

Frameworks

If potential ventures are viewed within a strategic context, it should be possible to identify a series of parameters or 'boundaries' that show the type of projects that are right for the particular organisation. This will enable people to identify those achievable areas worth pursuing as well as areas that should be avoided.

These boundaries need to be stated and specified and these determine whether an organisation should pursue an idea in the first place. Amongst these guidelines can be specified the following company strategy fit including:

- allowed financial boundaries (e.g. minimum return on investment, maximum development cost, etc.);
- allowed time parameters (e.g. maximum time to launch, – see Chapter 9);
- existing product range fit (including product phase out of the old and in with the new);
- delivery/sales channel fit (how it should reach the customer?);
- manufacturing fit (will you make it or out source?);
- market trends;
- technology trends;
- environmental considerations (including servicing and eventual disposal).

These guidelines set limitations as to what may be developed and boundaries around various company activities which (correctly) restrict the freedom of those responsible for developing new products. These boundaries can be thought of as a series of circles and the type of products that a company should develop should fit within the overlap of all these circles, (see Figure 4.1).

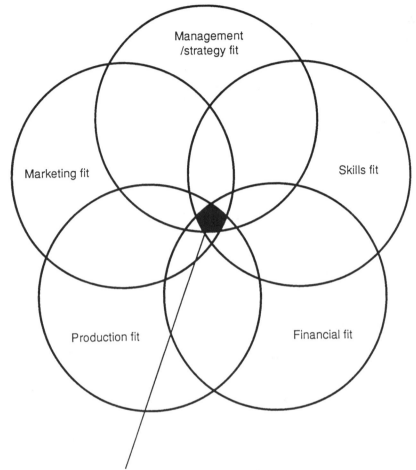

Figure 4.1   Organisational parameters

The budget can be directed into areas that are considered best suited for the company. Alternatively, areas which are outside the parameters described will be highlighted and a decision taken on the continuation of the design project in the light of these discontinuities. In other words, if ideas fall outside of these parameters it may be reason enough not to pursue the idea further. Alternatively, ideas that fall outside these parameters will be identified early in the process (before much money has been spent) potential problem areas. Having highlighted these, the potential difficulty should be appraised and a solution found before going any further with the development.

CASE STUDY – HOVER HORROR

We'll give you an example of product development without these frameworks. In the seventies, Bill was in charge of a small development department in a similarly small manufacturing company. One morning, the Managing Director strode into my office and announced,

'We are going into hovercraft'.
'Hovercraft?' said Bill.
'Big potential in hovercraft. Stop what you are doing and get on with looking into this.'

The M.D. must have had another bright idea on his way to work. It was pretty obvious that he was wrong and we couldn't spare the time in our over-stretched work load to deal with another of his whims, but he was the M.D. so we all jumped into action. It was great fun and in no time at all we had converted vacuum cleaners whizzing around the department. Two glorious weeks, but two wasted weeks and later the idea fizzled out and we went back to an even more delayed work schedule.

    Bill is older and wiser now and brave enough to say 'no' to Managing Directors. Now it could be shown that many of the products they wanted to create were really outside of their technical capabilities and their financial realities.

    This started an investigation which involved looking back at where new product ideas came from, in that company, and which were a success or otherwise. The results were surprising. Anything in the new product line that came from top management should be ignored. They were out of touch with the customers and often, it seemed, with reality. The most successful new products emanated from the Ministry of Defence in those halcyon 'cost plus' days. The sales force were pretty good at spotting potential winners, which is not surprising as they were in daily contact with the customers. Usually, their ideas were for existing customers and often resulted in increasing the product range without significantly increasing the overall market. How did Market Research do? Don't be silly, we didn't have such a department.

    Needless to say, some ten years after leaving the company it had drifted into oblivion, but oh what fun it had been. Bits for the Advanced Passenger Train, the TSR2 and many other less well documented failures had flowed from this factory. The company had no direction and no parameters by which to identify where they ought to be going. Eventually, they didn't even have a company.

Write a complete process for the service you are going to develop

The next few pages sound rather boring. They are but they are also perhaps among the most important few pages in this section of the book.

    First, it has been decided that the company will be developing a product or service for a particular market, and it fits within the strategic framework that has been specified as right for the organisation. Then, it is necessary to compile a complete model of the process for the development of this product. This will describe, in great detail, the stages that the product will have to go through in order to be developed into a saleable item. These should be taken right through to the termination of the project and also consider selling, the service side and the eventual disposal of the product, if this is relevant.

Of course, this is extremely difficult to do at the start and is bound to be wrong. It will be improved upon and updated as the development goes through the various stages of this process. Even though what we are advocating sounds very much like guesswork it is still absolutely vital that it is done, as will become apparent. Over a period of time, the more people in the organisation compile these models the better they will become at them.

> **THERE IS NO ONE MODEL OF THE PROCESS THAT SUITS EVERY PARTICULAR ORGANISATION, OR EVERY PARTICULAR PRODUCT OR SERVICE, OR EVEN THE SAME PRODUCT OR SERVICE REPEATED WITHIN THE SAME ORGANISATION.**

But there are sections and elements of models that are likely to be repeated from service to service and from organisation to organisation and there is certainly a broad sequence that can be shown, such as the one in Figure 4.2.

If you find a process model that appears to be repeated from one product to another then it is likely that you have not included sufficient detail. It was the Polish engineer Rohatyinski (1990) who said that it was the attempts to make these models universal that made them unworkable. Figure 4.3 is nearer to that which your organisation will need to develop, but even this falls far short of the complexity and detail that we recommend.

The most useful models are those that show what should be done and also the outcome or output from each stage of the process. The output of each stage become the input to the next stage so building up some of the 'small steps of the specification' as mentioned in the Introduction and described more fully later in this Time Frame.

> **THROUGHOUT THE PROCESS YOU SHOULD CONTINUALLY ASSESS AGAINST THE OBJECTIVES, ENSURE ADEQUATE FINANCE, CONTINUALLY REFER TO THE MARKET AND CONTINUALLY CONSIDER ABANDONING THE PROJECT.**

So why do you need so much detail?

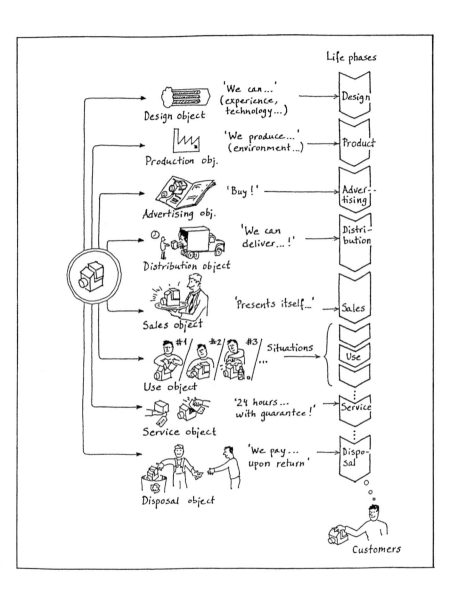

Figure 4.2   A typical broad model of the process
(Permission of M. M. Andreasen)

		ACTIVITY	OUTPUT

Management commitment

Before starting have:

		Quality and reliability	
		Reacting to market pull	
		Effective sales unit	
		Financial control	
		Organisational control	

	Layer 1	Identify organisational	
Business		Frameworks & Parameters	Main management
Environment		(Technological, financial, skills,	guidelines
		timescales, production,	
		implementation and other	
		competencies.)	
		Investigate business environment	

Select the product champion
Form core team   design circle

Overall business	Layer 2	Analysis of Objective	
objectives		Analysis of opportunitites	
		Identification of key activities	Business plan
		Idea generating	Trigger for perceived
			business & product
		Strategic specification	opportunities
		Initial marketing	Possible threats &
		specification	opportunities
		Budgetary requirement	Required return and
		Initial staffing requirements	maximum costs
		Preliminary service specs.	
		Objectives setting	Mission statement
		Main review (go/hold/abandon)	

Idea formulation,	Layer 3	Explanation, preliminary	Target market identified
analysis, and		assessment against objectives	
evaluation		Business analysis	Projected cashflow statement
		Market research/desk research	Complete process model
		Identify, qualify, quantify need	Review of past performance
		Competition analysis	Likely competitor response
		Relevant innovations	
		Initial costing	Multidisciplinary team
		Identify people	Roles and Responsibility
		Identify timescales	Matrix
		Segmentation analysis	

	Layer 4	FEASIBILITY STUDY	
		Main review: Assessment and screening	
		PRODUCT/SERVICE DEFINITION(S)	
		(go/hold/abandon)	

Planning	Layer 5	Product status specification	Blueprinting and process
		Find product status (macro	mapping
		and micro)	
		Service audit	

	Layer 6	Preliminary technical specification	
		Costings refined, service model	
		Preliminary marketing specification	
		Compromise	
		Expansion potential	

Figure 4.3   Process sequence for the development of products and services

		ACTIVITY	**OUTPUT**
	Layer 7	Assemble full specification	
		Main review: Assessment (go/hold/abandon)	
Concept	Layer 8	Concept identification Concept assessment/evaluation Concept selection Costings refined	Preferred option Final costings
		Main review: (go/hold/abandon)	
Development	Layer 9	Embodiment design Full technical specification Dynamic product design Staffing requirements identified	
	Layer 10	Static product design Dynamic process design Dynamic product testing	
	Layer 11	Detail design Dynamic process testing Static process design Maintenance and servicing facility design Main marketing strategy (promotion, pricing, distribution) Full cost of the design Contract negotiations with suppliers/purchasers	
		Main review: (go/hold/abandon)	
Implementation	Layer 12	The 'doing it' stage of the design Product prototype testing: trial, user test Implement/manufacture/production/construction Purchase and procurement Set up operation Prepare user manuals/training schedules/system manuals	Fine tuning of the process
		Main review: (go/hold/abandon)	
Commercialisation Product availability	Layer 13	Launch/announce/educate/promote Full operation Sell Use Evaluate project	
Monitoring in use **performance**		Assessment Evaluation (financial) Reaction Appraisal Update → Re-design On-going testing Update → Re-design	Product improvement Process improvement FEEDBACK
Termination		Terminate project Decommission Disposal of product	

NOTE: The activities in each layer are undertaken in parallel (Concurrent working).

1   Concurrency

Having written the process down in great detail and in a linear form, it is then possible to identify those stages of the process that can be done in parallel. Identifying the concurrencies has the effect of shortening the total time from start to finish. The previous work on concurrent engineering, simultaneous working or parallel processing, (it's all the same thing), is one of communication. Inadequate communication is where most attempts at simultaneous working fall down.

In 1990, Bishop stated that the concept of concurrent engineering was something 'which, by now, almost everyone has heard of but few practise'. A report on a survey undertaken in 1993 by The Design Council found that of 700 replies from UK industry fewer than 20% 'have adopted concurrent engineering as the preferred way to tackle product development'. This would appear to be a strange finding as there are apparently obvious advantages to concurrent engineering.

In spite of this, quite a lot of work is currently being undertaken on simultaneous engineering. Much of this has been unsuccessful and this may be partly due to failings in describing the design process. Wikstrom and Erichsen (1990) have determined that the design models currently used are inadequate. We can partially 'kill two birds with one stone' in this research. By looking at the early stages in detail and by identifying useful and useable models, these will be reflected in the sequence and content of the specifications used.

One observation on simultaneous working (Shelley 1994) was that for it to succeed 'everyone must have access to the data, and there should only be one version of it. Everyone should also be able to mark up their opinions and observations. On the other hand, it is essential that only certain people be allowed to make changes.' A good spec is, therefore, essential in simultaneous working.

Mortimer and Hartley (1990) quote examples of 50% reduction in lead time or 50% reduction in product costs being achieved. They also say that successful companies need to define clear goals. Leppit (1993) has stated that 'the right process' must be established and these 'have to be complemented by the correct organisation and infrastructure support'. Constable (1993) states that 'progress plans are needed to show what is due to happen when, also where and how concurrency of activity is to take place'. This suggests the need to describe the design process through a detailed design model.

Until a process for each specific design to be undertaken has been fully described it cannot be possible to specify which aspects can be done in parallel or what form the communication should take. In our research, by looking at the early stages in detail and by identifying the sequence and content of the specifications used, we believe that useful and useable models will emerge. This could make simultaneous engineering easier to implement and therefore generate a greater readiness for its adoption. Constable (1993) agrees:

> *Since the success of concurrent engineering depends critically on making the team fully accountable for achieving the results required, it is essential that these requirements (i.e. the brief) be defined with great care and clarity. If this is not done, concurrent engineering or no, the product will have to be redesigned downstream . . . Drafting well-considered design briefs is not easy. Unless such competencies exist, the adoption of concurrent engineering practices may be premature.*

2   People (roles and responsibility)

The next stage, with the model, is to identify who will be involved in each stage of the process. This is best undertaken by developing a roles and responsibilities matrix, similar to that shown in Figure 4.4. On the vertical axis is shown all the stages of the development process and on the horizontal axis is shown the various people who will be involved in completing that particular stage of the process. To do this effectively you need to include not only those who will be actually doing the work, but also those who need to be consulted, need to advise, need to be informed, as well as one person, and it should be only one person, who is responsible for the completion of that particular stage of the process. If you give the responsibility for completion to more than one person they will tend to leave it to each other. Specifically naming one person as being held responsible tends to avoid this.

Also, by doing this at the start you will identify shortages within the skills available, but at the start this need not be a problem. For example, if you discover at the start that in fifteen months' time you require three people with particular skills, but you in fact only have one person with these skills, there is plenty of time to either employ or retrain people or subcontract this stage of the work to another organisation. Problems are significantly reduced if they are predicted sufficiently far in advance so that it is possible to cure them before they become a problem.

3   Finance

When starting a new project it is normal to specify an overall budget within which it must be completed. With a complete process model it is now advisable to allocate the budget to various stages of the process

The activities as described in the sequence for the development of products and services shown in Fig. 4.3	The NAMES of JOB TITLES of those who should be INVOLVED at the various STAGES of the PROCESS						
	A	B	C	D	E	F	G
BUSINESS ENVIRONMENT	✓		✓			✓	
CORE TEAM							✓
BUSINESS OBJECTIVES			✓	✓	✓		
MAIN REVIEW	✓	✓			✓		
IDEA FORMULATION ANALYSIS & EVALUATION					✓		
FEASIBILITY STUDY	✓		✓				
PLANNING	✓	✓					

(And on through the whole process)

Figure 4.4   Roles and responsibility matrix

model. The first purpose for doing this is to see if it is actually possible to complete what is required within the money that is available. If it is not then either seek a bigger budget or don't bother to start. One of the four causes of product failure is financial failure. You may run out of money towards the end of the project but the root cause of this is that the organisation had not considered the finance that was needed right at the start of the project.

The other reason for splitting up the budget between the various stages of the process is to give an early indication when the project is going out of control financially. David Farrar, formerly of Cranfield University, plotted the expenditure of various aircraft developments and found that in all but one it was possible to see very near the start of the project that the costs were going out of control. But those developing the planes did not become fully aware of this until much later. The only aircraft that he identified at that time that was developed on budget was the European Airbus.

4   Time

The next stage, (remember this is still all done before any work is undertaken in earnest on the project), is to allocate the time that will be spent on each stage. Much like the allocation of the finances, allocation of the time allows those involved to determine whether what they are trying to do is possible within the time allowed to do it. If it is not it may be reason enough not to start. Ken Wallace of Cambridge University was involved, quite a few years back, in developing particular products for the Falklands War. The main criteria in the development of these products was that the item had to be on the beach ready for loading at a particular time on a particular day. If it was not the whole development was a waste of time. It was the time parameter which determined what could be included within the development. This tended to reduce the innovation or complication to that which it was certain could be completed on time. Budget, in this case, was less of a problem.

Now, in your particular organisation, you may have to finish the development for, say, a particular exhibition and by allocating the time to each stage of the programme you can see if what you are trying to do can, in fact, be completed by the time that it must be completed. Furthermore, similar again to the finance, you will be able to see, as soon as the development is slipping behind the planned schedule, when the actual time taken for each process stage is longer than that specified in the original plan.

5   Priority

Now, in any organisation there are, probably, several projects going on at the same time and several groups of people will be working on some, or all of these projects. Having developed the matrix showing the activities/people for each project that is being undertaken, the next stage is to place all the matrices on top of each other. This will show where there is a clash for skills and resources. This is where the senior managers should identify and specify priorities.

For example, if next November the same group of people are scheduled to be working on two projects it must be specified which project has the higher priority and on which project they will be working. The project with the highest priority, of course, will use the people and the project with the lower priority will be delayed. Now in many cases this doesn't matter, especially as it has been identified right at the start of the project. It might mean that the project will be delayed by a month, fifteen months in the future.

Delays are only a problem if they are disruptive and cause other people problems. For example, in concurrent working many activities are dependent on other activities and unanticipated delays in one area of the organisation can cause significant disruption in other areas. Delays predicted well in advance should not fall into this category. If, for example, two projects require the same skills at the same time and both programmes cannot be delayed – fashion is a good example of this – then it is a case of subcontracting aspects of the programme to overcome the problem. Once again, because there is sufficient advance warning of the likely problem the cure should be achieved with little panic or disruption.

The previous few pages may seem dry and rather tedious but you can see that, essentially, this is the key to managing a new service. It enables those involved to identify a programme and to predict many problems before they occur. It is then possible to manage your way out of these problems. The alternative is to continually 'fire-fight', as you blunder from one disaster to another.

The vital key is that the process that you identify, for the development being proposed, must be extremely detailed. It is well worth spending much more time than you are at the moment (from our experience it is usually insufficient) to develop the process before you wander off into the unknown.

This cannot be done by one person. Certainly, one person must lead it, the 'product champion', but the only people who can say how long each activity stage will take and how much it will cost will be those who have the skills in those particular activities. They need to be consulted and their answers accepted.

ZOO OF THE NEW

Developing new products and services and managing that development is a bit like running a Zoo. Each department is staffed by some pretty strange animals, that are usually separated almost by cages and, if you let them all out to mingle with each other, they may not go as far as eating each other but they may come near to it at times. Also, with new products, you should start off with a veritable menagerie of new ideas before you eventually home in on one. Hopefully, a successful product.

Organisation of communication is extremely difficult and it would be glib to overlook the difficulties of dealing with people and personalities. Having an effective process is vital but whether it works or not comes down to good leadership and co-ordination.

Choosing a Leader

When improving existing or developing new products and services it is necessary that this should be co-ordinated by an overall project leader.

This person takes overall responsibility, but this does not necessarily mean that this person does all the work or is even responsible for seeing that the various stages of the work have been completed, as much of this can be delegated. We call this person the 'product champion'.

The term 'product champion' generally has two definitions. In BS 7000 part 10 it is defined as a 'person dedicated to the promotion and introduction of a new product, although not necessarily responsible for any aspect of the programme'. This implies that it could be a director who actively supports the project, but need not be involved. Another description of a product champion and the one that we choose, is one who is actively involved in every stage of the programme. When developing a new product, various people with various skills will be involved at different stages of the programme. They will arrive when their skills are required and leave when they are no longer required, but may return later. The people who are involved at the various stages are indicated on the roles and responsibility matrix. This implies that there could be no one person who is involved throughout.

It is important that one person is involved at every stage, so that they know why, late in the programme, decisions were made earlier in the programme. Developing new products requires continuity. This person should be the product champion. The product champion must be given the power of a director for this product only. But you do not want a director undertaking this role, because it is a waste of a director's skills and an unnecessary cost to an organisation, especially as the director will, probably, be involved towards the end of the programme, when it is being implemented. Hence the product champion. As such, although the product champion is allowed to make the management decisions throughout the project, these decisions must be supported by the directors, they must trust the product champion. For example, if the product champion makes a decision concerning the project and next week this decision is overturned by the directors, the product champion will have no credibility in subsequent decision making.

The product champion must be an enthusiast and a realist. They must encourage those others involved in the project and push them to achieve what are often difficult targets within what are often tight financial constraints. On the other hand, they must be a realist, in as much as when things go wrong and it is apparent that the targets or specification cannot be achieved they should recommend that the project be abandoned. In reality, this often means that the final decision for abandoning is taken by the directors on the product champion's advice, having reiterated back to the earlier stages of the process to see if the problem could be overcome by, perhaps, changing aspects of the specification.

THE NPD JUGGLER

The product champion's job is a difficult one and the ideal person is one who is capable of seeing the whole picture. He or she has to be a bit of a 'juggler'. For example, in the development of a manufactured product there are natural areas of conflict. The production manager, wanting economies of purchasing, economies of scale in manufacture and, perhaps, to automate the process, would like to make as few variations around a standard product as possible. On the other hand, the marketing manager wants to give the customers precisely what they want and wants a large variety of products around the basic model. The product champion has to be able to see the whole picture and should be able to conclude 'having heard the arguments on both sides, I have decided to make (say) three variants.'

The product champion needs the ability to see the whole picture, but this does not necessarily mean they are in the most skilled or senior role.

Recently, we were involved in some consultancy in an organisation that made very highly technical products. At the early stage of the process of developing a new version, those involved were mainly directors, all over the age of forty and all very technically competent specialists in their own very narrow field. It was recommended to us that the ideal product champion, in this case, was a twenty-five year old, who had a degree but was otherwise not very senior within the organisation. This person was ideally suited, as he was capable of seeing the whole picture, when the well qualified specialists focused too much on their own particular area. This meant that, in effect, we were going to advise that a twenty-five year old was to 'manage' the older directors and this could have caused obvious problems. The solution turned out to be quite easy. We drew the directors together and explained why the product champion was the right person for the job, pointed out the possible conflict that could arise, but added 'it is a sign of your maturity to be able to operate within such a system'. Nobody likes to appear immature and the system worked well. The product champion was the right person for the job.

A product champion should start this role with small less important projects and having shown themselves to be successful they can then be given increasingly larger projects, which involve more people and a greater budget.

Design Teams

People come and go during a project as their expertise is required. The maximum number that should be involved, at any one stage, should be nine (Schein 1969; BS 7000 part 3, 1994; BS 7000 part 2 1997). Belbin (1981) suggests a maximum of ten. At the start of a project, after the process has been written and then the roles and responsibility matrix, it is possible to identify who will be involved at each stage. If more than nine are required at the meetings, at any stage, the process should be split into two groups for that stage and then joined together later in the process. For larger projects, it may be necessary to split the process into one controlling circle and peripheral circles. Effectively, each peripheral circle will need its own product champion and this person will attend the meeting of the main circle and provide their input into the workings of the main circle. This can cause problems: having put in a system as described, in one organisation, we were invited back because there were problems associated with it. What was happening was that teams in the sub-circles were agreeing amongst themselves a particular solution to that stage of the process and for their particular part of the product. The leader of the sub-circles would then go to the main circle and present their group's ideas. Of course, their solution had to fit in with the solution of everybody else and quite often it didn't. Compromises were necessary. Developing new products is all compromise. Having agreed the compromise in the main circle, the group leaders would then go back to their own circle and would be accused of 'selling out'. This resulted in conflict.

We developed an artificial product scenario that overcame this problem in quite a clever way. This consisted of three specific parts, which could be drawn up separately by three separate groups, but then had to all fit together to make one complete item. This was used in the organisation in a half-day workshop. The people involved were split into three groups, we having first been primed by one of the directors in the organisation, with the names of the three 'troublemakers' (for want of a better word). The sub-groups developed their own solution to the problem and then the three previously awkward group members had to decide between themselves the design of the overall product. Of course, this involved compromise. The product was chosen so compromise was inevitable. Having compromised, these three people had to go back to their own groups to explain why they had compromised, against a background of our accusations that they had 'sold out'. This simple exercise, apparently, solved the problem. Compromise is not selling out and compromise is inevitable, as long as it can be justified.

5

New Product Failures and How to Avoid Them in Your Organisation

If only they were as Bright as you are

If you wish to look for successes don't look at the large inventions, such as the Hovercraft (a failure anyway); look to the small items that are part of your everyday life. For example; paperclips (invented by a Norwegian – and there is a sculpture of a very large one in Norway to celebrate the fact), safety pins, zips and staplers.

Here, we look at the reasons for success and failure and how to avoid wasting time on pointless new products. By understanding what causes failure and success it is possible for an organisation to eliminate the potential failures and concentrate on the potential successes. This avoids lost opportunity, time and money and shows where management should direct their effort. Some of the great blunders of recent times could have been avoided if only somebody had applied just a few simple techniques, a little expertise and common sense – usually right at the beginning of the project. Through understanding what causes failures, these problems could then be avoided next time – perhaps, in your organisation.

We like failures (except our own) and one can learn so much from them. In more than thirty years of designing new products Bill has had more than his share of Concordes, Edsels and Sinclair C5s in his history. Fortunately, due to the small scale and lack of exposure we have managed to keep these fairly quiet. Amongst them were included the all singing all dancing safety system that nobody could afford and few wanted. This was fortunate because it couldn't be made either!

New products in this particular organisation usually started the same way. As soon as one of our salesmen would appear in the office, describing a new product wanted by one of the existing customers, a pencil would be grabbed and the creative juices would be allowed to flow. Innovations were ten a penny (unfortunately, innovations cost a good deal more than that). Invariably, only that one customer wanted the device . . . or something similar. Like Chinese whispers, the salesman had not heard it right, had mis-told me, who, probably, misheard him. The result was something nobody wanted.

Never mind, next week another salesman would appear and there would be a new project. I was busy, very busy, with a large number of new products getting into the market. The draughtsmen were working flat out to keep up with the demand for detailed drawings and production was constantly disrupted with short runs of product variations. The tool room was clogged with prototypes. We had a really lively new products programme . . . we had an expensive disaster on our hands.

Since that time, we have seen many new product departments and some of what has just described is apparent in most of them. There had to be a better way of organising and managing new products. But finding time to reorganise things, with the mountain of projects on my programme, made this impossible. This was the first mistake. Organising the management of new products reduces work and also reduces time and cost of new product successes.

The second mistake was to view the new product department as something on its own and not as part of a total process. Everybody who needs to be involved must have the opportunity to make a contribution. This causes communication problems that need to be confronted and overcome. Many companies seem to work on the 'over the wall' principle, as described in Time Frame One, where one department throws the information over the wall and the next department catches it, does their bit to it and then throws it over the wall to the next department. Once the project is over the wall the department can, hopefully, forget about it. Communication between departments is kept to an absolute minimum and management of each department is kept quite separate. Everybody is working hard but they are not working together. The net effect of this is that what the customer wants is not what the customer gets. These walls need to be broken down.

Management is about the planning, organisation and control of resources to achieve objectives. In other words, you cannot manage projects unless you look at the entire process.

SUCCESS	**FAILURE**
TGV	ADVANCE PASSENGER TRAIN
HARRIER JUMP JET	TSR2

VW BEETLE	FORD EDSEL
VHS VIDEO	PHILIPS VIDEO 2000
RADIAL TYRES	DENOVO TYRES
BAC 146	CONCORDE
DYSON VACUUM CLEANER	HOOVER 'FREE FLIGHTS' PROMOTION
SWATCH	SINCLAIR BLACK WATCH
SONY WALKMAN	SONY MINIDISC
COMPACT DISC	DIGITAL AUDIO TAPE
DRIVER'S AIR BAGS	ALLEGRO SQUARE STEERING WHEEL
SATELLITE TELEVISION	SQUARIALS
HYDROFOIL	HOVERCRAFT
MOBILE PHONES	TELEPOINT PHONES (RABBIT)
THE LOTTERY	JUNK BONDS
TELEPHONE BANKING	BARINGS BANK
VALUE ADDED TAX	POLL TAX
GOLDEN GATE BRIDGE	TACUMA NARROWS BRIDGE
FORD ESCORT	FORD PINTO
BUBBLE CAR	SINCLAIR C5
PETROL DRIVEN CARS	ELECTRIC VEHICLES
TRAMS	TROLLEY BUSES
FLUSH TOILETS	EARTH CLOSETS
BOEING 707	D.H. COMET
PRINCESS FLYING BOAT	SPRUCE GOOSE
THE UP-LIFT BRA	EDIBLE UNDERWEAR
TALKING BOOKS	BRITISH LIBRARY
CHEDDAR CHEESE	LYMESWOLD CHEESE

Did it Make a Profit?

Before we can look at failures we must first define success. **The only worthwhile measure of success is financial**, 'did the product make any money?' People often disagree with this view with platitudes such as 'it gave us good publicity' . . . 'it was a flagship product' . . . 'it completed the range' . . . 'it created excitement' . . . 'it was a celebration,' etc.

Put it this way. It is the products and services that your company sells that pay your salary. It is nice to have the other measures of success as well but these must be secondary measures. It is the same in the 'not for profit' sector. You either have to work within a budget, grant, or some other financially based guideline, which amounts to the same thing.

> AND YOU WANT YOUR ORGANISATION TO
> SURVIVE INTO THE FUTURE, SO YOU HAVE TO
> MAKE MONEY IN THE PRESENT.

What about the money made from spin-offs?

Another delusion is that an organisation can make a big profit from all the 'spin offs' that come from a new product failure. As a 'spin off' from a dish of mould, Penicillin was one hell of a profit maker (albeit for the wrong people) but there are cheaper ways of developing the space blanket and non-stick frying pans than going to the moon. David Farrar investigated 'spin-offs' from various products and found that pound for pound the 'spin offs' from Concorde and space race were actually lower than with most other products.

Failures are far more easy to track than successes. Most product successes are the result of somebody inventing, some other group improving and commercialising and then yet another group eventually winning with it. It can happen all in one group – such as the Sony Walkman or 'Post-it Notes' – but these tend to be the exception rather than the rule.

Are you so different in your choices of new products and services? With many of the failures described in this chapter those people involved started at the concept stage, missing out the market research and specification compiling stages. They suffered expensive failures as a result. What perhaps is worse is that whilst they were wasting time doing what they were doing they were not doing something that would have been more profitable. This is lost opportunity.

Of course, it is easy with the benefit of hindsight. But when one actually looks at the reasons behind these failures, with so many, it should have been obvious very early in the new product development process. Essentially, there are four reasons for a product or service failure.

MARKET FAILURE

TECHNICAL FAILURE

FINANCIAL FAILURE

POLITICAL FAILURE

Many people think that the most common reason is technical failure. This is because these make headlines. A plane crashing, a bridge falling down or a ship sinking is news. The real main cause of failure – overwhelmingly so – is market failure, failure to sell enough. A product, one week, is on the supermarket shelves, next week it has as gone. You don't even notice its departure and the void left by it is quickly filled by something else. Market failures probably exceed all the other failures put together.

Where do these failures occur in the process?

Consider where the root cause of these failures are in the new product development process:

Market failure is due to not having assessed the market correctly, not understanding the customer requirements, which should be done right at the beginning.

Technical failure can occur anywhere in the process, the wrong concept was chosen, problems in the detail or errors in manufacture or implementation (in the case of a service).

With **financial failure** you run out of money, usually in the implementation stage, but the cause is rooted in the specification, right near the start. If you haven't the money to complete the job, don't bother starting.

Political failure tends to occur with only very large projects. If the government is likely to be involved, ensure that you have found out what they are prepared to accept. You should do this, again, right near the start of the process, at the specification stage.

> **THEREFORE, THREE OF THE FOUR REASONS FOR PRODUCT AND SERVICE FAILURE ARE ROOTED RIGHT AT THE START OF THE PROCESS.**

And most of these failures can be identified and the idea abandoned before they reach the expensive end of the process. These lessons can be applied to any current product or service currently being developed. Identifying potential failures early on can allow one to stop the expense on these and put the resources more towards those products and services that are more likely to bring in a return.

Conversely – its success was its failure

M25 Motorway. Far more people than anticipated used this motorway from the time that it was opened, resulting in it being described a 'the largest car park in Europe'. It certainly is the busiest road in Europe. When it was first proposed it was suggested that it ought to have four lanes in each direction. This was more than the government were prepared to finance. At the time of writing, there are further hold-ups on this motorway as they put in the fourth lane. It has been said that one of the problems with the M25 is that there are too many slip roads on to it. Well, it certainly would reduce the congestion if they blocked off all the entrances!

National Health Service. Since the NHS was started, in Britain, shortly after the Second World War, it has always been used more than was expected. When it first started there were questions asked in the House of Commons querying why there were so many people applying for spectacles and false teeth. Not surprisingly, the answer was that a lot of people needed these but prior to the NHS these people could not afford them. Ever since, it has been a battle to provide a 'free' service that increasingly needs to incorporate the latest (often expensive) advances in medical treatment.

Its failure was its success

The Leaning Tower of Pisa. If this tower hadn't leant over then probably nobody would have been interested in it and it probably would have been demolished centuries ago. It can be seen that it actually began leaning during construction and those involved tried to compensate and straighten it up during building. Recent attempts to prevent further leaning resulted in the tower leaning further. When people were allowed to go up to the top, at each level one could step out on to the perimeter. There are no perimeter fences at all but the top level. Far more scary than the tilt of the building are the over excited student tourists that seem determined to use their back packs as bludgeons to evict other tourists off the tower.

CASE STUDY – BEWARE OF 'SPECIALS'

Companies often have tried to design in variation for every customer at a cost that is usually far greater than they realised. There was a manufacturing organisation that had a standard range of products but it was discovered that 25% of orders involved quite significant modifications from the standard. This caused a production nightmare which effectively had transformed their batch production to that of unit (one-off) production. What was worse was that these 'specials' were being sold at almost the same price as the standard product. It was stated to the Manufacturing Director that through not appreciating the real cost of these specials he was putting the whole company at risk. His answer was that he thought it was good business and he was going to encourage sales of these specials without introducing greater true cost 'awareness'. Six months later this well known and well respected company went into liquidation.

Not Enough Failures?

It was said earlier on in this chapter that the failure rate of new products and services is much too high and needs to be reduced. It will now be suggested that, perhaps, it is not high enough. What is too high is the cost of these failures.

Reducing the investment in failures can be a major step forward in the management of your products. Consider the cost of the various stages of the process. Initially, these are relatively low as there are not many people involved, no investment in capital equipment or materials and most of the work (market research, etc.) is still only on paper. As the design progresses the costs increase dramatically, especially during the implementation stage. The early stages or 'front end' is the low cost end. A product failing at the market research end of the process is much less expensive and therefore far less dangerous to your company than one failing after it has been put on the market. So, as a manager, you should emphasise your effort at the front end to identify and eliminate potential new product failures before they become a heavy investment, before they become financial disasters. Furthermore, because the cost of the front end is relatively small, it is possible to double the effort and the cost of these early stages, without seriously increasing the overall cost of the entire process.

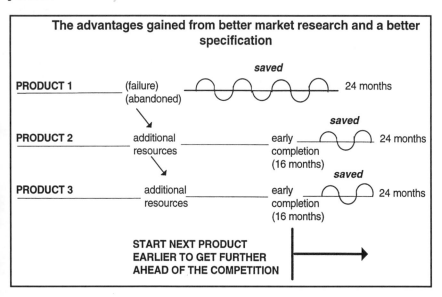

Figure 5.1   The advantages of identifying and abandoning an idea early in the process

EXPERIENCE

LACK OF MARKET RESEARCH =

FAILURE

Evaluation of all concepts and elimination of those most likely to fail must occur at the low cost, early stages of the process. The time, labour and financial resources can then be applied to the remaining potentially more successful projects. The additional resources when applied to these will reduce the time to market and hence reduce costs (e.g. interest repayments) and, probably, increase market share and profits (through skimming) – thus beating the competition. It also allows those in the organisation to start the next project earlier in order to get even further ahead of the competition.

In the future it should be possible to identify and eliminate most potential failures even before one starts. This will mean extending the process even further at the early stage and this is covered in Time Frame Four.

6
The Start

Important Stages in a Typical Process Model

As stated, there is no one model that describes the sequence of stages that a product or service goes through from start to finish. What is now described are the main points of consideration in a typical model of the process and you must develop your own that is right for your product in your organisation.

Triggers

This word was first thought of by Ken Rutter, when the first Design Management Standard was being written, back in the 1980s. It means that which may lead to a new product or service and so, kicks off the process. There now follows a list of triggers, taken from BS 7000 Part 2 (1997): (Reproduced with the permission of BSI):

a) *an order or enquiry from a customer;*
b) *a response to a perceived market need (market-pull);*
c) *government initiatives and charters;*
d) *a research finding, perhaps associated with the development of a new technology (technology-push);*
e) *a new way of applying existing technology that may result in an innovation;*
f) *a license or franchise agreement;*
g) *a creative thought from any source;*
h) *a change of company facilities or assets that may provide an opportunity to redesign the product;*
I) *problems, failures or deficiencies with existing products;*
j) *loss of sales to competitors, success of competitors or a decline in orders;*
k) *improvement to existing products to reduce their cost, simplify, rationalise or to 'stretch' the design;*
l) *complaints and ideas from, or surveys of, customers, sales staff or dealers, etc.;*
m) *published market research findings;*

n)   *new patent applications;*
o)   *inventors, academics, scientists and consultants;*
p)   *new regulations, legislation, standards and codes of practice;*
q)   *economic trends;*
r)   *quality circles and suggestion schemes (including customer suggestion schemes);*
s)   *observation, imitation or improvement of competitors' products;*
t)   *environmental issues;*
u)   *a change in the organisation's or competitor's vision or image;*
v)   *augmenting the product to get closer to the customer (for example, direct delivery)*
w)   *increased leisure time;*
x)   *community welfare need;*
y)   *experience and intuition;*
z)   *natural change (for example, the tooling of an old product needs replacing).*

Potential products and services will emanate from these which should all fit into the allowed strategic framework of the organisation. Fairly early in the process one will start to look at the market.

Look at the Market

For some time there has been criticsm on how companies do 'market research'. They often rely on the Panatela smoking salesman ringing up the head office from his car phone in between business lunches to describe his latest ideas for new product. He uses words like 'hunch', 'gut-feeling', 'intuition', 'seat-of-the-pants approach' and 'experience' to justify the need for the new product and for the lack of any formal market research.

It has always been said that this is absolutely wrong and that market research is vital. Then, in Britain, the General Election of 1992 was held. From it was learned one thing, that market research is a pretty inexact science. How can it be said that you must find out the customer requirements for form, fit, function, performance, aesthetics, ergonomics and price, etc. when, after this mammoth market research exercise, they couldn't even find out which box people were going to put a cross into, even after they had done it (exit polls)!

In spite of this, thorough market research must be advocated and Cooper (1988) once again confirms his earlier findings that the main source of product failure is and always has been, not understanding the customer's requirements. Just remember that market research is always a bit 'hit and miss' but, even so, it is still a more accurate way of finding out who your customers are than relying on the salesman in his Vauxhall.

ON THE OTHER HAND: DO YOU NEED MARKET RESEARCH AT ALL?

'Market research is bunk. I am an engineer'. Alec Issigonis said this and, of course, he was brilliant and designed the Morris Minor and Mini. When the Mini came out in 1959 it was priced at £490. This price was chosen because there was still some Ford 95E models available (the Ford Popular) and it was considered that as the Mini was the smallest car it ought to be the cheapest car. This showed that those involved with the marketing of the Mini did not understand the market. Much marketing is still based around the four Ps: Product, Price, Place and Promotion. If they had understood the market they would have looked beyond the Mini being just a small car. It was chic, it looked good in Chelsea, it would eventually be driven by stars, such as Peter Sellers, Sophia Loren, Twiggy and Marc Bolan. Small doesn't necessarily mean cheap and in this case it meant style.

It is well known that the Mini was a success. At that time, it was manufactured in Australia, South Africa, Italy, as well as in Britain. It was the second biggest selling car at that time, behind the VW Beetle. Yet, by being pitched at a low price, the Mini only made for its manufacturers £5 profit per car. This meant a great success, but the company was getting into financial difficulties with it, all because they didn't understand the market. They could have charged an additional £50 for the car and who knows what would have happened to the company then, with all this additional revenue. Marketing, marketing research and understanding markets is important. If one looks at the history of the Range Rover, BMC introduced the vehicle also well below the price it ought to have been, but fortunately did realise what the product really was in time to make money from it.

At least these were products that people wanted. Too often, companies drift into new products without a clue as to what the customers really want. Alan Topalian (1980) summed this up when he wrote:

'Managers and designers do go seriously astray when they begin to believe that they can be effective arbiters of consumer needs without first researching those such needs sensibly. When, in ignorance or shear arrogance, managers and designers begin to rationalise their private wants into fictitious or superficial consumer needs.' It is necessary to investigate and understand markets.

To get a crude but effective initial understanding of your market just looking at the advantages and disadvantages of any new product idea is an ideal way at the start to determine if it is worth pursuing an idea. To make a start, it is necessary to identify something to compare it to and hence the competition and market niche. This train of thought should be followed:

First identify the likely competition for the proposed product or service. The competition may be wider than you think, remember 'Marketing Myopia' by Levitt (1960).

- **Then list the advantages and disadvantages** when compared with
  the competition (of course, they will not be of equal value but focus
  on the most important).
- **Can the disadvantages be eliminated or turned into advantages
  through some modification of the proposal?**

If the market niche has too many disadvantages when compared with what
is already available then look at a different niche. If you can't find one
where the advantages significantly exceed the disadvantages then forget
the idea. If you can find a possible niche **then GUESS the following**:

- **Approximate size of market**
- **Approximate market share that could be expected**
- **Anticipated selling price**
- **And therefore the estimated turnover**

**What is the sensible amount that can be spent on the new product
development?**

- **Is it possible?/Is it worth pursuing?**
- **NO – abandon / YES – do market research (you haven't done
  any yet).**

The whole of the above is pretty hit-and-miss and, of course, only guesses
are used, but quite a full understanding of the new products potential can
be achieved in just one morning's work by a group of sensible people
sitting around a table. It is surprising how many non-viable ideas can be
eliminated through this simple method. If you want to try it look at the
viability of electric cars. Having convinced yourself that they are a waste
of time then start wondering why so many companies, big and small, are
wasting theirs.

This technique (it's really too simple to call it that) often also shows
what is needed to turn such a failure into a success. In the case of an
electric car it is something that gives it more range, more speed, quick
charging, which is low cost to buy and use – a new battery. So, they
should be developing that and not a car (or looking at someone who is).

In effect, the advantages are much the same as the benefits of ownership as described at the start of this Time Frame, which are the same as
USPs. These are almost the same as the most important elements in your
specification, which are described a bit later in this Time Frame. In a
way, it's a circular process which should have the same focus throughout.

It's all about identifying who you are aiming your products at, finding out what they want and then giving it to them.

THE DIFFERENCE BETWEEN MARKET RESEARCH AND MARKETING RESEARCH

Now you can impress friends at cocktail parties and win new clients and customers purely by voicing the difference between the two oft confused terms:

Marketing Research *addresses the question – 'What mix of qualities and price will attract customers to your company's products, rather than those of the competition?'*

whereas **Market Research** *is concerned with analysing the size and nature of a particular market – one aspect of a broader activity known as marketing research. (Engineering Industries Training Board)*

Knowing this was worth the price of this book alone!

7

Specifications and Subspecifications – The Control for New Products and Services

Introduction

In the early part of the design process it is necessary, as put by Elliot (1993): 'to turn the abstract and (usually) ill-formed idea of the customer (his "dream") into a concrete statement of requirements against which suppliers can tender and carry out detailed design (a "specification")'.

In BS 7000 (1989) the importance of specifications is confirmed: 'It is essential for success in the market that the brief should be comprehensive and complete and deal adequately with the requirements.'

The earliest spec was pointed out by John Doyle, of the Institution of Engineering Designers, and it appears in Genesis Ch. 6, Verses 14–16:

> *Make thee an ark of gopher wood; rooms shalt thou make in the ark, and shall pitch it within and without with pitch.*

> *And this is the fashion which thou shalt make it of: The length of the ark shall be three hundred cubits, the breadth of it fifty cubits, and the height of it thirty cubits.*

> *A window shalt thou make to the ark, and in a cubit shalt thou finish it above; and the door of the ark shalt thou set in the side thereof, with lower, second, and third storeys shalt thou make it.*

So if God thought it a good idea to issue specs then one is on pretty safe ground in stating that they are important.
Incidentally, Noah must have been a clever chap. He floated a company when the rest of the world was in liquidation.

Figure 7.1 reproduces part of a 200 year-old specification for the 'Cutting, Embanking, Lining and Puddling' on the Kennett and Avon Canal which has been reproduced with the permission of the Hampshire Record Office (their ref. 8M62/140L). It is quite a good specification and a lot better than many that people try to work with in today's more exacting age. (Again thanks to John Doyle.)

An analysis of specifications in industry show the main reasons for failure to be inadequate specifications. The situation is even worse with organisations that operate in the service sector. Manufacturers may write specifications badly, companies in the service sector often don't even write them at all! Evidence suggests that many companies are reluctant to compile comprehensive specifications since the process can be difficult and time consuming and there are few procedures on precisely how this should be undertaken.

Having taught Design Management, for several years, to post graduates on part time management courses and having given these students the theory, they were then set an assignment looking at a product or service development within their organisations. The main purpose of the assignment was to assess the understanding, knowledge and competence of the student. In effect, this provides a selection of up to 250 'case studies' every year written by those often actively involved in new products, of which over 95% are employed in the service sector. An analysis of these showed the overwhelming main reasons for failure to be rooted in inadequate market research and inadequate specifications, (and anyway, the former should be reflected in the latter).

The results also show that having been taught how to compile suitable specifications, the students are not only able to identify the errors made in earlier projects, they are also able to improve their performance in subsequent efforts. This indicates that it is possible to teach practitioners how to compile more effective specifications and hence improve the effectiveness of their organisation's products.

Writing a good brief is not easy. Several elements are dependent on others or are interrelated. The processes adopted, such as automation, depend on the potential number of customers, the technology available, the costs involved, as well as the facilities available and the actions of the competition.

How to Write a Specification

This must cover all the aspects of the product to be developed and provides a mantle around the subsequent stages of the development process.

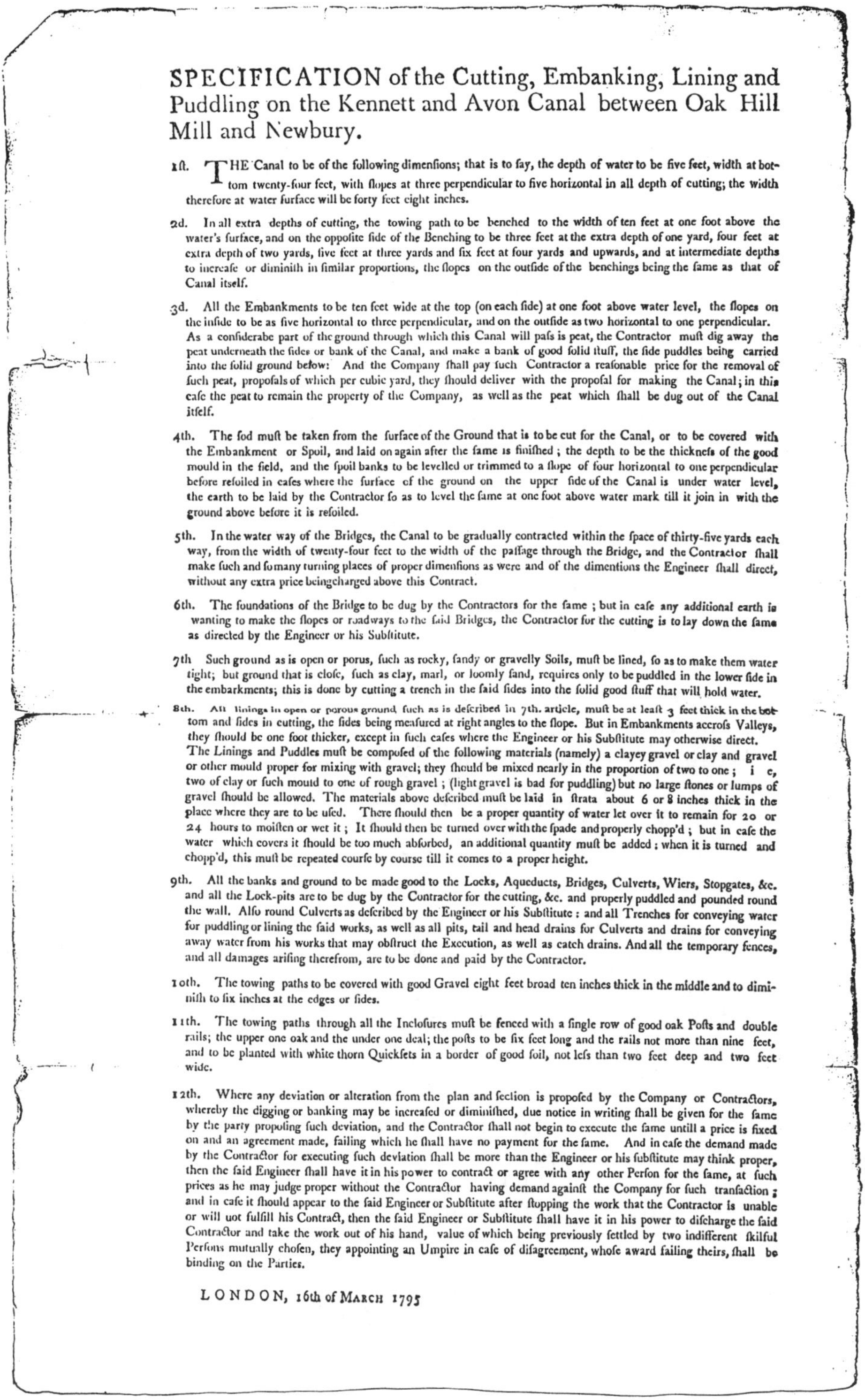

SPECIFICATION of the Cutting, Embanking, Lining and Puddling on the Kennett and Avon Canal between Oak Hill Mill and Newbury.

1ft.   THE Canal to be of the following dimensions; that is to say, the depth of water to be five feet, width at bottom twenty-four feet, with slopes at three perpendicular to five horizontal in all depth of cutting; the width therefore at water surface will be forty feet eight inches.

2d.   In all extra depths of cutting, the towing path to be benched to the width of ten feet at one foot above the water's surface, and on the opposite side of the Benching to be three feet at the extra depth of one yard, four feet at extra depth of two yards, five feet at three yards and six feet at four yards and upwards, and at intermediate depths to increase or diminish in similar proportions, the slopes on the outside of the benchings being the same as that of Canal itself.

3d.   All the Embankments to be ten feet wide at the top (on each side) at one foot above water level, the slopes on the inside to be as five horizontal to three perpendicular, and on the outside as two horizontal to one perpendicular.
As a considerable part of the ground through which this Canal will pass is peat, the Contractor must dig away the peat underneath the sides or bank of the Canal, and make a bank of good solid stuff, the side puddles being carried into the solid ground below: And the Company shall pay such Contractor a reasonable price for the removal of such peat, proposals of which per cubic yard, they should deliver with the proposal for making the Canal; in this case the peat to remain the property of the Company, as well as the peat which shall be dug out of the Canal itself.

4th.   The sod must be taken from the surface of the Ground that is to be cut for the Canal, or to be covered with the Embankment or Spoil, and laid on again after the same is finished ; the depth to be the thickness of the good mould in the field, and the spoil banks to be levelled or trimmed to a slope of four horizontal to one perpendicular before resoiled in cases where the surface of the ground on the upper side of the Canal is under water level, the earth to be laid by the Contractor so as to level the same at one foot above water mark till it join in with the ground above before it is resoiled.

5th.   In the water way of the Bridges, the Canal to be gradually contracted within the space of thirty-five yards each way, from the width of twenty-four feet to the width of the passage through the Bridge, and the Contractor shall make such and so many turning places of proper dimensions as were and of the dimentions the Engineer shall direct, without any extra price being charged above this Contract.

6th.   The foundations of the Bridge to be dug by the Contractors for the same ; but in case any additional earth is wanting to make the slopes or roadways to the said Bridges, the Contractor for the cutting is to lay down the same as directed by the Engineer or his Substitute.

7th   Such ground as is open or porus, such as rocky, sandy or gravelly Soils, must be lined, so as to make them water tight; but ground that is close, such as clay, marl, or loomly sand, requires only to be puddled in the lower side in the embankments; this is done by cutting a trench in the said sides into the solid good stuff that will hold water.

8th.   All linings in open or porous ground such as is described in 7th. article, must be at least 3 feet thick in the bottom and sides in cutting, the sides being measured at right angles to the slope. But in Embankments accross Vallyes, they should be one foot thicker, except in such cases where the Engineer or his Substitute may otherwise direct.
The Linings and Puddles must be composed of the following materials (namely) a clayey gravel or clay and gravel or other mould proper for mixing with gravel; they should be mixed nearly in the proportion of two to one ; i e, two of clay or such mould to one of rough gravel ; (light gravel is bad for puddling) but no large stones or lumps of gravel should be allowed. The materials above described must be laid in strata about 6 or 8 inches thick in the place where they are to be used. There should then be a proper quantity of water let over it to remain for 20 or 24 hours to moisten or wet it ; It should then be turned over with the spade and properly chopp'd ; but in case the water which covers it should be too much absorbed, an additional quantity must be added : when it is turned and chopp'd, this must be repeated course by course till it comes to a proper height.

9th.   All the banks and ground to be made good to the Locks, Aqueducts, Bridges, Culverts, Wiers, Stopgates, &c. and all the Lock-pits are to be dug by the Contractor for the cutting, &c. and properly puddled and pounded round the wall. Also round Culverts as described by the Engineer or his Substitute : and all Trenches for conveying water for puddling or lining the said works, as well as all pits, tail and head drains for Culverts and drains for conveying away water from his works that may obstruct the Execution, as well as catch drains. And all the temporary fences, and all damages arising therefrom, are to be done and paid by the Contractor.

10th.   The towing paths to be covered with good Gravel eight feet broad ten inches thick in the middle and to diminish to six inches at the edges or sides.

11th.   The towing paths through all the Inclosures must be fenced with a single row of good oak Posts and double rails; the upper one oak and the under one deal; the posts to be six feet long and the rails not more than nine feet, and to be planted with white thorn Quicksets in a border of good soil, not less than two feet deep and two feet wide.

12th.   Where any deviation or alteration from the plan and section is proposed by the Company or Contractors, whereby the digging or banking may be increased or diminished, due notice in writing shall be given for the same by the party proposing such deviation, and the Contractor shall not begin to execute the same untill a price is fixed on and an agreement made, failing which he shall have no payment for the same. And in case the demand made by the Contractor for executing such deviation shall be more than the Engineer or his substitute may think proper, then the said Engineer shall have it in his power to contract or agree with any other Person for the same, at such prices as he may judge proper without the Contractor having demand against the Company for such transaction ; and in case it should appear to the said Engineer or Substitute after stopping the work that the Contractor is unable or will not fulfill his Contract, then the said Engineer or Substitute shall have it in his power to discharge the said Contractor and take the work out of his hand, value of which being previously settled by two indifferent skilful Persons mutually chosen, they appointing an Umpire in case of disagreement, whose award failing theirs, shall be binding on the Parties.

LONDON, 16th of MARCH 1795

Figure 7.1   Part of a two hundred year old specification Better than many seen today

It is the main control document (or rather, documents). The information in specifications will be compiled by subgroups and these groups will usually be responsible for ensuring the implementation of the relevant stage. The specifications will:

1 Let all others involved in the design process know what each other is doing, then be used to aid decisions.
2 Identify 'holes' in the design before proceeding to the next stage of the process.
3 Be used to focus discussion in the design reviews. They will be compiled and worked to by different groups.

Make your brief concise, putting down only usable information and in a form that can be used by others. There is no contradiction between asking for a concise brief and stating that it will be long. If all the points are covered in sufficient depth, no matter how concise the writers have been, the document will be long.

Be quantitative rather than qualitative, where possible, put numbers to the parameters and then put tolerances on these. A common error in the brief is to specify parameters that are unnecessarily restrictive. This has a doubly damaging effect. Restricting certain aspects of design more closely than is necessary only increases the eventual cost of the product. Parameters should be specified, but keep all such requirements as broad as possible, but also so that they still meet the market requirements.

The other damaging effect is that an over-restrictive brief can limit 'flair'. Those involved should be given enough freedom to provide some intuitive or innovative design, if at all possible. The brief ensures that the overall product will still satisfy the findings of the market research. If, whilst doing this, the eventual product performs in a different manner to the competition, so much the better.

The brief should never be written by just one person. All those who have a role covering the various elements should provide an input. Developing new products and services is a multidisciplinary activity and it is no longer the case that one person will have the necessary knowledge to enable them to provide all the inputs. Furthermore, research undertaken at IBM showed that when people wrote specifications they tended to put too great an emphasis on the areas of their own expertise.

The iterative nature of developing new services allows for the brief to be changed and updated as markets and circumstances change. This may even lead to abandonment if the competition brings out an identical or superior service with which your company cannot compete. Alternatively, you may be unsure about aspects of a particular element and in this case you may need to do some more market research.

Whenever you have a change you must put an issue number and date on it. Although changing the specification is allowed, there is a point beyond which it is unwise unless it is absolutely necessary. This is where good management comes in, to know when to change and when to fix it to give some stability to the subsequent process. There is no simple answer to this. You must aim to minimise disruption, but at the same time keep on target towards a successful product. Updating and changing a brief naturally causes disruption and the later in the design process that the changes are made, the greater will be the disruption and its associated cost.

CASE STUDY – TIME TO CHANGE YOUR BRIEFS

Specifications are not cast in stone. The further you get through the process of any new product the more you will learn as new data becomes available. Markets move and change, competitors are not standing still either and technology has a habit of advancing. A suitable specification at the beginning of a long development can begin to look out of date as one reaches the end. Specifications must be updated as one progresses.

This is not a problem near the start. Most of the work should be in the form of pieces of paper and these are easily torn up and rewritten. Unfortunately, the further one gets through the process the costs and commitment rise, and so does the cost of any change to the specification. As the design approaches production alterations may involve the remake of tooling. This is both costly in terms of money and time and the effect may delay the introduction of the eventual product on to the market. This may result in the loss of competitive edge.

The trouble is that people always want to change things. Individuals who have only a passing involvement with the product like to make their mark on it by proposing 'improvements'. What is worse is that these persons are often from very senior management and you can't tell them (politely) 'no'. To make matters worse, the subsequent delays in incorporating the change are always blamed on you!

Bill has battled with this problem throughout (what is laughingly known as) his career. Several years back, as a Design Director in one organisation, the 'Technical Director', who was senior to the Design Director, and had about as much technical knowledge as a cabbage, always had to feel he was making his mark with any new idea. He never went to any of the product development meetings and so never made a contribution to the product or proposed any changes when it was the right time to do so (at the low cost early stages of the process). On the other hand, he liked to feel that he was involved in NPD. Whenever a prototype was brought to him he would have to make a change to it with some bright idea straight off the top of his head, whether it was needed or not. Invariably, this caused delays in the production and marketing and the Design Director would get a 'roasting' because he was the person in charge of the project.

After a period of time this began to irritate, because the proposed change always slowed the development down but never improved the product. He had to be stopped but murder, though justified, wasn't entirely ethical.

Bill was pretty efficient with the design process (even if I say so myself) and made sure that changes which were made were done, as much as possible, whilst the design was still just in paper form. As a result, the prototypes that I had produced were pre-production models and these were made just before the product went into production, and preferably made on the production tooling.

I still think my solution to this problem was inspired. I went down to the paint shop and selected the most horrible colour. 'Spray it with this' I requested. At first, the painter made disparaging noises so I explained my predicament. The Technical Director hated the colour, he talked about nothing else but the colour and even wrote a memo instructing that the colour should not be used for this product. My product and its development programme stayed intact.

When I told the painter of my 'success', he really entered into the spirit of the thing. I would send down all prototypes to the spray shop labelled 'the usual' and back they came looking worse each time. Once I was called down to the spray shop by the painter who informed me that there weren't any nasty colours available that day. As an early exponent of Empowerment I said 'what do you suggest?'

'How about runs and drips?' was his reply and duly obliged. The prototype looked a mess with bare patches, runs, drips, etc. The Technical Director went mad. Of course, there followed a memo from him to the foreman of the spray shop about the falling standards of workmanship in the department but the foreman was in on the ruse and promised that the following day standards would be back to normal, which they were.

Unfortunately all good things come to an end and one day it was requested that prototypes should remain unpainted until after they had been 'appraised'. This led me to think about when specifications should or should not be changed. This is my conclusion. At the start of the process people should be encouraged to propose and make changes as this is low cost and quick to do. Late in the process the reverse is true. If changes are requested late in the development process the following two questions should be asked. Preferably, this should be done on Friday afternoon and the answer demanded for Monday so that it ruins their weekend. Most people who want to make changes in the configuration of a product late in the process deserve to have their weekends spoilt.

QUESTION 1.   WHAT IS THE COST OF THE CHANGE?

QUESTION 2.   WHAT WILL BE THE LOSS IN SALES IF THE DESIGN IS LEFT UNALTERED?

The first question is possible to answer but people always underestimate the work and cost involved. Late in the process tooling may have been made, brochures printed, customers promised delivery dates and exhibition space booked. Changes to these may be slow, expensive, embarrassing or impossible.

The second question is probably impossible to answer, but it makes the person who wants the change think. If the product is likely to break and, as a result, there will be a loss in sales or company reputation then the change is justified. But usually the change is of a minor and often, of cosmetic nature. In this case, it would hardly affect sales at all. In such a case, just promise that the change will be

> *incorporated in the next model and that the existing configuration is the one that will be supplied first time out.*
>
> *The above two questions have saved a great deal of unnecessary work and heartache. There are several organisations who have incorporated these, or similar, questions when confronted with this problem.*
>
> **The cost of any change to the product specification must be compared to the loss in profit from leaving the design unaltered.** *If the loss in profit from the unchanged design is greater than the cost of the change, then change it. The first part of the equation is quite hard to calculate if you include lost opportunity costs, etc., but an estimate is not too difficult. The second part of the equation is very hard to determine. Few will even attempt it. What the equation does do is draw people's attention to the fact that most design alterations late in the process are really not worth the effort as the 'improvement' proposed will not significantly increase sales.*
>
> *On the other hand, where a change is really necessary it is often obvious that it should be included. For example, the device won't work, or cannot be made, unless the change is included. In these cases, it is often worth questioning if there is something wrong with the communication in your organisation's design process that failed to identify such a serious problem earlier, at the low cost end of the process.*
>
> *In practice, you will find that most small changes are unnecessary and can wait until the 'Mark 2' version and your programme can proceed unhindered. Try it on your boss when next cornered, get him or her to state how sales will be affected. You will find it works, they will back down and your life will be a little easier!*

There is another failing of some specifications. This is where constant changes – or moving the goal posts – can prevent completion of the product or result in an overpriced or unacceptable product. This has been called the 'Nimrod factor' (remember the AWACs plane whose nose grew and grew every time they changed the specification?) It is difficult to avoid with products that are being developed at the leading edge of technology. Some companies are not prepared to confront this problem and aim to be second in the race so that somebody else has ironed out the unforeseen difficulties.

The Most Important Elements

Not all elements in the brief are of equal weight. The important elements depend partly on the particular product, but there appear to be some that are more important with almost all products and these are:

Reliability, safety, aesthetics, maintainability, egonomics and price

It is, however, possible to grade the elements in your specification for importance and the easiest way to determine these important elements, having identified your market need, is to focus your market research to answer the question, 'why will customers buy this product or service?' The brief will highlight inter-relationships and compromises between elements. When you have identified the most important elements in your specification, through market research, you should not compromise on these. Instead 'de rate' some other aspect of your design.

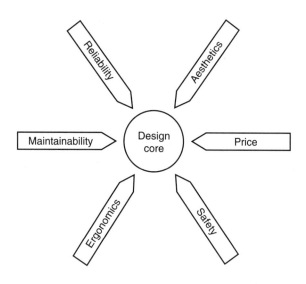

Reliability. This is 'the ability of an item to perform a required function under stated conditions for a stated period of time' (BS 7000 Part 10 1995). It seems to be the single most important aspect of design in almost every product. For example, the most important consideration regarding a car is that it starts in the morning and keeps going throughout the day. When stuck on the motorway hard shoulder with a broken vehicle the fact that it looks attractive and has good aerodynamics is a poor consolation.

Reliability is often linked to quality (fitness for purpose) because it takes quality in 'manufacture' to achieve reliability. Customers quickly notice when a product is unreliable and it puts them off more quickly than anything else. They then tell their friends and soon the company has a reputation for unreliability and its sales plummet. It is to a certain degree possible to protect a company from a poor reputation by giving the product a separate identity, by giving it a different brand name, but this does not get to the root of the real problem. In your specification make reliability at least as good as the competition (you should know how good the competition is).

What comes next in importance has not been so clearly determined by researchers but the following tend to come in the top six or seven main features of most products.

Safety. This is the odd element out because, in most cases, customers do not consider safety. When they make a purchase they assume it is safe, although with cars there has been greater consumer awareness of what is more safe. On the other hand, if we were really concerned would we ever charge about at seventy miles an hour in a tin box? Somebody who buys an electrical item is not afraid to plug it in. Although customers do not buy safety they do avoid anything they perceive to be unsafe, such as the Sinclair C5. It is also the law that any product be safe, which only adds to its importance.

Aesthetics. This comes from the Greek for how something is 'perceived through the senses'. Nowadays, this usually refers to whether or not a product has a pleasing appearance, but the original meaning is more useful in developing the right product. Generally, a manufactured product's appearance is important but consider also the other senses – sound (e.g. a sports car's exhaust tone), feel (a TV controller), taste (obviously if it's edible) and the smell (the smell of a new car or of new leather). Consideration of these can enhance your product offering.

Maintainability. The ease with which faults can be corrected is obviously important in manufactured products. It is even more important with services because, by definition, a service cannot be stored. If a hotel room is unavailable because the sink is leaking or a plane unavailable due to a technical fault, then you have lost that sale. With many products this is not the case because if you can't sell it today, you can tomorrow. Ensure that those products that interface with your product and services are reliable so they don't break down, but that if they do they can be quickly, easily and inexpensively corrected.

Ergonomics. This comes from two Greek words, 'ergo' meaning work and 'nomos' meaning natural law, and it is to do with the people side of products and services. In America, it is known as 'human factors engineering', in the computer industry as 'user-friendliness', but in each case it amounts to the same thing – ease of use. The interface between the user and your product must be designed so that your product is easy and obvious to use – and why not pleasant to use as well? We believe that improved ergonomics will be the main thrust in design in the future. It has been found that a typical consumer will not purchase another product of the same make if it is difficult to use or maintain (Woodson et al. 1992, Stephenson and Wallace 1996).

WHY IS LIFE MADE SO HARD?

It is a well known fact that prior to the introduction of things such as Videoplus nobody over the age of seven could program a video. Well, as you would expect, we live in a very classy and expensive part of London. And round here this is how we plan our families. We have a child, it reaches the age of seven and suddenly can't program the video any more – so we have another one.

More seriously, a new telephone system was installed in a university. It was so complicated that nobody could use it – and we are supposed to be fairly bright people. There was no point in reading the instruction manual because this was even more complicated and confusing than the phone. Eventually, the users had to have a ten minute, one-to-one tuition from an employee of the phone company to tell them how to use the phone! It was only a phone after all. Remember the time when all one had to do was stick one's fingers in a series of holes and twiddle a disc?

Why are products so difficult? If you can't use a product or service easily then it is the fault of the product – and the people and company that produced it and/or marketed it – not yours. But what are the services and products that your organisation sells?

Price. Kenneth Corfield chaired a committee that reported way back in 1979, stressing the importance of 'non price factors' in design. This has led to the belief, in some circles, that the price of a product is almost unimportant in helping potential customers to decide whether or not to make a purchase. Although it is true that people often consider other attributes in making a purchase more important than the price they have to pay, the price comes near the top in terms of importance. People tend to identify a price bracket that they can afford. They then look at the various features that are available on products within this price range. They make their purchase decision on the item that combines the best of these features.

When potential customers are asked their views, there will be some features that they consider are essential (needs) and others which they would quite like but if they weren't in the service they would probably still use it (wants). The 'needs' you must have to get on to the customer's shopping list. The 'wants', on the other hand, are probably the factors which the customer uses to differentiate between all the choices available to help them make their final decision to purchase.

It is now accepted that formal assessment of how well each generated concept satisfies the specification is an integral part of the design process. Specifications help with optimal concept selection and indicate if it is worthwhile proceeding to the next level of product development, and specification, or better to abandon the project at that point and seek an alternative product to develop.

CASE STUDY – HOW CAN YOU SELL IT?

*To give an example of the application of one of these parameters, some years ago Bill was called in to an organisation to improve the early stages of their product development process. Looking at which of their new products had been successful or had failed, it became apparent that **all** their successes had been products that could be sold and distributed to a well defined market segment. Every time this company had stepped away from this precisely focused area, their products had failed. The simple solution was to state, as an initial guideline, that the only new designs to be undertaken had to be those that could be marketed, sold and distributed through their very effective sales channels into this market, which was to local authorities.*

At first glance, this seemed to be very much a strait-jacket around new product development but, in fact, it enabled the company to expand into various areas that had not been previously exploited. This organisation continues to grow within these precise boundaries. The guideline focused their attention on those areas where they were likely to succeed and prevented limited resources being squandered in areas where they were more likely to fail. Isn't this much of what Business Process Re-engineering should have been promoting?

There are several such parameters which can be put around any company's design activities. If these are stated in writing before any design starts, the budget can be directed into areas that are considered best suited for the company.

Specifications Elements

The full specification embraces many factors and is a dynamic document. Checklists of the aspects which should be covered within these categories are still relatively new. Specification formulation is included in BS 7000 part 1 (1989) with 21 elements. Smith and Rhodes (1991) and Pugh/ SEED (1986) each specify 33 elements. Hollins and Hollins (1991) include one with 52 elements. Perhaps the most comprehensive listing of what elements should be included in a specification is taken from BS 7000 part 2 (1997) which lists 125 elements!

All these elements need to be considered with all new products and services (although each may not be relevant in every case) and here lies the main problem. Full specifications are difficult and time-consuming to compile. Furthermore, in most cases, it is possible to identify early on that a satisfactory product will not result and the project should be abandoned. In practice, there should not be just one document, but several compiled by various people and these specifications grow as the programme proceeds.

What is needed is a presentation of these in stages that will enable the user to investigate a potential product or service in increasingly complex steps. These will allow plenty of 'bale out' points where the project may be identified as being unsuitable without a significant degree of work.

Subspecifications

Subspecifications are becoming even more important as a control over the process. Although many of these methodologies appear to improve the development of products, often they are complicated and difficult to use.

In the late eighties, we devised a full process for the development of new products for a telecommunications company. After a suitable period the company was recontacted to find how the process was working. They agreed that the process did appear to work well but on further questioning it was discovered that although they were satisfied that the system worked, they did not use it for all their projects – because it was too difficult to use! The managers liked the process but those actually charged with doing the work were not keen. As one user put it: 'The process itself is seen as a hindrance to overall speed in completing a project and therefore stages are omitted or skimmed over.'

Eppinger et al. (1993) have also noted this: 'We have observed that in most large firms there is a huge investment in existing design procedures, often heavily bureaucratised. While these procedures seem to work well, they may have grown up organically and historically. Without having been subjected to careful analysis the internal inefficiencies or irrationalities remain largely undetected.'

Research into User Friendly Specifications – Refining and Simplifying the Process

We now discuss the findings of some research into the development of Product Design Specifications (PDS) which was undertaken by Dr Ken Hurst of Hull University, and Bill. The aim was to simplify the early stages of the design process (Hurst and Hollins 1995).

The key to simplifying the process, to make it more user friendly, was to break up the process by introducing a series of subspecifications. A series of small specifications are proposed in the early stages. Each subspecification includes enough information to enable the decision to be made to take the proposed new product to the next stage of the process. This can be analogous to someone dipping their toe in the water before going swimming. If the water isn't too cold one can go in a bit deeper, then deeper still, until one is confident enough to take the plunge. These stepped specifications allow one to appraise the situation at every stage whereupon a decision may be taken whether it is worth making the investment to go to the next stage of the process and the next step of the staged specification. In both the swimming example and developing products if it is decided not to take the venture any further you just abandon the whole thing and retire to the bar to plan your next venture.

These small specifications will eventually build into a full Product Specification. The focus on these various subspecifications will present stages that will enable the user to investigate a potential design in increasingly complex steps. These will allow plenty of 'bale out' points where the project may be identified as being unsuitable without a significant degree of work.

It is also necessary to identify who should be involved and who should provide this information and precisely in what form it should be presented. Bearing in mind the multidisciplinary, highly iterative, nature of this work it is far from easy. The result must be a relatively simple set of guidelines and procedures which enable organisations to explore the applicability of any new product without the need to embark on a large amount of 'up front' work.

The staged specification process identified simplifies the development of new products. Necessary compromises are confronted early on. This ensures that potential product failures are not pursued, allowing the organisation to devote more time to something potentially more suitable or move on to something more worthwhile. The subspecifications, thereby, determine the process by enquiring 'what do we need to know to do the design and when do we need to know it?' A typical build up to a subspecification is shown in the next section on how to justify the project to the accountant. This demonstrates that these subspecifications are needed right from the outset of the programme.

Perhaps each subspecification should also be linked to a short concept stage to show the 'general' idea. The systems that were developed also help with optimal concept selection and indicate if it was worthwhile proceeding to the next level of product development, and specification, or better to abandon the project at that point and seek an alternative product to develop. Product status can also be investigated as part of this. A subspecification to identify if, and where, innovation is needed will be included as part of the process.

> **TO SUMMARISE THE FINDINGS FROM THIS RESEARCH – THE HIGH INCIDENCE OF PRODUCT FAILURES CAN BE ATTRIBUTED, IN THE MAIN, TO A LACK OF CUSTOMER FOCUS AND COMPANIES' FAILURE IN DEVELOPING COHERENT AND COMPREHENSIVE SPECIFICATIONS.**

Effective specifications are one of the keys to successful products. Where potential failures are not identified at an early enough stage, a staged specification development process is advocated, based on agreed check lists of criteria with 'bale out' points.

CASE STUDY – A STITCH IN TIME . . .

Bill visited a quite successful organisation that made heating equipment to discuss with them ways to improve their product development process. It soon became apparent that the specifications they used were incomplete. These were compiled by the marketing manager (first problem, it should have been done by a multidisciplinary team with different types of expertise at their disposal). I showed the marketing manager a list of elements that should be included in a typical specification. She said 'if I had to write a spec. like that it would take me two days to write the specification, and I haven't got that amount of spare time'. I congratulated her on being able to cover all the elements that needed consideration and writing it up in only two days.

A little later, I was in the production shop and was told of an error that had occurred in the design of a large casting. This had delayed the introduction of the product by six months. This was because an omission from the specification had meant that the tooling had to be re-made and this took six months. I advised that they should seek an alternative supplier for this type of tooling, one who could supply in a more realistic time.

The problem lay not in the detailed design but in a feature that should have been included within the specification, an essential market requirement that had been talked about but had not been written into the brief. Because they had taken a short cut at the start of the process they had incurred an unacceptable delay at the end of the process, and the product was late to market.

The point was that because the person compiling the specification had not spent a small increment in time to do the job properly, the result was a much greater increment in time to put the omission right. Don't try and cut corners by writing incomplete specifications.

THE SPECIFICATION MUST BE **BIG**

8

How Do You Justify the Project to the Accountant?

Having identified a suitable idea, before embarking on what is usually an expensive process of developing new products, the accountant will probably want certain questions answered and, if not, those involved in new products should still have the answers to these questions. Once again, the focus is on eliminating potential failures early on.

This is all about money, as that is all that interests accountants! Most of the measures described in accountancy books relate to after the event. Return on capital employed, etc. is fine as an evaluation as to the success of a design project when it has been completed and is up and running. But you will have to convince accountants right at the outset that it is worth the organisation investing in the proposed new product at the very start of the project.

So How Do You Do It?

Initially, convince the money man of the importance of new and improved products and services in general. With no new products your organisation will slowly decline and fail. When discussing a new project proposal with accountants they are likely to want to know what rate of return is to be expected before they subscribe to the development. In almost all organisations the money to pay for the development of new products has to be borrowed or taken from investments. This means that interest has to be paid on this money, if borrowed, and that the return from selling the product must exceed this interest rate. In the case where money doesn't have to be borrowed there is still a penalty in the loss of interest from not just leaving the money in the bank. Money borrowed for new product development is considered a risky venture by banks and therefore the interest rate is likely to be high, about 5% higher than the minimum lending rate.

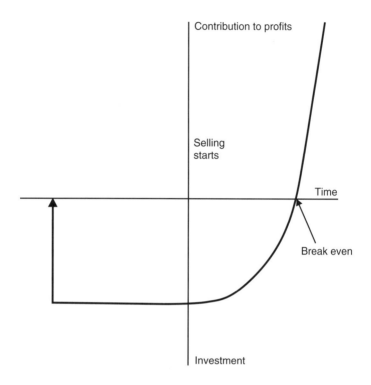

Figure 8.1   The basic total borrowing needed in the development of a new product or service

Research and Development, etc. should not be written down as an asset. This was the case in 1970 where Rolls Royce wrote down the cost of the development of the RB 2-11 jet engine as an asset and this caused the company to go into the hands of the receiver. Most new products only become an asset when they can be sold. Up until that time although a lot may have been spent on it the reclaimable value is small. An exception may be intellectual property which may have a market value – if anybody can be found to buy it.

To convince the accountant that it is a worthwhile exercise it will be necessary to show them that the anticipated return will be substantial. So there is little point in proposing a product that will bring in any less than the interest rate.

The accountant will also want to know when the money is to be borrowed. This is where accurate planning and a model of the process showing the detailed stages of the work to be done becomes important.

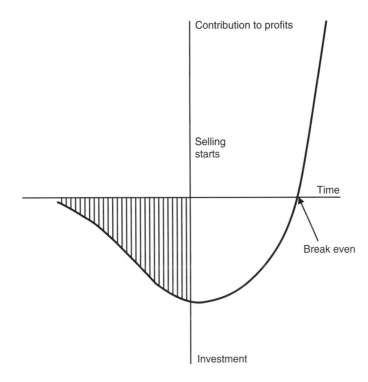

Figure 8.2   The stepped borrowing in the development of a new product or service

You will be able to tell the accountant specifically when each stage of the borrowing is required. For a manufactured product the cost of tooling is typically 45% of the total, therefore, the major stage of the borrowing is quite late in the process. By splitting up the cost of the stages of the detailed design process and setting it against a calendar it is possible to state precisely when each borrowing takes place. This alters the requirement for finance from Figure 8.1 to Figure 8.2.

The accountant will also want to know how fast he/she is going to get this money back. So they will need to know how many will be sold and the approximate profit from each. This, of course, is a very difficult equation because this discussion will be held before even the concept stage of the project has taken place, often before you know what specifically is going to be done (nobody said this was going to be easy – but it is still necessary). A guess must be made as to the sales over the life of the product. This must take into account:

1   the low level of sales which is normal at a product's introduction;
2   the sales will then generally build up and the rate of this build needs to be estimated;
3   an estimate is also required for the annual demand over the life of the product before it is replaced.

Demand Variation

This must include an estimate of the changes in annual demand. Many products sell better at different times of the year, e.g. 25% of the annual sales of cars in Britain are in the one month of August although this is likely to change now that the registration letter changes twice a year. This is when the registration letter on the number plate changes, and it shows your 'status' to have a car with the latest letter. Lawn mower sales are highest in Spring, most fireworks in the UK are sold for November 5th bonfire night and umbrellas sell best in winter – there are many examples. The demand pattern for most products can be identified and this may include combining the various demand patterns for the product in different countries if the product is to be exported.

CASE STUDY – YOUR CRACKERS

It isn't always possible to flatten the demand curve through export, for example Christmas Crackers are almost a purely British thing. This became clear to us when we had some Norwegian visitors stay at our house around the Christmas period. After a time and a few drinks we handed out the Christmas Crackers. Our visitors looked confused and had clearly never seen their like before. 'Pull them', we said. So they grabbed an end with each hand and did so.

Out popped the 'hat' rolled up, as usual, in an elastic band. They looked at it then threw it in the bin. Next they found the cheap and nasty plastic toy (we only invest in cheap crackers). This to went straight into the bin. With a little rummaging they found the 'joke'. It was thus:

'Q.   what happened to the man who couldn't tell the difference between porridge and putty?'

Now this caused some confusion. 'What is porridge?' one asked. After some discussion, we discovered that the Norwegian equivalent is called something like 'Gruel'. So:

'Q.   what happened to the man who couldn't tell the difference between gruel and putty? A.   His windows fell out.'

> *They looked at us, we looked at them, and then they looked at each other as the 'joke' was dispatched into the waste bin.*
>
> *At that moment in time we had a spark of realisation. We quickly handed round the drinks again and accepted that we Brits are almost the only ones daft enough to have fallen for such a crass con-trick as the Christmas Cracker, and if you are involved in this product then there is no hope of generating an export market.*

In effect, an estimate must be made of the product life cycle, and the much shorter model life cycle, with estimates of demand until the product goes into decline. With some organisations, such as in particular models of cars, this can be partially controlled by the organisation. They plan the life of the model to be so many years and, therefore, plan the development and introduction of the next new model and phasing out the old one. In many organisations, this cannot be controlled and demand is greatly determined by market forces or the actions of competitors. Promotion can affect the demand pattern and this can be built into the original calculations and will effect both the positive (increased sales) and negative (the cost of promotion) side of the balance sheet.

The return that pays back the money borrowed, plus interest, comes out of profit rather than turnover. An estimate must, therefore, be made of that profit, which is essentially the selling price less the costs of developing and producing that product or service, plus a contribution to the fixed costs.

In theory, the selling price should be whatever the market will stand, but at this stage, it is more usual to work on a 'cost plus' basis. That is, the total cost of the product plus a percentage of that for profit. Because of the contribution to the fixed cost there is likely to be a great difference between the actual cost to implement, produce and supply and the minimum acceptable selling price. In many organisations, a ball park figure for this can be given.

THE TRUE COST OF A PRODUCT

In an organisation in which Bill was employed, in simple terms if the manufactured cost was £10 the minimum selling price was £50. The difference between the two included profit, promotion, distribution, storage, selling costs, a portion to shareholders, the directors' salary, contribution to rent, rates, electricity, etc. and, of course, both mine and the accountant's wages. Knowing the ratio between the manufactured costs and the selling price is very useful. For example, if a competitor's product was selling for 100, it is, generally, fairly easy to determine whether your competing product could be designed within a maximum manufactured price of 20. If the likely cost was going to be significantly above this base line figure then it was reason enough not to start the development of the project.

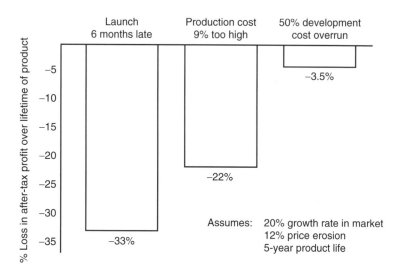

Figure 8.3   The effect of project overspend
(Design Council 1985)

From the information given you can see the curve in Figure 8.2 can be generated. On the left hand side of the vertical axis the time when the money is borrowed can be marked and the amount that is borrowed can also be marked. On the right hand side of the axis, after selling begins, the rate of return of money from the product coming back into the organisation can also be estimated. It is only when the line breaks the horizontal axis that this product is likely to go into profit. The effect of interest rates can be included, which is negative until the product eventually goes into profit, then it becomes positive – it pays money into the bank. This does not take into account the effect of inflation which can further distort the curve. The net present value should be considered.

The Design Council in Britain has undertaken research that shows that a product that is six months late on to the market loses 33% in after-tax profits over the lifetime of that product (Design Council 1985). This is a much quoted and much claimed set of results. This is shown on Figure 8.3. Blake (1998) quotes these figures, stating that it is 'a recent McKinsey & Company study', but adds that 'by improving time to market by one month, profits improve by 11.9%'. It can be seen from Figure 8.4 that a delay in the design programme would certainly extend the time that money is borrowed and the interest that accrues. Also, a product appearing late on to the market is likely to be less competitive, resulting in further loss of profitability.

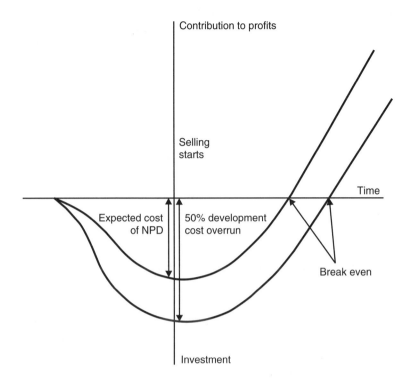

Figure 8.4   The effect of project overspend on the breakeven point of a project

In the same research, shown on Figure 8.3 the Design Council in Britain shows that a 50% overspend will lead to a reduction of only 3.5% in profitability after tax over the lifetime of the product. This reasoning is flawed. Looking at Figure 8.4, you can see that an additional 50% in the expenditure, even if the product does come out on time, will delay the product reaching the break-even point.

More fundamentally, consider that a certain amount of money has been borrowed from the bank. If the bank is then informed of the expected pay back rates, you can imagine the problems of going to the bank saying that you were wrong, that you require more money, 50% more money, and they will not be getting the money back until later (for example, consider the overspend problems of the Channel Tunnel). In many organisations having to do this may actually threaten the organisation's existence.

Less dramatically, most design and project departments have a budget in which they must work and an unplanned expenditure in one area will mean a reduction in investment in another new project area. Along with this, it must be remembered that, typically, less than 40% of new products succeed (Hollins 1995.2) and the profitability from any new developments must also include a contribution to pay for failures.

Operating Parameters

As already mentioned, it is possible to identify a multiplier which indicates a link between the manufactured price and the selling price. It is also possible to state some other parameters, which can usually be determined from experience. The purpose of these parameters is to determine whether it is worth or wise to start a new development project. These will be linked to the organisation's specified set of operating parameters (see Chapter 4) and may include:

♦ a maximum time scale in which a product can be developed;
♦ a maximum time scale after launch until the product becomes profitable;
♦ a maximum cost which can be incurred in the development of a new product.

There are restrictions that rightly envelope the type of products that may be developed and these encompass production, marketing, distribution and strategic restrictions. Most of these are usually financially based considerations. If these are calculated and this information given to designers, it will allow them to identify products that are not right for a particular organisation, thus preventing a waste of this valuable resource in pursuing unsuitable new product developments. These are usually financially based considerations and if these are calculated and this information given to designers, it will allow them to identify products that are not right for a particular organisation, thus preventing a waste of this valuable resource in pursuing unsuitable new product developments.

Of course, when determining the likely costs of development, tooling, decor, promotion, rates of sale, etc., it becomes obvious that these estimates cannot be made by one person alone. For example, in the failure in Britain of a detergent powder that put holes in your clothes, £32 million of the £53 million lost was the loss of wasted promotion costs, this information coming from the marketing department. All this further confirms the fact that developing new products must be a multidisciplinary exercise. This information must be obtained from the various people who are responsible for, and likely to know, the information that you require.

Reducing the Cost

There are some ways to reduce the costs or the level of borrowing:

1 With a suitably detailed process model, showing the stages to be covered in the project, it will be possible to identify precisely when the money needs to be borrowed, thus avoiding extra interest payments.

2 The cost of development can be shared (along with the risks) by going into partnerships. This is becoming common for large developments, such as aero engines, aeroplanes and pharmaceuticals.

3 The cost of development will be lower if innovations (developing new concepts) are kept to a minimum. This tends to encourage short termism, which is not a good thing. But innovation when it is not essential is also not a good thing.

4 Delaying the introduction of automation can also delay the investment that this requires, perhaps these costs can be paid for partly from profits that are actually coming in. This can only be done with certain products where the take-up is fairly slow, such as, with the first calculators, video tape players and video cameras. With other products, such as cars, this policy is not possible. It must be remembered that if you enter a market 'knife and forking' the product together with the unit manufactured costs will be higher and thus overall profitability lower.

5 Reducing the time to market means that the product comes on sale faster and money is borrowed for less time. This is why over 60% of manufacturing organisations in Europe are attempting to reduce time to market (Bishop 1992). This is best achieved by emphasising the front end of the process, which has the effect of reducing the number of changes at the latter, slower end of the project.

   Another way that time to market can be reduced is through concurrent working, essentially doing as much of the design process as possible in parallel (see Chapter 4 on process models).

6 The early stages of the design can be reduced by buying in designs, inventions and ideas from elsewhere. This can be done either by contacting inventors or by hiring in consultants to do the work.

7 The time for the later stages of projects can be reduced through subcontracting tooling or the manufacture of parts of the product or service.

8 Finally and most effectively, don't have any new product failures, which means having a suitable mechanism for weeding out these likely failures as early as possible. The above will go some way towards achieving this.

It can be seen that the only sensible measure of success is financial. This is why the accountant is so important and also why they need to be convinced of the importance of your work, usually before you embark on a new project.

Questions to Ask at the Outset

(– which make up one of the early subspecification)

Most of the initial information needed can be summarised in a short series of questions that need to be answered at the outset and shown in a preliminary specification. The following may give an indication:

1 Name of the product to be designed (just to put a label on it).
2 New product or update of an existing product (new products take longer and usually cost more).
3 Description of new product (what does it do?).
4 Features to be included (wants and needs).
5 Reason why the new product is required (this can be to satisfy an identified demand, as defence against competition, etc.).
6 Quantity to be produced in the first year, the second year, and the third year of production.
7 Maximum time scale or date for delivery of the first product to the customer.
8 Maximum total budget for completion up to the point of delivery of the first product to the customer.
9 Minimum selling price (including all overheads).
10 Other priorities, other parameters.

It can be seen that by answering these questions most of the data will be available for constructing the curve shown on Figure 8.1. Of course, these answers will be mainly educated guesses at that early stage.

Do not forget that often there is money to be made beyond the actual sale of the product. Canon make more money from servicing their photocopiers than they do actually selling them. The actual selling price of a laser printer is only 36% of the total cost of ownership. A further 46% is made up during the whole life cost of the printer by ink cartridges (Bush and Sheldon 1993), and who makes them? Try and build these additional likely returns into the calculations for your products (Figure 1.1 Time Frame One).

To Summarise

It is far from easy to determine and justify the cost of a new product or service at the start, but an attempt must still be made to do this so that those in the organisation can make a decision on investment. The estimations of cost will be quite inaccurate at the start but will be refined as the project progresses. Good process planning, organisation and experience will improve the accuracy of these cost estimations.

CASE STUDY – HOW LONG DO YOU WANT IT TO LAST?

Whenever we visit any country we try to seek out a selection of their past glories, this we call 'effort spotting'. Not long back we visited Carthage – not much there. The high spot for us was when our lad climbed up the side of what little does remain and, with some style, peed off the top. It summed up our opinion of the place better than mere words can.

Done Ephesus in the mid seventies when not so many people visited Turkey on holiday. Seen a few pictures of it again recently. There is a lot more of it now than when we went. Apparently, they have been frantically building up more of it since our visit. We wonder how much of the original we saw?

Valley of the Kings? Seen it long after the grave robbers had taken the best bits. Incidentally, when does grave robbing become archaeology? Jerusalem – great but is any of it original? On the other hand, if you have faith then does this matter? At least most of us already have the best guide book to Jerusalem already at home.

Troy? – nothing twenty years ago and nothing now. Pompeii was a different story but so are the circumstances. We even went on a walking tour of the sites of the Great Fire of London. Not much to see, not surprising really as it all had been burnt down.

When one considers that Carthage was flattened by the Romans, Barbarians, Goths and, probably, a few others, and then just used as a supply of stones for the building of Tunis, it is not surprising that very little remains. Even the guide's brave efforts failed, when pointing to a column set on a modern concrete plinth, indicating the height (32m) of the original bath house and saying 'you can imagine the magnificence of this, the fourth largest of 700 bath houses in the Roman Empire'. No, we couldn't.

Should one be surprised that often there is not very much left to see? After all, when you produce something how long do you expect it to last? If you think 'forever' then you are a mug and your products are likely to cost too much.

On the other hand, if you are one of those people who still believe in built-in obsolescence, to the point that your products are designed to last just longer than the warranty, then you have, probably, noticed your declining number of customers. Customers expect a longer life than the warranty. If your product fails them it may well be replaced – but not by your company's mark.

Bill worked for a company that thought it would be clever to apply a bit of 'built in obsolescence'. The product was designed to survive just outside the two year warranty. Unfortunately, somebody got their sums slightly wrong and droves of the product came back after one year and eleven months – when it was still under guarantee. Attempting built in obsolescence to that extent is, fortunately, a thing of the past.

Somewhere in between is the, so called, 'happy medium', where your products should be positioned. You want to 'delight' the customers by providing quality reliable products but at the same time your organisation has to make money. The best way to do this is to design products that last long enough but not too long. But how long is this particular piece of string? It depends on the product and 'forever' certainly isn't the answer.

The relatively limited life of our products shouldn't cause concern/surprise to us or our organisations. We need to appreciate the product life cycle and develop products accordingly. Some products may outlive their 'fashion' (any offers for a slightly worn pair of loons?) Of course, the basic concept may remain unaltered and only models become outdated, e.g. cars. Such an understanding can guide us in our decisions concerning the provision of spares and in planning the next product to replace this one. Of course, all this should feature as one of the important elements in your specification and you should consider current markets and also, if possible, future adaptations that may be possible to meet anticipated markets.

Now, the owners of Ephesus have twigged that there is now a completely new market and they are attempting to satisfy it. The point of the line from Shelley's poem 'I am Ozimandias King of Kings, gaze upon my works ye mighty and despair' is that there was little more than the plinth remaining from the magnificence that once was. We should only be amazed that even the plinth remained; clearly over designed and over engineered for outliving its usefulness.

Things you buy you want to be reliable, but not for ever. Generally, the longer you want the product to last the more it is going to cost. And then there is the provision of spares. How long is it right to expect to be able to service your washing machine? Five years or ten?

The cost of providing spare parts is considerable and this needs to be appreciated and considered early in the development process – as part of the specification. If you are providing spare parts do you make them all at once (for economies of scale) then store them? Or do you make them when they are required? If you have a stock of spares these must be stored where people can get to them (in the centre of town), they must be protected against the weather and theft, and people must be trained to fit them. Spares themselves depreciate fast and whilst you are tying up capital in spare parts you are not investing the money, perhaps more wisely. Of course, spare parts can also be a useful long term source of income. There are a lot of decisions to be taken early in the process.

Or you can make the product maintenance free. When it breaks the customer throws it away. This tends to pitch your product at the low end of the market. It also *causes difficulty in the design. If all the parts last twenty years and one part lasts only six months then the life of this product is six months. Another difficult decision and one that needs to be made at the specification stage of the design, as a result of an investigation as to what the customer wants and what the company can provide.*

Increasingly, companies are using less maintenance and fewer provision of spares and we have come to love throw away pens, razors, electric kettles and a host of other products.

How long should we expect spare parts to be supplied? Well, it depends on the product. For cars it is twenty years but you can still get spares for certain cars older than that. For many electronic products it is about ten years.

Vacuum cleaners seem to be a special case. Have you noticed that vacuum cleaners are passed down the female line? They don't often break down so when a new one is purchased mothers pass the old one down to daughters. Our house was no different. Gillian tried to get some bags for our old vacuum cleaner and was told that they were no longer available. I protested, to be told that the vacuum cleaner was over twenty years old! We had to invest in a new one.

The provision of vacuum cleaner bags has been a nice little earner for the suppliers for many a year, estimated to be a turnover of £100 million per year (presumably a long-term earner identified at the specification stage of their development process). Now thanks to Mr Dyson we can continue using our vacuum cleaners for ever. Will tourists and vacuum cleaner salesmen in year AD 3000 be looking at the remains of a Dyson cleaner and despair?

Subsequent Evaluation

Having completed the project and, after some period of the product having been sold, it is necessary to evaluate whether the development met up to the parameters originally set, along with those identified during the process. The following questions should be asked in this evaluation:

a) Were the targets met and, if not, why not?
b) Were the correct targets set?
c) Could the targets have been exceeded?
d) Were the communications systems used adequately?
e) Were the plans appropriate to the project?
f) Were the company-wide systems adequate for the project?
g) What hindrance to the successful outcome of the project needs specification for the benefit of new projects?

The purpose of this evaluation is not to lay blame on anybody, but to identify areas where subsequent projects can be improved.

◆ ◆ ◆

Summary of Time Frame Two

1   Start by considering new products and services as a total process. Management is about the planning, organisation and control of resources to achieve the objectives of the project. In other words, you cannot manage your projects unless you look at the entire process. This is a much bigger process and involves far more people than those traditionally called designers. The process is multidisciplinary and this means people other than those traditionally involved. It is also an iterative process, that starts with an idea and/or market need.

2   The main reason for product and service failure is the same now as it has been for over three decades and perhaps longer, that is, not understanding what the customer wants. In other words, poor or inadequate market research. Too often, companies have a bright idea and start developing it without finding out if there are enough people out there who want the product. Market research doesn't incur much time or cost in relation to, for example, the cost of tooling-up for manufacture or acquiring premises. Effective market research cannot guarantee that a product will not fail, it is not a panacea for success. But so many companies miss out the low cost first stages of the process, yet spend so much time and effort on the subsequent stages with a product doomed to fail. In many cases, very basic market research is all that is required to eliminate most potential failures.

     Therefore, whatever the 'trigger' that starts the process, always back this up with market research. Whatever the trigger, there must be a market identified for the new product, as Gisser (1965) said 'A product without a market is an exercise in futility'.

3   People buy products for specific reasons. Find out these reasons and ensure that they are in your product. The most important elements in a product are, generally, Reliability (achieved through quality), Safety, Price, Ergonomics, Aesthetics and Maintainability and these must be ranked high in your specification. Often, to this must be added **TIME TO COMPLETE**.

4   There must be a 'balance' between what products are being developed and what the organisation is capable of, or willing, to do. To state that a company must be market led is an over-simplification. Organisations should identify the type of products and markets that they ought to be in and know those that they should not be in. Select a project that utilises only those resources.

5   As the cost of the various stages of product and service development rises significantly, the further one gets through the process, the main management decisions should be made at the low cost, front end of this process. Consider how the various market needs and compromises can be met and even how the finished product can be disposed of. This should be written out in a full and thorough specification. The time available must be used both effectively and efficiently and a focus on these early stages can best utilise time. Furthermore, an effective specification written early in the project will ensure an appreciation of the work that has to be undertaken and also should indicate whether it is possible within the tight time frame. The specification should be written by a group of people rather than an individual.

6   Companies should not be afraid to abandon a project as soon as it becomes apparent that the resultant product will be a failure. The earlier this can be done the better. It is far less damaging to a company to stop a likely failure than to continue with development in the hope it may be a success. There are exceptions, but, generally, if one has reason to think it will be a failure, it will be. Far better to redirect effort towards something that will be a success.

7   Don't rush into making prototypes or models of the thing you are developing except if a) it aids understanding, or b) it proves a new theory or process.

8   Beware of too much 'sophistication' just for the sake of it, or too much variation. You are trying to satisfy all your customers but you must do this at a profit.

9   But, above all, have a detailed plan for developing new products and services. This means a detailed design model that should be prepared at the start of the project to ensure that the full implications of the work are understood. Again, this should indicate if the work is possible within the time and resource constraints.

10 This multidisciplinary, iterative process does not end when the product is sold to the customer. It continues beyond the implementation and through improvement stages and must include consideration of the final disposal of the product or service.

AND THEREFORE SURVIVAL INTO TIME FRAME THREE

Time Frame Three

New Products and Services by Innovation

9

Innovation

Introduction

In this section, the manager needs to consider some product tactics and some product strategy. So what is the difference?

It was 1917 and the Great War was at its peak. Thousands were being thrown into the carnage as the two sides battled to gain a few yards advantage in the mud between the trenches. After another pointless bayonet charge a group of British soldiers found themselves cut off in no-man's land. The small group of survivors were huddled in a soggy shell hole and considered their chances as the shells whistled overhead. A lieutenant looked around and tried to sum up the situation, looking at the fit and the wounded. Then, much to his surprise, he spotted a General amongst the number. He shouted to the General above the rattle of enemy machine gun fire.

'You're the highest ranking officer, sir, please take charge and get us home.'

The answer came back immediately.

'I'm a General and therefore in charge of the strategy that is going to win this war. How we get out of this shell hole is tactics and that is down to you. You get us home.'

Strategy is the appreciation of the overall direction of the organisation and tends to be the domain of the very top management, whereas tactics is the day-to-day operation of the organisation and how the company operates is generally down to those a little lower in the management hierarchy. There is no clear cut off as to who deals with strategy and who with tactics and it is wrong to delegate one to one group and one to another. Business Strategy is concerned with the adoption of a course of action and the allocation of resources necessary to compete in a business area (Coombs 1994) and the way one achieves it is through an effective product strategy.

Strategy is concerned with:

+ the scope of an organisation's activities;
+ the matching of an organisation's activities to its environment;
+ the matching of the activities of an organisation to its resource capability;
+ the allocation and reallocation of major resources in an organisation;
+ the values, expectations and goals of those influencing strategy;
+ the direction in which an organisation will move in the long term;
+ implications for change throughout the organisation.

It is dangerous if either tactics or strategy is ineffective or even missing altogether. Yet it has been reported that '40% of small and medium sized enterprises (SMEs) have no coherent marketing strategy' and 'only 20% present well developed strategies' (National Westminster Bank 1996). Furthermore, it must be a proactive strategy, one which, according to Handley (1995), 'must enable you to control or at least influence the rules of play'.

Tactics are equally important. Our complaint with much (academic or consultant) writing is that it tells people where they should be going but does not equip them with the nuts and bolts of how to actually get there. Tactics need detail for implementation.

Models of the development process are vital but do not work when one is considering the longer term future. Process models can be used to fill in the various slices of the 'Swiss roll', which is the organisation's future. Incremental change and product improvement are also not the focus of this section. Here, we are concerned with innovation, new concepts and the creativity needed to achieve a successful future.

By its very nature, what is being discussed is vague, rather 'fuzzy'. It is hardly possible to state precisely what to do in the future. But, if you consider and assimilate the following, you will be going in the right direction. As circumstances and situations alter over this journey into the future, adjustments of better strategy and tactics will be needed but – going in the right direction – these adjustments should neither be traumatic or catastrophic. Predicting much of the future doesn't require a crystal ball – it requires common sense. But as Bernard Shaw said 'the trouble with common sense is that it isn't very common'. This book is applied common sense and may help to point you in the right direction.

Organisational Issues

We now propose yet another set of boundaries around, and sequence of actions for, the concept stage of the process of developing new products and services processes. It is believed that these will focus concept selection and improve this stage of the process,

---

A woman walks into an empty pub, goes up to the bar and asks the barman for half of lager. He serves her then walks to the far end of the bar. The woman sips her drink then hears a quiet voice 'you're looking very nice tonight'. She looks around but sees nobody. She assumes that it was her imagination and takes another sip of her lager. Suddenly the quiet voice speaks again 'that is a very smart dress that you are wearing'. Again, she looks around but there is nobody else in the bar save the barman who is still at the far end of the bar. She takes another sip of her drink, thinking that she is just a little overtired and her imagination is playing up when she hears the voice again, 'that hairstyle really suits you'.

There was no mistake that time, she had definitely heard the voice. Calling over the barman, she says 'I'm sure I keep hearing voices but there is nobody but you and me in the pub. Am I going loopy?'

'No,' he answers, 'that's the complimentary peanuts'.

A daft story, but the daftest part is that such a thing is quite possible using existing technology. The trick would be to put the necessary electronics into the base of the peanut container. By the time this book hits the shelves there may be a talking bowl of complementary peanuts on every smart bar in your town!

This is what innovation is all about. The many small things that interface with your everyday life. And if they do, and if they emanate from your organisation, then your future is assured. But even with the daftest of ideas, these are more likely to come about and are more likely to be profitable if your organisation has a system that enables such opportunities to be identified then carried forward into fruition. It may not be without trauma, as Pablo Picasso said 'every act of creation is first of all an act of destruction'.

When is Innovation Needed?

This will provide another 'boundary' around the product development process. When is innovation needed and how should it be managed? This is the theory of Product Status.

Organisations are being told to innovate more. Innovation has a precise meaning and its management is quite different from product improvement. From top to bottom you are encouraged and ushered into innovating. For example, a few quotes:

'Everybody in management and politics agrees that innovation is the golden key to the future, and without innovation the future for the firm and the economy will be leaden' (Heller 1992). Some months earlier, the same journal, *Management Today*, announced 'innovate or die'. The DTI, in their '90s News' of March 1993 headlined 'Innovate or liquidate'. It seems vital to innovate and, apparently, we should be doing it all the time. Apparently, everybody is out there frantically reinventing the wheel. We suggest you stand back and avoid innovation unless you are sure that it's absolutely necessary. On the other hand, we're just lone voices speaking out against 'everybody in management and politics' as well as the DTI and what do we know?

Is Innovation Always Needed?

It is important to appreciate when an innovation is required in the total process, as the way that new products are managed and the activities that should be included in the process vary, depending on whether a product is 'static' (incremental or evolutionary improvements) or 'dynamic' (innovation). For example, if a product is static, aesthetics are more important, automation is more likely to be viable and necessary, larger companies are more likely to benefit and CAD will be more useable in the design process. The reverse will be the case if the product is dynamic. See the section on Tools and Techniques.

Knowing that a product is static or dynamic can show when managers should direct their emphasis towards innovating that product or making incremental changes. Throughout the process of developing new products or services through product status, it becomes more apparent what aspects of design become more or less important. This means that the design manager can accentuate or emphasise the important disciplines and diminish those that become less important.

Furthermore, certain elements in the Product Specification can be graded for importance. When a product is static aesthetics are more important, but patents less important. With a static product the concept stage of the design process will be of less importance and perhaps will be unnecessary. A static product which again becomes dynamic indicates when designs and research should cease on the old concept.

If a product is known to be static it is sometimes possible to identify the extent of an innovation necessary to end the static plateau. This, in turn, can direct a company when not to develop a new technology. For example, work on electric cars for most applications is unlikely to be successful until a low cost high powered, light weight battery has been developed. On the other hand, it can show when it is worth putting effort into developing a new technology. This occurs whenever an existing system does not reach the performance requirements of a changing or new market. The flurry of work into an AIDS vaccine would be an example of this.

If a company does not have sufficient disciplines associated with the product status of the new design, knowing what disciplines are associated with a particular status can aid the decision on whether they should, or should not, attempt to enter a market. For example, a batch production company should not attempt to enter a mass production market, such as the match industry, unless they are prepared themselves to become mass producers. This would, of course, involve a very large investment.

Similarly, it can show when a company should consider leaving a particular market. For example, innovators, identifying that a product has become static, may be unable to compete with the large organisations entering the market. They should, in such cases, 'cut and run'. If, on the other hand, they know that the particular product is still dynamic they will not be at such a disadvantage against these large organisations. They may then be able to hold their ground and compete for the next innovation.

Knowing the product status can show if investment should be directed by the company towards process design (the method of manufacture) or product design. With a dynamic product the emphasis must be towards product design, but with a static product, process design may be pre-eminent.

The product status can indicate, to outside funding sources, such as to the Research Councils (e.g. ESRC), whether the research direction being taken by a company or academic institution is worthwhile. If the product is static the funding may well be better used elsewhere on another (dynamic) product.

A large company, relative to the competition, benefits from a design being static whereas a small company may benefit from a design being dynamic because they are better able to compete with larger companies as a fast changing product and market prevents, in many cases, automation and economies of scale, which suit the large companies; this depends on the industry. Smaller companies tend to react faster to change, but in certain industries, such as pharmaceuticals and the aerospace industry, the high cost of innovation excludes all but the largest companies. If the product is static the smaller companies may be better directed to seek market niches away from the main competition.

If a product is static and looks like remaining static for some time, the market share becomes increasingly important as this enables greater volumes in relation to the competition. Therefore, a greater degree of static disciplines may be included. This will then allow the company to benefit from the economies of scale and lower cost production to further improve their competitive edge. Therefore, if a product appears to be static for some time in the future, a company should aim to increase its market share, improve learning curves, make larger (bulk) purchases of materials, make fuller use of machine and create more sales outlets. Larger market share may also allow the company to benefit from disciplines such as Just-In-Time.

In competition analysis, if a competitive company is known to be operating with a particular status it can indicate whether their new products are likely to be static or dynamic. It can, therefore, aid the planning of the defence against competition. A competitor is unlikely to discover a new concept unless they are actively looking for one. If a product is known to be static the future is more predictable and, therefore, corporate planning is easier. It can be undertaken with a great confidence of its accuracy. Subsequent stages of the design process become easier, such as the concept stage, and the product design specification is easier to write.

All this from the simple premise of product status, which has been developed into something that makes the design manager's job more structured and, therefore, (hopefully!) more easy. With the benefit of hindsight it is possible to look back at some products to show where consideration of product status could have aided decision making. The originators of video recording machines were producing an ever improving highly technical machine, but they failed to appreciate that the technology had reached the point where a cost effective consumer product could be marketed. With many technological innovations the price starts high, but rapidly declines in a curve similar to that shown on Figure 9.1.

This is because the producing companies become more experienced with the technology and begin to introduce improved manufacturing processes, which brings cost down. Also, with few competitors initially a high price can be charged, especially if the idea is protected by patents. The price declines as the supply increases. In the case of videos the dynamic phase of the design had come to an end and with a suitable injection of the disciplines associated with static design, in effect process

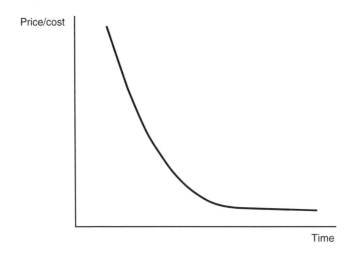

Figure 9.1   The rapid decline in cost for new products

design for low cost manufacture, a machine for consumers was possible. A machine could be produced at a price within the range of a wide consumer market. The originators failed to take this step and declined. The Japanese companies, who concentrated on this aspect of design using the innovations of the originators, took over this market.

Although there have been some significant innovations with the design of certain car parts, the basic car design has been static for some years. In the years from 1966, though, car companies have concentrated more of their effort and resources on the way in which a car is manufactured than its actual design. Once again, it was the Japanese who have led the way producing effectively and at a lower cost than the competitors, thereby taking a lead in world markets. Ten years later, the European manufacturers also started to adopt this policy. It could have been possible to have predicted this emphasis earlier and matched the Japanese in process design. Certainly, Henry Ford operated on this principle with the Model T and, although improvements in process design improved over the subsequent period, it took the Japanese to really show what could be achieved with process technology.

As you can see, the simple expediency of looking at your product status can fundamentally effect the health and even the survival of your company. Now, if you are a manager, or involved in the product or service, think for a few minutes, is the product static or dynamic? Now having decided that, doesn't this alter your emphasis in design?

Of course, it is rare that a new product or service is completely an innovation or an incremental change and it is possible for the product to be broken down into its various sub-components, some of which will be innovative and some will require incremental change. It is possible to identify if parts of a new product/market require static or dynamic design and also whether an organisation is best able to achieve it.

As most customers and hence most products do not require a new concept, the existing concept is good enough. If it is **known** that the product is entirely static then the concept stage and the search for new concepts may not be necessary in the process of developing new products or services. As long as the specifications, and hence the market research, is thorough and complete then, for some products, it may be possible to omit the entire concept stage.

What is Innovation?

Innovation is a misunderstood word. Do not innovate unless you have to. Jacob Buur, a Danish engineer spent twenty months investigating design in Japanese companies. He concluded: 'It seems that the emphasis in Japan is very much on developing products that suit customers, where European companies rather concentrate on creating original outstanding products' (Bradley and Buur 1993).

So what is innovation? The Department of Trade and Industry (DTI) defines it as 'The successful exploitation of new ideas' which is essentially correct although one cannot have the word 'successful' in a definition as it would still be an innovation if it were a failure.

Drucker (1985) defines it thus: 'Innovation is the act that endows resources with a new capacity to create wealth. It is the search for and exploitation of new opportunities for satisfying human wants and human needs.' In the latest Standard on design terminology, published in 1995, 'innovation' is defined as: 'The transformation of an idea into a novel saleable product or operational process in industry and commerce or into a new service' (BS 7000 part 10 1995).

> THE DEFINITION WE PREFER IS 'AN INVENTION IN
> ITS FIRST MARKETABLE FORM'.

The key here is that this means it has to be **new**, and not just an improvement on what has gone before. It requires a new concept and not

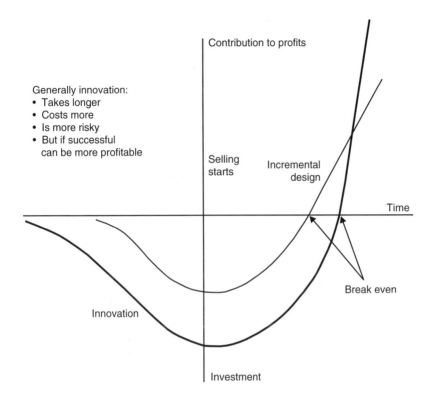

Figure 9.2   The comparison between innovation and incremental change

a rehash of what already exists. It also means that it must have been put on sale. New products must certainly be improvements but not often is a new concept needed. Do not just drift into innovating. Many do because it's fun but only innovate if it is required. Innovation appears in this part of the book because in the longer term your organisation will need to innovate to survive.

Take a look at Figure 9.2. The problem with an innovation is that it takes longer and so needs a greater amount of time than those parts where people are more familiar with the concept (you cannot rely on experience). Innovation thus costs more than a product improvement (time is money) and is more risky as it is more difficult to do market research on an innovation (but not impossible if you remember that people buy benefits). On the other hand, if successful it can be very successful as there is no exact competition and you are the only supplier. Therefore, an innovation should only be embarked upon when the market actually wants it and the company is able to provide it.

Regnis Sewing Machine from Singer
Rememberd for its value
Respected for its versatility.

- Feed drop mechanism
- Embroidery hoop facility.
- Forward & reverse stitching.
- Open type shuttle race.
- Dial type thread tension adjustment.
- Threadle operated.

Rs 4990/-

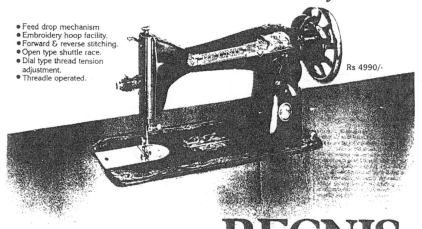

REGNIS
Sewing Machine -
built to last in the SINGER tradition

Reproduced by permission of Singer (Sri Lanka) Limited

So, innovating costs time and money yet 42% of so called innovative SMEs provide no resources for continuous innovation (National Westminster Bank 1996).

Does your market really want something new – all the time? An example is the introduction of electronic sewing machines in Sri Lanka. Bags of sophistication but few could afford them. Electric power could be a bit wayward outside of town and if the machines break down the local blacksmith or car mechanic couldn't fix them. The solution was to bring back the tried and tested mechanical variety that made Singer famous.

You think this doesn't apply in our sophisticated society? How many of you want the new electric plug we've just invented? It is smaller, lighter, better, and potentially cheaper than those big ugly things in your house. One drawback, you will have to replace all your sockets. Customers like the familiar and they like products that interface with their existing belongings (what format will be the next video that you buy to replace your current machine when it wears out? And if you buy a different format what will you do with all your old tapes?).

Innovate Throughout the Process

Walker (1998) says 'even well respected authors have written about the creative leap at the centre of the design process . . . as if creativity was a spontaneous hop, step and a jump. At best, creativity and intelligence are not condensed into one or two opening moments of inspiration but distributed and infused throughout the **whole process**. So creativity operates in the smallest details, such as a bolt for fastening, as well as at the level of inventive principle. Indeed, an inventive principle depends entirely upon the detail of process and component design to give it credibility – and ultimately to make it ruddy well work.'

Do not just limit innovation to the design of the product. There is growth through innovation in methods of manufacture and it is here that the Japanese have been successful. They started off by taking ideas from the West and then applied innovation to their production processes so that they were making things better cheaper and of higher quality. This is how they took over world markets. It is some years since they found that they had run out of things to copy and have now moved on to creating completely new products.

There is also innovation in marketing and this is probably one of the more successful areas that you should investigate. In fact, in work done by NEDO and reported in Stimulating Innovation in Industry (1992) it was found that marketing innovation is a greater growth stimulant than technical innovation. Sir Paul Girolami of Glaxo said 'I believe it is important that innovation should become an attitude of mind. As such, it should permeate the whole business – research, products, production, administration services and marketing. It is no good being effective in one department and not in another.'

As an example, take the marketing innovation relating to pizza. How many people would have continued to spend quite a lot of money on pizza (after all, it is only glorified cheese on toast) if somebody hadn't thought of home delivery and then included a guaranteed half hour delivery service? Home banking is another 'obvious' success, (only obvious when someone else has thought of it) which works because people do not want the bother of going out perhaps in inclement weather, between fairly narrow opening hours, to have to find a parking space in town centre and then to join a queue.

Serendipity plays an important part in innovation. It is said that the chap who invented Cat's Eyes for the road did so when he saw a cat walking towards him at night, the light caught the cat's eyes and they shone and hence the idea was born. If the cat had been walking in the other direction, he might have invented the pencil sharpener!

Product improvement takes time, seeking new concepts (innovation) takes even more time. We must re-learn to allow people thinking time and time to speculate and work for the future. We must also re-create a climate that allows time for consideration.

10

Innovation – Tools and Techniques

Product Status

There are many such activities that are related to the status of a product, and some are shown below.

Factors that tend to keep a product or service static

1 Customers not willing to change.
2 Stable technology.
3 A few large producers.
4 A reducing or stable number of producers.
5 No recent inventions.
6 Large inflexible infrastructure based on an existing concept.
7 Conformance standards.
8 User familiarity.
9 Large number of existing users 'locked in' to an existing system (e.g. VHS or the QWERTY keyboard).
10 Companies not willing to change.
11 Rigid legislation.
12 Existing patents.
13 More process design than product design.
14 Companies greatly influenced by shareholders.

Factors that can make a product or service dynamic

1 Customers willing to change.
2 Invention, innovation or new technology.
3 Many small producers.
4 An existing infrastructure that can be used with a new concept.

5   No conformance standards.
6   The product or service does not interface with other static products and services.
7   Limited recently purchased automation.
8   Companies willing to change.
9   Changing or new legislation.
10 Ill defined market infrastructure.
11 Flexible production methods.
12 Relative changes in the cost and availability between certain commodities and resources.

If you know that your product or service is static or dynamic, then you can emphasise the 'Disciplines' shown below.

Disciplines that accompany static design

1   Mass production.
2   Industrial design – aesthetics and ergonomics.
3   Use of dedicated machinery, automation, or CAD.
4   Short model life cycles.
5   Cost reduction.
6   Standardisation, specialisation and rationalisation.
7   Vertical integration.
8   Imitation.
9   Niche marketing, innovative marketing.
10 Economies of scale.
11 Just in Time.
12 Market pull.
13 Value analysis.
14 Robotics/CAM.
15 Energy conservation.

Disciplines that accompany dynamic design

1   Seeking new concepts, technology push.
2   Short product life cycles.
3   Flexible production systems.
4   Use of subcontract.
5   Labour intensive.
6   Patents.
7   Creative marketing.

How to Innovate – Reassessing the Lone Designer and Creativity

There appears to be a new paradigm emerging on the best methods to use in the generation of new concepts. Brainstorming groups have been accepted as showing an improvement in creativity compared with that of the individual designer. But brainstorming sessions, perhaps, do not draw the best from the capabilities of the individual. A combination of group work and individual 'contemplation' may be the route to finding better new concepts.

Developing new products and services is essentially a creative process but is one that requires rigour and systems to which one needs to adhere. At the concept stage of the total process we are amongst many who have been advocating that the 'days of the lone designer are over' (Hollins and Hollins 1992). We should be operating in brainstorming teams, co-ordinated by quite 'antique', but still valid, rules that were formulated in the thirties and published in the fifties (Osborne 1953).

De Bono has criticised brainstorming groups (de Bono 1993). He has said 'Brainstorming is non-productive because it lacks structure and control' (Bunce 1994). Of course, in these brainstorming sessions free thought is encouraged but here De Bono is out of date. In brainstorming procedures, the 'dos and don'ts' have always been structured through set rules and controlled by the chairman. Additionally, nowadays, brainstorming sessions should subsequently be controlled and the ideas assessed, through a thorough written specification, as we described in Time Frame Two. The elements, that require consideration, that should be included in the specification far outnumber the 'six different notional hats' proposed by de Bono (1986).

De Bono has stated that 'the creative idea must make sense and must work' (Bunce 1994). This is correct, but it must go much further, for our organisations to survive the idea must also sell. Although not entirely fans of de Bono, we have come to similar conclusions after exploring alternative areas. Something is not right in the way we think up new ideas. The creative process needs improvement beyond what can be achieved in brainstorming sessions.

A New Direction?

Lenin said that 'to see only one side is to be blind in one eye'. Academics tend to concentrate on their own discipline to the point of missing out on useful theories that are almost 'old hat' in other areas (we still see Maslow and his 1952 theories quoted – has nothing relevant to us appeared in medical psychology since?).

In a period of 'catholic' reading, we have recently explored and revisited psychology and philosophy that we have avoided since graduation day. In the years since, being closely embroiled in design theory, we have read the amateur blundering of designers exploring the left and right side of the brain to no apparent purpose. Knowing generally which does what in the brain does little in our work if we cannot actually utilise it. The right side of the brain deals with creativity and the left side more with the 'process'. Design today must be mainly a left side of the brain activity with many shots of creativity from the right throughout the process (in the innovation of product, production and marketing). The main area for the creativity and use of the right hemisphere of the brain is in the concept stage of the process and is covered in this Time Frame.

The individual

Looking again at psychology and philosophy through the eyes of a designer it can be seen that most views of 'enlightenment' identified by philosophers are all solitary experiences, though often achieved through some guide or teacher and nearly always after a long period of struggle. Designers can relate to this struggle for creating the new. Edison may have talked about the 5% inspiration and 95% perspiration, but that 5% is hard work and vital for successful products.

In Plato's 'Symposium' he is in effect saying 'don't be discouraged because the way of consciousness is difficult. Press on, and you will find that it will be more worthwhile than you can even imagine.' Creativity takes time and far more time than we can allow in brainstorming sessions – they are, after all, expensive operations taking a number of senior people away from money making activities. But perhaps individuals need more time than brainstorming group sessions can allow.

In our own experience most can relate to struggling over a problem for hours, or even days. Then, some time later, often when doing another quite unrelated activity, like gardening or lying in the bath, the solution suddenly flashes into our head. McCorkle (1994) points out that many such ideas are lost as, by then, the brainstorming activity in the organisation has come to an end, 'the ideas have already been evaluated and voted on'. We probably need that early struggle to get the flash of inspiration but we also need this diversion and incubation time to enable the inspirational flash to appear. Can both be built into the concept phase of the process? Our conscious and unconscious creative processing seems to work slowly but we need to capture these brain waves as part of the creative concept stage if we are to have successful products.

CASE STUDY – HEALER HEAL THYSELF

As recently as March 1994 the UK Design Council were advocating the following:

*It is the established approach of many academics that lots of options should be created during the concept phase and should then be sifted (according to some procedure or other) to determine the best. Such an approach may now seem somewhat dated. Provided the brief is sound and comprehensive, **THE FIRST SOLUTION THAT FITS IT'S REQUIREMENTS IS LIKELY TO BE GOOD ENOUGH** (OK, one may choose to sift through two or three options, but sifting through many may be unacceptably expensive and time-consuming – particularly in the light of current time-to-market pressures). Thus, this piece of teaching may need debate and perhaps revision.*

Eh . . . No! Time to market is important for the following reasons:

1   Lowers costs (less interest repayments).
2   Allows higher prices to be charged (skimming).
3   Achieves higher sales (you are in the market ahead of the competition).
4   Allows you to start the next design earlier (to get even further ahead of the competition).
5   Improves company reputation.
6   Can improve morale.

All-in-all seems to be a good thing!

but consider the following scenario.

It is a well known fact that all men tend to put their underpants on their heads and parade around their bedroom thinking that they are hilariously funny. Furthermore, they all do it but think they are the first person who has thought of this super wheeze. If you are male then you can't deny that you have done this, and if you truly haven't done this, then there is probably something seriously wrong with your up-bringing.

Of course, some people take it all a bit far as reported in The Big Issue (21–27 July 1997):

Robbers have been adopting some very strange disguises. In Washington, a man held-up a supermarket wearing a pair of badly soiled knickers over his head.

Well, seeing as so many men seem to put underwear on their heads, is there an unexploited market niche for such a product as 'head-pants' for the man who has everything? Specially styled boxer shorts that come in a complete range of head sizes.

Let us consider two such organisations, company A and company B, that discover this new product opportunity and start on the development process simultaneously. Company A appreciates the importance of getting to the market early and so they waste no time in attacking the stage of the total design process. After all, the advantages of getting on to the market fast are well documented. So, company A gets on with the process. Now, the Product Champion for this development is fairly well read in the art of NPD and has read the quotation above from the old Design Council. 'Makes sense' he thinks and blitzes on with the first concept that meets the specification.

The development department manager in company B has also done a lot of reading but she is a wily old bird. She spends longer in the concept stage of the process, a full two days longer than company A. In this two days were held brainstorming sessions in a nearby hotel with nine individuals from different departments. Expensive, but worth it.

After six months, Company A hits the high street with their natty head gear just in time for the New Year and the New Man. And do they sell? Well, actually no. Because company B had spent longer on the concept stage they had thought of all the additional gimmicks and added value that could be added to such a concept, roll-down ear muffs, sun glasses affixed and topped off with a flashing bobble crotch.

But weren't company B entering the market after company A? Not at all. Because they had spent longer in the concept stage, company B had thought of not only more and better features, they had also found a better way of producing this fashion item and were ready in the shops in time to exploit the lucrative Christmas market.

Having the wrong product, in this case, is known as 'concept vulnerability'. The moral is that although it is important to reduce the time to market for new products, this should not be done at the expense of thorough development.

A case of 'a stitch in time'.

The Design Council, as it was then structured, was disbanded in August of that year and reformed with one tenth of the staff and a much smaller budget. I showed the above quote to Angela Dumas, the then Training Director, and asked her views. 'it's rubbish isn't it?' was her reply – so things must be looking up.

The group

On the other hand, most creativity is nowadays done in groups ('Teamwork has replaced individual genius' – Enzio Ferrari). Group work is more effective for developing new ideas than (the sum of) individuals working alone. Research at Sheffield Hallam University found that 55% of industrial designers questioned stated that team working improved their capacity to generate ideas and that 70% reported that team working had led to better communication with colleagues outside of their own discipline (Fisher et al. 1996).

> Karl Marx once said 'the group seemed so ill-assorted as to risk being torn apart by their own internal contradictions' – seems to sum up most attempts we've seen at Total Quality Management and group creativity, no matter . . .

Various authors have written on how long should be spent in brainstorming sessions. McCorkle (1994) stated that many of the best ideas from brainstorming sessions can come in minutes, hours or days after the session because of incubation time. Majaro (1992) states that an effective brainstorming group should be able to produce 150 ideas in twenty minutes. Jones (1980) found that six people with a wealth of relevant experience to tap on could generate about 150 ideas in thirty minutes. Osborne (1993) refers to a study by Dr Sidney J. Parues (who has the widest experience in brainstorming) who felt that thirty to forty-five minutes is the best for brainstorming. According to Majaro (1992), the time for a full brainstorming session, designed for groups which are relative novices in the use of the technique, is approximately two days, three hours and fifteen minutes.

The period of time specified in all these examples may not be sufficient in the case of a large design project. However, this level of time should not necessarily be allowed for small projects for fear that time for marketing the product will be reduced, allowing competitors' products an advantage.

Until recently, people assumed that a brainstorming session of a couple of hours would 'drain' the group's creative abilities. Now, it is commonly accepted that at least two days should be allowed for an effective brainstorming session (BS 7000 part 2 and part 3), and that there will be periods of 'soaking' when nothing creative appears to be happening. You probably know this for yourself. You are thinking long and hard about something then you stop and dig the garden or soak in a bath and suddenly the solution pops into your head. This is the effect of this 'soaking' phase.

During a brainstorming session up to nine or ten people (Schein 1969, Belbin 1981) are otherwise unproductive. Although this is expensive, it is justifiable when compared with the enormous cost of developing the wrong concept into a saleable product only to be faced with competitors who have chosen a 'less vulnerable' concept, who subsequently take your market. The ability of those in groups to 'bounce' ideas off each other produces more, and better, solutions to a given problem. Therefore, we believe brainstorming sessions of a couple of days are likely to be more productive than individuals working alone.

Even this, we suggest, is probably insufficient time and too 'intense' to be an effective way of getting the best from those involved (the aim being

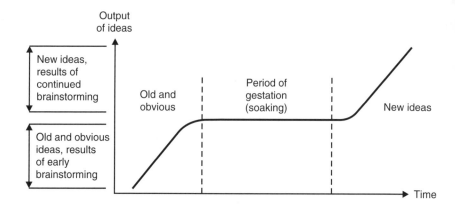

Figure 10.1   The effect of the 'soaking' period

the best design concept and subsequently, the most competitive product). A much greater period of 'soaking' is necessary, where individuals can mull over the problem to find this 'consciousness'. We are under utilising our personal capabilities by subjecting them to group decision making. We need to promote the thoughts and subsequent ideas of those in the group so that the best of the various individuals – as individuals – is fully exploited, and also maximise the best that the group situation can offer. But which comes first, the lone thinking or the group brainstorming?

Combination – a new way?

Let us now relate this to the more 'mundane' process of the concept stage of the process of developing new products and services. If organisations are using Total Design, as they should, the concept stage of the design process should be reached after the potential market has been investigated and the specification has been written.

The way by which we then achieve the 'best' product should be explored. There is truth in both the proverbs 'two heads are better than one' and 'a camel is a horse designed by a committee'. Group decision making is flawed (e.g. Groupthink) (Janis 1972). Solitary designers also have the propensity to fail, through, perhaps, too much focus (right-side brain activity?) and insufficient view of other areas such as the market and their organisation's capabilities (left-side brain logic?) What is needed is a compromise that develops the best of both worlds.

First, there needs to be a structure around the concept stage. There is still insufficient guidance to those seeking these new concepts. Some companies still start design at the concept phase without the necessary prior work that puts this stage into its correct context. Those involved need focus and guidance, which also needs to be built into the process and these parameters should be made available a week before the first brainstorming session. These will include:

1 Does the organisation need a product improvement (evolutionary design) or a completely new concept (innovation)? Knowledge of the product status (Hollins and Pugh 1990) should be ascertained and given to those involved.
2 Other necessary restrictions (financial return, timescales for development, production, market or distribution limitations) must all be provided as broad limitations. These may limit the flair and creativity of those ideas eventually selected in the final assessment but necessarily so within bounds acceptable to the organisation who are paying the wages and paying for the design. But as well as this, participants need to be encouraged to think beyond just the next product to the potential customer needs and benefits required further in the future.
3 Ideally, a full specification is required, This mantle around the design process will, ultimately, guide those involved toward the more useful (saleable) product. Organisations are still woefully bad at writing specifications and an inadequate specification will prevent the ideas that emerge from the creative phase from being adequately assessed to enable the 'best' concept to be identified.

This requires greater commitment, direction and understanding of design by those at the top. People keep writing this but, even now, in too many organisations the top management only become actively involved when things (usually costs) are out of control and panic sets in.

In answer to the question 'which comes first, the lone thinking or the group brainstorming?', after much 'chicken and egg' consideration we suggest that one full brainstorming group session is required with individual contemplation on either side.

Having put in place the structure around the concept phase as proposed above, the concept phase could follow these stages:

1 An initial 'introduction' where those in the brainstorming group confront the problem, understanding the limitations and boundaries to which any chosen concept must comply.
2 Allow one week in which those in the brainstorming group can think over the ideas on their own.

3 Hold the two day brainstorming session, including an initial assessment of concept proposals – using a concept assessment matrix (Hollins and Hollins 1991).
4 Allow another week for individual appraisal and contemplation.
5 Reform the brainstorming group for one further day to assess any additional new concepts and identify the 'best', as before.

This proposed method is expensive in terms of people's time. The whole concept stage is likely to take three weeks! This flies in the face of reducing 'time to market' and thus it should only be used for 'large' design projects where the anticipated return justifies this high cost. Furthermore, it is not proposed that individuals should devote themselves exclusively to the particular design problem but do it in parallel with other activities.

The message is that, as individuals, we have enormous untapped talents of creativity. Well run brainstorming sessions are supposed to release this potential but the very group situation and time limitations can stifle these. Even if the sessions are run for an adequate two or three days they cannot capture the sudden thoughts or release the intermittent unplanned spasms of creativity, the 'Eurekas' that ought to be harnessed in design. But the failure rate resulting from random inspirational sparks vastly outnumber the successes. The 'flashes of genius' from individuals are of little use unless they are funnelled towards organisational needs, strategies, and a planned product range. This section proposes a compromise that may capture the best of both forms of creativity.

Shaw says in *Man and Superman*, 'That as life after ages of struggle evolved that wonderful bodily organ the eye, so that the living organism could see where it was going and what was coming to help or threaten it, and thus avoid the thousand dangers that formally slew it, so it is today evolving a mind's eye that shall see, not the physical world, but the purpose of life.' We need be able to think beyond the next product improvement and seek greater purpose in our products. Likewise, even if we do harness and harvest a greater part of our creative talents we cannot expect the 'infinite streams of consciousness or spirit', or Samedta (God ecstasy) achieved by the Hindu saint Ramakrishna. But if this is possible, why can't we improve our performance by going part way along this road?

CASE STUDY – A NEW CONCEPT IN VACUUM CLEANERS

The vacuum cleaner was designed as a result of a Victorian Music Hall act which featured a device that blew dust off furniture. What a great evening's entertainment, 'let's not stay in tonight dear, there is some very impressive furniture blowing on at the Empire'. And they wonder why Music Hall died? Anyway, after this virtuoso performance a member of the audience went backstage and asked the performer why the device wasn't made to suck in the dust rather than just blow it over the orchestra pit. He was told that such a device was 'quite impossible'. Well, in spite of the diversions of the local entertainment, the spectator still found time to design the vacuum cleaner, as we know it today.

And that is the point, it is still essentially the same concept. Apart from Hoover adding 'it beats as it sweeps as it cleans' in the 1930s little has changed. Air and dust (and bits of lego) are sucked into a porous paper bag, the air passes through and the dust is left behind. The inefficiencies are obvious.

A friend, who was a repair man of electrical consumer durables, would ring his hands at the occasional plea of 'my Hoover is still working but isn't picking up the dirt'. He would tell the customer to return some hours later but fix the cleaner in a moment by removing the plastic bag that had been inserted and replacing it with one of the porous paper variety!

On a television design awards programme in 1995 there appeared the Dyson cyclone vacuum cleaner, the first major new concept in domestic vacuum cleaners this century. No clogging bag to suck through, a far more effective and efficient device. 'An obvious winner' you may think, but no. It was dismissed in a moment and, at least, ten times the air time was spent discussing the merits of a credit card torch designed by Sinclair, brother of Sir Clive. OK, it was a novel design with some good features but as a potential award winner I would have thought that there was no contest. And they wonder why Bill shouts at his television. Anyway, the rest is history. The Dyson went on to be a market winner with sales of the first model being double that of the nearest rival at almost twice the price. The moral is, don't put your trust in TV pundits or design awards.

Blueprinting Enhanced – a New Design Method for Improving Service

Blueprinting, as described in Time Frame One, shows how the customer uses a service. This is shown when the process is mapped out and this will identify bottlenecks and areas where the service quality may be improved. This also has the effect that service quality, which tends to be mainly qualitative and therefore difficult to measure, can be made more qualitative.

This process can be extended much further to improve services. Initially, compile the blueprint as before. Then, in parallel to what has gone before, look at the 'sensory' side of the customer experience and write these in the parallel boxes. What does the customer see, hear, taste, smell and feel at each stage? Then, related to each sense, propose how the service can be improved through the normal concept generation methods. This will allow potential service improvements to be focused more precisely in areas where they are most needed. What the customer feels about each stage and some ideas on how it could be improved should be collected reactively, for example by customer complaints, or better, proactively from customers using the service by interview or other form of market research.

For an indication of potential new products look also to stretching the process – extend the blueprint, adding to the service side.

Activity at each stage of the blueprint

WHAT DOES THE CUSTOMER:	TASTE? SEE? HEAR? SMELL? FEEL?	HOW CAN EACH BE IMPROVED?

CASE STUDY – BEWARE OF TOO MUCH FUN!

Do you like the concept stage of developing new products and services? Of course you do, it's jolly good fun. A nice clean sheet of paper, loads of self expression and a perfect excuse to while away the hours day dreaming. You cannot hurry the process if you are going to do it properly. The only way to steer clear of 'concept vulnerability' is to take your time and consider all possible variations on a theme and then to select the 'best'. Incidentally, how do you know that you have selected the 'best' concept? Short of developing all your ideas into products and seeing which is the most popular, which nobody in their right mind would ever do, you can't.

Design Methods is the term given to all these aids to creative thinking, such as analogy, inversion, combination, lateral thinking, etc. Wallow in these to choose the one with which you are most happy. As you can't know the best concept similarly, you can't identify the 'best' design method, accept the one you are most comfortable with.

The eventual product could be on sale for five years so it's worth spending a few days on the concept. Doodle away for a few days and all you will have to show for it at the end is a few sketches, and this is how it should be.

Remember that it has scientifically been proven that alcohol improves creativity. Well, you know this already. Go to a party, have a few drinks and it is amazing what 'creative' ideas come into your head. On the other hand, it has also been shown that marijuana makes one too focused, so stay away from the funny cigarettes and stay on the booze. You do have a well stocked drinks cabinet in your office – don't you?

Embourgeoisement

Around the 1860s, Karl Marx was telling us that those at the point of production would take over companies in a workers' revolution. His mate

Engels noticed that rather than take up cudgels against the bosses workers were, in fact, trying to copy their lifestyle (clocks for the mantelpiece, etc.). This was later called (by Bottomore) 'embourgeoisement of the working classes'.

The fact is that the things the rich have the less rich also want and eventually get. Unfortunately, the poor have to do without. Once, only the rich had foreign holidays, colour TV and electric windows on their cars. It is a good pointer to the new products of the near future. Look to what the wealthy have as part of their lifestyle. If popular, and if the costs can be brought down (often through better manufacturing methods or new technology) then these are likely to be the successful products of the next few years. By and large, the cost of technology reduces over time so embourgeoisment is likely to continue.

Identifying the Best Concept – the Concept Assessment Matrix

Having discovered various new concepts it is necessary to identify the 'best' for your organisation. Initially, the concepts should be appraised against the various specifications and this should result in the elimination of most. There should still be several concepts remaining and these should then be assessed for suitability against each other in a Concept Assessment Matrix. The one described below we developed in our book 'Total Design' (Hollins and Hollins 1991) and seems to work successfully. This is shown in Figure 10.2 below.

The matrix is split into several sequential stages. In the first, the proposed new products and services are considered with a view to their safety. It is the law that products and services should be safe and if they are not it is reason enough for them to be eliminated without further consideration.

In the next stage, the concepts are related to the company strategy. These will include management guidelines, which may relate to maximum time scales for implementation or other parameters, which have been specified. Financial aspects are also considered at this stage and will, probably, include limits on the amount of money that can be used in the development, the return on investment, etc. Also, considered here will be whether the organisation must produce the product themselves or can allow part or all of it to be subcontracted. The allowed parameters regarding the product distribution or the technology which is allowed are also appraised at this stage. Those products or services that fall outside

Figure 10.2 Concept Assessment Matrix

Concept	Strategy — Safety	Strategy — Management guidelines	Strategy — Production	Strategy — Distribution	Strategy — Financial	Strategy — Technology	Market — Maintainability	Market — Price	Market — Aesthetics	Market — Reliability	Market — Ergonomics	Combination
A	X	✓	✓	✓	✓	✓	1	5	1	2	2	
B	✓	✓	✓	✓	X							
C	✓	✓	X									
D	✓											
E	X											
F	✓	✓	✓	✓	✓	✓	2	4	3	(1)	5	
G	✓	✓	✓	✓	✓	✓	3	3	2	3	(1)	
H	✓	✓	✓	✓	✓	✓	4	(2)	5	4	3	
I	✓	✓	✓	✓	✓	✓	5	(1)	4	5	4	
J	X											? ? ? ?

Spec. level — Elements (Apparent overall best concept):

	1	2	3	4	5	6	7
	✓	X	✓	✓	✓	✓	✓
		Reappraise					

Criteria

Apparent overall best concept

the stated company-wide parameters for the development of new products and services can be eliminated at this stage. Alternatively, if the proposal identifies one area in which the company-wide parameters cannot be reached, it highlights where immediate consideration should be given to resolve or accommodate this problem area. In other words, for example, if the organisation does not have in place ways to distribute the potential product, this problem should be overcome immediately before the proposal is taken any further.

If the subspecifications had been well compiled these previous stages should be a formality, but it is surprising, in practice, how often these basics have been overlooked and the matrix highlights these specification deficiencies.

In the next stage of the matrix the most important elements of the specification are considered. Here, the concepts are ranked (not weighted) for importance and at this stage an overall best concept will begin to appear. In the next stage, combining concepts is considered. In those concepts which do not appear to be as good as others it may be possible to take some of the features of the other concepts to make an overall best concept. As an example of this, if a service was being developed in which parcels were to be delivered around town, one concept may be to use the local bus service and another concept could be to use old aged pensioners. By combining these two concepts a third, better, concept could emerge of OAPs delivering parcels by bus (using their bus passes).

The final stage of this matrix provides an overview of other important elements in the specification to ensure that these can be met, and where they cannot, suitable compromises can be achieved. The overall Concept Assessment Matrix has the effect of weeding out unsuitable concepts and indicating those which are most likely to be successful. Remember that it is just a tool and it should not be used to control the concept assessment process. The manager must always control the process and if an overall best concept emerges, which common sense suggests is not the best, then the manager should go with their understanding of what is required.

This matrix should indicate what the customer wants, what the organisation can do and why the proposed product or service is better than the competition.

GREAT PRODUCTS IN THE PAST – NOW WE WANT GREAT PRODUCTS IN THE FUTURE

In recent times, we have seen wonderful products such as that terrific device that clips on to the side of your plate which allows one at buffets to hold a glass of wine, the plate and still have a hand free with which to eat or gesticulate. There have also been great advances with Virtual Reality, which is just like real reality but you get the chance to wear a hat.

But we must not forget that we have a lot of work still to do. Below are some of the devices that need to be designed over the next twenty years. Sharpen your pencils and get to grips with the following eleven products that we need well before the next fifteen years are up:

BILL'S HOPES FOR THE FUTURE

1   I start with the impossible. There needs to be an optical device designed to make politicians see sense with a verbal attachment to make them speak it. Now let us move from the sublime.
2   When is somebody going to invent the non splashing urinal? If I stand too close I splash my trousers, if I stand too far away I splash my boots. (I suspect the eventual design will consist of some type of hole in a wall, and then there will have to be a National Standard for the size of the hole.)
3   Decent non alcoholic wine and beer, oh what the hell, I'll take a taxi.
4   A device for tailors to take inside leg measurements without causing the customers to smirk.
5   The undetectable wig – or has this already been designed and I didn't notice? If so, why do people still buy the other sort? We used to hold 'spot the Irish jig' competitions (as the cockney slang merchants would say). We got very good at it and could detect a 'syrup of figs' from fifty metres. The game came to an abrupt end on Savoy Circus in Acton, West London, when Gill shouted 'look at that one' on seeing a chap with a rabbit (from a distance it looked like hare). In eagerness to see the latest example, Bill nearly rolled the motor and just avoided causing a multiple pile up. As you see, the undetectable toupee is needed as any other type can be a serious hazard.
6   Another more obvious redesign is that old problem of the unsteerable supermarket or airport trolley. It can't be mere chance which makes them so difficult. I think the current designs are fitted with some form of rudimentary artificial intelligence that gives them a mind of their own as part of some much wider joke that I'm not party to.

Nothing makes me realise that a summer holiday is over more than being hurtled down the one-in-two slopes (that are a feature of London airports) with an uncontrollable accelerating trolley depositing my duty frees through a series of minor collisions en route to the inevitable major pile up just before the train ticket office. My design for this starts with three wheels.
7   Picture the familiar scene. You are watching TV at 7.30pm with your maiden aunt and your children of impressionable age. The playlet you view at a tiny tots Christmas party suddenly, without warning and for no apparent reason switches to a steamy bedroom scene full of nakedness, groping, grunting and heavy breathing. You sit there trying to think of some form of diversionary conversation or you pretend to have a fit that results in you hurling yourself across the room to land on the remote controller, thus switching to another channel. You feel embarrassed and responsible because it is your television. Well I'm no prude (well, actually I am) but there must be some way of avoiding these clammy situations.

The answer is the Squirmometer. It will constantly monitor the programmes and relate these to the sensitivity level of the viewer. When an embarrassment threshold is exceeded it will automatically play a suitable 'interlude' such as the 'potter's wheel' (readers over 45 please explain to those under 45) whilst recording the 'offending' part for later inspection, education and edification.

A simpler form can be made available without the recording device that will automatically come into operation during game shows, party political broadcasts, anything to do with the lottery or whenever Jeremy Beadle appears. I'm sure the technology is just round the corner and the designers are here today.

8   Now we are fed up with dogs that seem to select to foul the portion of pavement outside my front gate. What about an effective 'pooper scooper', preferably attachable directly on to a dogs hindquarters? A simple, hygienic device that ensures that dog owners will be entirely responsible for their dogs' entire digestive system rather than just what goes in at one end. On second thoughts the solution may be much simpler. I'll buy a blunderbuss.

9   An earring that would whisper in my ear the name of people I meet. This is perhaps the most useful of all of these pipe dreams. It would avoid me having to ask all those 'round-the-houses' type questions in the vain attempt to identify the complete stranger who seems to know me like a brother.

10 Any form of compact, low cost transport must be a good idea. Pushbikes, etc. are too bulky and, although rollerblades fit the bill, we are not alone in not being able to master them.

A few years back, Mazda held a design competition in their Japanese factory. The winner was the most absurd idea which confirms that even the Japanese are fallible and capable of some really awful ideas, (we wonder what came second?) It was a 'suitcase car'. Imagine your suitcase filled with internal combustion engine. All engine, no room for your poser phone and bar of chocolate. You were expected to sit on top of it and then hurtle down the road at up to twenty miles per hour. Your chances of surviving any confrontation with a juggernaught from your invisible position on the road would be nil, the nearest thing to a human hedgehog. But if you did survive, could you live down the ridicule of driving such a device? The coup de grâs for me was the fact that when (and if) you reached your destination it all folded up into a suitcase that weighed thirty kg – so you couldn't carry it anyway.

We reckon a better idea is the rubber bike that could be fitted in a suitcase and inflated from a cylinder of compressed air (helium for the racing version). When opened, the body of the case would be the bike frame. When deflated and packed away the case really could be carried. There you are, a concept just ready for detailing.

For an even more compact form of transport, how about this? The privatisation of public transport has certainly reduced the service round our area, so much so, that I've seen an increase in the number of people thumbing lifts. Coupled with this, there is talk of legislation proposing that certain lanes on roads should only be occupied by cars with more than one occupant, so they need to find a passenger. Combine these two factors and what results? Of course, it is obvious, the inflatable, illuminated hitching thumb. It would fit neatly into the waistcoat pocket but be quickly and

> *easily assembled into a beacon advertising from the roadside your desire to get home!*
>
> 11 *I need a 'spell check' that identifies the difference between 'new' and 'knew' and 'to', 'too' and 'two'. This may prove difficult; an easier (and serious) product that we need is a Fax for computer discs. We have been swopping quite a lot of information recently between others in far off places like Hull. Such a device would make our lives easier.*
>
> *As you see, there is still a lot to be done to improve the quality of life of mankind so get on with it!*

Not enough organisations have planned processes for innovation and in many it is still something that is only occasionally done. Gary Hamel stated at the Stockton lectures on the theme of 'Entrepreneurship and Innovation', 'We need to move from innovation as serendipity, or as the product of visionaries, to innovation as a deep capability [of organisations] – a product of activists' (MacLachlan 1998).

If you plan to innovate then you must learn to accept that in this difficult area things will not always go without a hitch. Dr William Coyne, the Senior Vice-President of Research and Development in 3M said, on instilling a tradition of innovation in an organisation: 'It also means that we must be tolerant of mistakes. People need to know that if they are tying something new and fail, they won't be punished. We would rather they ask for forgiveness rather than permission.'

> *One of the many joys of visiting Sri Lanka is the opportunity to read their newspapers, at least, those in English. They always provide us with insights hitherto unthought of by us. In their 'Sunday Times' of 23.8.1998 they had two adverts. The first demonstrates perhaps that if it is possible to fool enough of the people for enough of the time, then you can make quite a healthy living. On the other hand, we need not have gone as far as Sri Lanka, a close look at our politicians would have told us that!*
>
> *From the same paper comes the second advert. This shows that you can get almost eveything right but the devil is still in the detail.*

◆ ◆ ◆

Summary of Time Frame Three

During this Time Frame, management should be considering the strategy it needs to adopt to ensure the success of its new products and services for

English Day

The English study Cnetre of Maharagama will hold its English Day on August 23 at the Maharagama National Youth Centre at 2 P.M.

The programmes to take place are directed by English Advanced Technical Institute lecturer W. Lionel Srimanne and the chief guest will be Gateway International School Principal R.I.T. Alles.

the next five to ten years. We stress the importance of developing the right tactics so that the organisation can implement that strategy. We have suggested some tools and techniques to use for innovation and concept assessment for this next generation of products and services.

You are now ready to look into the long term future, as described in Time Frame Four, and you should have the confidence that your organisation will be supplying the products and services to get you there.

Time Frame Four

Part I   New Products and Services Over the Horizon

In times of drastic change, it is the learners who inherit the future. The learned usually find themselves equipped to live in a world that no longer exists.

(Eric Hoffer)

11

Looking a Long Way Ahead

Three Score Years and Ten

Two opinion polls took place in Britain in 1997, Mori found that 60% of the people they asked, and Gallup 63%, thought that the future would be worse than the present. A frightening finding in itself. We think that actually things will continue to get better but we will have to learn to cope better with the inevitable changes. With our background in design this will cause us no problem. We have made a livelihood out of change. You may find this to be more of a problem. But take heart, things are generally better than they were in our western economies. Rarely do people starve and people generally survive into old age. For most life is no longer 'Nasty, brutish and short' (Thomas Hobbes 1651).

So what are people worried about? Clearly, they have fears, but at the moment it is unclear what their fears are about. Finding these out, in the broad sense, will reveal a great deal that will stimulate your organisation into the development of new services. Homing in on the specific, it may be possible to adapt processes and products to avoid or alleviate these fears.

As an example, a small experiment was tried on a group of students. They were asked what did concern them about the future. Initially, they spoke about wars and the like, but then the conversation narrowed towards problems of everyday life – fear of a declining standard of living because of redundancy and fears of not being able to understand how to use things that arrive as part of their daily lives. Perhaps the former could stimulate a 'cradle to grave' insurance protection policy (as did the original promise of the welfare state). The latter certainly implies that there is a need to make products and services easier to use and have them better explained at their introduction. The easier it is to use a product the more likely it is that customers will adopt it. The 'training' for this may not be all that complicated, maybe only a 'helpline' for confused users.

Introduction

So the future doesn't come as a surprise. This is the most important section of this book for it is in this section that we look at how to develop products and services well into the future. The future is relative to your organisation and the type of business that you are in. In IT the future spectrum must be small as a lot is going to happen in the next five years. On the other hand, if your business is making furniture, electric plugs or selling pizzas or holidays the future is more predictable (but not unchanging) and we can be considering the next twenty years. But even in the fast changing areas there are aspects that will remain stable and in the slow changing areas there are likely to be interfaces with products in which change is happening fast. This will be down to the subinnovations that are occurring, and the product status.

The earlier three Time Frames have, hopefully, set you and your organisation in the right direction so that you arrive in the future in good shape and able to take on the competition. These early sections have also described the very latest thinking on how best to develop new services. These Time Frames have also introduced a series of tools and techniques, known to work from our consultancy, which will now be refined, and these provide the architecture that is used to plan your organisation's future. Much of what has been described is now developed further and taken a stage beyond to allow an organisation to develop products for more than ten years time.

For more than ten years we have been considering the future and its effects and have always perceived that, in the vast majority of areas, change is much slower than one would expect. To prove the point, below is part of an article that was written in 1989 when Bill was more of an out-and-out designer:

THE NINETIES, THE DECADE OF INVISIBLE DESIGN

A gentle touch on the brow, 'Good morning madam, it is eight o'clock and I've brought you breakfast in bed.' It's Erutuf the mark 3 model robot fully programmed to take care of your every need.

Our vision of the home at the turn of the century? We're afraid not, the best we can expect is a microwave teasmade to wake us when the tea is ready and not half an hour before with the gurgles and hisses that accompany the current designs on the market. When looking into the future we invariably expect great changes and are promised that new technology will bring forth devices that will solve every problem. Life will be full of leisure in which we can fulfil our ambitions and fully utilise our talents. Unfortunately, we have not yet solved the basic problem that leisure costs money and working for money takes time.

We are told that change is occurring faster than ever before and that there is an exponential rise in technology. This is true, but these advances are only in some areas and in most others things are not changing a lot. We will go into the next century driving cars with internal combustion engines and pneumatic tyres, only the road congestion will get worse.

To look forward in design it's sometimes best to look back on what has been important to the British way of life in the past ten years. Our suit pockets are now distorted by the Filofax and, probably, the biggest impact brought about by design has been that caused by drivers circumnavigating roundabouts whilst using their cellular phones. Most of us have bought products crammed full of integrated circuits that bring us features we don't know how to use and don't really need. Examples of these are videos, computers, telephones, word processors and now even on TV remote controllers. If you don't need a function or it is not obvious how to use it then this is bad design. This, we believe, is the key to design in the next decade, it will be more ergonomically sound, that is, more user friendly. Look at the design successes of the eighties. Products that are so simple and obvious to use.

One clear message for Britain, in the next ten years, is that there will be a skill shortage and if your company uses skilled people you must either train them yourself or design them out of the system. In some ways, this has been going on for years through automation (will the last person out of the machine shop please switch off the lights), but will spread to other areas such as driving tube trains and any form of ticket collection and dispensing. People will become more invisible in the design of the nineties, things will work but it will not be obvious how. This skill shortage will also spread to designers and they will become a scarce and valuable resource to be used wisely. This means good management of the total design process and a breaking down of the existing barriers so that designers are devoting their time to designing products people actually want.

Customers in this country are used to having a choice in whatever they buy and, as such, have taught themselves to increasingly appreciate and buy good design. This choice will increase as an effect of 1992 (this was when trade barriers were lowered throughout the EC) and, therefore, producers must themselves become even more design conscious.

Ecology and 'green' issues will dominate thinking in the next ten years and designers will have to focus more on energy and resource consumption in both production and use of their designs. Their thinking must stretch to consideration of the eventual disposal of the product.

Crime will continue to become more sophisticated and less easily detectable and more people will seek their entertainment at home, their castles becoming fortresses. Is this the direction of design and its management?'

Well, that estimation of the future, that we gave back at the end of the eighties, wasn't far out, although the microwave teasmade hasn't yet appeared, and what happened to the Filofax? Probably replaced by the Psion. We were also right about the emergence of greater interest in ecology.

Plan for the Future

Enough of patting ourselves on the back, hopefully our estimate of the next decade will also be right. But Peters (1997) says 'predictability is a thing of the past'. If this is true, we will be foolhardy to make any attempt at predicting what organisations should do to cope with the unpredict-ability of this future. We would be wasting our time writing this and you would be wasting your time reading it. But we don't believe it is. According to Handy (1994), even though the future is not linear it should be rooted in the past if it is to be real.

Should we be planning at all? Adrian Birtwell (1998) described it as 'the paradox of uncertainty, uncertainty means more planning'. If you don't plan at all, everything is going to be a surprise and you will spend your life 'fire-fighting'. If you predict and plan for the future you will, at least, be going in a direction. With the application of a few rules, you will be going in the right direction and this direction can be fine tuned as time passes.

The problem that we have is well demonstrated in a diagram from Gill Ringland from her work at ICL (1998) (Figure 11.1).

This shows that the further one looks ahead the greater is the range of uncertainties and less certain is the timing of when these things will occur. Certain aspects are more predictable, such as demography, the old age pensioners of the future and the pupils for secondary education in ten years time are alive today. Bearing that in mind, it is amazing that a London Borough actually closed and demolished a secondary school only to have to rebuild a new school on the same site a few years later. This is because they had underestimated the number of secondary school places that they would need only a few years later. Such obvious blunders should easily be avoided with a little research and even less common sense.

A common error made by people projecting into the future is that they assume things will be a simple projection of what has gone on in the past. In many cases this may be true but, often government (through legislation and laws) intervenes to shift this simple projection. An obvious example is the crowding on our roads. We keep being told that in a few years there will be gridlock on our city roads. This is unlikely to be allowed to happen. Road tax, increased petrol tax, toll roads activated by smart cards and difficulty in parking will have the effect of cutting down the anticipated road usage in the future. Perhaps there will be improved public transport – but this requires expenditure and planning and there is certainly no evidence that this will occur. Perhaps we will have to travel

The danger in forecasting is....

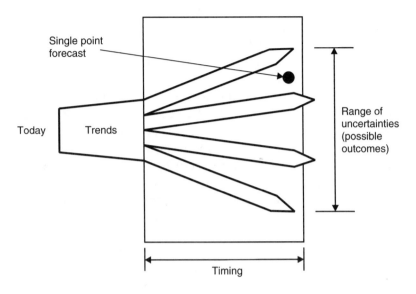

You can get it wrong!

Figure 11.1   Time against the range of uncertainties

less in our cities and this indicates that people will probably work at home more. It has been said that more people are researching home working as are actually doing it. Perhaps all their predictions promised to occur in the eighties may actually happen early in the 2000s.

Another assumption is that we assume people will all behave the same. There is little evidence of this looking back at the past. As Andrews (1998) said, 'there is not just one future – there are multiple futures . . . it is a mosaic'.

Future gazing has been undertaken, since the 1950s, in various countries. This tends to be done by national or government agencies. In the 1950s, the USA started developing Delphi and Scenario techniques, mainly to determine the direction for military developments. In the 1960s, Japan became involved and their science and technology agencies identified thirty year targets through Delphi techniques. In effect, these were goals, at which their industry would aim.

Plans for the future were developed in the 1980s by Japan, USA, Australia, Sweden, France and Canada. And in the 1990s the Nether-lands, Spain, Germany and the UK joined this group. The process used in nearly all of these includes scenario planning, Delphi techniques, interviewing experts and brainstorming. The first two are most popular and tend to have the opposite effect. In Scenario planning the viewpoint tends to expand, whereas in Delphi the viewpoint tends to focus in to one outcome. Scenarios are useful but Schwartz (1998) says that they are not about predicting the future, rather they are about perceiving the futures in the present. Whereas the Delphi method is described by Mintzberg (1994) as 'provides us with the average "guesstimate" of ignorant experts'. Most of these nationally led exercises have not been too successful and they tend to focus on particular sectors.

This book has taken a different approach, because we are proposing you look at what is likely to happen to actual products and services. There is, also, an attempt to set up a framework in which to view an organisation's offerings, so that one can take the approach 'we are here now, what is likely to happen to our products in the future, so how do we get there from here?'

Another aspect, which makes this book different from the national plans is that, unlike national future planning, we don't have any vested interest in any particular area, we are not pushing for funding from a government. We are not going to say 'our area is going to change fast and we need government money to help us.'

12

The Powers That Be

Does the Government Know Best?

CASE STUDY – THE MEN FROM THE MINISTRIES

Just in case you think the government have any idea of how to manage the future . . .
Bill was at a meeting of The Royal Institute of International Affairs at Chatham
House in London, where it was proposed by some of the British that as the UK were
good at design and the Japanese good at manufacture we should design products
and let the Japanese manufacture them. Those Japanese present, not surprisingly,
seemed delighted at the prospect of our 'decision makers' advocating such a
scheme. We design, you make, and we will buy them back from you. I sometimes
wonder where these people keep their brains – any suggestions?

At a similar such meeting, I met a very senior civil servant. He had reached the
top and was a whisker away from his KG. He told me that as a young man he heard
policy and saw the effect that it had and he didn't understand it. This didn't worry
him because he knew that 'they' must be working to a 'divine master plan up there'
and, because he wasn't party to all the facts, all would become obvious in the
future when he was older and wiser. Time passed and he became older and wiser
and was promoted up the various scales in the Civil Service. He still couldn't see
the rationale in many of the decisions taken. With each promotion he expected to
see a bit more of this master plan – but with each promotion, in this respect, he
was disappointed. This 'divine plan' became no clearer.

He had now reached the top and, having arrived, he realised the worst. Those
inexplicable cock-ups that politicians make, as they blunder from crisis to crisis in
their day-to-day running of the country, are not a piece of the jigsaw in some well
focused, well directed model of the future. The tragedy is that this master plan
doesn't exist. They really are blundering from one cock-up to another with self
interest being their only guide.

With the benefit of hindsight, over the past forty years of our industrial policy,
shouldn't that have been obvious? Next time the government (of whatever shade)
makes some apparently incredibly stupid decision – like closing the coal industry
whilst importing coal, or allowing our last mass produced car industry to be sold off
for the price it costs to develop one new car model, privatisation, monetarism –
don't assume that they know something that you don't or that they are brighter than
you, they aren't. They are, as you have always suspected, incredibly stupid.

Do not expect the government to be able to assist you in this long term planning of products. You may be able to convince them that you need money to build plant or premises or provide jobs in the future, but the actual detailed planning of these must be down to you.

They say that a week is a long time in politics, well, a ten year spectrum might as well be another thousand years as far as politicians are concerned. For example, in the last decade the government wanted Britain to become an all service economy. When it is considered that, using the government's own figures, we would need 55% of the world market for services to prevent us having a balance of payments deficit, the logic behind the thinking was obviously flawed. People like to own products and many services ride on the back of products. Therefore, there will always be a continuous flow of new manufactured products within a national or global market. Furthermore, there will also be new ways in which customers will use, own and interface with these products. These interfacing services are opportunities to benefit any organisation.

For example, if a new product is being developed, such as virtual reality, your organisation may not be able to benefit specifically from this actual product, but they may well benefit from all the additional opportunities that may arise from this product. For example, making the discs that hold the software or the box that holds the discs or the packaging around the box or the shop that sells the package. All these less technical systems are needed to accompany change.

Remember, we all operate in a world market. It is rarely possible and quite inadvisable for a country to operate in isolation. There is an initiative called 'Design For Transformation'. This group was set up in the United Kingdom to offer assistance to Romanian organisations. After many years of Communism, where markets were controlled, imports restricted and demand tended to exceed supply, the barriers to imports came down in 1990. Exposed to 'market forces' for the first time for many years, the indigenous industries were shown to be uncompetitive. Consumers preferred to buy imported products and the result was the closure of many Romanian firms and serious unemployment. A press conference was held during a visit in 1994. Many of those journalists attending insisted that the country was not operating in a world market even then. Just showing this group the origin of cars in the car park convinced these journalists that they were wrong.

Can we be a Low Wage Economy?

Obviously, in Europe, we realise that we compete in world markets both for customers but also against competitors. If companies want things made at very low costs they won't manufacture in Europe at all. Even within Europe (but outside the EC) a country such as the Czech Republic has labour costs which are only 7% of ours (according to Jurgan Gehrels, chief executive of Siemens UK (1997). Countries such as Poland and Romania have wage rates which are between 1/6th and 1/12th of our own and if you manufacture in China labour rates are only 3% of ours.

Trying to operate with low wages means that you will attract poorer quality workers. There is a lot of truth in the statement 'if you pay peanuts you get monkeys'. Furthermore, relying on low wage rates is really only valid if wage rates are a significant part of the operation. In many manufacturing organisations the labour costs of those involved in manufacture can be as low as 6% of the total costs of running the organisation. Forcing or holding these down doesn't really make great savings throughout the whole organisation.

A low wage workforce can also have the affect of slowing the introduction of the latest machines and automation. In a high wage economy, such as Sweden or Germany and now Japan, the costs of automation are more easily justified against the unit cost of labour. In a developing country the reverse is true and, therefore, developing countries often use cheap labour rather than introduce automation, whatever form it takes, from machine tools to IT to automatic cash point machines.

In this country, we are nearer the wage rates of Sweden and Germany than we are with those of India and China so we must automate. Automation also allows higher added value. These are the non-price factors that encourage people to buy products and services (Corfield 1979). The economies in these high wage countries survive certainly not by being the lowest price, but by offering products that are a combination of worthwhile features, improved quality and additional services associated with that product.

What Can You Control?

Japan was far more focused than most in the development of new products. In 1947, Japan formed MITI (the Ministry of International Trade and Industry). It had the aim of improving the nation's competitiveness through the development of new products. It is pretty clear who was the most successful. Following the Second World War, Japan had scarce resources, little money and fewer raw materials. They chose to identify particular products and channel their scarce resources into organisations working on these products. They aimed at being world leader within these particular chosen products and then planned over a period of years to fulfil this aim. The first product they chose was cameras, copying and improving upon the cameras that came from East Germany. They then moved on to other products such as motor cycles, radios, televisions, hi-fi, cars and machine tools. They identified potentially successful areas and planned their improvement of the product and subsequent domination of the world market over a period of years. This means they looked at the product, they looked at what the competition were doing, they used their educated workforce in a unified programme to move forward. Of course, we hear about the successful companies, quite a few failed on route.

Up to a point, futures planning in Japan (and elsewhere, such as Korea) has been shown to be self-fulfilling. Groups project the future and then strive to get there. To do this requires a combination of organisations, governments, banks and workers combining together to be successful. This only has a chance of working if you are big enough and powerful enough to organise such a meeting of minds. You are unlikely to be able to muster these groups. Even so, you can fulfil your projected aims and this is the approach we take here. Government agencies – MITI is the best example – can actually control their destiny.

What can your organisation control? You can have a say in standards, but not control over the eventual outcome. You can control your suppliers, if you are big enough and, whatever size you are, you can control your choice of supplier. If legislation protects/directs/controls your activities you can probably control your customers.

In simple terms, the smaller your organisation the less sway you have in controlling the future. But make a list of in what ways your organisation can influence the future. There are lots of things you can do within the firm: employ, invest, change, abandon. When you have completed such a list, you can assume that you can't change, influence or control everything else. This doesn't mean that you should ignore these areas. You should keep informed of everything that will impinge on your activities, ambitions or freedom.

Your Focus for Improvement

From your organisation's point of view, there is nothing to stop you doing the same as Japan did albeit in a small way. Identify a suitable product or service, in a growing market, which is within your capabilities, and then plan a slow but steady domination of that market. The Japanese did this by copying the competitors, but where they really scored was in incorporating a much improved level of process design, the design of the method of manufacture and production. This is where they were innovative. Nowadays, they have run out of competing products to copy and have to spend more time thinking up their own ideas. This is shown in their sharp rise in patent applications, compared with the rest of the world, in recent years.

In your organisation, there is nothing to limit you to improving methods of manufacturing or service implementation. Again, look at the service side, how you interface with the customers, what would make life easy for them, what can you do to improve the benefits of ownership, use, empathy and general enthusiasm about being involved and using your company. This is known as creative copying.

Also, by operating in a world market you can plan your entry into developing countries as they develop. On a recent visit to Sri Lanka it was noticed that many things that are current business practice in developed countries were not yet available in Sri Lanka. For example, when a credit card is used in the most more developed countries its validity is checked by 'swiping' it through a slot in a small machine. This is linked to a central computer at the end of a telephone line which will instantly either accept or reject the card. Another example is that the cost of purchases made in a shop are identified and totalled by 'bar codes' on all products. These codes also inform the central stores via a computer link that the purchase has been made and can activate a re-ordering process. This is called Material Requirement Planning (MRP).

As such practices are common and successful in Europe and America, it is just a matter of time before they come to Sri Lanka and other countries with similar economies. By being a follower in the use of some new technology, it is possible to identify the more successful ones and the best way of introducing them. The problems of the initiators can be avoided, and the unsuccessful new products and technologies can be avoided altogether. Using knowledge of what has gone before reduces business risk.

Users in these countries do not necessarily follow the same 'line' of product adoption. It is also possible to 'leap-frog' in the introduction of new technology. For example, when it was decided to introduce new telephone systems in China, the most up-to-date systems were purchased, missing out several generations of technology from their original systems. Furthermore, among those who can afford them, mobile phones are being accepted into the Indian sub-continent almost as fast as they are in Europe. The product is almost the same but the type of consumer is different.

13

A System Rather Than a Process

Introduction

Certainly, it is necessary for organisations to be able to move, seamlessly, into the future. This must be done through a constant supply of well designed competitive products. For the actual design of these products the work on process models and processes must continue. To make sure organisations are moving forward in a logical manner the work on the strategic links must also continue. There must also be a further dimension that links in with these. There must be a view of the future so that the strategic plan has a target at which it can be aimed, an 'estimation' of what **your** products and services are to be like more than ten years ahead.

You can read about the best managed and most successful companies and you may learn from these, but there are only a handful. Perhaps it is better to make headway and be successful, but not necessarily be world beating. If you plan where you want to be then set off to achieve it. Your chances of reaching your proposed destination depend on how ambitious your initial plan is.

If you don't set your sights too far you will probably get there without too much difficulty, but don't be surprised if you are left behind the rest of your competition. If you set your sights too far then you may not be able (to afford) to reach them. Be ambitious, but realistic, bearing in mind your capabilities and your existing track record. The further you aim the more skills you will require, the more you will need to grow and the more it will cost.

The Current Situation

It is possible to predict a great deal of what is likely to happen and it is also possible to build a system within an organisation that can evolve with those changes and cope with the unexpected. This section can take the management of new products and services further ahead, beyond current models. Process models must still be used as a guide to manage the actual stages of the process, the budget, the personnel to be used, and help to subdivide the total time available for the project between the various activities. Such models are also needed to show, first in a linear form, those activities that can then be identified as those which can be undertaken in parallel.

What is also required is an overall system in which these various process models can be fitted. This is likely to take the form of a top management forum who will turn a company strategy into products that will fulfil this strategy. The leadership and most of those involved will be at director or senior management level.

So How do you Plan for Even Further Ahead?

At the 'Scenarios for 2026' Conference (1996), there was general agreement that thinking should be at a systems level, rather than at a business unit, departmental or individual level. Senge (1993) has said 'systems thinking is a discipline for seeing wholes, it is a framework for seeing interrelationships rather than things, for seeing patterns of change rather than static snapshots, . . . humankind has the ability to create far more information than anyone can absorb, foster far greater interdependency than anyone can manage . . . organisations break down . . . because they are unable to pull all their diverse functions and talents into a productive whole.'

Rehearse what might happen and how to react to various situations. The problem with scenario planning, as it is currently undertaken, in most situations, is that it is often too vague and those involved do not put boundaries round their 'system'. For example, consider scenario planning recently undertaken by a large authority. In an attempt to view the situation ten years ahead, they were building into their system the anticipation of new roadways and monorail systems, the initiation of which was outside of their control and were not currently being planned by any other authority.

> **SCENARIO PLAN ON WHAT YOU CAN CONTROL OR WHAT YOU KNOW WILL HAPPEN. The key is to ring-fence your scenarios.**

CASE STUDY – CAN YOU FORETELL THE FUTURE?

Many people seem to think that they, or their ideas, are ahead of their time. Now, Leonardo Da Vinci was one whose ideas were – brilliant ideas for products that were centuries ahead of their time, such as helicopters they couldn't make and which wouldn't even fly if they could as well as various dubious fighting vehicles, etc. In fact, most of Da Vinci's ideas would not work and only a few of his designs that did work were actually made in his lifetime. Amongst these was a mechanism for controlling the flow of water in a canal and some defensive structures. Is this the kind of chap you want controlling the future in your organisation? Sounds like a certain recipe for rapid company decline.

We have met people who were ahead of their time. Sidney Gregory was a grand chap who was writing things about design in the sixties that, only now, we fully appreciate. Apparently, he used to lecture to students whilst standing and staring out the window. His lectures were crowded as people came to tune in to his brilliance. He was a great design thinker and great company.

Bill attended Sidney Gregory's presentation at ICED 85 in Hamburg, which he decided to give in German and which Bill tried to follow on the simultaneous translation. The translator couldn't follow Sidney's German and nor could the German speaking audience. He reached the end and nobody realised until he walked off the stage. Some time later, I asked him why he did it. His answer was immediate, 'I hadn't done it before'. He may have been a great design thinker but he was a lousy linguist.

The trouble with being years ahead of your time is that you actually live and work in this one. Ideas for the far off future never look so attractive when you appreciate that it is these that probably pay your wages – and you want to be paid next week.

This is not a plea for short termism. We need plenty of new products and services that reach the market quickly to pay the immediate bills. These also keep shareholders happy, as shareholders only have a six month span of 'patience' where their money is concerned. We also need those more risky long term projects that help to ensure that a company exists beyond the immediate future.

Markets are constantly changing and, increasingly, marketeers are having to try and think beyond what consumers want now, to what they will want when the new product becomes available, or anticipate even beyond that. This is where being ahead of your time can be useful. If you can think and plan beyond the next corner to the one after that then you are giving your organisation that competitive edge they crave.

So you need to see into the future and if you are able to do this your bosses will love you for it. Assuming that the average boss can't see into the future, why not tell them you can – whose to say you can't? Don't just blurt this information out, be subtle, let the bosses 'deduce' this themselves. To start in this new exciting role, first get yourself a pair of big earrings and a crystal ball. Subsidise your crummy salary by fortune telling, let your clairvoyance creep up on them. Let it be known that you are the youngest of seven brothers and that you have six uncles. Promotion to 'Futures Director' is bound to follow along with all the power, glory and financial reward that you can handle.

One small tip though, keep an eye on the job market. After two years of the good life, somebody may realise that perhaps you weren't so far seeing as they first thought and that your future should continue elsewhere. On the other hand, just perhaps . . .

One of the major keys in planning the future is consumer prediction. There is little purpose in using conventional marketing research for this when trying to plan a decade into the future. Asking consumers now what they want will result in answers that focus on what is already on the market. Likewise, you cannot ask these customers about products that have not yet been designed.

For the same reason, conventional competition analysis is of little use for planning well into the future. What the competitor is doing now is already history. It is necessary to predict what they will be doing ten years from now. This is far from easy to do. So probably, a better course of action is to ignore the competitors and aim to develop your products and services so that the competition is following you. Marketing myopia (Levitt 1960) will be as true in the future as it has been in the past. The competition must be considered as being much wider than is often considered the case. In addition to this, designers must also add the consideration that with the number of products and services that are becoming available outstripping the rise in disposable incomes in most economies, there is a greater propensity for consumers to decide not to buy at all.

Evolutionary

Reproduced by permission of Chan Sow Yan at
chansy@pacific.net.sg

process

14

The Effect of New Technology

Introduction

One of the excuses why people do not plan for the future is that they say that they cannot predict changes in technology. It may not be possible to predict the actual working of potential technology, but often it can be considered as a series of 'black boxes' which can be incorporated as they appear. It comes as no surprise that people are working on a new battery breakthrough (it doesn't have to be a battery, perhaps it could be a capacitor). We can even say what benefits should be in the new battery. It must be low cost, high power, lightweight, quick to charge and operate at room temperature. Now, knowing this, we could either start to design such a battery, or more likely, wait until someone else does and then build it into our products. The lesson is that we need to be constantly looking for such breakthroughs.

New technology is one of the commonest causes for otherwise healthy products to be superseded, but do you search for new technology that may affect your products? When asking managers how they keep informed of new technology regarding their products, one is usually told that they read their trade magazines and visit their trade exhibitions. This is a blinkered way of seeking technological change. The majority of companies look no further than their immediate competition and spend most of their energy imitating them, often to miss out on the major changes that are occurring just outside their field of view.

Jewkes et al. (1969) have also shown that many major innovations are not pioneered by those companies currently involved in a market, but are most likely to emanate from other companies. Other work (Hollins and Pugh 1990) has shown that there is sufficient time in most cases for a company to identify such potential threats and act in their best interests to benefit from these changes. This is providing that they are seeking these innovations by reading scientific and technical journals and visiting exhibitions, other than those which are more obviously concerned with their market.

It is essential to look far wider than your own market if you are to identify possible threats or opportunities. Threats can be identified early enough to be opportunities from which you can benefit. This function is not necessarily product related and should be an on-going process, carried out by those in organisations. It is considered that one person limited to one day each month is sufficient to do this 'innovation seeking'. Seniority is not important for this function; an ability to see applications for new inventions in your products is the necessary skill.

> **TO LOOK FOR YOUR RADICALLY NEW PRODUCTS FOR TEN YEARS TIME, LOOK AT INVENTIONS BEING MADE TODAY. You will not be caught out by new technology if you are constantly seeking it.**

Commentators perceive that technological change occurs so fast that it is impossible to state where we will be in the not too distant future. It is commonly said that change is exponential and our lifestyle, only a few years from now, will be quite different from what it is today. This is almost certainly **NOT** the case. Radical change and exponential change is occurring but only in a few areas and it is possible to identify these areas through using Product Status (Pugh 1983, Hollins and Pugh 1989, Hollins and Hollins 1991).

It is a myth that things generally change fast and that the rate of change is accelerating. Certainly, in most areas, improvement is continuous. But this improvement is at a level of incremental change to existing concepts. It is only occasionally that there is a discontinuity in this continuous improvement and a radical change occurs. We have always assumed that things are changing faster than they are. To confirm this one has only to look back at what authors and film makers predicted would occur in the technological future. They invariably guessed too far ahead or what they believed would happen just didn't.

We were all going to dress the same in shiny aluminium one piece outfits. In fact, men are still wearing a pointless piece of cloth round their necks when they want to look 'smart', the same as we have been doing for more than one hundred years. Also, the air was going to be thick with personal autogyros. We can be thankful that this never came to be realised. British male readers may remember Dan Dare. His exploits were first published in the 'Eagle' in the 1950s. There were 'Mekons' flying around on half walnuts in a futuristic world that was all supposed to be based in 1996! The world as depicted in the film 'A Space Odyssey, 2001' still seems a long way off, yet the computer 'Hal' in that film was supposed to have been built in 1997. We have come a long way in computers but not all that far. It took a great deal of development before a computer was developed that could actually beat a human in a game of chess.

In 1935, it was predicted that by 1955 we would be able to fly fifty miles home from work in five minutes (600 mph) in our helicopters. Not only can't helicopters yet do that but it seems we can't even get a commuter train to arrive on time and we are still using 'mph' instead of the long preferred 'miles/hr' when, anyway, we should be talking in kilometres (fortunately, the metric hour also seems some way off). Pan Am were predicting in the 1960s that by the year 2000 they would be flying 'hyperjets' that would have a speed of 4000 mph. Not only didn't they achieve that, they didn't even survive the end of the century, going out of business in 1997. As recently as 1990, we were being told on the British TV programme 'Tomorrow's World', by the Department of Trade and Industry, that by the end of the century we would have domestic robots that would 'do the cleaning, clearing away dirty dishes and put them in the dishwasher, and then vacuum the house'. If only.

Don't get us wrong, we're not saying that things won't change, quite the reverse. Bill, being a designer, relies on things changing for his security of employment. But we will be more secure in our jobs if we spend our employed hours doing things which are more likely to sell. We can, perhaps, steer our bosses away from their feather-brained excesses if we show them that although all of your products can be improved, we would do well not to go blasting off in many dubious directions.

Actually, change in most areas is slow, steady and, therefore, much of the future is more easily predicted. Try looking around your room. What did not or could not, have existed twenty years ago? Change is fast but only in a few quite precise areas, typically electronics, communications, new materials, pharmaceuticals and biotechnology. Even in this area the investment in computers and information technology capital equipment in organisations is only currently running at 3% per annum of their total investment in the United States (Clipson 1996). This is small, when it is realised that in the early part of this century, in the United States, capital expenditure on the railways ran at 18% per annum. Organisations working in these 'fast track' fields must have the key to coping with radical change to survive now. For other organisations to survive long term they will need to look to what these organisations do and follow their pattern, albeit at a slower rate. So what patterns do these fast track organisations have in common? They make the present pay so that they can survive into the future and they invest in long-term research funded by the present.

We often hear about 3M and their '15% rule' in which people in this organisation can spend that amount of time on highly speculative (often daft) ideas. The example often given is Post-It Notes, which in itself could hardly sustain an organisation the size of 3M! What is forgotten is that this means 85% of their time is spent doing the bulk standard product improvement that sustains the company now and pays for the more speculative and risky projects to be supported.

In most other areas change is rather plodding with constant product improvement and incremental change and thus it is far more predictable. In other words, static design. This is how most of us like it. At most times, certain products change fast but then plateau out to centre, in a more stable form of improvements, around an existing concept. Take cars as an example. What have been the fundamental changes in car design over the past ten years? Brakes, suspension and the fuel flow system have experienced the greatest changes but are these changes really radical? Now look at the changes that occurred in car design between the ten years of 1895–1905. The steering wheel, carburation, pneumatic tyres, inline engines, electric lighting, glass in the windows and quite a few other fundamental differences. Now these were radical changes.

> *Incidentally, when was the car invented? It depends on how you define a car. If a train comes off the tracks is it a car? The first ever mechanically powered vehicle was the steam carriage of 1784 invented by William Murdoch from Ayrshire (1754–1839). David Trevithick also developed a steam carriage in 1799. Gold-worthy Gurney (1793–1875) formed the 'Gurney Steam Carriage Company' that ran steam carriages (unsuccessfully) at 15 mph between London and Bath.*

Also regarding change, in a British TV programme 'The Aviators' (BBC 2, 6 May 1998) it was said, on the rate of change in planes and flying in the late 1920s early 1930s: 'Every day there was records. What was state of the art today was old hat tomorrow.'

With every product and service there is a time when change is fast and at other times (most of the time) change is slow and is more incremental in nature. And, in fact, people in most organisations would do better to look at the incremental changes that they can make to their products and services (Time Frame Two) rather than panicking that they are about to be left behind in a helter skelter of change. Furthermore, people do not like much radical change in the products and services that they use. They like improvement but not fundamental change. This being the case, then it is fair to assume that in the next ten years there will not be radical change in many items.

Radical change occurs in new ideas as they come to market. Often, they mimic the old concept and this is known as 'the horseless carriage syndrome' Then the design settles down, gets its own personality and general improvement occurs. Then, mainly through new technology, there is another surge in radical change and then things settle down again and change is back to general improvement. During the period of gradual improvement certain areas of design tend to change faster, such as aesthetics and ergonomics. This means that if your products are on this 'plateau' you can focus your efforts more in these areas of product development and on the methods of manufacture or implementation and you can spend less time seeking new concepts.

Roy et al. (1995) also have described how the introduction of a radical new concept often causes a surge in improvement in the older concept. They state:

> The figure for revolutionary/discontinuous technical changes [Figure 14.1] has two S-curves where the switch from one to the next is the result of radical innovation. What should be noted is that the switch is a **technological discontinuity** and that the switch from the first to the second is frequently before the performance of the first has reached its limit. For example, about one hundred years ago, steamships represented a technological discontinuity, but the earlier generation of sailing ships continued to accumulate incremental innovations. This postponed the day that steamships could surpass sailing ship performance, leading to a clear switch from one technology to the other. This pattern repeated itself about fifty years ago when steamships were replaced by high speed diesel engines for commercial ships and high speed turbines for military ships.

> ◆ The switch from an established technology to a new technology is a period of intense **technical competition**, often with the established technology producing a spurt of incremental innovations before finally being overwhelmed by the invading new technology.

> ◆ It is exceptional for the new technology to be developed by organisations which are already producing established products with the older production processes. Many established organisations die with their older technologies and seem unable to learn how to make the necessary shift to the new, emerging, more radical technologies.

> Forty years ago, the first commercial jet airliners had a higher cost per seat mile than the most advanced radial piston-engine aircraft. Only in the late 1950s and early 1960s did commercial jets, when they had accumulated numerous incremental improvements on top of the original radical innovation, begin to get into the high growth part of the S-curve and achieve substantially lower costs per seat mile. During the crossover or overlap period, there was intense technology and innovative competition between the two technologies. This was further complicated by technological hybrids which produced turboprop aircraft. The switch from continuing with incremental innovations to more radical innovations which only promise new advantages in the future, is neither easy nor obvious.

> In principle, the revolutionary and evolutionary patterns of technical change seem to represent clear alternative strategies. In practice, there is something of a hybrid that occupies middle ground.

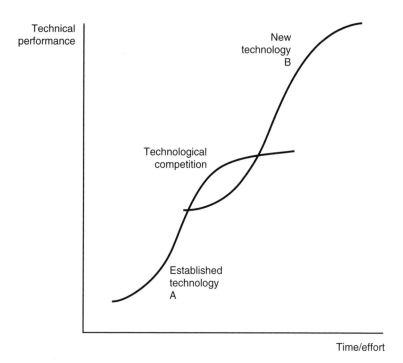

Figure 14.1   S-curve for revolutionary/discontinuous technical changes

Part of this work on the older concept is an attempt to put off the inevitable demise of the new (which may be a bad thing) but part is to better focus the old concept towards still thriving market niches (and this is a good thing). To state how organisations should look well into the future a good starting point would be to look at organisations currently working in areas which are changing fast. Computers and IT certainly are fast growing areas, but look at most other products that interface with your lifestyle. As we said, look around the room in which you are sitting. Excluding the electronic items, how many items, in your line of sight, did not and could not have existed twenty years ago? Most have existed in the same basic concept for many years. If you operate in a fast changing area you need to take a faster view of change. 'The faster you drive the further your headlights must shine' (Godet and Fabrice 1996).

> **MOST PRODUCTS DO NOT CHANGE MUCH OVER THE YEARS.**

And even when change is bound to happen it may still take a long time to occur. The standard for the thirteen amp plug was brought out in 1946 yet many houses still had the old round pinned plugs and sockets well into the 1960s. The latest European standard calling for a universal sixteen amp plug to replace our thirteen amp plugs actually came out in 1996. Yet we are still building houses with thirteen amp sockets. It will take at least twenty years before the sixteen amp system is widely adopted.

> **IT IS EASIER TO IDENTIFY THE AREAS WHERE CHANGE IS FAST. IT IS THEN QUITE SAFE TO PREDICT THAT, IN MOST OTHER AREAS, CHANGE IS UNLIKELY TO INVOLVE A RADICAL NEW CONCEPT.**

Furthermore, people do not like radical change which does not fit in with their existing lifestyle. Most products interface with other products. Our whole lives are tied up with 'user standards' that will require a significant improvement in any new concept to shift us away from these. The ease with which we are prepared to accept these changes depends on the comparison between the perceived advantages of the improvement to the consumer over that which already exists balanced against the disruption (or additional cost) of that improvement. For example, many people with cars that do not have catalytic converters are prepared to use unleaded petrol as there is almost no alteration to their car. They are less keen to use LPG as there is more disruption. The next video player they buy will probably be VHS so they can play their existing tapes. They expect a compact disc that they buy will operate on their player and any new player they buy must play discs from their existing collection. Our whole lives are tied up with standards that are very difficult to shift. It is, therefore, quite easy to predict and plan for the future in these areas.

More than two decades ago the economist Burton Klein (Klein 1977) endeavoured to measure the 'quantity' of improvement needed to make people or organisations alter from the status quo. He identified that, for aero engines, it would need a 10% increase in the performance from a new engine before users would be prepared to consider changing from existing engines (and away from the existing stock of spare parts).

In your organisation, you should be able to identify a similar 'percentage improvement in performance' that relates to your products and services. In many cases if the existing 'infrastructure' can be made to adapt there may be no specific minimum product improvement necessary. In other words, if there is no 'downside' to any improvement in the eyes of the customer then they will welcome any improvement.

```
e " ' ( – e _ c a )
A Z E R T Y U I O P ^      User standards are
Q S D F G H J K L M        extremely difficult
W X C V B N , ; : !        to shift
Barre d' espacement
THE FRENCH KEYBOARD
```

Are you likely to be caught out by new technology? The answer here is that you shouldn't. Again, history has shown that it generally takes about ten years from an idea being patented to it appearing on the market. Electronic calculators were invented by the Bell Punch Company of London in 1963 and appeared on the market about 1974. The inventions that made the digital watch possible were made around 1970 and the first digital watch appeared on the market in 1976. Robinson (1996) has implied that it may take even longer than ten years: 'It is unusual for a technology to develop from a scientific concept to prevalence in the marketplace in less than 25 years.' So we actually have plenty of time to act as long as we keep our eyes and ears open as to what is going on around us.

We already know that some market areas are growing for the long term. Crime is still growing, so will developments in crime prevention. Populations are growing older – though these groups have less disposable income than some other groups. Those with higher disposable income are actually working longer, so have less time to spend their money. These people may make fewer but higher value purchases. They may also seek less time consuming ways to own their products through different forms of purchasing and less maintenance, etc. People are becoming better educated and populations are growing bigger. But although a growing number of people have access to on-line facilities we should also remember that half the population of the world have never even seen a telephone.

Companies need vision and to have a strategic framework to achieve this vision. Furthermore, they have to have the right competencies to defend their position against emerging competition. Organisations must be prepared to cope with radical change and be prepared to plan for it within the organisation of their design management. If potential ventures are viewed within a strategic context, it should be possible to identify a series of parameters or 'boundaries' that will show the type of projects that are right for a specific organisation. This will help people to identify those achievable areas worth pursuing as well as those areas that should be avoided. These frameworks (rightly) restrict the designers' freedom of design direction, they provide focus. These boundaries need to be stated and specified and these determine whether an organisation should pursue an idea in the first place.

What don't People like About the Present?

When looking at people's future needs it is worthwhile finding out what people do **NOT** like about their current lifestyles. This will render far more information than asking people what they do like. For example, if you ask people what they like about their spectacles they will comment on comfort, aesthetics, cost and strength, etc. – all leading to incremental improvements. For radical change, you need to ask what they don't like about wearing glasses. This will also include proposed incremental improvements but also indicate directions for innovative progress. For example, they don't like restricted vision, but contact lenses are uncomfortable, but operations may be expensive and risky – so where do we go from here? We don't like travelling to work, does this indicate home working or 'beam me up Scotty'?

As consumers, we do not have time to spend understanding our products. In most cases, we should not be expected to read instruction books. If it is not obvious how to use a product, it is, probably, a bad product. Products are currently being sold on the fact that they are 'user-friendly'.

CASE STUDY – TO MAKE THEM WANT IT, MAKE IT EASY

Bill was at a conference in Paris and Alec Robertson from De Montfort University was making a presentation. In it, he showed a picture of an early cash register made by NCR. On it was the notice 'this registers the amount of your purchase'. The idea of cash registers was new and people needed to be shown the purpose of the machine. Of course, now we all recognise the machine and the notice is superfluous. It seems obvious, but it needed this picture to make me realise that, if something is new then often consumers need to be told how to use it. If the way to use the product is tricky and if customers are not told how to use it, then they probably will avoid it. The product may be brilliant with many more benefits than the competition but it can fail on this point alone.

Innovations need greater attention to explain how to use them, like Apple Macs or just be easy to use, like pencils or microwave ovens. Some products manage to survive in spite of being almost impossible to use. People considered that it was worth the hassle of trying to programme a video because they really wanted the device, and all the machines the market had to offer were just as bad as each other. At long last, manufacturers have realised that we are tired of missing the last part of a serial because we blundered with setting the timed recording. We have the most wonderful collection of video recordings set to the wrong channel. Now that there are easy-to-set videos, the days are numbered for those others that are not.

One of our favourite examples concerns cameras. In the 1960s came the Instamatic. All you had to do was drop in the film cassette, pull the lever on the side to position the film then look through the one hole and press the one button and there you were, a photo. A fuzzy photo because they were only cheap cameras, but anyone could operate them.

Then came the micro revolution. Manufacturers could offer consumers lots of exciting new features at very little extra cost, so they did. It seemed that all new designs from the mid 1970s to the late 1980s had to be packed with every available feature including the obligatory digital watch and calculator. It did not matter that people perhaps did not want many of these 'space age' advances. No one who was not a keen enthusiast or professional could set them up properly and the usual result was not only a fuzzy photo but also a bored look on the faces of those who had waited ages, through all the dial setting, to have their photo taken.

Camera designers seem to have led the way in coping with low cost electronics. You can now buy cameras that are packed full of sophistication, but all the electronics and 'hard work' is on the inside. You drop in the film and it winds on automatically. The camera focuses automatically and flashes (if required) automatically. The film then winds on automatically and at the end of the film it automatically rewinds the roll. This is invisible design and it is good design. It is just as easy to use as the Instamatic of twenty five years earlier but now it also takes good photos.

The focus here is Ergonomics – ease of use, user friendly. Now, is this part of total design or TQM? Actually, it doesn't matter which. Customers want the products to work, and keep on working safely. It must perform well and look good. Increasingly, people want their products to be easy to use. Companies are realising this and are spending more design time ensuring that their products are also easy to use. They also make a feature of this in their promotion – 'your money back if you can't use this in five minutes' type slogans.

We have already said in Time Frame Two that, to our mind, telephones have become difficult to use. It was a doddle when there was a dial but not now. Most of us haven't the time to lark around with an impossible array of buttons, we just want to get the job done. We have had many a 'Please will you transfer me to the right extension?' type phone call. No chance, haven't a clue how to use this new phone and nor has anyone else around here. Read the manual and press the buttons and, low and behold, there they were – gone, along with their 10p.

Furthermore, the greater the innovation the more it needs to be explained – even in promotion – what it is and why it is better than what went before it. When the product eventually becomes well known advertising takes the form of reminding, such as cigarettes or Kit Kat, but this can take years to happen. Customer 'fear' of the technology in new products is one reason that causes innovations, and often advanced products, to fail on the market.

The moral is that if you want people to want it, then make it easy. It has to be down to you. You also must realise, if you want to make it, so that people want it, then make it easy to make (if that makes any sense) – which is also down to you. Products that are easy to make, not surprisingly, also tend to be lower cost and are more reliable. This is one of the central themes behind TQM.

When you think of a new product or service you must also think about how it will be produced and who are the people who are going to produce it. These are *your internal customers and they are every bit as important as those outside of your organisation who will queue up to buy the fruits of your toils.*

It may even be possible for you to plan the whole range of improvements in your products and phase these in over a period of time. These are called 'Platform Products', which was first written about by Wheelwright and Clark (1992), who worked with the US car industry. For example, if you are designing tooling for plastic mouldings, include the bosses to position the additional buttons for the year after next's model. Just think how much more simple it will be to incorporate that improvement when it becomes necessary. We need to be able to think ahead and plan ahead and this has to be down to effective communication. Another well publicised requirement of TQM.

So you must also make it easy for your internal customers. When did you last stroll around your organisation to actually relate what you are doing to what they (or your subcontractors) are doing? If it wasn't in the last week, put down this book immediately and get strolling.

'EASE OF OWNERSHIP' DESCRIBES THE PRODUCT PROFILE OF THE FUTURE

An old word that dates from about 1350 that seems to be reappearing is 'concivinity'. This is what makes information easier to process through symmetry, harmony and elegance and perhaps should also be the future focus of new products and services.

Arnold Cambell of Nortel Technology (1997) has said that the emotional responses that they wish to generate when people interact with their machines is as if they were other humans and therefore they can be used to make new products more user friendly. Research has found that women's voices are best for emotional advice but men's voices were more believed when talking about financial matters.

On the other hand, new technology allows you to do far more but do not include it in the design unless the consumer really wants it. Over-complication and sophistication can put off potential users, but with the reducing price of electronics the urge is to include additional complication, because the additional cost is not all that great. Just because it can be done does not mean that you should. See how this relates to your potential products and services and inventions that have recently emerged. Remember that you are also consumers, so why not ask yourselves the same question first?

The lesson here is to identify the advantages of ownership that you can offer potential consumers with your new designs over what is already available on the market, or will be made available in the foreseeable future. Why not take this further? Hamel (Van de Vliet 1997) advises us to 'build joy of use into all you provide'.

> JUST BECAUSE TECHNOLOGY ALLOWS YOU TO
> DO IT DOES NOT MEAN THAT CONSUMERS
> WANT IT.

The Effect on Manufacturing Capability

At the start, the costs of any innovation are high for several reasons. There is a need to pay off the cost of R & D, there are high promotional costs that are needed to educate the potential consumer and new products are often manufactured through less than efficient means. There is a learning curve to follow in manufacture and fast market introduction often precedes the process design and automation. There is also an element of 'skimming' with a new product.

In the past, we have plotted the selling price of several products (e.g. video recorders and pocket calculators) and identified the fast, almost exponential, decline in selling price of these items at the start. Customers, at the start, tend to be the technical/professional user or the enthusiast. After a period, the price will plateau and the market opens up for the consumer. With hindsight, it is possible to identify the point at which this occurs. (There was one interesting feature regarding the curve for video recorders where, in 1963, Sony wrongly predicted this plateau and the potential consumer market. Their reel-to-reel recorder was a failure.) More importantly, the type of producer changes as the product moves from the high cost specialist producer to the producer for mass markets. The smaller producers do not invest in manufacturing technology for efficient mass production and either stay as small specialist producers or (more usually) fall out of the market. As a result, there is almost a quantum leap required for a small firm to move from being small to becoming a mass producer, although outsourcing can partly solve this problem.

> DECIDE WHAT TYPE OF ORGANISATION YOU
> PLAN TO BE IN THE FUTURE. If you plan to remain
> small then you must plan to move quickly in and out of
> certain markets and products and into something new.

It is necessary to explore consumers' perceived future benefits and try and anticipate their future emotions. It is possible to anticipate benefits and, furthermore, it is possible to prioritise these benefits. It is often more easy to find consumer dislikes than their likes. A rather impractical example of this is reputed to be carried out by Tibetan tailors. They live with a family for a week and watch how they live. They then make their clothes. This user centred design is not to be recommended but we do propose that you:

> **ASK PEOPLE WHAT THEY DO NOT LIKE ABOUT THEIR CURRENT PRODUCTS, SERVICES AND LIFESTYLES.**

15

Idea Generation for the Future

'There has been more progress in the last 25 years than in the previous 2500 years.' This was said by Ian Pearson of BT's Advanced Research Unit. Ian Pearson is thinking of a very narrow area, probably, concerning his organisation's operations. In reality, the house in which he lives, the main drainage, the power supplied, the transport he uses, the education offered in the local schools has hardly changed in those 25 years. Yet, in the previous 75 years, all the above mentioned things have changed quite significantly and you can add to this the changes in life expectancy and the reduction in infant mortality in this and other developed western economies.

This can lead to consideration of what actually changes within our daily lives, the wider effects of invention, innovations and especially new technology. The invention of the computer, in its present form, is nowhere near as important as the wider effect it has had on the things interfaced with our daily lives. Having already described those areas that are changing fast, it is necessary to look at the implications of these fast changing areas. These are going to not only affect our daily lives but also provide the opportunities for possible business opportunities to those organisations who don't necessarily actually produce or perhaps even use this new technology.

As an example, let's look at the future of retailing. Much has been said about virtual retailing. Customers may access services through digital television or the internet and perhaps 'walk' through the shop selecting their purchases. They can order goods without having to leave their homes. This is not so far away. In America in 1997, 39% of 25 million people who use the internet have made purchases on line. Nortel is developing systems that will allow the internet to be fed from the mains (no telephone connection needed). This will open a new dimension that could herald the end of industrial exhibitions. Why travel to and walk round an exhibition site when the same products are displayed on your computer?

There are many advantages in on line home shopping as it means that people can shop whenever they want to. They can shop during the night or at holidays and also they don't need to travel out in their cars on increasingly crowded roads, perhaps travelling long distances to the shopping centre, then have to find somewhere to park. So, all in all, it seems a 'good thing', with sufficient benefits to make virtual shopping a likely success.

Having decided that, think of the other things that have to be associated with the implementation of a virtual shopping system. Apart from the supply and installation and maintenance of the equipment in people's homes, there is a whole chain of services that need to be provided to make such a system viable. The majority of these may use aspects of the fast growing areas, but there are large profits to be made that do not rely on these. There will be a market for those who can provide the information for the ultra informed sales staff on the virtual system who can answer all sales questions and provide a history of the product for those who need it.

The products have to reach the purchaser's dwelling, they have to be picked and loaded on the lorry. Due to crowded roads, it seems likely that these home deliveries will be made at night. The purchases will be put in secure containers outside of the dwelling, as the home owner will not wish to be disturbed at night. Will your organisation design, make, supply, or fit these containers? It seems increasingly likely that the same group of people who deliver may also have to collect and dispose of packaging and other equipment. The logistics of such a system needs to be worked out if such a process is going to be able to work. For a start, will only bulk purchases be allowed, thus excluding a large number of potential purchasers who live alone?

There is another dimension to this, we always assume that everybody will operate these new systems in this way. Do you really think your kindly, old, grey-haired grandmother will choose to be stuck at the computer terminal to do her shopping? Secondly, the computer system required will cost quite a lot of money. And with the ever increasing gap between the rich and the not so rich, there are a large number of people who will not want to afford such a system and will stay with more conventional ways of shopping. Furthermore, as roads become more jammed and there are increased pressures and costs for individual car ownership these people are less likely to be able to afford their own transport. Public transport will also be slower on more crowded roads. Does this mean the return of the corner grocery shop, supplying these people?

And what of packaging in virtual retailing? At the moment, the purpose of packaging is to attract, promote, ease filling on production, inform the consumer of the contents, cover the legal requirements on information regarding weight and contents, etc. It has also to protect the product during delivery and take up an 'acceptable' amount of shelf space. With virtual retailing, the uses of packaging become separated between those of the virtual product (to attract, inform and promote) and those of the real product (to protect, inform but in a different way, and to ease filling on production). What side of this packaging will your organisation need to consider? The virtual package can be as environmentally unpleasant as you wish, the actual packaging used can be as green as grass.

The example in itself is unimportant, it is the way of thinking that needs to be developed within your organisation, regarding the accessibility and use of new technology. Your organisation should endeavour to contemplate the wider ramifications for the lifestyles of people. This will indicate a whole parallel series of new services that can come about through others' innovations. With specified boundaries within which your organisation plans to work it will be easy to eliminate those areas in which you have no interest and then take further those which are likely to fit into your plan.

The development of cable television and digital TV will probably mean more people will stay at home to see films and sporting events. This could mean the introduction of home delivery of beer and popcorn for those wishing a night in. Perhaps more education could be undertaken by cable TV, and distance learning programmes could be organised around this medium. Perhaps libraries could 'lend' books in the form of CDs or even down cable.

On the other hand, if more of us can work from home and be entertained at home will we choose to stay at home? We are gregarious beings and rather than be lonely we will still want to meet our friends and make new ones. Where will we meet? How will we get there? What will we do when we all get together? Perhaps pubs and clubs are the answer but perhaps not the complete answer. What can your organisation offer us for the future?

Products and Services to Solve Today's Problems

Think what problems could be solved if certain products existed. Then seek out these products or develop them yourself. For example, what limits the height of buildings? When you get beyond the structural problems and the effects of nature one of the most serious problems is the lifts. It was the invention and development of lifts that made skyscrapers possible. It is the lifts that often are the thing that now holds us back. For example, supposing you want to build a 100 storey tower block. How many lifts will you need to put in? Remember that you may have at least one person waiting on each floor who each want to return to the ground or go to the top. This requires a lot of lifts and each takes up an expensive area of space on every floor of your building. In many buildings, this problem is partly overcome by having each lift do just part of the journey to the top of the building,. For example, lift A goes from the ground to floor 33, lift B goes from floor 33 to 66 then lift C goes from 66 to the top. In practice, this will partly solve the problem but will require users travelling all the way to wait for three lifts. Currently, architects have to install several lift shafts, all being an area of not saleable/rentable space.

The solution? Lifts that can pass each other going up or down in the same lift shaft. This would allow quite a few lifts to use the same shaft. Easy eh? Well no, but if you could solve this problem then buildings could be taller in those areas where the high cost of land warrants it.

Business Cycles

Nicolai Kondratieff, who worked in the Agriculture Academy in Moscow back in Stalinist days of the 1920s predicted the long waves of business cycles and his work appears to generally still hold true. He did this by predicting the booms and busts of economic activity of about fifty-four years. This work has been subsequently refined and built upon and the short term waves were added to the theory, called the Kitchen Cycle or Inventory Cycle, which lasts about six to eight years. To this can also be added the nine to eleven year cycle of the French economist Clement Jugler, these predict booms and busts at the end of each decade (Houston 1996).

It is possible to broadly predict the boom and bust of business cycles. The capital generated during the boom needs to be invested to cope with the inevitable downturn. This needs to be linked to the organisation's funding of their new product programmes. Too often, organisations cut this expenditure during business downturns which make them poorly positioned to benefit from the later upturn.

> **PLAN THE ANTICIPATED BUSINESS CYCLES INTO YOUR PRODUCT DESIGN FUTURE.**

A Green Future

Concern about the environment is not just a current fad but definitely an important area for the future. This will go beyond bottle banks and buying environmentally friendly washing up liquid. We must, though, remember that many people within organisations are sceptical of the real marketing advantages of implementing a company wide environmental policy. Of course, when questioned, most managers would say that it is 'a good thing' to be concerned about the planet and its future. This should not be taken as an indication that they are prepared to invest in that direction without some clear marketing advantage. If you are to develop new product and services in this area then you must be clear how these new services benefit the customer – on the bottom line. Focus on the financial benefits, the other benefits are obvious. Energy savings often mean savings to customers, so let them know it.

CASE STUDY – SAVE THAT TREE AND IMPROVE YOUR DESIGNS!

(A plea for ecology)

Carbon paper was invented in 1806, which allowed people for the first time to easily reproduce copies of their work for circulation to others. The photocopier was invented in 1936, although they did not reach these shores until after World War Two. Now they are cheap enough to be everywhere and most of us copy and circulate everything to everybody whether they are interested or not. CAD allows fast alteration and variation and we can quickly print these to show off our latest ideas. Laser printers mean we can rattle off additional copies in a moment to send our dabblings on the keyboard to everyone we have ever known. Mother Nature can hardly keep up with our desire to destroy trees so that people can be kept informed of our latest thoughts. Everybody is frantically writing to everybody else and the point is being reached where they are so busy writing that nobody has any time left to read.

Do you remember the promise of 'the paperless office'? It coincided with our first dealings with computers. Each week, the large valve-driven mainframe would cough out yards of 'data' and we all were delivered a pile from the computer centre. Very useful it was too, turn it over for an endless supply of scrap paper that would be replenished every Friday. The paperless office never materialised as we all desire 'hard copy' to keep in our filing cabinets and to circulate for everyone else's filing cabinet. Apparently, 70% of all information put into a filing cabinet is never ever needed again (how do they compile such statistics?) The filing cabinet was only invented 100 years ago so our forebears managed to build an Empire without them and their contents, as did the Romans, Greeks and Moguls before them.

We are always being told that data is vital for decision making, and we agree. So many new products fail because insufficient information was compiled about the market, and specifications were insubstantial and incomplete. But how many new products fail because all the really vital stuff was lost in a blur of unnecessary claptrap? We should guard against confusing our colleagues with a barrage of paper so they miss the important bits. We have all played the game of 'neutralising' the company nuisance by swamping them with memos to deal with. This gets them off your back and allows you to get on with your job. (You haven't tried it? You should, it works.) We must be careful that we don't do this, unintentionally, to our colleagues, or worse, they do this to you. Often, we are only trying to keep them informed, though occasionally, we suspect, it is a valiant attempt to show everyone how busy we are!

When Bill was a company director, each month's board meeting was preceded by the board reports. I didn't read them, I was too busy, but I always weighed them. A normal meeting was 1kg (that is a lot of writing!), the worst went up to 2 kg. At each board meeting, I would wait in trepidation for the MD to say 'What is your opinion, Bill, of the second paragraph on page 73?' This was the ultimate paper-as-a-weapon sketch because I knew that whatever I said he would refer me to some contradictory paragraph somewhere else in the manuscript. I realise now that this ploy allowed the MD to run the company without opposition.

*Most of the time, you actually want to work with those around you in the most effective manner, so when it comes to notes, reports and memos, **less is often more**. So next time you think about circulating paper why not think again? With a small output of relevant and important points of information your notes will be read, appreciated and remembered. Your colleagues will not miss these vital points and your company's products will be better and, therefore, more successful. Your organisation will become market leaders and you will be promoted.*

How Products and Services Change

We can benefit more from change if we understand how it occurs. As described earlier, with most products and services change is in the form of incremental improvement. Then after a period of time, there is a radical improvement, often involving a change of concept and the 'performance' of the product or service changes by a great deal. This is innovation. The radical improvement then flattens out so that change, once again, is gradual. This is shown in Figure 15.1 (status s-shaped curve). How products are managed in the innovative phase is quite different from how it is managed in the improvement or incremental change phase.

What Causes Products and Services to Change?

The most common cause of change in a product or service is new technology. Companies generally keep developing and improving on familiar lines, then a new technology comes along, which causes a radical change within that product. Radical new products and services need not necessarily involve new technology, for example, the Sony Walkman. People consider this to be an innovation, the innovation is the product

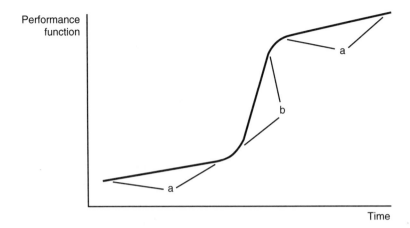

Figure 15.1   How products and services change over time

itself and does not involve new technology. Akio Morita of the Sony Corporation, when speaking at the Department of Trade and Industry Lecture at the Royal Society back in 1992 (reported in *Eureka* March 1992), stated about the Walkman, 'many have called it an innovative marvel, but where is the technology? Frankly, it did not contain any breakthrough technology, its success was built on product planning and marketing.'

So change can also be brought about by putting existing technology in a new form and by marketing. The process by which a product or service is produced, the blueprint, indicates another area where change can occur. This blueprint can be 'stretched', usually at the selling end, to introduce new profitable opportunities. For example, pizza deliveries again. This is where Relationship Marketing also becomes part of the process. If you look at your products and services in such a way it is possible to see, not only new products, but also the skills and services that go with these. J.D. Powers undertakes an annual audit of what owners think about their cars. Most of the complaints, and hence the 'bad' cars, are due to customer dissatisfaction with the service end of the process, with the treatment that they get when things don't go right after the car has been delivered to the customer.

What else goes with these?

If it is possible to identify what causes change, it is therefore also possible to identify what products and services are likely to change and see if these then relate to your product offerings. We have already stated the five main areas where change is occurring and taken the assumption that the technology in other areas is likely to be fairly stable.

Where change, in the form of new technology, does occur, is this a threat? Well, of course it is. But as any SWOT analyst knows, many threats can be turned into opportunities. If you identify that your product is likely to be replaced by better new technology in the future, you can always do something about it. Initially, you must identify if the new technology is a threat. We have talked about people buying benefits, look at that new technology and see if the benefits that it offers now, or the further benefits that may be offered from this technology in the future, actually outweigh those of your products and services. Often they do not. The television programme 'Tomorrow's World' is littered with inventions that we never ever see again, because close scrutiny shows that they are not as good, in the total sense, when compared to that which is already available. The most common reason being that the new benefits are not worth the higher cost of existing technology.

Having identified these threats, does your organisation have time to act? Well, here the answer is yes, but only if your organisation has sufficient warning of these threats and you only get warning of these threats if you are looking for them. If your organisation has a mechanism for seeking potential threats as soon as these 'inventions' are announced, you will have plenty of time to act. Patent searches in areas that relate to your area of operation will certainly show up these inventions. A patent application must be made right at the outset and there is a period of time before the product associated with this application appears and then a further period of time before it is developed away from the specialist market to the really large market, that for the consumer.

Services cannot be patented and, therefore, it is more difficult to identify that people are working on them until they appear. This need not be a problem, because quite often the infrastructure associated with services is not so great, so that it does not take so long to copy them and because services cannot be patented they can be copied.

If you allow one person two days each month to investigate potential threats you should not be caught out by these threats. You will have time to neutralise them or turn them into opportunities. The seniority of the person doing this invention seeking is unimportant. The type of person who is required is somebody who has a lively mind and can read across from new concepts to possible new products for your organisation. So, your organisation should be aware of potential threats to your existing products and in sufficient time to do something about it.

What can you do about these threats?

There are three things that your company can do. If it is a service it can be copied, but if it is a patented product copying is less easy but not impossible. If the new technology is worthwhile, your organisation could try and buy into it, perhaps by paying a royalty. With a patent, because the application has to be made so early in the life of a product, it is quite possible that the product is then developed extensively and actually does not meet its own patent specification. If the initiating company has any sense often they will have taken out a new patent to cover the product that is eventually put on to the market. It is easy to check if they have and if they have not, again, you may copy it.

With any such patent it is often possible to find a way round it. Towards the end of the patent, after the description, it states 'what we claim is' and then follows a series of numbered claims. Most relate to the first claim, for example, 'a claim as described in claim one that'. This means that if you can find your way round the first claim you have avoided the protection of that patent. This may seem a bit underhand but, after all, this is your livelihood you are protecting. Any patent must actually describe a working principle and not an idea. Of course, patents are written by authors that use all encompassing terms to avoid somebody copying the idea. For example, a patent will not say 'held by a spring', but will say 'held by resilient means', to stop you replacing the spring by a piece of rubber. It will not say 'the item is bolted together, but 'held by fixable means' to avoid you copying it by gluing it together. In spite of this, it is often quite easy to find one's way round patent protection.

Some years ago, Bill worked in an organisation where the major competitor had a good product which was patented and which we wanted to copy. Bill looked at the product patent and found that they had, in the first claim stated that the two major parts were held together by a 'plurality of lugs'. By avoiding lugs altogether we avoided their patents and thus came on to the market with a very similar competing product. On the other hand, just blindly following competitors isn't usually the best course of action. 'Me too' products are generally unsuccessful. Customers are suspicious of companies that just copy other people's products. It is necessary to offer other benefits or USPs (Unique Selling Propositions) as well.

Supposing you can't compete?

If you are unable to compete do not dismiss the direction of change as being outside of your company's operations. With any product there is a plethora of ancillary products and services that are associated with the new. Could your organisation provide spares, undertake warranty or servicing, provide add on features and updates or even arrange the eventual disposal of the new? There is a whole gambit of tools, techniques or skills associated with the above that your company could provide.

In spite of this, over a period of time, your organisation's products and services will fade and die, to be replaced by new ones. If you are aware that in the next few years one of your companies offerings will be replaced by a competitor, it is still possible that your organisation could do well from it by withdrawing from the market. But, during this withdrawal, your organisation maximises profit. If you know the product demise is inevitable in, say, five years, you can plan the withdrawal over that period. Your aim is to make as much money as possible with this product over the five years and this means keeping costs as low as possible. Limit the amount of new machinery bought that is associated with this product and maintain the existing machinery as little as possible, in order to arrive at the product withdrawal with essentially scrapped machinery. Virtually eliminate any development of the dying product with the exception of aesthetic changes. Certainly, those involved with new products should be working on new products rather than spending their time on the old. What your organisation should be doing is making an orderly departure from the market. In the 1970s Bill was working for a company that designed and developed suspension systems for military vehicles. A new competitor on the market (it is often a competitor who was not previously in the market) appeared with a product that rendered ours obsolete. Over the next few years, we hammered our machines to death and put nothing into the development of the product or the processes used. This was probably the most profitable period of this product's life. We focused our efforts in a completely different and growing direction.

Most marketing books state that during the decline period of the product's life cycle profits fall. If you are aware that the product is in decline the total profits will be smaller but the unit profit can be higher. For example, if you supply parts for Morris Minors or Betamax tapes you may not sell many but those who want them will be prepared to pay a lot for them.

How you can deal with change

If it is possible to identify which types of products are changing fast and which types of products are changing slowly it is possible to link this knowledge to your products and services. You can then start to manage the future. There are a series of disciplines that can be associated with products that are changing radically or incrementally. Some disciplines will be required whatever the type of product, but others are more important depending on whether change is fast or slow. These are listed below:

1 **Process improvement**. This is the method of manufacture or service delivery. These processes change more quickly and more is spent on these when the basic product or service concept is static.

2 **Aesthetics/decor**. When the basic concept is stable there are often many organisations trying to compete with similar products and services using the same level of technology. When this occurs, more effort should be put into changing the way the product or service looks, the aesthetics. For example, realistically, cars are not changing all that much and much more effort is put in to the way they look.

Skills Audit – a Reminder

From the above, you can see that once you have identified the type of direction a product is going in, you can see the type of disciplines that are associated with it. Now, all of these require certain skills, which may or may not be within your organisation. Should you require these skills you can, as said before in Time Frame Two, employ, train or sub-contract. If you are in a large organisation with various types of products going in different directions an appreciation of the status of these products will allow you to focus the skills within your organisation towards those products and services that most need them. Of course, to do this you need a skills audit. The skills audit can take someone as long as a month to do and should be done at a 'quiet time', if such a time exists. As people come and go their skills are identified and listed or deleted. You may also need to compile the skills of your major suppliers or sub-contractors.

In Time Frame Two was briefly mentioned the roles and responsibility matrix that identifies the people requirement when developing a product in the short-term. In this section, we are looking much further ahead in the direction that our products are going and, as we identify the general direction, we can also identify the skills that we are likely to need. Any skills that we need but do not have we can seek.

Are You an Innovative Organisation?

We have already said in Time Frame One that companies must be willing to change. Some companies find it easier to change than others. There now follows two lists. The first shows factors that tend to restrict change:

1 A few large customers. If this is the case then whether you are able to change often depends on them.
2 New products and services must be an extension of your existing product range. Many organisations insist that new products and services can only be developed in a very narrow direction.
3 Must new products use existing machinery, sales force, outlets or other methods of marketing?
4 Is time to market one of the most important considerations in the development of new services? Of course, time to the market is important but if this is considered as being more important than most other aspects of developing a new product then this is bound to restrict or even eliminate innovation.
5 Using existing tried and tested knowledge or experience. Certainly, these ensure reliability but it is necessary to 'break out' from what has gone before.
6 Is there a large infrastructure based around your existing products or services (software is an exception)? It is always difficult to move forward, even in the longer term, if to do so means a radical change to that which already exists. Such a change not only involves altering the large infrastructure of buildings and equipment, but also involves a lot of re-training to cope with the new.
7 Conformance standards. If you produce something which is specified by, for example, the British Standards Institution it is difficult to move away from that which already exists.
8 An example which need not be a restriction but often is, occurs when a few large companies dominate a particular market and all tend to copy each other. Large companies, in general, tend to keep a product or service from changing. Often, it is because they have such a large infrastructure (as described above) in the form of dedicated machinery, automation or delivery systems (similar retail outlets) that they eschew change. Being large, they command economies of scale and, therefore, low unit prices. When they try to change they lose these economies of scale and come under pressure from small companies. This can often be seen if a market becomes increasingly dominated by a decreasing number of competitors.

9   If you cannot financially afford to change. Change is more expensive than leaving things as they are and you can only change if you have the money or can obtain the money.

Factors that encourage change are:

1   Of course, new technology or other such technical advances.
2   Problems with an existing system. If something doesn't work properly there is more likelihood that people will want to change it.
3   If the potential price of something new is lower than the existing, then it is more likely to be a success. This usually has to be coupled with other benefits, an example being the digital watch compared with the clockwork variety.
4   If your organisation actually controls your market niche then there is little to stop you changing.
5   Changes in the world at large may result in change within your organisation. These changes may be economic, legislative, environmental, economic or even changes in 'raw material' (such as more old people).

CASE STUDY – IT'S GOOD TO BE GREEN – ISN'T IT?

You should question much of what you hear especially as many 'facts' do not stand up to close investigation. After the greedy, grabbing eighties there was supposed to be the caring nineties. Not a lot of evidence for that. The streets around London and most cities still present the tragic sight of homeless people. When we first went to Italy and saw homeless beggars in the late 1960s it horrified us that such a wealthy society could not/would not give a helping hand to those people. It shocks us even more that we are prepared to put up with such misery on our own streets in this 'caring' age. If you are still so naive as to think they are all 'drunks who want to live like that' you may be interested to know that their main cause of death is suicide – more than five times the number who die of alcoholism.

Bill seriously wanted to design a flat pack cardboard shelter for homeless people. The idea was to distribute these from hostels when they were full. Purely as a design exercise it is quite a tricky problem. Unfortunately, nobody seems to want to fund it.

We may show little charity towards these individuals but we do appear to be concerned about the wider environment on our planet. We have all become 'green'. We worry about the ozone layer and extinction of the white rhino. But, when it comes to getting in the planet's good books, do we think logically about our behaviour?

Do you use unleaded petrol? If you have a catalytic converter on your car you have no choice, but what of those of you who don't have such a new car? People puff out their chests and feel proud that they use unleaded petrol. They put 'we are green' stickers on their cars and think they are doing the rest of us a good turn. Lead was put into petrol for a reason, as an 'anti-knock' agent and it also helps to lubricate the valves. So leaving it out must have some penalty attached to it. Never mind, it is about 8% cheaper so we are making money out of it – aren't we? Well actually – no. You get about 10% less power from unleaded fuel. You tend not to notice this because you just put your foot down '10%' further to achieve the same level of power as before. And you almost certainly don't notice the fall in fuel consumption from, say, 33mpg to 30mpg. You save the lead going into the atmosphere but (without a cat.) you increase, by 10%, all the other nasties – carbon dioxide, sulphur dioxide and all the other NOX's. The result, more pollution and a bigger hole in the ozone layer.

Is there any clear evidence that the lead in petrol is really doing any harm? The research reports about the possible hyperactivity of children brought up in the exhaust polluted areas of Spaghetti junction around Birmingham were far from conclusive. We often make snap judgements that affect our behaviour based on the crudest of data.

You may also save bottles and papers, etc. for your local bottle/paper bank. How much fuel do you use driving to the bottle bank and how much fuel is used taking the bottles away from there? If you really want to be a good citizen, just drive less – leaving more room on the road for us.

In a recent study on the ranking of nations that pollute the planet the US came first, Japan second and Britain third. It's nice to see that we still lead the world in something. Having travelled in Eastern Europe, it seems hard to believe that we can be worse than what is coming from their chimneys. Perhaps we are just more honest at admitting our short-comings.

When it comes to being green, an excellent article in the IEE News (5.10.95) took a slightly different point of view. It said that many of the conclusions drawn from environmental scare stories were, frankly, untrue. They cite the unfulfilled fears concerning the environmental damage caused by acid rain in the US and Canada and oil spills such as Exxon Valdez in Alaska and Braer in the Shetlands. They also remind us that it was claimed that oil fires started in the Gulf War were supposed to burn for three years but were actually extinguished in a matter of months. Part of the reason is that scare stories make better newspaper fillers than good news.

But we ought to care about our planet and its future, and we can certainly care more when we work. Most of us should already consider our products and services as far as, and including how to dispose of the product at the end of its life – as part of the specification. We can avoid certain toxic materials such as cadmium, which could eventually pollute our rivers and we are now considering reclamation and reuse of the materials used. Just including an identification number of the material used engraved in moulds is a big step forward. When it eventually becomes time to scrapping the product these numbers will allow the material to be identified, reclaimed and reused.

In April 1994, The British Standard BS 7750 was published. This is the environmental standard and operates very much like BS EN ISO 9000 (formerly BS 5750). You can now be audited to ensure that your waste is correctly managed. The first companies to be audited against the five points achieved certification in April 1995. In autumn 1995 EMAS – the Environmental Management Audit System – was introduced. This includes the first five audit areas of BS 7750, plus two more. This is a EC initiative and there is EC money available to help you conform to the system. When BS 5750 appeared there were obvious advantages to be gained *through the better quality that (in theory) would accrue and certification also gave a definite marketing edge. It is not so clear that BS 7750 will provide such an effective marketing edge.*

Even so, we are improving our consciousness of the environment. If you want an example of how far we have come: In the late 1970s Bill was talking to someone from some place or other that were using precipitators to clean flu gases. These structures were powered up by electricity and they attracted the dirt particles of smoke that passed through them. Showing an over active interest in the working of these, I asked, 'and how do you clean these?' The answer made me cringe even in those bad old days, 'we wait for a moonless, dark night, switch them off and blow the muck out of the chimney stacks.' I hope those days have gone forever.

Other long term decisions that need to be taken, beyond product invest-ment decisions, are those concerning training, recruitment and location. For example, the cost of replacing an employee has been estimated by the Institute of Personnel and Development, in 1998, at up to £15,000 depending on the skills and experience of that individual and therefore such planning ought to be a fairly long term consideration.

The first two really fall outside the area of this book but the last perhaps ought to be considered here. The products that you produce in the future may be better produced elsewhere. Alternatively, if those in the organ-isation decide that they cannot or do not want to relocate then this is another boundary around those products that ought to be developed.

Plant and Business Location

When siting a business there are many factors that need to be taken into consideration, and it is likely that several will need to exist in order to make it an attractive place in which to relocate. The following should be considered. When siting a business your organisation may need to be:

1 Near to customers – this cuts down on transport costs but, also, your customers will not have to travel so far to reach you. Example, a bakery.
2 Away from competitors – if there is a limited number of customers being too close to a competitor subdivides the market. Example, you wouldn't site a fish and chip shop next to another fish and chip shop.
3 Near the competitors – certain areas become known for a particular type of product and people will visit there to purchase. Example, in the UK, Saville Row for suits, Hatton Garden for jewellery, Tottenham Court Road for hi-fi equipment.

4 Where there are good road links – the building of the M4 motorway west of London resulted in many companies setting up along the edge of this motorway (ribbon development) because of the ease of transportation.

5 Where government grants are available – several areas of the country are less successful in attracting business and the government provides grants to encourage organisations to set up in these areas.

6 Near raw materials or suppliers – the steel industry was established in South Wales to be near the coal and near to the ports where iron ore was imported.

7 Near to available cheap energy – the aluminium industry was established in Scotland, because of the available low cost electricity from hydro-electric schemes. Aluminium is smelted from bauxite. Bauxite is available in many locations but the high cost of electricity needed to obtain the aluminium from the ore determines where the industry is located.

8 Near to available skills – the car industry in Great Britain is sited in the Midlands, where traditionally the relevant metal working skills have been prevalent. The Nissan factory was also set up in the North East where there was a ready availability of skilled labour.

9 Away from traditional labour practices – Toyota chose Derby to site its factory, an area not previously used by car makers. This was chosen to avoid the heavy unionised working practices prevalent in other car companies.

10 Near to sea and airports – if the product is to be exported, this may determine the site of the factory, (lightweight/high value near to airport. High weight/low value near to sea ports).

11 A nice place to live – when the electronics industry was initiated, in the UK, companies needed to attract physicists from Universities. Scotland was chosen (Silicon Glen), as it was considered that it would be a sufficiently nice place to live to attract the necessary labour; the same is true of Silicon Valley in the United States.

12 Where there is low cost land – the customers of hypermarkets and DIY centres generally come by car and, therefore, large car parks are required. So, these businesses are sited where sufficient car parking space can be obtained relatively cheaply.

13 In a Free Port – some areas are designated Free Ports and in these duty is not payable. Although most are, these do not have to be on the coast. As an example, we visited the Free Port of Manaus in Brazil, which is 2000 miles from the sea.

14 In the right climate – if a company is involved in, for example, agriculture, they will site their business where the climate is ideal.

Example, one would not try and grow pineapples or coffee commercially in many places in Europe.

15 Near test facilities – example, Newbury is where racehorses are stabled and trained, historically it is the place for 'testing' horses.

16 Where there is cheap labour – example, often the main reason for setting up a manufacturing plant in China is the availability of very cheap labour.

17 Avoiding potential Political/Cultural problems – example, it is unlikely that you would find pig farming in Israel and throughout the Arab world.

18 Where the environment is right – example, if noise was a problem the plant would be sited away from residential areas, the same may occur with waste disposal.

19 Where the region is right – example, Champagne can only come from the designated area for Champagne.

20 Where the production process involves bulk reduction – (for example, iron ore to iron) the plant would be located near to the site of the availability of raw material.

21 Where there is an increase in bulk volume of the product – (for example, tin boxes from sheet metal) the plant could be located near the customers.

22 Away from crowded roads – example, if the roads in one particular area are liable to heavy traffic, delivery of raw material or supply of the finished goods may be difficult. Example, the London Arena closed in 1991 because transport links were insufficient for customers to easily get to the events.

23 Away from high insurance cost areas – example, certain areas have high crime rates and, in these areas, insurance premiums are higher, this may deter an organisation setting up in these areas.

24 Where patent rights can be exploited – example, if a competitor has patented a product or process, only in certain countries, it is possible to set up in other countries and supply to these or third countries.

25 Away from legal restrictions/regulations – (for example, gun shops in the UK).

26 In safe places – (for example, fireworks manufacturers away from the town).

27 Away from geological problems – (for example, nuclear power stations over geological faults).

28 Where there is an availability of capital or lower interest rates.

29 Where there is political stability – do you fancy relocating to Albania?

30 Where the boss wants to live!

So far in this Time Frame we have been talking about innovation in products and services. Why stop there? The principles described here work in a much wider area than the obvious. For example, have you considered how they could be applied to sport? This is a worthwhile direction to take as it is not only a fast growing market but also a multi-billion pound set of big businesses. These are set to develop further as people become more health conscious and also more interested in both taking part or watching sport as a leisure activity.

Anyway, below are our own opinions on this important dimension that is set to expand over the next decade – and where we think it could be taken. In the next part of Time Frame Four a sequential process is proposed, that can be used to develop the products and services that your organisation will need beyond six years into the future.

Time Frame Four

Part II   The Process

16

How to Find the Future

For the foresight of things to come, which is providence, belongs only to him by whose will they are to come. For him only, and supernaturally, proceeds prophecy. The best prophet naturally is the best guesser, he that is most versed and studied in the matters he guesses at; for he hath the most signs to guess by.

(T. Hobbes. 'The Leviathan' 1651)

Introduction

In this section, the process by which you can plan for the future is outlined. Companies need vision and to have a strategic framework to achieve this vision. Furthermore, they have to have the right competencies to defend their position against emerging competition. Organisations must be prepared to cope with radical change and be prepared to plan for it.

If potential ventures are viewed within a strategic context, it should be possible to identify a series of parameters or 'boundaries' that shows the type of projects that are right for the particular organisation. This will enable people to identify those achievable areas worth pursuing as well as areas that should be avoided (Hollins 1995 2). These boundaries need to be stated and specified and these determine whether an organisation should pursue an idea in the first place.

Furthermore, it is necessary to recognise and understand the driving forces for change. Identifying the future is pattern recognition and this involves learning from past experiences and 'rehearsing' what might happen in the future.

The methodology for this section

There is no favourable wind without direction.

(Seneca (French writer))

A framework in which organisations can plan their products and services well into the future is now proposed. As said before, you cannot expect such a system to be exactly right but we suggest that it will put you in the right direction. Of course, the entire process will be highly iterative and subject, perhaps, to radical change over time and as circumstances alter. As circumstances change, you can adjust this direction so that your organisation stays on course for your future. You can adapt the process to suit your own particular needs but keep it simple. You don't know enough to make it complicated. There is no point in trying to work to three places of decimals when you are only dealing with glorified guesses. The need to have a flexible structure is a view supported by both Mintzberg and Hammer (Gibson 1997) 'in an environment of change, you don't want a very rigid organisational structure. You want one that allows you to adapt.'

Essentially, the question that needs to be asked is: Where would you like to be in (say) ten years time? Can this organisation contribute to any aspect of this through products or services that either impinge directly on this or are ancillary to it? How? Knowing this, how do we get there from here?

Some techniques, such as competition analysis and benchmarking, are too short term to be part of this process and innovation seeking will become invention seeking. Focused patent searches will be worthwhile but an investigation of the workings of things that are already on the market will not allow a sufficiently long term view. As you move into the future, the earlier sections of this book will become more relevant and this section will be used for the new future of that time.

Specify long term corporate objectives, then achieve them through long term corporate strategy. Therefore, you need clear corporate objectives, which are, where possible quantifiable – put numbers and tolerances on them – then people will know when they have been achieved. Of course, they must also be achievable. They need to be clearly documented. The corporate objectives must involve the whole gambit of the organisation's disciplines and must be clearly described so that all contributors may be harnessed to their full potential to achieve the set corporate objectives.

The process is presented in a series of layers and each should be completed in turn before you move on to the next layer.

Resources to run this long term process

You can't do anything if you haven't allocated the (financial) resources to do it. We propose that you set aside an additional 1/12th of what you currently budget for new products to finance the management of long term products. Most organisations do not spend enough on developing new products, especially compared to what their overseas competitors do. Whatever percentage you do budget really depends on what markets you currently serve. The faster your products change the more you need to invest to keep competitive. If you are operating in one of the very fast changing areas then the percentage of your turnover that you need to invest will be in the teens. You know what is best for your organisation and an additional 1/12th will now be needed to finance that proposed in this Time Frame. That is, just to run this long range viewing process. The existing R&D budget finances Time Frames Two and Three, which will be the ideas that come out of this long range process.

Although there will be financial parameters which specify the new services, the actual running of the process must be financed from a budget allocated from retained profits. This work certainly can't be written down as an asset (as was the case in the RB211 development described earlier). There will be a return but as this is so long term, the rules described in Time Frame Two on justifying the work to the accountant do not apply. Oddly though, the questions used in that section are not unlike those described in this section. The cost of this long term planning must be specified as a running cost to the organisation and written off as such.

Sequence of the process

There are risks and costs to a programme of action. But they are far less than the long range risks and costs of comfortable inaction.

(John F. Kennedy reported in Tora (1993))

The group

The top managers and directors (excluding those with share options whose interests are probably short term) must first specify the parameters in which any long term developments must fit. If the company is part of a larger group the managers should be drawn from the company but be advised by the directors of the holding company as to some of the allowable parameters. We suggest those which are, perhaps, most important

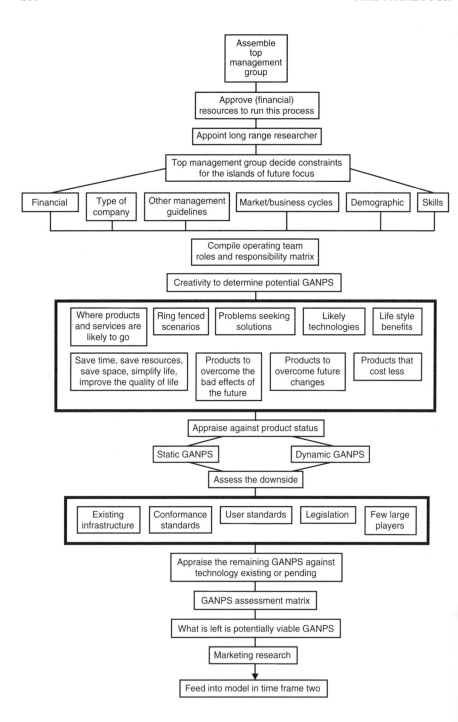

Figure 16.1   Sequence of the process

but, depending on your organisation, you may need to specify more. Also, do not specify a parameter if it is not necessary. Each will restrict the action of those developing new products and services and, hence, do not restrict their actions in areas where you don't have to, leave these open.

Islands of Future Focus

In Time Frame Two, frameworks were described. These were a development of the early stages of product development, earlier than models of the process. These frameworks allowed those senior managers in an organisation to specify the various parameters in which the organisation would be allowed to operate. This principle is now developed and what will now be described are 'Islands of Future Focus'. Organisations need to select all or several of these islands, depending on where they want to go. These islands identify and articulate real targets for the future within the organisation. Once you have these islands their totality is the 'innovation universe' in which the organisation works.

As before, the type of products and services that ought to be developed will be those that fit into the overlap between these overlapping circles, similar to that shown on Figure 4.1 and are now shown on Figure 16.2. The heading of these Islands will be Main Management Guidelines, on the Type of Company, Finance, Market/Business cycle, Demographic and Skills and may include other resources or parameters. Do not only think of what your organisation can do now or what business you are in, though this is of prime importance, think also of what business you could be in. This is a case of avoiding marketing myopia from the development side. Don't just be in the business of trains, be in the much wider business of transport and travel. You are trying to determine:

> **WHERE SHOULD WE GO? CAN WE DO IT? DO WE
> WANT TO DO IT?**

Most, but not all, of the most important parameters are financial parameters. The following parameters should be specified.

The financial island

What is the maximum that the company can afford to develop the product or service? This must include all the investment and promotion

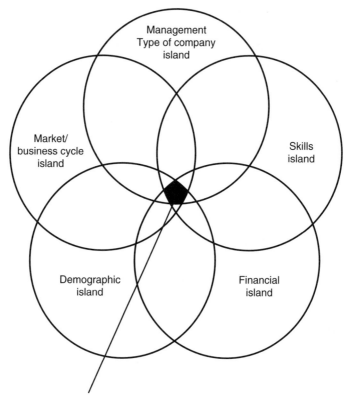

GANPS should be undertaken in the area of overlap

Figure 16.2   Islands of Future Focus

costs, spread over several years, up to the point that the product runs into profit. Essentially, what is the maximum debt that we can sustain? For example, Sky broadcasting had to absorb weekly losses of £14 million before sufficient customers made extraterrestrial broadcasting profitable. Only the very largest of organisations could have supported such losses. There are various cut-off points beyond which an organisation should not venture (especially on borrowings) otherwise the whole organisation will be at risk. BSkyB currently makes such large profits as to render their earlier losses as being almost insignificant which shows that, for them, the risk was worthwhile, but most other companies would have been bankrupted by such a product.

This financial parameter is for all the developments being undertaken. It is unlikely, in view of the high failure rate of new products and services, that your organisation will only be developing one product. In all the potential developments, including the short term ones, the total investment should not exceed the specified figure. This should be specified year on year and will alter as the short term products come on the scene and (hopefully) the organisation grows. In this case, the maximum 'risk' money will also be allowed to grow. Consider it as the 'maximum debt that we can sustain'.

The minimum rate of return on investment should also be specified. This will show if the new venture is worth the effort or (at least) if it would be better to leave the money in the bank. At a minimum level, this should be higher than the rate of interest that the company is getting if the money is invested, or above the minimum borrowing rate if borrowing is required to finance new products. There needs to be an additional per cent added to the ROI to allow for the risk. In view of the failure rate of products (about one success for every 2.6 products put on the market (Hollins and Hollins 1991)) this should be 2.6 times the percentage cost of money. To explain: If you are a typical company and experiencing that high failure rate, then the failed 1.6 products have to be supported by the one successful product, that also has to pay for itself. If your organisation has reduced the rate of failure of new products to something sensible, which is possible if you follow the procedures as explained earlier in this book, it should be possible to reduce this figure to under two times the percentage cost of money.

On the other hand, it is equally dangerous to specify a rate of return on investment that is too high. At one time, when Xerox were making a very large return from their photocopiers, it was specified that any new product had to generate a similar rate of return. This had the effect of strangling most of their attempts at new products. It is necessary to be realistic about both the minimum and maximum return of investment allowed. The return on investment is usually based on the number sold and the price of these. Err on the side of caution here as, over time, generally, the total delivered cost per unit sold is decreasing.

We are talking of a potential long term investment and, therefore, it is important to consider discounted cash forecasts. Even with low inflation rates the value of money now is not what it will be when the product eventually appears on the market in over six years' time. During the long term, over which the development will take place, there will be regular cash calls. These will be low at any one time for most of the process and will become high near the end. The organisation may be called upon to make too large a cash injection if the development of the later stages of several products coincide. This can be avoided through prioritising and planning early in the process. The revenues generated over a period of time and the anticipated margins achieved will identify the profits and payback periods.

The type of company island

This also determines the type of products and services that can be taken on. As described in the 'Hover Horror' case study in Chapter 4 of this book, beyond financial parameters there are other parameters beyond which a company should not step. The first is to decide if the organisation will stay with being mass, batch or unit production. A big company is unlikely to want to develop batch production products and services and a small company may not be able to move into mass production products. It is possible to move from one to the other and, of course, almost all large companies started out small. There is also enough time to be able to do this. But it has been shown that there is a dip in profitability when an organisation moves from being small to large as there is a significant increase in the number of 'non profitable' administrators needed. This reduction in profitability can be overcome by increased economies of scale but you may then be competing with other organisations that also can utilise the same benefits.

It has also been shown that many organisations actually don't wish to grow above the size at which they are currently operating. Speaking for ourselves, we are happy as a 'two man band' and will not wish to expand as a company. Consider realistically whether your organisation really wishes to take on all the trauma of planned growth and if you don't then exclude ideas that fall outside your existing scope and ambitions. This is another specified parameter.

Which markets are the organisation prepared to enter? This will depend on the type of products that will be developed and which markets are likely to grow. So, it is more a case, at this stage, of stating which markets are unacceptable. This will be mainly product areas but will also include countries and regions that will not be approached. Some companies, which are part of larger foreign owned organisations, are not allowed to sell in certain countries. Some companies do not wish to trade in countries where there may be insufficient customers who can afford the product or service or areas where it may prove difficult to take profits across borders. There are other dimensions to this, for example, a pet shop owner will not be able to become involved in animal trading with other countries whilst our anti-rabies laws are in place. There are several such parameters that need to be specified relating to both inside and outside of the organisation. In general, it is easier to change the marketing parameters without causing significant problems, but each of these must be judged on their own merits.

Must new developments be complementary to the existing portfolio of products and services? This may be the case in the short term but in the longer view that is being taken here, it is perhaps an unnecessary restriction on the directions which the organisation is being allowed to take. Be brave, there is plenty of opportunity further down the line to put the brake on things before there has been unnecessary expense on them. All this is being done at the low cost end of the process.

The market/business cycle island

A slightly different feature that needs to be built into these islands of future focus is the likely effect of business cycles over the next twenty years. As it is possible to broadly predict when the market is looking up or down, it is possible to identify when it is the best time to introduce particular types of products and services. In a recession, it is hard for all businesses but it is harder for some than it is for others. When there is a recessionary climate and unemployment tends to be higher, there is a period of entrenchment and customers are less likely to make large purchases, such as cars. People move less, so demand for housing falls and people take fewer overseas holidays. Conversely, people do up their existing houses and maintain their existing belongings rather than replace them with new ones. This means that, relatively, demand increases for DIY products and maintenance services. Also, relatively, the demand for holidays in this country increases compared to the number taken abroad.

Therefore, it is often unwise to schedule the introduction of new products, especially high cost ones, during a recession. The rate at which a new product or service can be produced is slow when it is first introduced. This is due to being at the start of the learning curve, and not having fully introduced the automation that would speed up production. It is often a good time to plan a product introduction just at the end of a dip in the economic cycle.

Also, part of this island is to consider demand variation. It is possible, at this stage, to identify where there are likely gaps in the annual activities of an organisation and then favour products and services that will go some way towards filling these voids. Demand variation was discussed in Time Frame Two. Although the plans are for a long way ahead, it is unlikely that all the company's existing products and services will be obsolete in the period ahead being considered. Identify the likely survivors and note the demand pattern for these. This will be annual demand for products and annual and daily demand for services.

It is unlikely (and unwise) to only be planning one product for the long term future so also look at the likely demand pattern for these other products in an attempt to plan a smooth operation in your organisation's future.

Demographic island

What will be going on in the world and what will its people be doing in the future? We have mentioned our ageing population and its composition is altering. Fewer people are remaining married and the extended family is less common. This means a change in the size and type of housing. There are many parameters that need to be identified and these will indicate worthwhile growing areas and those that are dying and should be ignored.

Conversely, small companies can often make a sufficient return in dying market niches which no longer interest larger organisations. The turnover will be small but the unit profit may be quite high. For example, few people now own a Betamax video player but those who do will pay quite a lot for the tapes, low turnover but high profit. VHS tapes are a low price but are sold in large quantities. So it is often worth looking at declining areas and demographies to identify profitable corners, if you are that type of company.

Skills island

What skills have you got within the organisation? More to the point, what skills can you realistically obtain and use, bearing in mind the type of company yours is and the type of company they plan to be in the next few years? This island will be iterated back to during the later stages of this process but can be compiled near the start. It will mainly show the type of skills that the organisation will **not** be able to aquire, manipulate or use and hence potential ideas that need such skills will be excluded.

What are you best in the world at? Handley (1995) has reported that Philips's key competence is fusing metal to glass, Shell is to find oil at 1,200 feet or below, Federal Express to 'track, trace and control packages' and 3M's skill is 'the application of polymer chemistry to coatings and abrasives'. What skills do you master, can you master or be prepared to master? Again, there is time to obtain new skills in technology, producing or marketing. But realistically, do you want to? Can your organisation afford these skills and if you obtain and use them what other organisations will your organisation now be competing with? For example, do you want to employ people with software skills and then be in competition with the new low wage software centres such as Bombay? The other direction that you can take is to use their skills. The decision then is to determine how much of your core competencies your organisation is prepared to sub-contract. If you outsource that which is your marketing edge than your organisation can become very vulnerable. When outsourcing was at its peak some companies outsourced as much of their organisation as they could. This gave them greater flexibility and made change easier. It also cut down on much of the administration costs. Unfortunately, some of these companies became known as 'empty organisations' in which there was almost nothing to them but a name. Some found that they had left themselves too vulnerable, having traded security for a fast short term profit and did not survive. In spite of this, there will still be areas where it would be beneficial to use outside skills.

GANPS

Long-term products and services need to be treated separately from your other products and services and so we have given them a separate name. These type of products are called 'GANPS'. This stands for Generation After Next Products/Services. These are more a series of long-term product ideas that you can identify and then feed into the process given in this Time Frame and also fit inside the various frameworks. The best of these will eventually be developed into new products and services but none of these will be available for at least six years. Of course, this depends on your market. Remember, we are dealing with the generation after next and you should know what that is for your offerings. If it is possible or likely that these could be developed now then you are not thinking far enough ahead. You are thinking of 'triggers' not GANPS and these should be developed as described in Time Frame Two and Three.

Of course, GANPS eventually become new product concepts, if they survive that far. Don't just identify a single GANPS, develop a whole interlocking interrelated portfolio of GANPS. It is also worthwhile anticipating the risk of the GANPS being developed. A mix of lower risk and high risk should avoid jeopardising the organisation while at the same time allowing some high risk but very high rate of return projects to be built into the portfolio.

People leave

The core skills need to be specified and those that are core will need to be sustained and maintained as part of the process. We are considering a period where new products will become available from over six years to around 15 years. How many people stay at the same job for 15 years? Younger people tend to change jobs more than older people and it is a natural part of running an organisation. If the core skills are specified as part of one of the parameters then as those with these skills announce that they are to leave steps will be taken to replace them. Additional competencies will be specified as the GANPS that are to be developed are agreed upon. As these may be important to the likely new products then these will then be added to the list of core skills and treated in the same way. The personnel department can then organise their manpower operations into the future. The Skills Audit described earlier in this section and also in Time Frame Two will assist in this activity.

Subspecifications

The chapter on Subspecifications in Time Frame Two is another one of the keys. Linked with each Island will be a series of subspecifications and these will be compiled within a series of questionnaires similar to those described in that section.

Remember to review and update

Over the years that the system is to be used there will be changes as circumstances change. Change is allowed and those involved in developing these long term (and short term) products and services must be informed of these new parameters as the changes are made. Any reduction in the parameters is certain to cause disruption so those involved must be careful when specifying the parameters in the first place and also must avoid too many changes to the allowed parameters in which people and the organisation must work. In short, endeavour to maintain some stability with the parameters.

Communication

The process will operate in a fairly loose system of communication. The rules of Design Circles, Brainstorming and the Product Champion will still be used for meetings in the same form as described in Time Frame Two. But this is not a system that will work in a few short meetings. The system that will be described must not be allowed to degenerate into the 'handicapped design' scenario as described in Chapter 3 in Time Frame Two, albeit in more formal surroundings. There is a need for Brainstorming but only to provide ideas which will then feed into the Islands. It will not be a substitute for the full process to be described. Furthermore, the process will provide the focus in which the creativity will be allowed to flourish. The longer term type of creativity, as also described in Time Frame Three, will be more useful.

The organisation needs to be guided to be in the right place at the right time with the right structure and the right resources with the right people and the right creativity to ensure that serendipity occurs. This is much more than scenario planning. It is focused scenario planning and then implementation.

The team

Having identified and developed the Island of Future Focus in which the new products and service will fit it is now necessary to draw together those people that will seek out these new products. This team will certainly not be the same people who identified the Island but may include one, or at the most, two. What is needed is a group of under nine people who have lively minds and cover a complete cross section of those employed and preferably more of those types of people that make up your likely customer base for the type of products under consideration. Of course, the work which is being done must remain confidential as it is the organisation's future products and hence their future existence that is being decided upon. On the other hand, the fact that it is being done should be broadcast throughout the company as it shows that the organisation is concerned to survive as a healthy entity for an indefinite period and is doing something to ensure that it does.

The group must be co-ordinated and led and this should be done by a senior member of the management team. It is a worthy use of their time and it should not be delegated. The team should be creative people, but realists, as the type of thinking in which they will be involved can easily spiral out of control from the achievable to the unlikely to the impossible. By all means pipe dream but keep a firm hold on what is likely to be reality. Keep remembering that in most cases most things don't change much.

A process is described in this section, but don't forget that more than 50% of processes are people and a great percentage of that is politics. People may have their own private agendas and we would be glib if we believed that everybody is in tune with the process and wants to go in the same direction. Winning people over to this programme will be a continuous part of this process.

Another difficulty is confidentiality. How can an organisation arrange for the free flow of ideas to all without risking the sensitive nature of the

THE DESIGN CIRCLE
It should be a jolly time

THE DESIGN CIRCLE
but it is usually more like this!

information? Certainly, it is important to identify the less crucial information and encourage the flow of this throughout the company. The commercially confidential material must be confined to a 'need to know' basis. Suspicion from others should be eliminated, or at least reduced, if it is made clear that such information relates to that which will make the company grow and the jobs of those within the organisation more secure. Clearly, this will only work if there have not been any recent attempts to 'rationalise', 'downsize', 'rightsize' or any of the other expressions used which mean kicking people out of employment. As this book is about surviving in the present and thriving in the future these problems need not arise.

Roles and responsibility matrix

In Time Frame Two, the Roles and Responsibility Matrix (Figure 4.4) was described, which is a way to identify, at the start of the process, those who will be involved throughout the process. The same system will also work here and should be compiled at the very start when assembling the top management group. It will also help to determine who should be involved with the development of the Islands of Future Focus and the subsequent stages of creativity. Therefore, a typical matrix, which will include the type of roles that will be needed throughout this process, is suggested. The Islands will be developed concurrently. As before, the vertical axis will show the various sequential stages of this process and the horizontal axis the people who will be involved.

Creativity

To create is to be a poet.
(Samuel Smiles 1863)

In the earlier Time Frames, it was first stated that market research precedes the concept stage of the process. This is what the majority of the recent literature on developing new products states. In Time Frame Three, we took this a stage further to show that, near the start, there is constant iteration between concept identification and looking at the market. In reality, it is very difficult to state which comes first and both of these activities can occur at the same time. But when looking long term the creative part comes first. It is necessary to explore what is likely, what is possible and what your organisation wants to do before investigating the market. Furthermore, marketing research as normally undertaken will not work as you are trying to find out what people are likely to want quite a few years before they can get it and perhaps before they even know that they want it. So, the creativity comes before the market investigation. Now is the time, as Alan Topalian says, 'to slap your brain cells'.

In Time Frame Three, the latest thinking on creativity was described. This can now be taken and used to develop the areas that need to be considered. There will be no specification for this creativity but it may be constrained by the Islands of Future Focus and other parameters as identified at the corporate level, which will indicate **REALISTICALLY** what the company should aim to be in the future through their products and services. The aim will be more to identify and specify GANPS and broad conceptual ideas. When these have been generated the sections in Time Frame Three come into play as the Time Frame diminishes. In Time Frame Two, it was stated that people buy benefits. This is one of the keys to the future. Much of the creativity will focus on what benefits people want to their lifestyles and then guide the organisation towards providing products and services that provide these benefits. A checklist of likely lifestyle benefits will be described and these can act as a starting point. If the focus is made on lifestyle benefits then it is possible to do market research on people to find, initially, what benefits they want and then to discover how many people do want these. These can be listed in just a couple of pages. In some cases, the invention seeking will show when what the customers require becomes technically possible. The other Islands will indicate whether your organisation should be the one that provides the eventual product or service.

Although it has been that innovation is all that will be required, there will still be a need for product improvement. Product Status is the key here. It can been adapted to show the areas where improvement around the existing concept is more likely than radical change. But in those areas where there is not an overall radical change in concept there are many subinnovations. The most obvious example is the change in aesthetics in products that otherwise have changed little – the basic concept has remained the same (from curtains to cars). There are other examples which, once again, will allow those decision makers in your organisation to better focus on what to do in the future and, hence, how to manage the future.

Most of the rules of brainstorming work here. The meetings will need to be held regularly, say every month, and it is quite likely that the discussions on GANPS will be carried over from one meeting to the next. This builds in the necessary 'gestation' period that improves creativity. The point of the meetings is to identify realistic long term future developments and so there must be the aim of producing an output which will eventually be developed into a product.

This is an ongoing process that, in theory, will last for ever. As a result, people will leave and be replaced and so there needs to be a thorough recording of what has been decided or rejected and why. It may be that a brilliant idea was rejected as the technology was not in existence and then, some years later, the technology becomes available and the idea suddenly becomes viable. Recording such ideas on an electronic data base with an emphasis on easy retrieval becomes a vital part of such a process. With most new product brainstorming sessions the failed output is of little use after a period of months. Not so this system.

Tools and Techniques for Time Frame Four

It's very easy to predict the future, people do it all the time. The thing you can't do is get it right.

(A. Norman. Apple Computers. 'Open Saturday' BBC 2 TV 19.9.98)

All investment must be linked closely to these objectives. The strategy must be communicated throughout the organisation. There will need to be regular audits of plans and progress checked against the overall strategy. Plans must be adjusted as need be. Bring in extra skills and resources if you are not meeting objectives. If you cannot do it look beyond in house resources, then call in consultants. If you do choose to use consultants then be sure that they have a precise specification to work against. This specification should include the various outputs required and a timescale and cost to achieve these. Only use consultants if you have first fully utilised the knowledge of your internal experts (companies are full of them) and read the available literature on the topic under investigation.

Plan the level and timing of cash calls and estimate the revenues generated over a specific time. Later in the programme this should be done with the aid of the model of the process to be followed (see Time Frame Two, Chapter 4). At this early stage, costs need to be identified. Near the start, the costs are very closely related to people's time and the Roles and Responsibility Matrix will aid this calculation.

GANPS Assessment Matrix

In Time Frame Three, the Concept Assessment Matrix (Figure 10.2) was described, which can be used to identify the most suitable concept of those that all meet the specification. Here, it is developed to take a longer term view of product and service and has been adapted into a GANPS Assessment Matrix. This can be used to whittle down potential new products and services to those that are likely to be more successful and more suitable for a particular organisation in the time frame over six years into the future.

At this stage, the GANPS will not have been developed as far as concepts. The object is to eliminate those that do not suit your organisation or

GANPS

A	B	C	D	E	F	G	H	I	J	Criteria 1 **Judge against the islands**
										√ = accepted X = rejected
√	X	√	√	√	√		√	√	X	Main management guidelines
√		√	√	X	√	√	√	X		Financial fit
√		√	√		√	√	√			Type of company fit
√		√	√	X	√	√	√			Type of market/demographic fit
√		√	√			√	√			Possible skills fit
										Criteria 2 **Judge the benefits against the downside**
7		9	4			11	6			'L' Life style benefits (number)
7		4	2			8	5			'D' Downside points (number)
0		5	2			4	1			L − D =
Y		Y	Y			Y	N			Time to reach market (over, say, six years) Y/N
										(eliminate those under seven years and consider as part of Time Frame Three)
Y		Y	N			N				Technology needed already invented Y/N Eliminate N
N		N								Are existing competitors likely to be a threat Y/N Eliminate Y

$$\frac{√}{C}$$ **Overall 'best' GANPS?**

Figure 16.3   GANPS Assessment Matrix

are 'unrealistic' opportunities. As before, in the matrix, the ideas are assessed through a sequence of viewpoints and in each sequence the unsuitable ones are eliminated.

In the first part, the GANPS are judged against the islands and those which are eliminated are those which are not right for your organisation. The next phase explores the possible time for completion through all stages of development until it will appear on the market. Anything less than six years will come under the earlier Time Frames and should not be part of this. Anything over fifteen years should be put on hold for a period.

It was said earlier that all new products and services, when viewed in the broad sense, compete with something. All right, so it is still just an idea, but it should still be possible to identify the potential benefits/advantages/USPs that the GANPS has over that already on the market. List the number of these lifestyle benefits and the 'downside' points. Can any of these downside points be neutralised with a bit more design work? Although the benefits are not of equal value and the downside points are also of different value, subtract the downside points from the benefits. This will give a comparison between the different GANPS under consideration. In simple terms, the GANPS with the highest total from the subtraction is likely to be the one with the most potential. You can rank the benefits for importance but do not try to weight them as this cannot be undertaken with any degree of accuracy.

The next stage is to see if the technology needed has already been invented (but not necessarily available). It should have been if the idea is viable. The final phase of the matrix is to try and identify if existing products or competitors are likely to be a threat. There is more chance of success if the potential threats are less.

Having undertaken the matrix an overall 'best' GANPS should appear and several should have been eliminated. Continue to view the operation of this assessment matrix with some scepticism. It is clearly a vague process and being used to judge things a long time into the future. On the other hand, it will draw together the various features that should be considered at this stage and enable those GANPS, that are not as good as others, to be eliminated.

What would you want your lifestyle to be in ten years time? The important thing to consider here is that you are comparing what is available **now** with what you can do in (at least) seven years time. You need to make an attempt to extrapolate the development of the current product or service to determine what form it is likely to be in the time scale now under consideration. In some cases this is possible, as we shall explain, but in many cases it is not. For example, you wouldn't come up with the idea for the photocopier however long you spend considering carbon paper. The type of thinking needed is to anticipate what people want to do in their future lifestyles and then try to anticipate the type of product that could fulfil these 'dreams'.

But, as it has already been explained, almost all products improve, but most improvements are in the form of static incremental changes. You will need to assess if the competitive products and services are likely to be developed along static lines – and therefore types of changes more easily predicted, or on dynamic lines – and the type of changes radical. To overcome this apparent dilemma it is proposed that first various (realistic) lifestyle benefits are proposed. Then look at what is already available that goes part way to fulfilling these identified potential needs. This will show if there are aspects of existing products and services that could be adapted or changed, perhaps with a newly available technology, to enable this new product to become a reality. This ties in with product status. Whole areas of existing products will not require radical change and can be improved through static design. Other entirely new products will be indicated and this means the whole may be a dynamic design.

To take the carbon paper analogy, if it is realised that people will want to make lots of copies of the same thing it is clear that multiple sheets of carbon paper is not the answer. A new system must be found that can make multiple copies. This would suggest (at that time) printing (hot metal then) or photography/film. These potential directions could each be explored, bearing in mind the cost/demand implications. Of course, we have the benefit of hindsight in this example and when you are trying to look over the horizon the process is far more difficult and those involved are more likely to end up with the wrong idea. As already said, learning to live with failure is something that managers must be prepared to tolerate when trying to judge the longer term future.

When thinking over 'over the horizon' products try the following:

Where are products likely to go?

Look at existing products and break them into their sub-components and the benefits that these provide. Then look at what is likely to happen to each through (probably existing) changes in technology. Which are the areas that are likely to change dynamically and which will improve in a static manner?

A product example – the computer. To give a more realistic example, we could look at the likely development of the computer. This is an outsider's view and those involved in this business should question the suggestions made below. The point is that it shows how people should try and appraise their products in the longer term.

This is a product in a fast growing area and thus there are likely to be some radical improvements over the next ten years. The product can be split down into its broad component parts and each needs to be considered. Improvements in the memory capacity of the microprocessor has been stunning. Robinson (1996) has observed that 'Semiconductor technology has improved at approximately 30% per annum for the past forty years. This improvement will continue at the same rate for the foreseeable future.' This aspect can be considered as a 'black box' that can be fitted in as and when it appears. It is also right to identify what peripheral services can be added in the light of these improvements. This is an aspect where scenario planning can be used focusing just on this one area of improvement.

The keyboard will be used less but will still be needed. It will change little because the QWERTY user standard will not change. Furthermore, the size of the keyboard is governed by the optimum ergonomics so its size cannot be reduced and this is another aspect that fixes the design. This means that work on improvements to the keyboard should be directed towards aesthetics, reliability and cost reduction. The obvious likely development here is a verbal input to replace the keyboard. Improvements in this area need to be watched closely. The large players have all made attempts at these and the difficulties of voice recognition are well understood. Ten years should see a more acceptable version.

Technology improvements will allow a smaller and lighter configuration of the Central Processing Unit, but it will still need to be big enough to be maintained. The likely improvements to the screen are probably going to be incremental in nature. It may be possible that flat screen LCD technology will be available at a sufficiently low price by then and the developments in this area need to be watched. Otherwise, we can assume that the TV parts of our computers will be as they are today. Again, this means a focus on cost reduction, aesthetics, ease of use and reliability.

There are so many cables needed to join up the parts of a computer when it has been delivered to the customer. Through radio or infra red could the system just operate by being in the vicinity? And, if this could be made to work, could parts of one desk top system be organised to work others in the room – when required? For example, the one printer that will work from all the computers in the room without a myriad of cables?

The use of the Internet will increase, especially if it is possible to put the information down the mains cable. This will make it potentially available to a wider market. And what happens to all those old computers? With such a short life where capacity tends to determine obsolescence rather than actual mechanical failure, what about the potential money making opportunities from computer disposal? In 1997, a quarter of waste from computers was recycled. Can we make money from the other three-quarters? This will not necessarily involve the electronic or computer companies. Other, less glamorous, players will make their business there.

Ring fenced scenarios

Scenario planning has been around for fifty years and has been taken to new levels of sophistication recently. The four main approaches have been to attempt to forecast in four dimensions. These drivers have been **cost, technology, quality and environment**. The most important of these is (again) the cost driven scenario. Public spending is being reduced and companies are not keen to embark on grandiose projects without the support of government. When looking at scenarios in the light of your organisation it should be appreciated that the financial realities will override all other main directions for scenarios.

In Time Frame Two, it was proposed that organisations should look to 'stretching' their products and services, especially at the service end. Looking only at your existing products and services, consider how, with the use of new technology, legislation or other opportunities, it may be possible to offer a new or improved service.

A product example – a restaurant home delivery service. Home delivery of restaurant prepared food and home banking already exist and are very successful. But these particular companies can go much further. If these companies are then linked to the internet a whole range of new services can be supplied via the lines. Local food delivery can be organised on national lines from a central point via a whole franchise (or similar) group of restaurants. The Automobile Association uses many small garages in an organised arrangement so that the nearest deals with a breakdown. Benchmarking this system to restaurants means that the latest forms of communication can be used to run such a system. This means that many of the existing services will remain and these can be linked to the new system of delivery. Each restaurant will work to the same basic menu and cover a particular designated delivery area.

Problems seeking a solution

Having undertaken blueprints (Time Frame One) of your organisation's products and services, bottlenecks or other problems that require solving begin to emerge. This is more apparent the more the detail is included in the blueprint. By using technology or other things that are already available consider ways in which the product or service could be improved. Do not focus on only the problem areas. By taking a broader view of the whole product or process it may be possible to eliminate the difficulty and improve the functioning of the whole.

A product example – luggage transport for airline passengers. A blueprint of the parallel processes that happen as people fly from an airport was described in Time Frame One. It shows that the bottleneck is actually getting people on and off planes. This suggests the focus on which new products and processes could be developed, many of these in the short or medium term. What has not been considered is the apparent anomaly that people are separated from their luggage, almost reunited on the plane, then separated again before finally coming together in the baggage collection point in the airport (if you are lucky!). Could the system be made more effective if the luggage and passengers are separated and not brought together again until the arrival at the final destination? This means that luggage could travel separately from the passengers and perhaps in advance. A whole new infrastructure could be developed around this theme which could mean that one large trunk would be collected from your door a day or so before your journey. You meet up with your luggage again in your hotel room. The passengers would have an easier journey to the airport and fewer luggage trolleys would be needed. Checking in could be done automatically by swipe card tickets a short while before boarding. Baggage handling would be undertaken some way from the passenger terminal and the existing terminal would be (virtually) for dealing with people and their hand baggage only. There are, of course, security implications, but is this a possible GANPS?

Linking technologies

As said earlier in this Time Frame, the fast growing areas are electronics, communications, new materials, pharmaceuticals and biotechnology. This means you must consider how these are used in, or interface with, your products and services. If you operate in areas or with products that are the fast growing areas, consider how likely improvement may be linked together to form new products or services. For example, floppy disc faxes, where digital information can be fed to a floppy disc at the other end of a telephone (or electric mains?) line.

Life style benefits

Another way of identifying potential GANPS is to take a broad view as to what people want to improve their lifestyle. It should then be possible to propose products and service areas within your organisation, Islands of Future Focus that could eventually fit into these niches. Again, you must think long term. If, when looking at a niche, a clear configuration of the full product or service can be imagined, then you are not thinking far enough ahead. If such ideas do spring to mind, then they fit into the type of product and service dealt with in Time Frames Two and Three. When seeking improvement in their lifestyles people and society seek products and services that:

Save time, save resources, save space, simplify life, improve the quality of life. (These will give you a competitive advantage and are related to lifestyle growth areas.) To these broad headings can be linked many of the types of attributes customers seek – as described in Time Frame Two. There is not a simple link to each of these and there is an overlap between some. Below, we have linked the broad areas of lifestyle improvements to these attributes – we have also shown, in brackets, the direction that these **may** take. Some of these will be static changes and, as such, the concept may not change. This will still be correct for GANPS which are still likely to be static ten years hence.

SAVE TIME
Faster
Easier Installation (e.g. no wires)
Easier to obtain (e.g. home delivery)
Altering time frames (e.g. video)
Home entertainment (touch, taste and smell virtual reality)
Labour saving
Time saving (e.g. home banking, home delivery, one-stop or internet shopping)

SAVE RESOURCES
Easier communication
Easier to dispose of. (e.g. biodegradable)
Environmentally cleaner (including opportunities in waste disposal and collection)
New forms of packaging (e.g. packing that can be fed to the birds)
Do it yourself products

SPACE SAVING PRODUCTS
This, essentially, means making things smaller. This may, or may not require a new concept.

SIMPLIFY LIFE
Easier to use, more simple (if it isn't obvious how to use it, it is the fault of the product not the user)
More reliable (hence the need for Total Quality Management)
Easier to obtain (e.g. home delivery)
Less anxiety (products that always work as they should, to insurance schemes)
Home entertainment
Labour saving (e.g. self-cleaning cars)
Time saving (e.g. home banking, home delivery)

IMPROVE QUALITY OF LIFE
Greater security (e.g. crime prevention measures for the home and car)
More reliable (hence the need for Total Quality Management)
Better performance
Less anxiety
More adventure ⎱
More enjoyable ⎰ Holiday ideas
Easier communication
Keeping fitter
Keeping well
Healthier foods (e.g. less fat)
Products to make you look good/look young (between the years 2000 and 2021 the number over the age of 65 will increase from 21% to 24%. And in the same period the number of 50–65 year olds will increase by 30%)
Products and services associated with sport
Gender products (e.g. make up for men)

Products to overcome the bad effects of the future. We are currently walking less than we used to. In 1978, the average person walked 250 miles each year. Now this is down to an average of 200 miles in 1998. This suggests a need for more exercising equipment, health clubs, and dietary aids – and what else? Litigation is increasing and thus so will the services associated with this and protection against it.

Products to overcome changes in the future. In 1964, 62% of the UK population didn't have a car. In 1979, this was down to 43% and in 1994 to 32%. In the same period, the number of people who had more than three cars had quadrupled. It has been estimated that in the next twenty years in the UK there will be an additional 10 million cars on the road. The effect of this would be gridlock. It is unlikely that this would be allowed to happen and it is speculated that legislation will be introduced to prevent this from happening. Such legislation will probably restrict the actions of certain individuals (e.g. by making car parking in towns more difficult) but will also introduce opportunities and new (transport?) products and services.

Products that cost less. Emerging technology often allows 'more for your money', or more features for the same price. 'Emborgeoisement' has been described in Time Frame Three and this may come about as technology makes things cheaper.

Incremental improvements. These will be needed for static products even when taking a long term view. These improvements may also be included with new radical products: more economical/cost reduction, (what the rich do today we like to copy tomorrow – greater economies of scale); better aesthetics; better ergonomics; casual fashion items.

And other problems seeking a solution. (But at a profit.) Like just being completely different.

The above shows the type of thinking that can be adopted to realistically guess at the future of an already existing, but fast changing, product type. Only a shortened version is described but, in reality, the logic should be taken much further to fully appraise the direction that can be taken with existing products or GANPS.

The 'downside' of the potential new product or service

The next stage of the process is to look at the 'downside' of your proposal. This has two functions. If the proposal has too many disadvantages compared with the potential of the current product then it is reason enough not to bother. Remember that the benefits and disadvantages are not of equal weight. An idea with many apparent advantages may be brought down by one disadvantage, e.g. it is potentially unsafe. Consider the benefits and disadvantages for various market niches. The benefits often alter or are eliminated when the comparative niche is varied.

There are really only a few major broad aspects that make a GANPS unlikely to be accepted and therefore a probable failure. These tend to keep a product static:

1 A large existing infrastructure around the existing product or service that cannot easily be adapted to be used with the new product. To replace the internal combustion engine would require a great leap of an improvement for organisations to be prepared to 'dump' their existing knowledge and equipment to make or service a new system.

2 There are conformance standards (e.g. BSI or ISO) that specify the existing product. These tend to be updated about every five years and perhaps can be altered in the light of new developments. This can be a risky thing to try and take on.

3 There are 'user standards' that mean potential customers will need to change what they have already. For example, these could include a collection of CDs that would not work on a new system and the customers would need to be convinced that what you are offering makes it worthwhile disposing of an existing collection. Look at the tight hold the VHS system has. We prefer to keep a less than ideal system as we all have so many tapes of the old format.

4 European or national legislation that fixes a particular configuration. In the longer term, are these likely to alter?

5 If there are a few large players in the market then, unless your organisation is one of those large players, it is very difficult to be a maverick and change things if there is no desire to or if there is no profit to be made from the change.

Most other things may be resolvable or may just show that the proposal is not really worth the effort of eventual development. The second function of identifying the potential downside is to focus on aspects that may need to be improved with the idea. Can the disadvantages be eliminated by the application of new technology? Does this new technology exist yet? When is it likely to appear? Will your organisation be able to obtain it, master it and use it?

Competitor activity

Your organisation must keep a view on what your competitors are likely to do in the long term. But, as said, most companies do not think very far ahead so don't be surprised if you find that this is the case with your competitors. Most of your direct and familiar competition will be using the same technology and are unlikely to be very different from you. Therefore, they need not be a threat if you move forward at least as fast as them. If you rely on competitive analysis you will always be following the herd. In many cases, the skill is not to try to surpass the competition but to take steps to neutralise it.

The major threats will come from further away. Competition should be viewed as anybody or any organisation that takes the money of potential customers away from you. On the other hand, your opportunities may not be an opportunity for others. They may not have your advantages.

Technology

If the proposal for the product still looks good the next stage is to look at the technology needed to bring it to fruition. Existing technology may be patented, can you obtain the patent rights (for use in at least seven years time)? Can you leapfrog the existing technology and enter into the next stage of the lifecycle?

Remember that what is possible is very different from what is likely, what many want and many will be able to afford. Furthermore, the cost may just be too high (in more than financial terms) to make many projections become reality. Regularly, the press makes a forecast of the future. In the light of what has just been said is the following likely, accepting that it is not the best source of reference, (all from *The Sun* 20 February 1998)?

In the year 2000, we will have 'Thinking Dustbins' that will automatically sort our rubbish into recyclable piles. One year later, 'every house' will have a large screen home cinema. The following year, we will be wearing 'singing shirts'. In 2011, we will have 'household slave robots' to do our housework (again). And so it goes on until in 2020 we will be living underground, in 2044 there will be space colonies on Mars and in 2050 there will be cheap space travel and we will have 'virtual sex partners'. Eh . . . no. We have just taken a trip forward fifty years. If you now look back fifty years, we live much the same. Change is not frantic.

As said earlier, it generally takes about ten years for a new technology to reach a marketable form. It may be that long until you are able to include it in your service. Those who own the technology may not wish to be in your market and with these perhaps you can go in for some kind of joint venture. If it is a competitor who has access to the technology, then this may be reason enough to make a planned exit from the market, as described in Time Frame Two. As described there, it should be possible to plan your departure from that particular market and maximise profit whilst so doing. There is plenty of time and opportunity to move into new products and markets.

There are also other opportunities for joint ventures. Perhaps you can go in with another company which has synergistic skills that will allow for both of you to benefit from the development but, combined, be strong enough to defend your stance against the competition. There may even be cases where you can develop the GANPS with the competition. They may be stronger than you but they may not have thought of the idea. There are obvious dangers with this and, again, the risks must be judged against the potential benefits.

Also, as has been said earlier, in this Time Frame, it is necessary to ring fence your scenarios, if you cannot develop the necessary technology and nobody that you know is actively working to develop it. Then, until you hear otherwise, you must assume that it will not appear. The principal of developing a product with a 'black box' in which to fit in potential new developments as they occur only works if they are likely to actually appear when you need them. You will need to keep a focused look at developing patents or, again, consider joint partnerships with a company which is capable of developing this 'black box'. And if they say that they can't within the period under consideration then you should seriously reconsider the sense of moving in that direction.

Are you proposing something that will be produced in large, medium or small quantities (mass, batch or unit production). In view of this, are you still the right type of organisation for this GANPS? If you are not at the moment you probably have time to adapt - if you want to. Most organisations do not wish to alter their potential production volumes. Moving from, say, batch to mass production can cause significant disruption in organisation as well as requiring a significant investment. Likewise, a mass production outfit may not want to become involved in a small market niche. Whatever is the decision, with this long-term planning at least you have the time to implement your decision.

Does the GANPS fit into your organisations growth areas? What other organisational changes are you likely to have to make? Can you succeed in your current location? If not are you prepared to move (see the list on business location)? What are the limits to the technology that you are currently using (speed, operations per hour, etc.)? For example, optical fibre has 250,000 times the capacity of copper wire but is more expensive to lay in the first instance. When considering the additional cost, it is worthwhile speculating on all of the additional services that can be supplied, both in the short term and the long term within the life of the cable, when taking the decision on which to lay.

If you decide that you still want to do it, you have an indication on the areas on which you must focus – what has to be done and what aspects of your organisation will need to be improved or changed. Do you still want to do it? Carry on. If you do not want to do it, **START AGAIN**. It is important to know when to stop and the best indication is when the GANPS fall outside the Islands of Future Focus.

If you still have a list of suitable GANPS, the next stage is to be realistic and consider what other organisations could also develop this potential product. Are you really the best outfit to attempt to do this? This may mean that you do not develop the idea as the likely competition will be too fierce. You may still be able to develop the idea because the likely competition may not have considered the potential of the particular GANPS. If you can control enough of the development to be able to keep it a secret until it appears on the market than you may have a lead over your competitors which will make it worthwhile continuing. Perhaps, if it is a product (you can't patent services) you can protect your intellectual property through patents – if this can be afforded within the budget. If, during the development, it becomes known that the identified stronger competition are developing a similar product it may be reason enough for your organisation to abandon it.

You may still have too many GANPS to cope with and, therefore, here you need to apply Pareto to help you focus on those ideas that are likely to give you the biggest return for the smallest financial outlay.

As well as identifying these generations after next products and services it's also necessary to (broadly) plan the likely methods of production and implementation. Plan the shift from product to process design. It was this 'jump' that many companies were unable to do at the start of the 1980s that caused the demise of the majority of players developing biotechnology.

Who Finds Things Out?

Having identified the GANPS, there needs to be one person who must spend two days each month compiling the information related to these potential products – a 'long range researcher'. The seniority of this person is not important but they must have the ability to see how technical breakthroughs, patent applications or just other activity can be applied in the areas under consideration. What is needed is a lively mind. This person is likely to be a technical librarian as much of the research needed is similar to that undertaken by technical librarians. They also need to be able to absorb knowledge from the local scientific community so that your organisation can create new knowledge. Proposed new legislation that forms a threat or opportunity needs also to be tracked by this individual. Also, this person will need to validate speculation about the future regarding demographics, purchasing habits and likely changes in life styles.

Francis Bacon said that 'knowledge is power'. The problem today is not the availability of data and information, it is being able to access the right information easily whenever you need it. It has been said that more information has been produced in the past thirty years than in the whole of the previous 5000 years (and here is another chunk). The information must be stored and archived in a form (probably electronic) that can be easily accessed and the relevant bits accessed when required. What is important is data storage, retrieval, processing and disposal.

All this may sound a lot for one person to spend only two days each month doing. This activity needs to be carefully controlled and focused to only investigate things relevant to the GANPS. It is one of those activities that can easily conform to Parkinson's law and grow to fit the time given to it, however much time is allowed.

Re-use and evaluation

Study the past, if you would devine the future.
(Confucius)

If the role is to be extended then consider learning from experience. We seldom bother to assess what might be done differently if we could have the particular experience over again. Twenty-twenty vision, afforded by hindsight, is a marvellous asset to increase our chances of future success (Topalian and Stoddart 1997; Wassermann and Moggridge 1990). So, to quote the US philosopher and poet George Santayana (1863–1952), 'Progress, far from consisting in change, depends on retentiveness. Those who cannot remember the past are condemned to repeat it.' Such repetitions lead to time and resources being wasted on fire-fighting and re-working old territory unnecessarily. Though dissatisfaction with the status quo can act as a drive to unlock creativity, irritation and frustration more often wear away our enthusiasm and blind us to fresh insights; they stunt our ability to break loose and create radically different futures. We constrain ourselves to incremental development at best.

The future presents multiple possibilities, some beneficial, some threatening. To cope with these eventualities we need to 'map' them out and formulate strategies to avoid or deal with them (Topalian 1995). To quote Alan Topalian (Topalian and Hollins 1998), 'dealing with the future innovatively may frequently feel like getting on a crowded moving escalator moving the wrong way: it is harder to make headway and you have to look further ahead to give yourself more time to cope with the future that is coming at you faster than you wish. Visualisation is a key tool for "previewing" those futures.'

Take your time – you probably have plenty

The assessment matrix is far from easy to implement and the temptation is to cut corners to speed up the process. Remember that what you are attempting to do is identify your likely product and service offerings that will maintain your organisation's survival. In that light, it is worth putting in a fair degree of time and effort by those people who have been designated to work on the company's future products and services; this group may be known as the 'futures circle'. And as you are considering quite a time into the future, there is really no need to rush. Far better to get it right by taking your time and doing it thoroughly. And don't worry if you seem to be spending a lot of time and have, apparently, little to show for it. As the Nobel Prize winning scientist Marie Curie said: 'One never notices what has been done: one can only see what remains to be done.'

Part of this is to plan in the whole life cycle of the organisation's existing products and then plan the introduction of the new. When will your current markets decline? Of course, this goes on with the introduction of any new product but here you are trying to plan for the product generation after the product generation after next – and the timings of introduction and deletion are far more vague.

Marketing research

Predicting markets is harder than predicting technology
(Robinson 1996)

Having identified the GANPS, the next stage is to do some rudimentary market research (you haven't done any yet). Peter Hutton (1995), director of the marketing research organisation group MORI, has said 'Marketing in the past has been about developing products in response to well defined needs. Marketing of the future will be about developing products in response to newly emerging needs which reflect the under-lying value shifts in society.' This must be borne in mind when seeking products and services for the future. Your organisation has some possible new products and they are still years away. The form of the market research must look at benefits as the GANPS have not yet been formed much beyond these, and not yet even as far as a concept. The team have identified a series of perceptions as to what the likely product should be able to do. It is now necessary to find out how many people outside of the organisation actually agree that this is the type of thing that they want. This must be done anonymously. If potential customers believe that a particular product or service, which is still some years away, is imminent then it will damage the sales to your existing customers. They may wait for it rather than buy what you currently do.

To summarise the process

As can be seen, the process described is quite different to that normally described for product development. The parameters are described at the beginning and then a type of concept stage is held in which GANPS are identified. These are then assessed and, having completed this, rudimentary market research is then undertaken. This system cannot be market led as the market does not know enough about what it wants and, furthermore, much of what the market actually wants for the future is neither possible or advisable for your organisation. The market will be offered possibilities within defined parameters and they can then confirm, or not, whether they want products and services of this type – whether they really want these benefits.

Ease of use v. technology improvements

As users get more used to new technology it is possible to make the systems more complicated. When a new concept is first introduced users need to be introduced to it (through promotion) and trained in how to use it. As new developments appear, associated with this product, the knowledge can be built upon using the existing knowledge as a base. In other words, things get more complicated. This flies in the face of our call to make things easier. It must be remembered that if the complication grows quickly the company introducing the improvements may alienate the new users, because there then becomes too much to learn in one go. The effect may be to limit the users to the existing users, and the market stagnates.

Therefore, with increasing complication that may come with increasing technology there must also be an increase in the application of ergonomics to make the systems usable to an ever wider group of people. This book was typed on Word 6 and Windows 97 and the latter is considerably more difficult to use than the former. Lots of improvements but also lots more complication and, probably, insufficient consideration of exactly what the user actually needs.

To Summarise this Book

You are here now with this product or service. Using Time Frame One of this book, you can find the tools and techniques to improve the product now. This ensures survival now. Through product status, it is possible to identify those areas where it seems likely that a type of product will go. Therefore, it can direct those of your products and services that are changing incrementally (static design) and those that are changing innovatively (dynamic design). Static design requires product improvement and this is covered in Time Frame Two. Dynamic Design requires innovation and this is covered in Time Frame Three.

You can then identify the organisational areas that need to be accentuated in the development of your new product and services and the tools and techniques needed to improve or innovate or abandon the product are identified. This ensures survival into the future with this product or enables the organisation to move in a new direction. Therefore, you can arrive in the future with the right product.

So, now you are in the future with competitive products and a healthy organisation. Having arrived here, over the past few years you have been developing first a process and from this the products and services that ensure your continuing survival and profitability. The average age of survival for new companies is only twelve years. On the other hand, many companies survive for more than one hundred years. Your organisation is going in the right direction to being one of these. On the other hand, 'if space and time are, in fact, the same thing the future may be happening somewhere else right now', said Omaat on Einstein's work in 1924.

Now you know in which direction the organisation is likely to go you can now formulate a realistic Mission Statement and a suitable Corporate Identity (see Time Frame One). You can also start to obtain and/or train people to get you into your future. This is how you should use empowerment. We are not alone in believing that the main discriminator between the successful and unsuccessful companies of the future comes down to how they use their people. 'People should be viewed as the principle source of sustainable competitive advantage for firms' (Bigler 1996). 'People are the only source of sustainable competitive advantage' (Pfeffer 1994).

Employees need direction but they also need space to think, plan and make that future. They need new skills, which means training and education and they need motivation. They need help and training to deal with fears. Then they will be in a position to be truly empowered to participate in creating the future.

End Note

In this book, we have endeavoured to take new product development beyond that which most people are currently considering. Do we understand the management of new products and services in the long term clearly enough to be able to specify a future for others to follow? Well, we think this has been achieved but we will have to wait and see. A lot of what we have said is unexciting and may now seem fairly obvious. If it is, then why are so many people predicting quantum leaps into the unknown in all areas. It is the unsurprising predictability of so much of the future that not only makes it tolerable, it also makes it manageable. We hope that we will promote further discussion on how (and if) managers and practitioners can prepare for the future.

It will not be easy, as a Chinese Proverb says, 'Forecasting is difficult, especially with regard to the future'.

Whatever happens, you shouldn't fear the future. Not only should you welcome it, you should also help to bring it about. The future is about change and change is easier if you control your destiny. Ambrose Bierce, in *The Devil's Dictionary*, first published in 1911, described the future as 'that period of time in which our affairs prosper, our friends are true, and our happiness assured'.

> **May you always live in the future – Bill and Gillian Hollins**

References

Anderson N.G. (1975) *From Concept to Production: A Management Approach*. Taylor and Francis.

Andreasen M. (1994) *Design Model*. *WDK Workshop on Evaluation and Decision in Design*. Technical University of Denmark, Lingby. May 2–3.

Andrews B. (1998) Student Presentation. Part time MA Design Strategy & Innovation. Brunel University

Anon (1995) 'Enhancing quality in service industries'. *Journal of Services Marketing* **10** 3:3–4.

Belbin R.M. (1981) *Managing Teams: Why they succeed or fail*. Heinemann, London.

Bierce A. (1958) *The Devil's Dictionary*. Dover Publications Inc, New York.

Bigler W. (1996) 'A blueprint for regenerating firms'. *Long Range Planning* **29** 2 April.

Birtwell A. (1998) Student Presentation. Part time MA Design Strategy & Innovation. Brunel University

Bishop R. (1990) *Teamwork route to product success*. Eureka Transfers Technology. October

Bishop R. (1992) Editorial Comment: 'CEO attitudes of what is important in European Manufacturing Organisations over the next five years'. *Eureka*. **12** 2:3. Findlay Publications.

Blake P. (1998) 'Accelerating Product Development Using Rapid Prototype Systems'. Time Compression Technologies.

Bradley D.A. and Buur J. (1993) 'The Representation of Mechatronic Systems'. Proceedings International Conference on Engineering Design. The Hague. August.

Brown M.A. (1993) 'Why does TQ fail in two out of three tries?' *Journal For Quality and Participation* **16**, 2 March.

Brown P. (1996) 'Understanding our own history'. *Strategy*. *Strategic Planning Society* **5**: 2, May.

BS0 (rev. 1997) *A Standard for Standards*. The British Standards Institution

BS 4778 Part 1 (1987) Quality Vocabulary, International Terms. London: British Standards Institution.

BS 7000 Part 1 (1989) *Guide to Managing Product Design*. London: British Standards Institution. (now withdrawn)

BS 7000 Part 1 (1999) *Guide to Managing Innovation*. London: British Standards Institution.

BS 7000 Part 2 (1997) *Design Management Systems: Guide to Managing the Design of Manufactured Products*. London: British Standards Institution.

BS 7000 Part 3 (1994) *Guide to Managing Service Design*. London: British Standards Institution.

BS 7000 Part 4 (1996) *Design Management Systems: Guide to Managing Design in Construction.* London: British Standards Institution.

BS 7000 Part 10 (1995) *Design Management Terminology.* London: British Standards Institution.

BS 7373 (1998) *Guide to the Preparation of Specifications.* London: British Standards Institution.

BS 7750 (1994) *Environmental Management Systems.* London: British Standards Institution.

BS EN ISO 9000 (1994) *Quality Management Systems.* London: British Standards Institution.

Bunce A. (1994) 'The original lateral thinker'. *Professional Manager.* 3 5, September.

Bush S.A. and Sheldon D.F. (1993) 'Whose Cost is it Anyway?' Proceedings International Conference on Engineering Design. The Hague. August.

Cambell A. (1997) 'Contextual Design – Design in Context'. The European Academy of Design Conference. Stockholm. 23–25 April.

Camp R. (1989) *Benchmarking.* ASQC Quality Press, Milwaukee Wisconsin.

Church J. (ed.) (1996) *Social Trends.* CSO. HMSO London.

Clausing D. (1998) 'Reusability in Product Development'. Design Reuse: Engineering Design Conference '98. Brunel University. 23–25 June.

Clipson C. (1996) Talk, Brunel University. 18 June.

Confucius (551–479 BC) Quote taken from the Analects.

Constable G. (1993) 'Concurrent Engineering – its procedures and pitfalls'. *Engineering Management Journal.* 215–218. October.

Coombs R. (1994) Innovation Management Seminar. University of Warwick. June.

Cooper R.G. (1983) 'A process model for industrial new product development'. IEEE Transactions of Engineering Management **EM30**, 1:2–11.

Cooper R.G. (1988) *Winning At New Products.* Kogan Page.

Corfield K.G. (Chairman) (1979) *Product Design.* London: NEDO.

Crawford C.M. (1987) 'New product failure rates: a reprise'. *Research Management* July/August 20–24.

Cox B. and Nelson T. (1996) 'The shape of the future'. *Strategy* Issue 06. The Strategic Planning Society. June.

Cronin Jr J.J. and Taylor S.A. (1992) Measuring service quality: a re-examination and extension. *Journal of Marketing* **56** 3:55–68.

Crosby P.B. (1979) *Quality is Free: The Art of Making Quality Certain.* New York, McGraw Hill.

CSO (1996) Labour Market Trends.

de Bono E. (1986) *Six Thinking Hats.* Viking.

de Bono E. (1993) *Handbook for Positive Revolution.* Harper Business.

de Geus A. (1997) in Michael Johnston. 'Managing for profit or survival'. *Strategy* Issue 12. February.

Deming W.E. (1986) *Out of the Crisis* 2nd edn. Cambridge Press.

Design Council (1985) *Innovation. Study of the problems and benefits of product innovation.* London: Design Council.

Design Council (1993) *Take-up of Concurrent Engineering in UK Industry.* Engineering.

Design Council (1994) *Comment on the Draft for Public Comment of BS7000 part 3.*

Droz D. (1995) 'Prototyping: a key to managing product development'. *Business Strategy.* May/June.

Drucker P. (1985) *Innovation and Entrepreneurship.* Heinemann.

DTI (1993) 'Innovate or liquidate'. 90s News. March.

Eder W.E. (1990) 'Engineering education: needs and recommendations for a design-based curriculum'. Proceedings International Conference on Engineering Design. Dubrovnik. August.

Elliot C. (1993) 'Turning dreams into specifications, pt 2'. *Engineering Management Journal*. April, 3.

EMAS (1995) EC Eco-Management and Audit Scheme for Local Government. Dept. of Environment.

Engineering (1997) Editorial. April.

Eppinger S.D., Whitney D.E., Smith R.P. and Gebala D.A. (1993) 'A model-based method for organising tasks in product development'. Working paper. Sloan, MIT May.

Eureka (1990) 'Technology speeds up time to market'. *Comment*. August.

Farish M. (1996) Editorial. *Engineering*. January.

Fisher E. (1994) 'Total Quality: hit or myth?' *Accountancy*. April.

Fisher T., Press M., Chapman G., Rust C. (1996) *The Management of New Product Development: Creativity and Teamwork*. Art & Design Research Centre. Sheffield Hallam University.

Gerrels J. (1997) Comment. *Eureka*. December.

Gibson R. (ed.) (1997) *Rethinking the Future*. Nicholas Brearley, London.

Gisser D. (1965) 'Taking the "chances" out of product introduction'. *Industrial Marketing*.

Godet M. and Fabrice R. (1996) 'Creating the future: the use and misuse of scenarios'. *Long Range Planning*. **29** 2: April.

Handley R. (1995) *Strategy News*. November.

Handy C. (1994) *The Empty Raincoat*. Arrow.

Haynes R.M. and Du Vall P.K. (1992) 'Service Quality Management: a process-control approach'. *The International Journal of Service Industry Management* 3: 14–24.

Health and Safety at Work Act (1974) London: HMSO

Heller R. (1992) *Management Today*. November.

Henley Newslink (1996) 'Innovation by Satellite'. Spring

Hobbes T. (1651) *The Leviathan*. Penguin.

Hollins W.J. (1988) 'Product status and the management of design'. *Engineering Designer*. **14** 4:13–15.

Hollins W.J. and Pugh S. (1989) 'Product Status and the Management of Product Design – What to do and when'. Conference Proceedings. International Conference on Engineering Design. Harrogate. August 1989.

Hollins W.J. and Pugh S. (1990) *Successful Product Design: What to do and when*. Butterworths.

Hollins G. and Hollins W.J. (1991) *Total Design: Managing the Design Process in the Service Sector*. Pitman, London.

Hollins W.J. and Hollins G. (1992) 'An International Perspective on Keys to Managing the People Side of Design'. The Design Management Institute's West/92 Conference Santa Cruz, California USA, March 1992.

Hollins W.J. (1995. 1) 'Quality Starts With Designers'. *The TQM Magazine* 17 2. MCB.

Hollins W.J. (1995. 2) 'How Do You Justify a Design Project to the Accountant?'

Proceedings of the 11 International Congress of Project Engineering. Bilbao 4–5 October. San Sebastian. 6 October.

Hollins W.J. (1996) 'Are Current Management Practices Damaging Long-Term Design Management Effectiveness?' Proceedings 8th International Forum on Design Management Research and Education. Barcelona. 20–23 November.

Houston W. (1996) *Riding the Business Cycle*. Little Brown, Boston

Huda F. (1997) 'Total Quality Management in Voluntary Service Organisations: Residential and Nursing Care Homes'. PhD Thesis. University of Westminster.

Hurst K. and Hollins W.J. (1995) 'Improved Product Design Specification Compilation'. Proceedings International Conference on Engineering Design. Praha. August.

Hutton P.F. (1995) Talk at the Auto Fellowship Meeting. March.

IBM/London Business School (1996) 'Made in Europe 2: An Anglo-German Design Study'.

IEE (1995) Scientific Morality 2 IEE NEWS. October.

Janis I. (1972) *Victims of Groupthink: A psychological study of foreign-policy decisions and fiascoes*. Houghton Mifflin.

Jewkes J., Sawyers D. and Stillerman R. (1969) *The Sources of Invention*. 2nd edition London: MacMillan, New York.

Jones J.C. (1980) *Design Methods: Seeds of Human Futures*. Wiley.

Johnston M. (1997) Managing for Profit or Survival. *Strategy* Issue 12. February.

Katz A. (1993) 'Eight TQM pitfalls'. *Journal for Quality and Participation* **16** 4: July/August.

Klein B.H. (1977) *Dynamic Economics*. Cambridge, Massachusetts: Harvard University Press.

Kotler P. (1988) *Marketing Management: Analysis, Planning, Implementation and Control*. Prentice-Hall.

Lauterborn R. (1993) IAS Agency Seminar. London. December.

Leppit N. (1993) 'Concurrent Engineering: a key in business transformation'. *Engineering Management Journal*. 71–76 April.

Levitt T.H. (1960) 'Marketing Myopia'. *Harvard Business Review*. July–August.

Lewis B.R. and Entwistle T.W. (1990) 'Managing the service encounter: A focus on the Employee'. *International Journal of Service Industry Management* **1** 3:41–52.

MacDonald A. (1992) *Aesthetics in Engineering Design*. SEED (Sharing Experience in Engineering Design)

MacDonald J. (1992) 'Reasons for failure'. *The TQM Magazine*. August.

MacLachlan R. (1998) 'An imaginative leap from serendipity to capability'. *People Management*. 14 May.

Majaro S. (1990) 'Innovation and top management'. *MBA Review* **2** 1: March.

Majaro S. (1992) *Managing Ideas for Profit: The Creative Gap*. McGraw-Hill.

Mattsson J. (1994) Improving service quality in person-to-person encounters: Integrating findings from a multidisciplinary review. *The Service Industries Journal* **14** 1:45–61.

McCorkle D.E. (1994) 'Climb out of the cellar of your mundane brainstorming session'. *IDM Exchange*. Issue 1 Autumn.

McMaster M. (1996) 'Foresight: exploring the structure of the future'. *Long Range Planning*. **29** 2: 149–155 April.

Mersha T. and Adlakha V. (1992) 'Attributes of service quality: The consumer's perspective'. *International Journal of Service Industry Management* **3** 3: 34–45.

Mintzberg H. (1994) *The Rise and Fall of Strategic Planning*. Prentice Hall.

Moorhouse B. (1997) 'Selling a vision'. *Design Management Journal.* Winter

Morita A. (1992) Lecture for the DTI at the Royal Society. Reported in *Eureka.* March.

Mortimer J. and Hartley J. (1990) *Simultaneous Engineering.* Dept. of Trade and Industry.

Morup M. (1993) 'Design for Quality'. PhD thesis. Institute for Engineering Design. Technical Universty of Denmark. Lyngby.

Murrell K.F.H. (1969) *Ergonomics: Man in his working environment.* 2nd edition. Chapman and Hall.

NatWest. (1996) *Innovation Briefing 3 Marketing.*

NEDO (1992) *Stimulating Innovation in Industry.*

Nesbit P. (1992) 'Common barriers to successful TQM implementation'. *Quality Forum* **18** 2: June.

Osborne A. (1953) *Applied Imagination.* Schibner.

Osborne A. (1993) *Applied Imagination.* Schibner.

Peters T. (1997) *Thriving on Chaos.* Harper & Row.

Pfeffer J. (1994) *Competitive Advantage Through People.* Harvard Business School Press. Cambridge. Mass.

Pugh S. (1982) *Total Design Method.* Loughborough University.

Pugh S. (1983) 'The Application of CAD in Relation to Dynamic/Static Product Concepts'. Conference, ICED83, Copenhagen, 15–18 August.

Pugh S. (1986) *Specification Phase.* SEED (Sharing Experience in Engineering Design).

Pugh S. (1991) *Total Design.* Addison-Wesley.

Parnaby J. (1996) 'President calls on city to back innovation'. *IEE News* 112: 4th April.

Randall L. (1993) 'Customer Service Problems: Their Detection and Prevention'. Service Superiority Conference. Warwick Business School 25–26 May.

Rawlinson G. (1994) *Creative Thinking and Brainstorming.* Gower.

Redmond J. (1995) 'Design Philosophy and Product Research'. Procs. ICED 95. Prague.

Ringland G. (1998) *Scenario Planning: Managing for the Future.* Wiley. p. 92.

Robinson G.W. (1996) 'Technology Foresight – The Future of IT'. *Long Range Planning.* **29** April.

Rohatynski R. (1990) 'Process of Technical Design Operational Approach'. Proceedings International Conference on Engineering Design. Dubrovnik. August.

Roy R., Weild D., Gardiner P. and Potter S. (1995) *Innovation Design Environment and Strategy. Block 4 Innovative Product Development.* The Open University.

Santayana G. (1863–1952) *The Life of Reason.*

Schein E.H. (1969) *Process Consultation; Its Role in Organization Development.* Addison-Wesley.

Schwartz (1998) *The Art of the Long View.* Wiley.

Senge M.P. (1990) *The Fifth Discipline: The Art and Practice of the Learning Organisation.* Century Business.

Shelley T. (1994) 'Managing data for optimum efficiency'. *Eureka Transfers Technology.* November.

Shostack G.L. (1984) 'Designing services that deliver'. *Harvard Business Review.* Jan/Feb.

Skinner C. (1997) 'Mock the title, heed the message'. *Management Today.* April 1997.

Smiles S. (1863) *Industrial Biography*. David & Charles.

Smith D.G. and Rhodes R.G. (1991) 'Specification Formulation – a structured approach'. Poster Session. International Conference on Engineering Design. Zurich. August.

Smith P.G. and Reinertsen D.G. (1991) *Developing Products in Half the Time*. Van Nostrand Reinhold.

Spottiswoode C. (1996) 'Blockbuster meeting'. *Strategy* Issue 08 September 1996.

Starr M.K. (1963) *Product Design and Decision Theory*. Prentice Hall.

Stephenson J.A. and Wallace K.M. (1996) 'Design For Reliability for Mechanisms' (in Huang G.Q. (ed.) *Design for X: Concurrent Engineering Imperatives*, London: Chapman Hall 245–267)

Thompson J. (1996) Paper presented at The Agile Organisation Conference.

Topalian A. (1980) *The Management of Design Projects*. Associated Business Press. London.

Topalian A. (1984) 'Corporate Identity: Beyond the Visual Overstatements'. *International Journal of Advertising*. **3**. 55–62.

Topalian A. (1995) 'Design in strategic planning. Proceedings of the Challenge of Change'. 3rd International Conference on Design Management. University of Art and Design, Helsinki. August.

Topalian A. and Hollins W.J. (1998) 'An innovative approach to developing the new British Standard on innovation management'. Design Research Society Conference Quantum Leap managing new product innovation. UCE. 8–10 September 1998.

Topalian A. and Stoddard J. (1997) 'New R&D management: How clusternets, experience cycles and visualisation make more desirable futures come to life'. Proceedings of Managing R&D into the 21st century conference, Manchester, July 1997, Volume 2.

Tora B. (1993) *The Second Financial Revolution*.

UK Government (1994) *Helping Business to Win*. Government 1st White Paper on Competitiveness. May.

Van de Vliet A. (1997) 'Build joy of use into all you provide part 4: Hamel in Perish not the Thought'. *Management Today*. April.

Vaugon M.R. (1996) *Business Monitor SDQ 11: The UK Service Sector Quarter Two*. Office for National Statistics, HMSO, London.

Walker D. (1989) 'Design or Decline'. Video, Design Management Series. Open University.

Walker D. (1998) 'Design Has Been Stolen'. *Engineering Designer* **24** 2.

Warihay F. (1993) 'Total Quality in service organisations'. *Journal for Quality and Participation* **16** 3: June.

Wasserman A. and Moggridge B. (1990) 'Learning from experience – An approach to design strategies for product success'. Proceedings of Product Strategies for the '90s Conference, London; *Financial Times*. October.

Wheelwright S. and Clark K. (1992) *Revolutionizing Product Development*. Free Press, NY.

Wikstrom K. and Erichsen S. (1990) 'Design Models Used in the Development of North Sea Oil Installations Compared with Theoretical Design Models'. Proceedings International Conference on Engineering Design. Dubrovnik.

Woodson W.E., Tillman B. and Tillman P. (1992) *Human Factors Design Handbook*. McGraw-Hill 2nd edn, New York.

Index

ALIEN ARRIVAL

SALVATION or DESTRUCTION

MICHAEL FITZGERALD

Schiffer Books are available at special discounts for bulk purchases for sales promotions or premiums. Special editions, including personalized covers, corporate imprints, and excerpts can be created in large quantities for special needs. For more information contact the publisher:
Published by Schiffer Publishing, Ltd.

4880 Lower Valley Road
Atglen, PA 19310
Phone: (610) 593-1777; Fax: (610) 593-2002
E-mail: Info@schifferbooks.com

For the largest selection of fine reference books on this and related subjects, please visit our website at **www.schifferbooks.com.**

We are always looking for people to write books on new and related subjects. If you have an idea for a book, please contact us at proposals@schifferbooks.com.

This book may be purchased from the publisher.
Please try your bookstore first.
You may write for a free catalog.

CONTENTS

INTRODUCTION

A liens are among us already and their activities have increased enormously with the arrival of the new millennium. There is strong evidence that extraterrestrial visitors played a part in creating and developing human civilization in earlier times.

Many people claim to have made contact with aliens. Most of these encounters are peaceful, but sometimes witnesses give accounts of having been kidnapped by extraterrestrials. They have given remarkable descriptions of advanced alien technology and a superior extraterrestrial civilization.

The Moon and Mars are the two closest planets to Earth and both show strong evidence that, at least in the past, there was intelligent life upon them. Now it seems highly probable that the same is true of Jupiter's moon.

Throughout the history of the period that UFOs first became recognized as a unique phenomenon, there have been numerous examples of cover-up and conspiracies by the authorities. The whole UFO field has been dogged by concealment, suppression of evidence, and deliberate disinformation from an early period.

The way in which human evolution has been affected by alien "genes" in the past is considered, as well as the possibility of future genetic interaction between humans and extraterrestrials. It has been claimed that we will find definitive proof of the existence of life on other planets within the next twenty-five years. If that is true, it would be one of the most remarkable and powerful events in the history of the human race.

The question of why the extraterrestrials are arriving on Earth in such large numbers is also addressed and reasons suggested for their visits and activities. We shall examine their motives and propose an explanation for their often baffling behavior.

ALIENS AMONG US

Extraterrestrials have been visiting earth for thousands of years and perhaps even longer. From the time of the Second World War onwards, they have been observed in ever greater numbers, and the beginning of a new millennium has seen a sharp increase in both sightings of UFOs and in reported cases of contact between humans and aliens. The volume of traffic between our world and extraterrestrials is now so immense that we could almost speak of an alien invasion of our planet.

Why are they coming to earth in such numbers? What do they want with our planet? Have they come to harm us or to bring us the wisdom of the stars?

There are many theories about why the aliens are coming to earth in such large numbers. They may wish to destroy the world, exterminate humans, and replace us as the dominant species on earth, enslave us, steal our natural resources, harvest our crops, or seize animals— and even humans—as food. There are also stories that human brains have been extracted by them as tissue.

There are many accounts of humans being kidnapped and subjected to strange and often sinister medical experiments. Abductees have also reported a possible breeding program designed to produce a hybrid species that is half-human and half-alien, combining the best features of both species.

Many aliens appear malevolent, but others appear to be messengers from more advanced civilizations who have come down to earth to bring us their wisdom and help us save the planet. With the threats of war, increasing natural disasters, and growing environmental problems, the space travelers could have come to earth to heal the planet and show us the way forward into a new and better future.

Humans and aliens interact in a variety of different ways. Some aliens appear instantaneously, seemingly arriving out of nowhere, while others are observed entering or leaving spaceships. A few are only visible to one or two observers, while others are clearly witnessed by large numbers of people.

The number and variety of aliens arriving is surprising. They are often perceived as being humanoid in form, but also appear as animals, insects, robots, substances, or even holograms. At times, no physical entity is observed, but a process of thought transference takes place rather than, or as well as, physical sightings. This type of mental interaction often precedes direct contact.

Contacts between humans and aliens are also made in a number of different ways, which will be discussed in detail in the next chapter. An equally relevant question is why it is that, on the whole, ordinary people rather than political and military figures report contacts between humans and aliens. Is it that extraterrestrials consciously avoid such authority figures or is it perhaps that such contacts do take place, but the details are withheld from the public?

DIFFERENT TYPES OF ALIENS

There are approximately ten principal types of alien beings. These are the main categories with their various subdivisions:

HUMANOIDS

Including the "human" type that is indistinguishable from ordinary human beings; humanoids that seem nearly the same as humans, but with subtle differences; flying humanoids; giants; and apparent children.

GRAYS

Small grays, tan grays, officers, Supreme Commander (almost always described as being a tall female).

ROBOTS

Metallic robots, fleshy robots, slabs.

ELEMENTALS

Beings resembling fairies, elves, dwarves, and similar creatures from mythology and folklore.

ANIMALS

Big cats, reptiles (sometimes referred to as "reptoids), insects, birds, hairy mammals, and dolphinoids.

MONSTERS

The best-known example of this type is the Cyclops.

"SUBSTANCES"

Blobs are the best-known example of this type.

HYBRIDS

The result of alien-human genetic experiments, also almas.

SPACE BROTHERS AND SISTERS

Wise, benevolent beings, the males often being bearded.

HOLOGRAMS

Apparently holographic creations, rather than physical realities.

HUMANOIDS

The most common type of aliens reported by observers, contactees, and abductees belong to the humanoid category. Some are entirely indistinguishable from ordinary humans and that group, in particular, has generated fierce controversy among Ufologists. Although, technically, the Grays belong to the humanoid class, their often striking differences and the variety of sub-forms among them make it more appropriate to treat them as a category on their own.

HUMANS

There are a number of theories about this type of being:
1. They are humans assisting aliens;
2. They are humans engaged in secret government projects;
3. They are the offspring of human-extraterrestrial mating;
4. They are human beings carrying out hoaxes;
5. They are non-human entities revealing themselves to us in a form that our human awareness is able to grasp.

Hilda McAfee and her mother made a remarkable sighting in 1972 at Las Cruces in New Mexico. They described seeing two human-looking figures standing between five and a half and six feet tall. The men were wearing blue overalls with matching boots, belts, and gloves. Their faces were covered with helmets and they were working on some sort of vehicle, though neither woman was able to give a clear description of the craft. They said that it appeared to be surrounded by a bright blue light, which hid the true shape of the object from them. Near the two men were some small black rods. The figures took no notice of the women and one even had his back turned to them. By the time their car had driven by, the women looked back cautiously and noticed that the object had now vanished.

The bright light they saw earlier seemed to have been turned off. Their impression was that it had been switched on to avoid collisions. Both women said that their bones hurt, their chests ached, and that they had suffered burning. This case probably represented a secret US government experiment, rather than an encounter with genuine aliens.[1]

HUMANOIDS

Reports of humanoid type figures similar to ordinary humans, but with subtle differences, such as a greater or lesser number of eyes, the absence of a mouth or ears, limbs that lack hands or feet, or that appear to be attached to the torso, rather than a continuation of it, have all been described by observers. In other respects, they are identical with ordinary human beings. This class of alien is one of the most frequently reported.

FLYING HUMANOIDS

Reports of humans flying in the sky date back for thousands of years. The first sighting since the age of the recognition of the UFO as a separate phenomenon seems to have taken place on 6 January 1948, when Bernice Zaikowski in Chehalis, Washington, was standing outside her barn at three o'clock in the afternoon and heard a peculiar noise coming from above her. As she glanced upwards to the sky, she was astonished to see a man flying straight past with a pair of silver wings on his back. He was flying at a height of somewhere around 200 feet above the ground. What makes this sighting particularly impressive is that it was also witnessed by a group of children who had just finished school and were making their way back home.

The man, observing his "audience," then began performing maneuvers in the sky, before finally placing his hand on his chest and appearing to touch some sort of button. He immediately ascended vertically higher into the air and disappeared.

Not surprisingly the story attracted the interest of the local media. Here is part of the coverage by the press.

CHEHALIS, WASH. — (UP) — THE STATE OF WASHINGTON, WHERE THE FIRST FLYING SAUCERS WERE REPORTED, OUTDID ITSELF TODAY. A WOMAN REPORTED THAT SHE HAD SIGHTED A "FLYING MAN."

MRS. BERNICE ZAIKOWSKI, 61, CHEHALIS, SAID SHE SAW A MAN WITH WINGS ATTACHED TO HIS BACK FLY OVER HER BARN AT AN ALTITUDE OF 200 FEET AND DISAPPEAR TO THE SOUTH.

MRS. ZAIKOWSKI SAID THE UPRIGHT BIRDMAN MADE A "SIZZLING AND WHIZZING" NOISE AS HE CLIMBED AND BANKED IN FLIGHT, BUT THAT HIS WINGS NEITHER FLAPPED NOR ROTATED. SHE SAID SHE COULD SEE NO MOTIVE POWER SUCH AS PROPELLER EITHER ABOVE OR IN FRONT OF HIM.

On the morning of 18 June 1953, in Houston, Texas, three neighbors, Howard Phillips, Judy Meyers, and Hilda Walker, were all sitting on the porch of their apartment block when they saw a huge shadow passing over the lawn. At first, they thought it was a moth caught in the reflection of a nearby street light, but then they saw it stopping in a tree. To their utter amazement they saw that it was a man with wings similar to those of bats. He stood about six feet, six inches tall, wore extremely tight clothes with a cloak or cape, and appeared to be emitting a peculiar gray light. He remained in full view for around fifteen minutes, before slowly appearing to fade and disappear. The three observers heard a loud noise and then saw a white object that they said was shaped like a rocket vanishing.[3]

BATWOMAN IN VIETNAM

In August 1969, three US soldiers serving in Vietnam saw a truly bizarre example of a flying humanoid. At one o'clock in the morning, they saw a trace of movement in the skies above. As it came closer, they stared in bewilderment to see a naked woman with wings like those of a bat. The witnesses described her skin as jet black and yet also shining with a weird, green light. She flew right above them, only around seven feet over their heads. The batwoman was completely silent until she was about ten feet away from the soldiers' camp, when she began flapping her wings vigorously. As they watched this extraordinary sight, they noticed that there seemed to be no bones in the female's arms.[4]

THE OWLMAN

The best-known modern "flying humanoid" is the strange Owlman that has visited the West Country of England and is particularly active in the region of Mawnan in Cornwall. The first reported sighting of him occurred on 17 April 1976, when June Melling and her sister, Vicky, saw a large man hovering over the village church, wings attached to him.

On 4 July, in the same year, two teenage girls on a camping holiday heard an unusual noise in the woods. As they gazed in astonishment, they saw a figure standing in the trees only about twenty yards away from them. One of them stated that the figure resembled a large owl and had bright, red eyes that seemed to glow. Both girls thought it was a practical joke until, to their amazement, they saw the figure take off and fly away.

The following morning, another woman saw the creature. She described it as being "like a full-grown man, but the legs bent backwards like a bird's." When it saw her, it rose upwards and flew into the trees. She noted the red eyes, adding that it had a large mouth, and a body of silver-gray, as were its feathers. The legs reminded her of the claws of a crab. Between 1977 and 1978, there were a number of sightings of the Owlman in the region of Mawnan church.[5] The entire phenomenon was witnessed by many different people and remains a baffling mystery.

ORANG BATI

The Indonesian island of Seram has a story about a flying humanoid known as an orang bati. The local population claims that it lives inside the extinct volcanoes on the island. It is described as standing about five feet tall with red skin, large wings like those of bats, and a long tail, but having an otherwise human appearance. At night, the orang bati are said to leave their homes in the volcanoes and venture out to the human dwellings, where, from time to time, they steal a child and take it back to their volcanic homes.[6]

GIANTS

Sightings of giants long predate the age of UFOs. They are infrequently reported in connection with UFO sightings, though some contactees and slightly more abductees have spoken of meeting or at least observing them.[7]

APPARENT CHILDREN

There are two main types of this form of ET: the "wise babies" and the tuyul. Wise babies take the form of normal human children, but appear to be exceptionally advanced compared with the young of our own species. It has been suggested that they are the result of human-extraterrestrial mating.[8] The tuyul, like the orang bati, is native to Indonesia and is described as a bald, completely naked, child with very red skin and huge eyes. In other respects it bears a considerable resemblance to the Grays. One unique aspect of the tuyul is that when it moves, its feet never touch the ground.[9]

GRAYS

In recent years, the "Grays" have become the most commonly reported type of alien, particularly in the United States. They have almost become fashionable and some of the more committed Ufologists refuse to accept sightings of any other type of alien as being a genuine report. In spite of this dogmatic approach, the grays are by no means the only type to be reported credibly and in any case they too have a number of sub-groups among them.

SMALL GRAYS

These are generally described as standing between three-and-a-half to four feet in height and as having gray or grayish-white skin. They are extremely pale and have exceptionally thin arms, legs, and trunks. Some appear to have neither knees nor elbows and tend to have disproportionately big heads. On the whole, they have no signs of a nose or body hair and their ears are either missing altogether or extremely small. The mouths are either non-existent or no more than a tiny slit. The most pronounced feature about the small grays is their huge, almond-shaped coal-black eyes. These are often spoken of as their means of communication with humans. The small grays have often been compared with the "worker" ants or bees and their behavior frequently appears robotic and purposeless.

TAN GRAYS

The "Tan Grays," sometimes referred to as the "Tall Grays," often work in tandem with the Small Grays. They have a darker-colored skin and are usually around five feet tall. The Tan Grays appear to supervise the various medical tests that are performed on abductees and many of them even claim to be doctors.

OFFICERS

These Grays tend to be around six feet in height and appear to be in charge of the other groups around them. They vary slightly in terms of their physical description, but there is general agreement that they are taller than the other Grays and make the decisions.

Sometimes they are described as being more similar to humans in their physical development than the other types of Grays. They certainly appear to be more intelligent than the robotic small Grays, who are the most frequently observed specimens of their type.

SUPREME COMMANDER

This being is said to be around seven feet tall and to have very dark skin, though, sometimes, its skin will be extremely pale. It is almost invariably said to be a female figure and she will generally wear a veil, cape, or cloak.[10]

ROBOTS

Two different types of robots have been reported and both demonstrated an entirely mechanical form of movement. There are "metallic robots" that look like chunks of metal or tin cans. "Fleshy robots," sometimes called "androids," either resemble humans or, less commonly, animals (generally reptiles).[11]

Particularly unusual types of robot aliens are the strange entities seen in Prospect, Kentucky, on 27 January 1977. Lee Parrish, then aged nineteen, was driving back home in his jeep when he saw a large UFO burning brightly in a rectangular shape, hovering above the trees nearby. The radio of his car broke down, and Parrish found his jeep being drawn irresistibly towards the lights of the UFO, but then it shot straight up into the sky. It was only when Parrish returned home that he found his trip had taken him half an hour longer than it ought to have. His eyes were also bloodshot and painful.

Undergoing hypnotic regression to try and find out what had happened during the "missing time" period, he recalled that his jeep had been drawn up into the air by a powerful force and he had found himself inside a circular room within the spacecraft. Then he saw three strange beings, one of which stood at the colossal height of twenty feet and was shaped "like a suitcase," having a raised section on top in the shape of a semicircle. The entity was black with a single arm. The second alien stood at about six feet, was red, and also had only one arm. The third was also six feet, white with a curved profile, and a head shaped like a wedge.

Parrish sensed that the second alien was frightened of him, but it came towards him slowly and touched him with its arm. When it did so, the youth felt extremely cold. Then all three of the entities faded into one another and vanished, whereupon Parrish found himself back in his jeep once more. After the encounter, he had the sense that they would contact him again, but no further communication or experiences followed.

ELEMENTALS

AWAY WITH THE FAIRIES

Under this heading are included a variety of sightings where the creatures resemble the fairies, elves, dwarfs, goblins, and similar beings from folklore. One of the most striking modern cases where "fairy" types of entities were involved is a remarkable story from Rowley Regis, near Birmingham, in the West Midlands of England. On 4 January 1979, Jean Hingley had just said goodbye to her husband and she saw him leave for work. She was about to go back into her house when she witnessed a large, orange globe directly above the garage, measuring about eight feet.

To her astonishment, her dog suddenly fell unconscious and, to her even greater amazement, she saw three tiny figures flying out of the orange sphere and entering her house through the front door, which was still open. They made a "buzzing" noise and she rushed inside, following them into the living room. There they shook the Christmas tree violently before landing on the settee and jumping up and down.

When Hingley, with remarkable presence of mind, demanded some sort of explanation, they touched a button-type device on their tunics and mumbled gibberish back at her. She then, still in a state of shock, offered them a mince pie. The aliens tried to eat the pie, but were unable to do so, after which they became angry. They "zapped" the unfortunate woman with laser-type beams of light from their helmets. The beams hit Hingley on her head and blinded her temporarily, as well as burning her skin. Then the creatures picked up a number of objects, such as videotapes, and looked at them.

After about an hour, they flew out of the house through the back door and entered the orange sphere before flying off and vanishing. Not surprisingly, the woman was badly shaken by her experience. She managed to telephone her husband and also called the police. A forensic team examined the landing site and saw clearly two parallel lines in the snow.

She described her visitors as around three-and-a-half feet tall, without any hair on their heads, but with huge, black eyes that stared at her from inside their bubble-shaped helmets. They wore long silver tunics with silver buttons and on their shoulders were some sort of glimmering streamer-type material. They had large, round wings similar to a butterfly's.

It was about a week after her unfortunate encounter that her sight returned to normal. It took several months for the burn marks inflicted by the lasers to heal. She also found that their radio and television sets no longer worked and the cassette tapes that the aliens handled were also inoperable.[12]

ANIMALS

ALIEN BIG CATS (ABCS)

Sightings of these animals seem to be largely confined to the British Isles, principally England, although often seen in North America as well. A considerable number of the animals have been photographed.

Perhaps the most famous alien big cats (ABCs) are the "Surrey puma" and the "Beast of Bodmin." During the 1990s, four wild leopards were found dead in Britain and over 300 sightings of ABCs were reported.

Sheep and calves have also been found dead with claw marks upon them and the flesh stripped away from their bodies. Farmer Rosemary Rhodes twice videotaped a black leopard on her farm after four of her sheep were torn to pieces. Experts believe the "Beast of Bodmin" is probably to blame.

It has been suggested by some people that the animals are extraterrestrial in origin and that they enter our world through "space warp portals" in order to prey upon wildlife.[13]

REPTILES OR "REPTOIDS"

These are technologically advanced ETs, described by witnesses as tall, strong, having green-colored, scaly skin, and faces like those of lizards. Reptoids are claimed, especially by abductees, to be hostile and malevolent beings. They are said to be the masters of the essentially robotic Grays.

Reptoids look on the Earth and its inhabitants as something to be exploited for their benefit, used as "lab rats" for medical experiments, "brood mares," or sperm banks for their genetic programs, and as resources to be used, even as food.[14]

LIZARD MAN

The "lizard man" that was seen in July 1983, at Mount Vernon, Missouri, was one of the most unusual and remarkable sightings of its kind. It began with Ron Watson and his wife, Paula, seeing some flashing silvery lights coming from a nearby field. They watched through a pair of binoculars and saw two figures wearing silver suits moving their hands over a black cow that lay in the field.

As they started pulling their hands upwards, the cow was dragged up into the air, as if it was being winched up by some invisible force. It then floated into a nearby UFO, shaped like a cone, with a mirror-like surface that was so highly polished that it was almost undetectable by the naked eye.

The Watsons then saw two more aliens at the side of the UFO. One was about six feet in height, looking like a giant lizard with green skin, large eyes, and webbed hands and feet. The other alien reminded them of Bigfoot.

Ron Watson told his wife that he meant to get up closer to see if he could have a proper look at what was going on. Paula managed to talk him out of the idea. Then the three aliens went inside the UFO, which promptly disappeared.

Later, the farmer in the neighboring field told them that one of his black cows had gone missing. When the Watsons told him they had seen his animal abducted by a UFO, he refused to believe them.[15]

SCAPE ORE MONSTER

This is another reptilian type of creature found mainly in the bayous and swamps of the American South. In 1988, the "Scape Ore Monster" was seen in the region of the swamp in South Carolina from which it took its name.

On 29 June 1988, seventeen-year old Christopher Davis was driving home. As he crossed Scape Ore, his car tire was punctured. He pulled over to the roadside to try and repair the damage. Just having finished fixing the tire and about to go back home, he saw a strange seven-foot-tall humanoid figure running towards him from the field nearby. Its eyes were fierce and glowing red in the darkness around him.

Davis leapt into his car and drove off just before the creature reached him. He fought to get his car back on the main road as the reptilian creature pushed its hands through the window of his vehicle, which was still wound down. Davis saw three long fingers, green skin, and black nails. As he drove away, he saw the creature pursuing him.

To his horror, he realized that it had jumped on top of the roof of his car and its long fingers were fastened to his windshield, trying to hold on. Davis, not surprisingly, gunned the motor and, as the car accelerated away, the creature leapt off the vehicle. With considerable relief, he made his way home, but refused to get out of the car until his father came out of the house to meet him.[16]

INSECTS

These sightings are among the most controversial in the whole field of Ufology. As with similar phenomena, such as ABCs, many simply refuse to regard alien types other than variants on the "Grays" as being genuine ETs. Others point to the rich diversity of life on Earth as counter-examples and question why life on other planets should be any less varied than our own.

The most famous sightings of insectoid types are the "Mothman" events that occurred in Point Pleasant, West Virginia, during 1966 and 1967. For thirteen months, over a hundred people saw a huge, headless, winged being. All agreed that it was seven feet tall with massive red eyes that glowed from its upper body. The "Mothman" was dark gray in color and had huge wings. These wings remained completely still, never flapping when it was airborne.[17]

Less well known, but equally dramatic, is the account of Baltimore University law student Mike Shea. Shea was on his way to meet a friend in Olney, and driving along the road with plenty of time to make the appointment, when he saw a bright light over a barn around 150 feet away from the road. The light seemed to come from a large object that hovered above, and a bank of yellow and red lights flickered on and off from the craft.

When the light switched off again, Shea continued his journey, but had an eerie sense that he was being followed. As it dawned on him that the UFO was flying directly overhead, he became extremely nervous. His anxiety increased when he sensed an electric current running along his back. Then he reached Olney and went to the bar to meet his friend. When he arrived, he found that the time was nine o'clock at night—not seven as he had thought.

Ten years after this frightening event, Shea contacted the abduction expert Budd Hopkins. He was hypnotically regressed and Shea recalled seeing four figures standing by the side of the road. They were dressed in a sort of black armor with huge eyes and black heads. They had six legs and Shea described them as looking like grasshoppers. Then he stopped his car and was taken on board the craft for a medical examination, a number of different samples being taken from him.[18]

GIANT BIRDS

One of the most remarkable sightings of giant birds was seen in Salt Lake City, Utah, on 18 July 1966. On that day, the residents saw a huge bird, described as being "about as big as a Piper Cub airplane," which circled the city. An equally spectacular sighting took place in December of the same year in Gallipolis, Ohio, where one of the four pilots who witnessed it exclaimed in horror and amazement: "My God! It's something prehistoric!"

This type of sighting is rejected by many Ufologists, but more and more of them are coming to understand that the phenomenon is far wider than simply the ubiquitous "Grays" and that creatures, such as giant birds, do have a part in the UFO story.[19]

MOCA VAMPIRE AND CHUPACABRA

The "Moca vampire" came to the notice of researchers in the 1970s. At that time, an outbreak of inexplicable animal deaths hit Puerto Rico, particularly around the town of Moca. Ducks, pigs, geese, and goats were all slaughtered and all of them had been drained of blood. Strange lights were also seen in the sky at the time these killings took place. No actual sightings of the beast were made and it has been suggested that it was simply the same as the better-known chupacabra.

The chupacabras (goatsuckers) began to attack animals (principally, but by no means exclusively, goats) and drain the blood right out of their bodies by making small holes in the animals, often at the back of their heads.

Unlike the mocas, chupacabras have been seen and are described as having strong hind legs, thin forearms, with sharp claws, and standing about four feet tall. The creatures have fangs, pointed faces, and big red eyes. Their activities began in 1995 at the town of Orocovis, but they soon widened their sphere of operations. As with the mocas, inhabitants also complained of seeing bright lights in the sky whenever the unexplained killings took place.[20]

HAIRY MAMMALS

Probably the best known examples of this species are the Bigfoot (Sasquatch) and Yeti (Abominable Snowman). The Bigfoot is a tall and extremely large apelike creature, covered with extensive body hair and found principally in the Pacific Northwest region of America. The Yeti is most commonly seen in the Himalaya mountain areas.

Another hairy mammal type sometimes observed is the yeren. This is principally found in the Shennongjia Mountains in the central Chinese region. It is described as being between five and six feet tall, with large feet and having long, shaggy, red hair.[21]

Sightings of these creatures long predate the UFO phenomenon, which makes many Ufologists deny any relationship between the two. All the same, they have sometimes been seen in the same vicinity as UFO activity.[22]

DOLPHINOIDS

These are aquatic aliens with the ability to communicate with humans through the use of telepathy. Unlike the Reptoids and the Grays, they are benevolent beings wishing to help humanity and they struggle against the Grays and Reptoids and work towards harmony, peace, and a better environment. In many respects, they are a more contemporary version of the Space Brothers and Space Sisters.[23]

MONSTERS

CYCLOPS

On the evening of 28 August 1963, three boys in Belo Horizonte, Minas Gerais, Brazil, stumbled upon a terrifying entity. The three of them were out in the back garden of their home when they saw a ten-foot wide orb over the house. It was a transparent globe and the boys saw a number of aliens inside the craft wearing helmets and spacesuits.

Two sharp and bright beams of light were then directed onto the ground by the craft and one of the aliens floated down between the two streams of brightness. As the entity landed, the boys saw with horror that it had only one eye and no body hair. It stood at about ten feet tall and walked towards the boys. The "Cyclops," as they christened it, spoke to them in a language they did not understand and made some sort of movements with its hands.

The eldest of the three boys picked up a rock and was preparing to hurl it at the alien, when it turned to face him. On the front of his suit was a small box-like object and the entity sent out a ray of light from it that struck the boy on the hand and forced him to drop the rock. Then the alien tried to speak once more, before giving up and floating back upwards to the UFO, which then flew away.

The boys told their parents about the encounter. The father looked at the garden and saw a number of triangular marks in the earth where the "Cyclops" had been walking.[24]

SUBSTANCES

BLOBS

In the early morning of 20 December 1958, two Swedish men were driving along the road when, at about three o'clock, they saw a thick fog blanketing the road that compelled them to reduce their speed. The road was in the middle of a forest, but, not far off, stood a clearing from which they could see a dazzlingly bright light shining.

They left the car to take a better look, but as they got closer saw that the light came from an object in the form of a disk that stood on tripod-like legs about two feet in length. The disk "seemed to be made of a peculiar, shimmering light that changed color."

At this point, the men saw a number of beings that they described as "blobs." They were blue and looked "like protozoa, just a bit darker." The entities leapt about the disk "like globs of animated jelly." Then they moved towards the two men, trying to pull them towards the disk.

They had great physical strength, but it was the overpowering stench of them that the men noticed. The men described it as smelling like "ether and burnt sausage." Making a supreme effort, one of them managed to escape from the blobs and run to the car. He began sounding his horn to try and draw attention. The noise appeared to frighten the aliens, who then retreated and went back inside the disk. Soon after, the UFO ascended into the sky and flew off at a tremendous velocity.

The two men went home and, to their horror, found that the appalling smell of the beings clung to them for days. It made them feel extremely nauseous and they went to see a doctor, who could find no apparent signs of illness or injury. Then they reported the encounter to the government and the Swedish Defense Staff interrogated them about the events of that morning. During the course of the investigation, officials discovered some marks in the ground where the strange craft had stood. The men were also later questioned under hypnosis and it was concluded that they were telling the truth.[25]

HYBRIDS

ALMAS

The almas are mainly found in the Altai Mountains of Mongolia and the Tien Shan mountains of China. They are said to be half-human, half-ape, and there are even drawings of the strange creatures.

A female alma was found in the forests of Mount Zaadan in the Caucasus at the latter part of the nineteenth century. She became pregnant by one of the villagers and gave birth to a number of children.

It has been suggested that the almas represent scattered survivors of Neanderthal tribes, but of course it has also been suggested that they might be the result of mating between humans and extraterrestrials.[26]

HUMAN-ALIEN CHILDREN

These beings, often referred to as hybrids, feature prominently in many alien abduction accounts. Many abductees report seeing on board the spaceships a kind of nursery in which they see incubators, fetuses floating in vessels, and even crèches with hybrid children. These infants are generally described as rather sickly and the abductees are frequently either encouraged or ordered to hold and even nourish them. It is clear from some of the accounts by the abductees that artificial insemination had taken place and that subsequently the foetus had been removed from the female's body during a subsequent abduction.

The probability is that experiments of this type appear to be genetically motivated and many researchers suggest that the aliens are trying to create a new species with half-human, half-alien DNA.[27]

SPACE BROTHERS AND SISTERS

These entities were very commonly reported during the 1950s and 1960s. Since that time, they have been seen far less frequently. They are worried about the future of the human race, particularly its warlike nature and lack of regard for the environment, and they came to warn humans to mend their ways.

The Space Brothers and Sisters looked exactly like any other human being. Their planets of origin were very varied, both within our own solar system and from different, faraway stars. They were always said to be tall, handsome (or, in the case of the sisters, beautiful) and golden-haired. Although they still occasionally reveal themselves to humans, they are now, sadly, a rarity.[28]

HOLOGRAMS

Some aliens, and particularly some of the worlds in which the contactees and abductees find themselves, appear to be more in the nature of holograms or of a holographically created world, rather than physically real in the ordinary sense of the word. The cases of Cynthia Appleton and Carlos Diaz are particularly good examples of this.[29] Various scientists, particularly David Bohm and Karl Pribram, have found the notion of a "holographic universe" one of the most useful tools for unlocking the mysteries of quantum theory.

THE ROSWELL INCIDENT

One of the most remarkable of all UFO claims concerns the strange events that occurred at Corona in 1947. That something unusual happened in that region at approximately the time claimed is not disputed by the most hostile critics. Precisely what that was, however, has long been a matter of furious contention among Ufologists.

As the Roswell affair has been more extensively written about than most other aspects of Ufology, only a brief discussion of it will be given here.

Essentially, at some time between late May and early June 1947, two objects crashed: one at Corona, where its wreckage was discovered by local rancher Mac Brazel, and another at San Agustin. There have been numerous books on the subject and the most probable explanation is that what crashed on Brazel's ranch and was taken away for analysis by the Roswell Air base was a top secret military balloon. The San Agustin object was probably one of the secret projects carried out by former Nazi scientists recruited to the service of the US government under Operation Paperclip.

The film of the alleged "alien autopsy" has long since been exposed as a fake. There were bodies found at Roswell, but they were almost certainly not those of aliens.[30]

VARGHINA THE BRAZILIAN ROSWELL

On 13 January 1996, the fire service of Varghina City, in the state of Minas Gerais, Brazil, received a telephone call asking them to rescue a strange animal that had been observed in the local park. When they arrived, the fire-fighters saw a humanoid creature with brown skin, big red eyes, three ridges on its head, and standing about three-and-a-half feet tall.

The senior firefighter immediately contacted the military base at Coracoes. The rest of the crew managed to catch the entity and place it inside a wooden crate, which they then gave to the military on their arrival.

Strange enough, later that day at half past three in the afternoon, three women saw another creature in approximately the same area. They screamed and ran away. Then a crowd gathered around the mysterious being and, once again, the fire service was called in. This time they arrived together with the military, who caught the creature with a net and took it away.

These two aliens were witnessed by no fewer than sixty different people. The second one was taken to the hospital, where it is said to have died on 22 January 1996. The doctors who carried out the postmortem said that it had no clothes and no apparent sign of any sexual organs, navel, or nipples. From the corpse came an overpowering smell of ammonia. The dead alien was then taken away by the army and nothing further is known about the matter; nor is there any word on what happened to the first captured alien.

Three months after the two entities were captured, a woman saw yet another one outside a local restaurant where she was eating. Only three weeks after that sighting, a man driving his car saw yet another alien as he was turning a corner. The entity was startled by the headlights of the car and vanished.[31]

MYSTERIOUS APPEARANCES

THE CHILDREN OF WOOLPIT

Throughout history, there have been a number of cases involving people who seem to have literally appeared out of nowhere and even more where they have abruptly and mysteriously vanished without trace. The case of the "children of Woolpit" dates back to the eleventh century A.D. and is certainly baffling. It seemed as if the children emerged from a crater in the earth. They spoke no English and were green-skinned in color. The girl was aged about twelve and her brother slightly younger. Beans were the only item of food they appeared able to eat.

After a period of adjustment, they were taught English and told their hosts that they came from a land known as St. Martin's. They had no idea how they had appeared suddenly in Woolpit. As they gradually became accustomed to their new home, they lost their green color and took on an ordinary human appearance. The boy died young, but the girl went on to become a domestic servant before ending her days married to a man from King's Lynn in Norfolk.[32]

KASPAR HAUSER

An extremely famous and well-documented case of an appearing person is the story of Kaspar Hauser. He first appeared in Nuremberg in 1828. A cobbler noticed a young man staggering in his direction with a strange look on his face and hardly able to stand. He held out a letter addressed to the captain of a cavalry regiment in the town. The only phrase he seemed able to say was: "I want to be a soldier like my father was."

Before long, he was taught German and he gave his name as Kaspar Hauser. He had many marked peculiarities, being at first able to eat and drink nothing but bread and water. He also had a strong intolerance to light, which gave him severe headaches, and he was almost incapable of using his hands and feet. A Professor Daumer took an interest in the young man and soon told the world about his extraordinary life before he was discovered wandering the streets of Nuremberg.

Kaspar Hauser claimed that he had spent the whole of his previous life in a tiny cell where two windows were permanently blocked up and neither sound nor light penetrated. His cell was maintained at a constant temperature and was always lit from a power source that he was unable to see. The only food and drink he ever had was bread and water and he had no idea of any difference between day and night. Until his arrival in Nuremberg, he had never seen another living thing. Only once did he become aware of someone's presence when a hand from behind him guided his own hand in tracing his name and writing the letter that he brought with him to the city.

He remembered being carried out of his cell one day and led down some steps, before being brought by an unknown companion into Nuremberg, where he was abandoned after boots had been placed on his feet.

Some time after he had related his strange story to Daumer, the first of two attempts were made on his life. The first attempt was when he was stabbed with a knife, but the wound was not deep and soon healed. Later, he received a note asking him to meet someone in the public park. Soon after his arrival there, he returned home in a state of collapse with clear signs of a stab wound in his chest. He claimed that both stabbings were the work of the same man, the one who had first brought him to Nuremberg. Soon afterwards he died.

There are a number of curious features about the Kaspar Hauser case that make it quite possible that he was an alien who had landed on earth from a spaceship. His physical difficulties in walking, his intolerance of sunlight, and the fact that he had a lump at the back of his knee instead of the normal hollow, all hint at some genuinely strange experience lying behind his story and possibly some unusual genetic condition.

Most puzzling of all is the fact that, in 1828, there was simply no way of keeping a room at an even temperature or maintaining a light burning night and day. All these conditions, however, could have been obtained on board a spaceship. It is impossible to see how he came to invent details about the constant temperature and ever-burning light, when no such technology existed on earth. On the other hand, if Kaspar Hauser was brought to earth from a spaceship, such conditions could and would have been entirely possible.[33]

NAKED MAN IN CHATHAM

A bizarre incident involving an "appearing person" took place at Chatham, Kent in 1914. Shoppers were stunned to see a naked man literally appear out of nowhere. A moment earlier he had not been there and yet suddenly and inexplicably he appeared.[34]

MYSTERIOUS DISAPPEARANCES

GONE FROM THE LINCOLN TUNNEL

Cases of people disappearing into thin air are perhaps more common than mysterious appearances out of nowhere. One of the most startling and inexplicable cases took place in 1975 when Jackson Wright and his wife, Martha, were driving towards New York. As a result of snow that had formed on the windows, they stopped the car in the Lincoln Tunnel. Jackson got out to wipe the windshield and Martha, who had gone to clean the rear window, simply disappeared.

She did not die in the tunnel, which was searched extensively, and nor were the police able to find any clue as to her whereabouts. A tunnel is hardly the most obvious or even the easiest place in which to disappear, and yet that is exactly what happened. Martha Wright literally vanished into thin air in the middle of the Lincoln Tunnel.[35]

GONE FOR FIVE

An equally baffling case is Armando Valdes, a corporal in the Chilean army. In 1977, in full view of six of his men, he suddenly vanished for a period of fifteen minutes. On his return, his men noticed that the calendar on his watch had gone forward five days and he had a five-day growth of beard on his face.

Valdes remembered nothing about his disappearance and could give no account of what had happened to him or where he had been during the "missing" period. Yet, in the presence of six witnesses, the corporal had vanished into thin air and reappeared fifteen minutes later.[36]

It is hard to find rational explanations for any of these events. The circumstances of Kaspar Hauser's descriptions of his captivity strongly suggest a spaceship and, with the truly bizarre nature of the cases of Martha Wright and Armando Valdes, it is not at all surprising that alien abduction has been proposed as a possible explanation. We will be examining that area of Ufology in the chapter on abduction.

ENDNOTES: CHAPTER ONE

[1] APRO Bulletin. December 1975.
[2] *Sheboygan* (Wisconsin) *Press*, January 21st, 1948.
[3] Loren Coleman, *Mysterious America*, Simon and Schuster, 2006.
[4] Reported to Ufologist Don Worley by Earl Morrison, one of the witnesses.
[5] Janet and Colin Bord, *Alien Animals: A Worldwide Investigation,* Book Club Associates, 1980.
[6] Karl P. N. Shuker, *The Beasts That Hide From Man*, Paraview Press, 2003.
[7] Ari Berk, *Giants: The Secret Histories*, Templar, 2008.
[8] Jenny Randles, *Alien Contact: The First Fifty Years*, Sterling Publishing, 1997.
[9] Mike Dash, *Borderlands,* Heinemann, 1997.
[10] Jack Cohen and Ian Stewart, *Evolving the Alien*, Ebury Press, 2002.
[11] Patrick Huyghe and Dennis Stacy, *The Field Guide to Extraterrestrials: A Complete Overview to Alien Lifeforms,* New English Library, 1997.
[12] Randles, alien contact.
[13] "Alien Big Cats in Britain," *Fortean Times,* February 2003.
[14] *Commander X, Underground Alien Bases*, Abelard Productions, 1990.
[15] Colin Wilson, *Alien Dawn: A Classic Investigation into the Contact Experience*, Llewellyn, 2010.
[16] Dash, op. cit.

[17] John A Keel, *The Mothman Prophecies*, IllumiNet Press, 1994.

[18] Linda Moulton Howe, *Glimpses of Other Realities,* Earthfiles, 2002.

[19] Keel, op. cit.

[20] Scott Corales, *Chupacabras and Other Mmysteries,* Greenleaf Publications, 1997.

[21] "Mysteries of the Unexplained," *Reader's Digest*, 1985.

[22] Karl P. N. Shuker, *The Unexplained*, Carlton Books, 1996.

[23] Ahmad Jamaludin, *Two Generations; One Mission; In Search of Elusive UFOs and Aliens, Singapore Paranormal Investigators*, 2005.

[24] Alan Baker, *The Encyclopedia of Alien Encounters*, Facts on File, 2006.

[25] Lynn Picknett, *The Mammoth Book of UFOs*, Carroll and Graf, 2001.

[26] Myra Shackley, *Still Living?* Thames and Hudson, 1986.

[27] Maximilian de Lafayette, *The Grays, Alien Abductions and Genetic Creation of Humans Hybrid Race*, Lulu, 2010.

[28] Helen and Betty Mitchell, *We Met the Space People*, Saucerian Books, 1959.

[29] It is noteworthy that both Appleton and Diaz make much play of the strangely holographic nature of the alien worlds they experienced. Appleton's account is particularly interesting and valuable because, of course, her encounters with aliens took place before holography had become part of the scientific repertoire.

[30] The best accounts of Roswell are given in: a) Michael Hesemann and Philip Mantle, *Beyond Roswell*, Michael O'Mara, 1997; b) Stanton Friedman and Don Berliner, *Crash at Corona,* Marlowe, 1997; c) Tim Shawcross, *The Roswell Files*, Bloomsbury, 1997.

[31] "Brazil Goes Nuts Over Aliens." *Fortean Times* issue 90.

[32] John Michell, *The Flying Saucer Vision*, Abacus, 1974.

[33] Ibid.

[34] John Grant and Colin Wilson (Editors), *The Directory of Possibilities*, Webb & Bower, 1981.

[35] Ibid.

[36] Jenny Randles, *Abduction!* Robert Hale, 1988.

CHAPTER TWO

CONTACT

Thousands of cases of contact between humans and aliens have been reported since the end of the Second World War. These encounters remain one of the most baffling mysteries in the history of the UFO phenomenon.

The three basic methods of communication between extraterrestrials and humans are the use of some kind of translating machine, telepathy, or the ability of the alien to speak the contactee's language. Of the three methods, the use of a translating machine seems to be the last resort and is certainly the least frequently reported. Telepathy, or the aliens' knowledge of Earth tongues, appears to be the main method of communication.

FIRST CONTACT

JOSE HIGGINS

The first reported close encounter since the recognition of flying saucers as a separate phenomenon comes from Brazil, that most psychic of countries. The case began with a simple sighting on 23 July 1947 at Baurau by a group of survey workers. They saw a large, metal disc descend and land. All but one of the workers ran away.

The man who remained, Jose Higgins, seems to qualify as being the first contactee of modern times. He saw three beings about seven feet tall getting out of the craft carrying boxes on their back and wearing overalls. When they became aware of his presence, they gestured towards him and invited him to enter their strange craft. As soon as they did so, he ran away and took cover, observing their activities. They spent some time simply leaping around in what appeared to be purposeless behavior, before digging some holes in the ground and beginning to move boulders.

In spite of his concealment, Higgins noticed the aliens must have been aware of his presence, because they drew his attention to their actions by pointing to the seventh hole. He interpreted that as meaning they claimed to come from Uranus. They also drew what he thought was a map of the solar system, after which they re-entered the craft and flew away.[1]

The fact that the occupants of the strange craft were clearly aware of the presence of Higgins even after he had refused their invitation to join them on board their spaceship, and that they made a point of gesturing towards the seventh hole that they were digging, qualifies it as the first contact report of modern times.

It is hard to interpret the actions of the aliens. Possibly, as Higgins imagined, they were claiming to be visitors from Uranus. It is curious that many aspects of their behavior seemed like playfulness, rather than purposive action. Higgins remains the first indubitable contactee and his story is genuinely puzzling.

GEORGE ADAMSKI, TOURIST TO VENUS

Higgins may have been the first human to have been contacted, but the wave of reports of contactee stories began with George Adamski. One of the most colorful characters in the world of Ufology, Adamski knew how to tell a good story and had a keen eye for publicity. He was the first person to claim that he had been invited aboard a flying saucer.[2]

Following the publication of Adamski's book in 1953, a wave of contactee stories followed. He undoubtedly changed the public perception of the UFO phenomenon. Before his book, the general attitude towards the saucers was one of fear, paranoia, and suspicion. Under Adamski's influence, religion entered into the Ufological mix. Soon, reports of wise, loving, and benevolent beings from Venus and other planets and stars began to surface. People began to claim that concerned aliens from outer space were coming to Earth to help guide humanity towards peace and love and away from the threat of nuclear destruction.

In hindsight, many of these books were clearly expressions of human fear cast in the form of an extraterrestrial encounter. It is also curious that it was quite a while after the publication of Adamski's book before variations in the descriptions of aliens began to be reported. For a number of years, almost every contact story gave the same "message" from the aliens and reported the same physical characteristics.

Adamski himself was partly a dreamer, partly a gifted psychic, and partly a religious prophet. He certainly produced some obviously faked photographs, one so clumsy that it has been described as a "flying dustbin." His claims to have traveled throughout the solar system and the descriptions he gave of the planets he had "visited" have long since been exposed as exercises in creative imagination.

On the other hand, he also had some curious "hits." Most impressively, he described the Van Allen belt of radiation surrounding the Earth years before it had been detected by astronomers. He also mentioned "fireflies" that he saw dancing in space, a phenomenon that was also later reported by astronauts.

Ironically, Adamski's work raised the public awareness of astronomy and generated a genuine interest in outer space. It was partly the effect of his "contacts" that not only inspired the Soviet and American space programs, but also helped secure public support for the huge sums of money it cost to fund them.

LYDIA STALNAKER, THE CHOSEN ONE

In 1955, a nine-year old girl, Lydia Stalnaker, was out on the road outside her farm in Jacksonville, Florida, playing with two friends. Suddenly, there was a blinding flash of light, after which a man appeared in front of them on the road. The children "blacked out" for a moment and, as soon as they recovered, they ran straight home screaming in terror. The sky had turned dark by the time they returned. Their concerned parents asked what had happened, but the children were too frightened to speak coherently. From that day onwards, they had recurring nightmares during which they repeatedly screamed that "they" were going to "get" them.

Following another strange encounter in 1974, Lydia underwent hypnosis. During the session, she became so emotionally disturbed the practitioner was forced to snap her out of the trance state abruptly. Later, she underwent further sessions, during the course of which her strange story finally emerged.

At the age of nine, Lydia claimed to have been taken on board a spaceship and her head tightly clamped by the aliens. Then they "took knowledge out of my head—they knew all about me."[3]

Lydia was also told that she had been "chosen" and that the aliens would return later. Sure enough, they did, and their second visit, in 1974, triggered her visit to the hypnotist the following year.

ELLECIA GRUEN AND THE DOCTORS FROM OUTER SPACE

In 1956, Ellecia Gruen, a young girl from an orphanage in Toledo, Ohio, was lying in bed and found herself surrounded by aliens. They were busily exploring her body with strange machines. She described the figures as being grey, with claws instead of fingers, though they did have thumbs.

In 1976, Ellecia found herself the victim of what she described as a sustained campaign of intimidation by UFOs, lasting for a period of three months. In the end, she simply yelled at them to go away and, after one final visit, they did leave her alone.[4]

Even more remarkably, another girl from the same orphanage also remembers aliens running machines over her body. Unlike Ellecia Gruen, this woman refused to "go public" with her story. She is a fundamentalist Christian who does not believe in the existence of extraterrestrial life since it conflicts with her religious convictions.[5]

JESSICA ROLFE, STUDENT OF ALIEN HISTORY

One night, lying in bed trying to sleep, five-year old Jessica Rolfe got the shock of her young life. Opening her eyes, to her astonishment, she saw three figures appear out of thin air. They stood at the foot of the girl's bed.

Jessica described the men as tall and having golden hair and skin, with perhaps a hint of brown streaking the gold in their hair. They appeared fit and even a little handsome, but they did not seem to use their mouths to communicate.

One of the men approached Jessica and lifted her out of bed. Without saying a word, he began communicating with her telepathically. The thought that he transmitted was actually a question. He asked the girl if she would like to come with them on a journey, pointing out of the window with his hand. Jessica, amazingly unfazed by these strange and scary events, calmly shook her head and told him that she was happy where she was. He said that was fine and tucked her up in bed once more. Then they simply vanished.

Jessica immediately rushed into her parents' room and told them her strange story. They replied that she must have had a nightmare and put her back in bed once more. Her strange encounter made it difficult for her to sleep and, curious about her unexpected visitors, she lay awake, wondering who they were and where they had come from.

For the next nine years the men returned, night after night, to the young girl's bedside. Jessica listened spellbound as they taught her about their world, customs, and history. She was fascinated by what they told her.

At the age of fourteen, she asked if she could travel with them on their spaceship and the visitors agreed to her request. She found the experience of space travel exhilarating and came to look upon the aliens as her mentors and friends.[6]

The account she gives of this alien race, which she calls Kuran, is fascinating. She claims that their propulsion system is "simple," being "a combination of magnetic energy and the energy of the navigator."[7] She also claimed that "one fifty-foot ship could tow Earth from its orbit and they can travel right through the Sun."[8]

Even more interesting is her account of their origins. According to Jessica, they do not live in outer space, but share the planet with us as fellow inhabitants. They have a number of bases on Earth, notably in Florida, Argentina, and the Amazon basin. Although they travel in space regularly, their home is on Earth.[9]

Rolfe's account of human history is also interesting. Basically, the Kuran told her that we began on a planet that broke up and became the asteroid belt. The Kuran rescued survivors of this catastrophe and took them to Earth to begin a new life.

When humans arrived, dolphins were the superior form of life upon the planet. Human aggressiveness soon changed that. Even early humanoid types were murdered or driven underground. Before long, black magicians from Mu caused chaos on Earth, as they tried to institute a theocratic tyranny.

Anxious to turn humans away from this way of life, the Kuran came to the people of Earth and established Atlantis. Mu, jealous of the new empire, made war upon it with catastrophic results. Their actions led to the downfall of both empires, the reversal of the Earth's axis, and the coming of the Ice Ages,

From time to time, the Kuran have tried to intervene in human affairs. The impression Rolfe gives is that they are well-meaning, but incompetent. She adds that the concepts of God or religion are seen as meaningless by the Kuran. Apparently, they also told her that twelve different alien races have visited Earth during the course of its history.

All these events took place between 1958 and 1967. It was not until the death of her stepfather, in 1977, that Rolfe felt able to tell her mother about her strange experiences. To her surprise, her mother said that she had suspected something odd about her daughter for many years.

Jessica Rolfe's series of contacts are highly elaborate, not to say spectacular. They are perhaps among the most interesting and impressive of the many cases of contact between human and non-human entities.

SPACE BABIES

THE FIRST SPACE BABY

Elizabeth Klarer claimed that extraterrestrials contacted her between 1954 and 1963. She flew light aircraft and had studied meteorology. Soon after reading Adamski's books, she announced that she had also been contacted by aliens since her childhood, transmitting their messages telepathically through an extraterrestrial by the name of Akon.

On 17 July 1955, she photographed what she claimed was a spacecraft from the Drakensberg Mountains in her native South Africa. The next year, on 7 April 1956, his ship landed. Akon took her on board and they orbited the Earth before finally arriving at his home planet of Meton in 1957. Meton was apparently part of the star system Alpha Centauri.

On the planet, Klarer and Akon had sex and she became pregnant, giving birth to a son called Ayling. He remained behind on Meton to be brought up in the ways of his father's people, while Elizabeth returned to South Africa. She claimed that from the moment of her departure from Earth to her pregnancy, giving birth, and returning home, took less than four months.

It was not until 1980 that Klarer published a book about her experiences.[10] She died in her native South Africa in 1994, and a film is now being made about her story.[11]

CYNTHIA APPLETON AND THE BABY FROM VENUS

Between 1957 and 1959, a series of strange events occurred to Cynthia Appleton, a woman then aged twenty-seven and married with two daughters, who lived in Birmingham, England. They began on 18 November 1957, when, shortly after lunch, her life was about to be turned upside down.

She went into the lounge where the baby girl was sleeping in her pram. Cynthia became aware of a mugginess in the air, as if a heavy storm was about to take place. To her astonishment, a figure appeared in front of her, standing in the middle of the room.

Her description of the alien, though in most ways similar to those reported by other contactees, has some bizarre touches of its own. As well as the seemingly obligatory long hair, it was tall and blonde, wearing a plastic rain coat with a collar in the form of a ruffle. The effect was so incongruous that Cynthia would have laughed if she had not been so utterly frightened by what she saw.

It communicated with her telepathically, asking if she knew where it could find a metal called "titium," presumably a mistake for titanium. Then it vanished as abruptly and unexpectedly as it had entered. It might seem strange that the alien should make a mistake about metals, but it is even more implausible that Appleton would have done so, as her husband was a metal worker.[12]

During the period of her various experiences, Appleton was interviewed by the psychologist and UFO researcher Dr. John Dale.[13] According to his account, Cynthia's troubles began earlier on 16 November 1957, when she suffered an unexplained black-out while she was cleaning the house. Apparently, her visitors later told her that this had been a "failed attempt at contact."

He told her that he knew all about the space programs on Earth, but that they were using the wrong techniques. Instead of trying to overcome gravity by ascending, they ought to travel "with a sideways attitude." Then he opened his arms and a device that Cynthia said was like a "TV set" materialized between them. From her description of the object, it is strikingly like a holographic image, in full color and three-dimensional. Holography, of course, was not even invented in the 1950s, a striking corroboration of her truthfulness.

She referred to the device as being a "living image" which showed the classic UFO shape, but "they seemed to take off and hovered in space for two or three seconds, went off to the left, then they went very quickly to the right." At Dr. Dale's request, she made a drawing of the power mechanism of the craft, which showed a central hub, with spokes leading off from the center. Apparently, they "collected power" from the atmosphere by rotating.

Uniquely for contactee reports of this period, the alien told her the name of the planet from where he came. It was called "Gharnasvarn" in his language, but the people of Earth referred to it as Venus. He then told her that he would come back, after which the TV set cut out and the extraterrestrial vanished from sight.

After her visitor had gone, Appleton saw that he had been standing on a piece of newspaper and it now bore clear signs of scorch marks. Dale also saw this and described it as resembling the effects of a "lightning strike or small electrical discharge."

The local vicar became interested in the case and surprised his congregation when, on 12 January 1958, he made Cynthia Appleton's story the main plank of his sermon. Then the Birmingham Psychic Society became involved and asked her to take part in an experiment to re-enact her encounter with the alien. We do not know if it ever took place or, if so, what the results of it were.

On 7 January, Appleton was visited for a second time by the Venusian. As on his previous visit, he materialized abruptly in a flash of rose-colored light. This time, however, he did not come alone. He had brought a companion with him and told her that he was his "superior."

A number of subsequent visits followed, during which the aliens stopped simply materializing and instead arrived at her house in a large black car with tinted windows. They also began dressing in black suits and wearing homburg hats. During the six visits Cynthia received from the Venusians during 1958, she was given considerable information about their world and their philosophy of life. Apparently, they told her that time had no objective reality, but was simply an idea constructed by humans to try and make sense of the world around them. They also told her that individual existence was also an illusion and that, in reality, all life was totally interdependent and "one." They also spent considerable time discoursing on the true nature of the atomic world, claiming that it possessed the ability to cure cancer. According to them, God "dwells at the heart and core of the atom."

Not surprisingly, Cynthia Appleton protested that the concepts they were speaking about were far beyond her comprehension. They took no notice and continued to relate the battery of scientific and philosophical ideas, which she struggled dimly to explain to Dale in their sessions together.

A bizarre incident occurred when, on one visit, the Venusian visitor told Cynthia that he had burnt his hand. He asked her to bathe it in boiling water and, startled as she was by the strange request, did as he asked. When he left, she saw a piece of skin at the bottom of the bowl and it was tested by scientists at Birmingham University. The results of the tests were evidently that the skin was not human, but perhaps came from a pig. A reporter for the *Sunday People* asked her daughter Susan, four years old at the time, if she remembered the

Venusians' visits. She answered, "Yes, I remember Mummy bathing the hand of a man with funny long hair and a fur collar."

On 10 May 1959, the Cynthia Appleton story took a new and even more bizarre turn. That day the *Sunday People* proclaimed: "I'm going to have a baby from Venus." Underneath the banner headlines were the words: "This is the biggest crackpot statement a woman has ever made." When the reporter suggested that Cynthia had an overactive imagination, she replied, "But it's true, and my husband believes it, too. " She then added that her Venusian visitor had also made a series of predictions, including her pregnancy.[14]

Apparently, on a visit by the alien in September 1958, Cynthia had been told that she was "in the state of being with child." He added that she would give birth at the end of May 1959 to a boy. She was instructed to call him Matthew and was informed that he would weigh exactly 7 pounds, 3 ounces. From the age of fourteen, he would become a world leader.

Not long after his visit, Cynthia, to her surprise, found herself pregnant. She was somewhat nervous about what might happen, but waited for her pregnancy to take its course. On 1 June 1959, she entered labor and gave birth on 2 June, at two minutes after midnight to a male child with blonde hair, weighing just over 7 pounds, 3 ounces. Naturally, the boy was called Matthew.

Not long after she had given birth, Appleton received another telepathic message announcing that her Venusian visitor would return shortly, accompanied by a friend from the planet Uranus. Her husband said that: "I believe everything Cynthia has told me, but I would love to have a yarn with him. If he shows up, I'm going to tell him I'm Matthew's father. If he doesn't give me the right answers, I'll crack his 'delicate features' with a crowbar. His mate from Uranus will get the same."

No more contacts followed, nor was there any further news about the Appletons. Then, after Matthew's first birthday in 1960, a newspaper ran a headline declaring that "The 'Venus' baby is so normal" and announced that then thirteen-month old Matthew was fit and healthy. Cynthia, however, was bemused and disappointed, complaining that she had not heard from her Venusian visitor. "He used to pop in quite regularly every seven or eight weeks," she said. "When he left, after forecasting Matthew's birth, he said he would be looking in again soon. But he never returned. I just can't make it out."[15]

That newspaper reference, in July 1960, is the last time Cynthia Appleton or her family attracted the attention of the media. None of the predictions made by the aliens came true and Matthew Appleton never became a world leader. Even so, the Appleton story is one of the most striking and unusual in the history of contact between humans and aliens.

FLYING HOUSES, CAVES, AND BEAMS OF LIGHT

JAN WOLSKI AND THE "FLYING HOUSE"

In 1978, a highly unusual case occurred in the village of Emilcin, Poland. A seventy-one-year-old farmer, Jan Wolski, was riding through the forest in his cart pulled by horses, when he saw two extremely small figures running along the road in the direction he was traveling. Wolski noticed how unusual their movements were, stating that they reminded him of "deep sea divers." As his cart drew level with the "men" they leapt aboard and made signs to him to continue his journey. They also tried to communicate with him, but he was unable to understand whatever language they were using. As his cart approached a clearing in the woods, he saw a strange, white object hovering steadily above him in the sky.

The UFO that Wolski saw was one of the most unusual craft ever reported. He said that it was in the form of a house and had "a roof like a barn." Each corner of the UFO had a device in the shape of a barrel with two black rods extending upwards from them and the rods rotating in corkscrew-like movements. On the underside of the vehicle, there were four cables, each of which seemed to support a device rather like an elevator in the form of a box. As his cart drew nearer, the "elevator" descended.

Wolski then heard a loud humming sound that he compared to bumblebees, when his two unexpected passengers leapt off his cart and went inside the "elevator." One of them then invited the farmer to join them on their craft and he accepted.

Wolski described the inside of the spaceship as being dark, with the only light entering from the world outside. He noticed that there were seats against each wall. He saw no evidence of any kind of mechanical controls, but did notice two black tubes which ran across from one wall to the other and also two small holes into which the aliens placed black rods. Wolski also saw ten black birds that he thought might have been rooks, which lay on the ground and appeared to be paralyzed.

He described the aliens as being short and slender, around four feet in height, dressed in one-piece gray suits, tightly fitted. The suits covered all their bodies except their hands and face. They had large heads with almond eyes, small noses, and no lips.

Wolski was then given a "physical examination," in the course of which he had to strip naked and then had some disc-shaped instruments passed over his body. His clothes were then returned to him and he was requested to leave the spaceship. He and the aliens then bowed to each other and Wolski left.

Naturally, he rushed home to tell his family and they—along with some equally curious neighbors—went with him to the "landing site." They saw a number of footprints in a rectangular form as well as black feathers (presumably from the rooks he saw on board the spaceship), some corn, and branches of trees. Bizarrely, on the same day, a neighbor's child had also rushed in saying that "a little house" had flown above their home. The child's and mother's house was only 800 yards away from where Wolski had his strange encounter with the aliens.[16]

CARLOS DIAZ AND THE ALIENS IN A CAVE

One morning, in January 1981, while the sky above was still dark, Carlos Diaz was sitting in his car in the area of Ajusco Park near Mexico City. As he looked around, he saw a distinct yellow glow from the valley beneath. To his amazement, it rose up from the valley and came nearly 100 feet (thirty meters) from the hood of his car. Diaz immediately picked up his camera and took a series of photographs. That day was to launch a trail of contact events over many years.

He was followed home by the as-yet-unknown presence. Before long, he began to develop a sense of when "they" would be coming. He took many 35mm photos of the UFOs he saw—some in his own garden and others around the mountains behind his home.

Before long, his story attracted the attention of Mexican television. Soon, his claims began to be scientifically investigated. Professor Victor Quesada at the Polytechnical Institute of the University of Mexico made a thorough analysis of the transparencies that Diaz had shot and came to the conclusion they were genuine. Dr. Robert Nathan of NASA's Jet Propulsion Laboratory in California also arrived at the same verdict.

Anxious to obtain more striking footage, the TV presenter Jaime Maussan gave Diaz a camcorder. Soon afterwards, he got a call from Diaz announcing that he had succeeded in capturing the UFO on film. The video displayed the object in exactly the same way as it was on the 35mm stills, but the camcorder also revealed the presence of a dark gray "membrane" that emitted a kind of "pulse" from within the object. Its appearance was similar to a large jellyfish.

During his various contacts with the aliens, Diaz was told that he was not allowed to enter the spaceship except through the side doors. On one of his visits inside, the vehicle was parked on a ledge within a cave. Diaz reported seeing stalagmites that had been carefully carved into sculptures resembling those found in Mayan art. Then he was taken to another smaller cave where he saw seven glowing balls shaped like eggs. He was told that they were "storage devices."

Strangely, he described the landscape within this world as being like a forest. However, he found it was impossible for him to touch the trees and other flora he saw there and it was almost as if he were viewing a holographic representation, rather than an actual physical environment. This curious detail reminds us irresistibly of the holographic-type events described in the 1950s by Cynthia Appleton.

Diaz claims that the aliens live among us and have done so for thousands of years. They look like ordinary humans, drive cars, and generally behave in the same fashion as any other humans. His UFO encounters, photographs, and films have continued from their first beginning in 1981 to the present day. They are some of the most remarkable evidence in favor of the reality of human-alien contact.[17]

THE MCGREGOR FAMILY: LIFTED INTO SPACE ON A BEAM OF LOVE

Kevin McGregor had seen UFOs before. On 7 May 2010, his latest sighting was also witnessed by his two daughters and a neighbor. A flaming plasma ball of light, blue-white in color, came down from the sky. He was sitting in his garden at the time, looking up at the night sky, when he saw a light in the distance that appeared to be flashing.

His elder daughter, aged twenty, was watching television, and his younger daughter, aged fourteen, was in the kitchen making a meal. His wife was upstairs in the bedroom as she was feeling unwell.

The light appeared to be coming from the direction of Livingstone, a town in Scotland near Edinburgh. As it drew closer, Kevin McGregor realized it was totally silent. Opening the back door, he spoke quickly to his elder daughter, saying the single word: "UFO." Promptly, both his daughters rushed out into the garden and gazed up at the sky above them.

The light approached ever closer, still maintaining its same fiery, but not blinding, intensity. Soon, it hung over the McGregor house. The elder daughter was staring at it and clearly frightened, while the younger girl was excited and even a little amused. A neighbor of Kevin's opened her window and stared in obvious horror at the light above his house. She then closed the window, drew her blinds tightly shut, and ever since that fateful night refused to speak to him.

Kevin said that what made this sighting different from the others he had witnessed previously was that "something invaded my thoughts in a way that can only be construed as some sort of communication." Apparently, he was filled with an overwhelming sense of love and peace, and saw a mental image of the Voyager spacecraft and its gold plaque as well as seeing the figure of a man with his arm raised in friendship engraved upon the plaque. Kevin raised his own hand in salutation, showing that he was not afraid and wanted to demonstrate his friendship.

Kevin felt the light stopping and "looking" at his family. Then he felt as if he was being lifted right out of his body and "was aware of a vibration, a crazy fluttering deep inside my chest." He was filled with an overwhelming sense of love and harmony with the universe as he underwent his strange out-of-body experience. He heard inside his head the words: "I am the herald" being spoken in a way that he described as being "not with words, but more a feeling."

Kevin's younger daughter simply said: "Wow!" His elder girl was struck dumb with astonishment, disbelief, and utter fear. Neither of them had the presumably telepathic contact that their father experienced, but both of them, as well as the disapproving neighbor, saw the light clearly and were in awe of it.

As the light disappeared over the roof of the house, Kevin stared at it with a sense of wonder. He watched it "collapse into a triangle" and then continue its journey, traveling to the left of the Edinburgh ski course and over the Pentlands hills that border the city.

His eldest daughter was so shocked that she left home for good, but the younger girl said that she was very "happy" about the experience adding: "they want you for something!" Although she only saw the UFO and did not have the mystical contact experience that her father had undergone, she did add that "time stopped and something happened." The experience made her feel "warm and loved."

As a result of his encounter, Kevin became a much calmer person. He had been a drinker and prone to occasional bouts of violence. Not long after his experience, he made his peace with his mother to whom he had not even spoken to for over ten years. He believes firmly that his extraterrestrial visitor helped him to change as a person.[18]

ENDNOTES: CHAPTER TWO

[1] Judith M. and Alan L. Gansberg, *Direct Encounters*, Coronet, 1980.

[2] George Adamski and Desmond Leslie, *Flying Saucers Have Landed*, Neville Spearman, 1970.

[3] Rowan Wilson, op. cit.

[4] Gansberg, op. cit.

[5] Ibid.

[6] Ibid.

[7] Ibid.

[8] Ibid.

[9] Ibid.

[10] Elizabeth Klarer, *Beyond the Light Barrier*, Light Technology Publications, 2006 (first published 1980).

[11] A film based on *Beyond the Light Barrier* is being produced in South Africa in 2011.

[12] *Birmingham Evening Despatch*, 1 January 1958

[13] Notes of sessions between Dr. Dale and Cynthia Appleton, transcribed by Jenny Randles.

[14] *Sunday People*, 10 May 1959.

[15] *Empire News, July* 1960.

[16] Testimony of Jan Wolski in an interview with Henryk Pomorski, July 1978, Emilcin, Poland.

[17] *Ships of Light: The Carlos Diaz Experience*, 2001 (film).

[18] *Marianna Paranormal Examiner*, 4 June 2011.

CHAPTER THREE

ABDUCTION

As well as the more peaceful forms of contact described in the previous chapter, many humans have reported being kidnapped by aliens. The stories of these abductees vary, but contain a number of common features. In the first place, the humans are abducted against their will rather than by some kind of voluntary agreement. Secondly, there are nearly always reports of some kind of medical examination. Finally, in most (though not all) cases, there appears to be a sexual element involved, even up to being impregnated by extraterrestrials.

The stories of Betty and Barney Hill in 1961[1] and Travis Walton in 1975[2] are so well known and so well documented that I will not deal with them here. Instead, this chapter will focus upon less well-known abductee cases, with the exception of Antonio Villas-Boas. His status as the first person indisputably to claim that aliens had abducted him and the baffling nature of his experience makes it impossible to leave him out.

FIRST ALIEN KIDNAP VICTIMS

SARAH SHAW AND JAN WHITLEY

Allegedly the first abduction, this case is claimed to have taken place in 1953, but sadly was not reported publicly until 1975. On 22 March 1953, at two o'clock in the morning, Sarah Shaw and Jan Whitley, then aged twenty-one and twenty-two respectively, saw a bright light passing over their house in a regular manner. Shaw gazed out of the window to get a better look and immediately felt giddy. She checked the time on her watch and saw that it was four o'clock in the morning. Two whole hours of her life had gone "missing."

It was not until 1975, when she underwent sessions of hypnosis, that she recalled in a state of trance how both she and Whitley had been taken aboard a UFO. Both girls were stripped naked and examined by aliens dressed in black. Bizarrely, they told Shaw that vinegar could cure cancer.

Shaw admitted that she found the attention she received from the male aliens pleasurable. The girls were then "floated" back home, just as they had been "floated" up to the ship, on a beam of light. Back indoors, they immediately lost any memory of their strange experience.

It is worth pointing out that although Shaw had called UFO researcher Ann Druffel twenty years after the original experience and Druffel had recommended that she undergo a course of hypnotic memory regression, the story she told was also confirmed in all essential details by Whitley. Like Shaw, she remembered being abducted by aliens and the sexual attention that they focused on the two young women. She also mentioned that, in 1956, she began to experience recurring nightmares focusing on the theme of alien abduction.

In addition, Whitley revealed that she had also experienced an abduction scenario of her own. This time it did not involve Shaw, but another young female, Emily Cronin. In 1956, both girls were driving home when, immediately after they had pulled up in a rest stop, they saw a bright light. They described its color as "yellowish-white." Both girls immediately became paralyzed and Cronin saw a man watching them through the rear window of a car. With a tremendous effort of will, Whitley managed to move a single finger, after which the effect of paralysis stopped.

Whitley also claimed that, in 1967 and 1968, she had woken up and found herself unable to move a muscle and saw "ugly little faces" hovering in the room above her head. She describes her state of mind at that time as mirroring exactly the feelings she had when she and Shaw had first experienced their alien visitation in 1953.[3]

Not surprisingly, it has been suggested that Shaw's abduction testimony, especially the part where she describes her enjoyment of the attention she received from the male humanoids, was expressing an inner dissatisfaction with the lesbian relationship in which she was involved with Whitley at that time. Although this is obviously a possibility, particularly as her "memory" was not "recovered" until over twenty years had passed, there are sufficiently unusual and original details in it to make us at least suspend judgment.

The mere fact that Whitley, entirely independently, gave the same account of the experience as Shaw and that she had also undergone similar phenomena, both on her own and with Cronin, strongly suggests that the three women are telling the truth.

SEDUCTRESS FROM OUTER SPACE

ANTONIO VILLAS-BOAS

One of the most colorful accounts of an alien abduction and, certainly, the first to be publicly recorded was given by Brazilian farmer Antonio Villas-Boas. He claimed that on the night of 15 October 1957, an object shaped like an egg flew towards him "at a fantastic speed," while he was out ploughing his fields.[4]

Boas sat in his tractor mesmerized and watching the craft as it came closer. When it landed, "three metal supports—like a tripod—appeared out of the underside of the object about 16 feet (a few meters) above the ground.[5]

At this point, Boas decided to start up his tractor and try to run. However, after only managing to drive for a short distance, his engine failed. Baffled and thoroughly frightened, he jumped down from his machine and tried again to get away. As soon as he did so:

> SOMEONE GRASPED ME BY THE ARM—A SMALL, STRANGELY DRESSED BEING WHO REACHED UP TO MY SHOULDER. I TURNED IN DESPERATION AND GAVE HIM A PUSH, WHICH MADE HIM OVERBALANCE. THE STRANGER LET GO AND FELL BACKWARDS ONTO THE GROUND. I TRIED TO RUN AWAY, BUT WAS GRASPED BY THREE OTHER STRANGERS SIMULTANEOUSLY FROM BEHIND AND FROM THE SIDES. THEY HELD MY ARMS AND LEGS FAST AND RAISED ME UP, AND I WAS UNABLE TO DEFEND MYSELF. I TWISTED AND KICKED, BUT THEY HELD ME TIGHT AND DID NOT LET GO.[6]

After dragging him into the machine, he found himself inside a room. They undressed him forcefully, rubbed some sort of fluid over his body, and took a blood sample. Then he was left alone for a while, after which he came face-to-face with a humanoid female.

> AFTER AN ETERNITY, A NOISE FROM THE DOOR WRENCHED ME FROM MY THOUGHTS. I TURNED ROUND AND SAW A WOMAN COMING SLOWLY TOWARDS ME. SHE WAS STARK NAKED AND BAREFOOT JUST LIKE ME. I WAS SPEECHLESS AND SHE SEEMED TO BE AMUSED BY MY EXPRESSION. SHE WAS VERY BEAUTIFUL, QUITE UNLIKE THE WOMEN I KNEW. HER HAIR WAS SOFT AND BLONDE, ALMOST PLATINUM BLONDE—AS IF BLEACHED—AND CURLED INWARDS AT THE ENDS, DOWN THE NAPE OF HER NECK. HER HAIR WAS PARTED IN THE

MIDDLE AND SHE HAD LARGE, BLUE EYES, WHICH WERE ALMOND SHAPED. HER NOSE WAS STRAIGHT. HER FACE WAS UNUSUALLY SHAPED WITH EXCEPTIONALLY HIGH CHEEKBONES, MUCH BROADER THAN THE SOUTH AMERICAN INDIAN WOMEN. HER POINTED CHIN MADE HER FACE ALMOST TRIANGULAR. SHE HAD THIN, UNOBTRUSIVE LIPS, AND HER EARS, WHICH I DID NOT SEE UNTIL LATER, WERE EXACTLY LIKE THOSE OF OUR WOMEN. SHE HAD THE MOST BEAUTIFUL BODY THAT I HAVE EVER SEEN ON A WOMAN, WITH HIGH, WELL-SHAPED BREASTS AND A NARROW WAIST. SHE WAS BROAD IN THE HIPS, HAD LONG THIGHS AND SMALL FEET, NARROW HANDS, AND NORMAL FINGER-NAILS. SHE WAS MUCH SMALLER THAN I, AND HER HEAD ONLY REACHED TO MY SHOULDER.[7]

After some foreplay, the woman seduced Boas. She also took a sperm sample from him. Then she pointed at her stomach and the sky, whereupon one of his abductors returned with the farmer's clothes. He got dressed, trying to notice every detail of his surroundings as he did so. Eventually, he was taken off the ship by other aliens and watched the strange machine ascending vertically into the air. Going back to his tractor, he checked the time. He had been captured at 1.15 a.m. and released at 5.30 a.m.

Boas then began to suffer terrible headaches, constant burning and watering of the eyes, hypersomnia, and the sudden appearance of unexplained sores on his body.

Unfortunately, it was some months after these symptoms first showed themselves that Boas consulted a doctor. The man he saw, Dr. Olavo Fontes, examined the farmer and found that there were burns on his body, "which suggest radiation poisoning or exposure to radiation, but, unfortunately, he came to me too late for the blood examinations that could have confirmed such a possibility beyond doubt."[8]

In spite of the extraordinary delay in time between Boas' experience and his visit to the doctor, this remains one of the most credible and baffling of all the abduction cases. There is hard physical evidence of some kind of exposure to radiation, and not even hardened skeptics regard his account as being a hoax.

KIDNAPPED SPACE BABIES

DEBBIE JORDAN

On 30 June 1983, in the Copley Woods region of Indiana, Debbie Jordan saw strange lights in her garden. When she went outside to get a better view, she saw a UFO and her presence was immediately noticed by the inhabitants of the craft. They took her aboard their spaceship and she was subjected to a series of medical experiments. During one of them, a small device was implanted in Jordan's body and then she blacked out, waking to find herself lying in her garden dressed only in her nightdress. She also bore physical evidence of her ordeal in the form of bleeding, which she attributed to the various medical procedures the aliens had forced her to undergo.[9]

This abduction experience was the first by Jordan to be reported to researchers in the field. However, during a number of hypnotic regression sessions, she also declared that she had experienced repeated abductions from her childhood onwards. Her mother had tried to protect her by making her hide in the wardrobe, as she had been previously abducted herself and wanted to avoid her daughter going through the same traumatic experiences.

Jordan also claimed that, on one occasion, she was on board a spaceship and met a young boy whom she believed was her own child as a result of an alien-induced pregnancy. In December 1977, according to her hypnotic testimony, she had been abducted from a car, although the other occupants were unaware of her abduction and were unable to confirm her testimony. Jordan claimed that she was given a gynecological examination by the aliens and they also made her pregnant. However, she was abducted once more and the fetus removed from her body.[10]

In November 1983, Jordan again claimed to have been abducted, given further medical tests, and had some of her eggs removed. She also announced that her young son had been abducted at the same time and that he, too, became another target for alien abductors. In April 1986, she was again abducted and this time presented to two infants. She was allowed to hold them and even give them names. Possibly these were the children of her earlier insemination by aliens. Even though she was only shown two children, they told her that there were nine in all, presumably also the results of her various abductions. In spite of the bizarre nature of some of her claims, Jordan is generally regarded as one of the most plausible abductees.[11]

UNDERGROUND ALIEN BASE

CHRISTA TILTON

Christa Tilton claims a long history of alien abductions dating back to when she was ten years old. At that time, she was on a visit to her aunt in Tucson, Arizona, and witnessed a huge ball of orange fire falling to the ground. A short time afterwards, she saw small gray aliens and the two of them bizarrely exchanged rocks. She then blacked out and woke to find herself on a table with a man standing over her, who told her to call him "the doctor."

On board the spaceship, young Christa was subjected to a series of medical procedures, including having scrapings taken of her skin. She reported that they used a device to examine inside her abdomen and she was conscious of a sharp object entering her ear.

That was the first abduction, but many more followed. During one of them, she became pregnant by the aliens, but, in 1971, while she was in New Orleans, her fetus was removed during another abduction.

The most remarkable of Tilton's abduction cases, which otherwise are fairly similar to those of other witnesses, took place in July 1987. She drove into the desert and saw a spaceship parked on top of a hill. Two aliens stood there, apparently waiting for her to arrive. Although she locked the car doors, somehow they managed to open them. In spite of her attempts to struggle against her captors, they subdued her and took her back to their spaceship. They gave her a drink and she remembered nothing more until she was led out of the vehicle, which apparently was parked outside a cave.

Tilton was then taken to an underground "base" that she claims is in the Dulce area of New Mexico. They took her inside and made her undergo an extremely long and tough "security check," before leading her through a number of separate "levels," at each of which she had to undergo further security checks. As seemed to be normal with her abduction experiences, she was also subjected to another set of medical tests. Then they took her up to what she described as "level six." However, her guards informed her that she would not be allowed to enter that particular part of the "facility." Instead, they returned her to "level one" and let her go.

Inside the underground base, she saw a man "dressed in a red military-style jump suit" who wore "some type of patch" and carried an automatic weapon. Inside the facility, Tilton saw "huge large tanks with computerized gauges hooked to them and a huge arm-like device that extended from the top of some tubing down into the tanks." They stood about four feet high and she believes that the underground base is connected with the military in some way. She considers that the tanks were used as artificial wombs for genetic experiments on human-alien hybrids and they smelled strongly of formaldehyde.

As soon as they took her back to her car, Tilton drove to her aunt's home and went into a sound and dreamless sleep. The next day, her friend saw some angry red scratches upon her back that Tilton claimed were incurred while she fought with her alien abductors.[12]

Tilton has also written a book giving more details about the mysterious underground facility that she encountered in the course of her 1987 abduction.[13]

KIM CARLSBERG—FROM "BAYWATCH" TO ALIEN BABIES

Kim Carlsberg is a photographer and camera operator who has worked on television shows like *Baywatch*. It was while she was going out with the producer of the program, in 1988, that she had her first UFO experience. Carlsberg said that she was on the beach at Malibu when she became aware of a huge, spherical object that reminded her of the Moon. She had the sense that it was responding to her thoughts.

A week after her first sighting, Carlsberg underwent her first abduction experience. She passed out and woke to find herself strapped to a table, which she described as being both "horrific and devastating," but also "the beginning of my consciousness."

Since that first encounter, Carlsberg claims to have been repeatedly abducted by aliens. In 1995, she published a book about her experiences in which she made a number of striking claims.

Carlsberg believes that alien abduction is "hereditary." She has not only undergone numerous medical examinations, but has also become pregnant by aliens many times. She says she has given birth to a number of babies who were "alien hybrids," one a thirteen-year-old girl called April. Carlsberg claims that she and other abductees are part of an extraterrestrial genetic engineering program.[14]

After the publication of her book, in 1995, Carlsberg fell silent and concentrated on her mainstream career in the media. Then, in 2010, she published another book, giving accounts of alien life with many colorful illustrations. Carlsberg claims that there are over twenty alien species visiting Earth and that their motives and activities vary as widely as those of humans do.

In spite of the frequently unpleasant nature of her encounters, Carlsberg does not believe that the aliens, even the ones who have subjected her to repeated medical tests and enforced pregnancy, are evil. In her second book, she expressed the view that "aliens aren't emotionless. I've experienced more profound love in an instant from aliens than from any human I've met."[15]

EXTRATERRESTRIAL GENETIC ENGINEERING

LEAH HALEY, GENETIC ENGINEERING AND INTELLIGENCE AGENCIES

Leah Haley claims that she was first abducted by aliens at the age of three. However, it was not until she was in her early thirties that she became aware of what her experiences meant. Even then, at first, she dismissed them as being bad dreams. It was not until 1990 that she recognized her earlier encounters as being alien abductions. She sought counseling, as well as undergoing hypnotic regression therapy.

During the course of these sessions, she recovered memories of her very first alien abduction at the age of three. She saw a "creature" while she was in the woods, but her parents, who were "lying on the grass nearby," had no idea that anything was going on. When the alien told her to come with him, she protested that her mother would be angry and he told her that he would: "make things okay with your mother." Apparently, the mother noticed nothing strange at the time, except that her husband was very ill.

Haley claims to have been abducted "dozens of times" during the course of her life and, though she admits that she wishes her extraterrestrial encounters would stop now, says that she no longer finds them frightening. She also claims that the aliens give her telepathic instructions.

Haley's accounts of her various encounters with aliens are interesting. She maintains that they generally begin when she is sleeping. She finds herself suddenly woken by some kind of "force field" that pulls her right out of her bed and then she loses consciousness. When it returns, she finds herself lying on a platform in a spaceship with aliens subjecting her to medical examinations. She describes the beings who examine her as standing at between four and five feet tall. They have neither hair nor ears but large, almond-shaped eyes of a deep black color. Their hands only have four fingers and they have no joints in either their knees or elbows. They have no reproductive organs and communicate telepathically using their hypnotic, black eyes. Their skin is what she calls "an off-white" color.

Haley claims that the purpose of these and similar types of experiments is genetic research to further the survival of both their own species and the human race. Although she has seen more than one type of spaceship, the one that she has encountered most often is shaped like a sphere with portholes. It is extremely bright inside the craft, but she is unable to see any obvious source for the light.

Haley says that she has met the same extraterrestrials on many occasions. One in particular, whom she calls CETO, is the alien who injects her before the start of her medical experiments. She explains that she is completely unable to fight them off and describes her state as being "much like a person feels right before surgery, drugged and groggy, incapable of fighting."

She has physical marks from her encounters, including mysterious bruises, scars, punctures, and injection marks that appear and disappear overnight. Once, she remembered an object being pressed into her nostrils and on another occasion she was pierced behind her ears. Since she went public about her experiences, in the 1990s, Haley's life changed dramatically. Her husband divorced her, her daughter refused to speak to her, and many of her friends broke off contact. She also attracted the attention of the authorities. Haley was seized by armed government officers who demanded that she give them "information." She was taken to a secret military base in a helicopter and subjected to aggressive interrogation by them. Haley said:

> I WAS STRUGGLING WITH THEM AS I WAS COMING OFF THE HELICOPTER. I DON'T UNDERSTAND WHY THEY'RE TAKING ME IN THERE. I FELT A SUDDEN CHILL. IT'S COLD. THERE'S A MAN ON EACH SIDE OF ME HOLDING MY ARMS TIGHTLY. THEY'RE TAKING ME INTO A BUILDING.

She saw a number of men sitting at what she described as "a conference room table." Some of them wore military uniforms and insignia of rank. She was held tightly by her captors, forced into a chair, and then given an injection in her right arm. As she began to feel dizzy, one of the men who had kidnapped her said, "Here she is. She's a cocky little bitch." A man at the other side of the room replied "We'll take care of that."

Haley was aware of someone putting a jacket round her shoulders and then her memories of the scene are perhaps understandably somewhat confused. She has no recollection of any of the questions the men asked her, but did remember tolerably well how they behaved after they had finished their interrogation. Haley said: "There's a man talking to me. He is telling me I haven't seen anything." She could not see who it was because she was so dizzy from the effects of the drug, that her head was leaning over. The man came right up to her and kept telling Haley that she had not seen anything, that she did not see any spaceship, that "they" were angry with her and that it was "none of your damn business." She also remembers a woman dressed in some sort of blue uniform bringing a tape recorder into the room and placing it on the table. Haley was then warned to say nothing more about her experiences and was eventually released.[16]

ALIEN KIDNAPPERS FOILED

AUSTRALIAN KELLY CAHILL

This case took place on 8 August 1993 in Belgrave, Victoria, Australia. Kelly Cahill, then aged twenty-seven, was in a car with her husband as they drove home. Suddenly, both saw a spaceship hovering right above the road immediately ahead. The light from the craft was so bright that Kelly was forced to shield her eyes from its glare by raising her hand to cover them. Then things went blank and as soon as she recovered consciousness, she asked her husband what had happened. Neither was quite aware of the answer to that question, but as soon as they arrived home, they realized that the journey had taken them an hour longer than it should have. Kelly also, to her horror, saw a "triangular mark" upon her navel.

Then they began remembering what had happened to them that fateful night. It had been Kelly who had told her husband to stop the car and investigate the bright light. They had both gotten out of the vehicle and then saw that the large object in front of them was actually some kind of black creature, one that was completely unknown to both of them.

She also saw more of the aliens standing nearby. Then a group of them began moving towards her. She saw another group turning towards another car that was also on the road and had stopped to investigate the bright light. Cahill was seized with an overwhelming fear and a deep sense that the aliens were evil beings. As they grabbed the woman, her husband shouted at them to let her go. She also yelled and screamed at them and suddenly felt violently sick. Then the two of them found themselves back in their car again.

Ever since that strange event, Cahill has had recurring nightmares about her experiences. She claims that one of the creatures not only bent over her body, but appeared to want to kiss her stomach. The aliens were described as being black with fiery red eyes that reminded her of those of flies. Their arms and legs were thin, but they were very tall, her estimate being that they stood at a height of seven feet.[17]

This case is one of the rare abduction experiences where more than one witness was present to confirm the truth of the abductee's story. The description Cahill gave of the aliens is also quite different from the general pattern and that, too, is a further argument in favor of the genuineness of her experiences.

ABDUCTION VICTIM CAUGHT ON CCTV

In December 2010, a woman called Sonia (not her real name) was abducted by aliens. Not surprisingly, she was frightened and emotionally upset by the experience.

A few days before she saw the UFO, Sonia noticed a black helicopter hovering over the field near her house. She became certain that the men inside it were staring directly into the windows of her home. Although it made her feel uneasy, she dismissed it at the time.

A few days later, Sonia was lying in bed when she found herself unable to sleep. She rose from bed and became aware of an intensely bright light in the same field where a few days earlier she had seen the black helicopter hovering. She had a sense that the light was watching her and she saw it drawing ever closer to her house. The craft was shaped like an egg and about the length of fifteen cars laid end to end. It was orange-white in color.

Sonia went back to bed, still restless and unable to sleep. Then her daughter came into her bedroom and said that something kept pulling at her leg. She told the girl it was probably the cat and she should try and go back to sleep.

Soon afterwards, Sonia found herself lying on her back, but not in her own room. To her astonishment, her other daughter was kneeling at her side and speaking to her. She told her mother that it was her "turn" and that "they" would not hurt her.

Then Sonia found herself being pulled sharply by her heel and had the sensation of entering some kind of tunnel. She found herself in another room that was covered with a series of grid lines that seemed to be suspended in mid-air. Sonia described the lines as being holographic rather than physically real. She had the sensation that she was floating in the air and that she was being poked or prodded. Then she heard a mysterious sound, mechanical but with almost the rhythm of electronic music.

Sonia was then put through a number of medical procedures, some of which she was extremely reluctant to talk about. She was frightened, but kept sensing the aliens telepathically reassuring her that she would not be hurt. There was even a kind of screen on which she could watch the tests being carried out on her. She also saw a tall, slim man with long arms and legs. He had dark and prominent round eyes and a large head. Sonia said that the legs and torso of his body did not appear to match, but gave the impression that they had been welded together, as if he had no waist.

Then the medical procedures were completed and Sonia found herself back in her room once more. She was lying in a different position from the one she had been in before her abduction. To her surprise, she was also naked. Not surprisingly, she woke up her husband and told him what had just occurred. Both of them were extremely worried and for the next few days Sonia was too frightened to be left on her own.

She tied a length of string to her wrist and her husband's wrist when they went to bed so that if she was taken again, her husband would also be woken up. In spite of these and other precautions, she continued to be frightened and, after four days of terror, her husband set up a closed circuit television camera in the bedroom in an attempt to reassure her.

On the first night after it had been installed, nothing happened. On the second, however, six days after her first abduction experience, Sonia was taken away once more. This time, it was while she was sleeping and she had no memory of the event. It was not until the following morning she remembered that she had been abducted again and told her husband what had happened. He went off to work but showed Sonia how to look at the footage on the CCTV. Naturally, he expected that the film would show her sleeping peacefully in bed and that she would then realize that it had been nothing more than a bad dream.

On viewing the CCTV footage she got the shock of her life. As she looked through the film, she came to a section where she literally vanished. Although her husband was working, her son and daughters were both at home. She called them in and all of them watched the film in a state of stunned disbelief. Sonia called her husband at work and he returned home at once. Like the rest of the family, he gazed at the footage in a state of utter astonishment.

The CCTV footage clearly shows Sonia and her husband sleeping peacefully in bed. Then she vanishes for a period of thirteen minutes and then reappears instantaneously, pulling the covers of the bed back over her. Her husband turns over in the bed and they both go back to sleep.

Sonia has experienced a number of psychic and unexplained events during the course of her life. One of her earliest recollections is of witnessing a UFO together with her father. The two of them watched a bright light in a field. The following morning, reporters came and took pictures of the field where a large, circular burn on the ground was clearly visible.

Sonia said that the events of those nights completely changed her life. She now felt considerable fear and that her whole life had been shattered by the experience.[18]

ENDNOTES: CHAPTER THREE

[1] John G. Fuller, *The Interrupted Journey*, Corgi, 1981.

[2] Travis Walton, *The Walton Experience*, Berkley, 1978.

[3] Rowan Wilson, op. cit,; Ann Druffel and D. Scott Rogo, *The Tujunga Canyon Contacts*, Prentice-Hall, 1980. Both books leave one with the impression that there is at least a considerable element of truth in Shaw's testimony and that it is certainly not a hoax of any kind.

[4] Druffel and Rogo, op. cit.

[5] Charles Bowen, (editor), *The Humanoids*, Neville Spearman, 1969.

[6] Ibid.

[7] Ibid.

[8] Ibid.

[9] Jenny Randles, *Abduction!*, Robert Hale, 1988

[10] Ibid

[11] Debbie Jordan and Kathy Mitchell, *Abducted*, Carroll and Graf, 1994.

[12] Christa Tilton, "I Was Held Captive in an Underground Alien Base," *UFO Universe*, April-May 1991.

[13] Christa Tilton, *The Bennewitz Papers*, Inner Light Publications, 1994.

[14] Kim Carlsberg and Darryl Anka, *Beyond My Wildest Dreams: Diary of a U.F.O. Abductee,* Bear and Co, 1995.

[15] Kim Carlsberg, *The Art of Close Encounters*, Rainbow Ridge, 2011.

[16] Leah Haley, *Unlocking Alien Closets: Abductions, Mind Control and Spirituality*, Greenleaf Publications, 2003.

[17] Bill Chalker, "An Extraordinary Encounter in the Dandenong Foothills," *International UFO Reporter*, September-October 1994.

[18] Sonia—case investigated by Andy Lloyd and Martin Cosnette.

CHAPTER FOUR
UFO SIGHTINGS

KENNETH ARNOLD

THE SIGHTING THAT LAUNCHED THE "FLYING SAUCER" PHENOMENON

The air over the mountains was perfectly clear. The pilot circled the once-volcanic peak of Mount Rainier slowly, looking for a missing U.S. Air Force plane. There were no clouds at all to be seen in the sky, only the bright gleam of the snow on top of the mountain.

The pilot, Kenneth Arnold, had often discovered lost aircraft. There was also a reward of $5,000 for finding this particular plane. Slowly and carefully, he searched the harsh terrain around and beneath him, looking for the missing craft.

Arnold's attention was suddenly caught by a flash of brilliant light that seemed to be reflected off his own plane. For a moment he felt a surge of panic as he wondered if he might have flown too close to another aircraft. Then, after checking the sky around him, he saw that the nearest plane was far away in the distance (flying from Seattle to San Francisco).

As he looked around to see what else might have caused the brilliant flash of light, he saw, about a hundred miles away in the distance, a whole flotilla of flashing lights. There were nine in all, and they seemed to be flying in formation and at an incredible speed.

The speed of the craft baffled Arnold. As an experienced pilot, he knew of no kind of aircraft that could possibly fly as fast as the objects he was watching. What was it that he was seeing? Was it a top secret U.S. military project? Or was he observing a Soviet invasion of America, using ultra-advanced technology?

As he approached more closely, he was astonished to see that the strange objects displayed signs of having neither wings nor tails. They looked like flat disks, shaped rather like pancakes, slightly rounded at the front and curved at the back. They appeared to emit a radiant bluish-white light.

Determined to obtain as good a view of the craft as possible, Arnold pushed up his window. Against the dazzling white background of the snow that clung to the mountains, he had a perfect view of them. As he watched them, they shot right past the peak at an incredible velocity. From the position of the craft as, one by one, they flew past Mount Rainier, Arnold was able to estimate that the flotilla of strange objects stretched out for at least five miles. By comparing the distance they had traveled with the time on his watch, he realized that these anomalous objects had managed to fly at a speed of 1,700 miles an hour.

The whole period of the sighting had lasted no longer than five minutes. However, it had so aroused his curiosity that Arnold was no longer interested in searching for the missing aircraft. He urgently wanted to tell people about the strange sighting he had made that day. At the back of his mind was also the thought that he ought to inform the authorities in case he had witnessed some kind of Soviet penetration of U.S. airspace.

When Arnold was asked by journalists what the objects looked like, he replied: "Like saucers when you make them skip upon a lake."[1] From this chance, off-the-cuff remark, the name "flying saucers" arose.

In a confidential report dated 16 July 1947, the U.S. Air Force commented: "It is difficult to believe that a man of [Arnold's] character and apparent integrity would state that he saw objects and write up a report to the extent that he did if he did not see them."[2]

It was Kenneth Arnold's sighting, in 1947, that first caught the public imagination and added a new phrase to the English language. Because Arnold's experience was so effective at raising public interest, it is often forgotten that a wave of UFO sightings took place over Scandinavia during the previous year.[3]

GHOST ROCKETS

The first hard news of the 1946 wave came on 19 July 1946. It described how "bright meteors, traveling at fantastic speed"[4] had been observed crossing the skies of southern Sweden. By 27 July, it was revealed that over 500 sightings of "rocket propelled projectiles" had been made across Sweden.[5] By 9 August, a Swedish lieutenant had referred to the objects as "a sphere of fire surrounded by flames of bright yellow."[6] It was also reported that the craft "do not follow a straight trajectory. Some of them change direction, either slowly or abruptly."[7] By 17 August, the first Danish sighting was reported and described as "a new rocket."[8] An even more enigmatic report came from Helsinki on 16 August. This announced that "a flying bomb exploded on Tuesday afternoon over the city of Tammerfors, Western Finland. Witnesses heard a loud explosion, then saw a cloud of smoke in the middle of which appeared a luminous phenomenon. Another rocket has been seen over Helsinki on Tuesday night."[9]

Following an exhaustive investigation by the Swedish Air Force, a few hard facts about the mysterious sightings began to emerge on 26 August. Their findings were that:

THERE ARE TWO TYPES OF PROJECTILES, THOSE WHICH HAVE A LEVEL FLIGHT AT EIGHT HUNDRED KILOMETERS PER HOUR [APPROXIMATELY 487 MPH] WITH A BRIGHT LIGHT IN THE REAR, AND THOSE WHICH FALL VERTICALLY FROM A GREATER HEIGHT WITH A SUPERIOR SPEED.

NONE OF THE PROJECTILES HAS EXPLODED ON THE GROUND. NO ONE HAS BEEN WOUNDED AND NO DAMAGE HAS BEEN DONE. SOME OF THE PROJECTILES MAY HAVE EXPLODED IN THE AIR, BUT NO FRAGMENTS HAVE BEEN FOUND.[10]

Before long, more startling details were added to the already perplexing accounts. The Stockholm correspondent of the *Daily Telegraph* claimed that "some of the objects are said to change their direction of flight after landing, when they go back towards their place of origin."[11]

These sightings of what became known as "ghost rockets" created such a fervor across Europe that the *Daily Mail* decided to mount its own investigation. Although its correspondent was honest enough to admit that atmospheric phenomena and balloons were probably responsible for many of the sightings, he made matters worse by publishing what he called "facts on which all of them [i.e., the witnesses] agree." This list has added extra layers of confusion and mystification to the already mysterious saga.

He claimed that all the witnesses agreed that the objects were cigar shaped; that their tails projected orange or green-colored flames; that their height was between 300 and 1,000 meters [approximately 984 and 3,280 feet]; that they flew about as fast as, or slightly slower than, an aircraft; and that they made no noise, other than a faint whistling sound.

It is worth comparing this list of "facts" with the careful investigation carried out by the Swedish military authorities. They make no mention of shape at all; flames are not mentioned;

the height was at two levels only, not the wide range mentioned by the reporter; that they were not similar in speed to an aircraft; and no mention was made of any kind of "noise" associated with the objects. Presumably, the one that exploded in mid-air must have made a considerable noise. It is difficult to come to any other conclusion than the reporters for the *Daily Telegraph* and *Daily Mail* were either recycling confused gossip or exercising their creative imaginations to make the story more dramatic!

All the same, in spite of the "improvements" added by journalists, the facts are frankly baffling. There seem only two possible explanations of the strange phenomena. One, which is almost certainly the correct answer, is that the Soviet Union was testing secret weapons acquired by them from the Germans at the end of the Second World War. The old V-rocket factory at Peenemünde had been taken over by the Russians, and it is difficult to imagine that they were any less keen to pursue the German research as actively and effectively as the Americans did when they came upon Nazi technology and scientists. The other possibility is that they were advanced extraterrestrial craft.

CLASSIC UFO SIGHTINGS

One classic UFO sightings since 1947 is the tragic sighting that led to the death of Captain Thomas Mantell in 1948. Others include the "Chiles-Whitted Incident" in the same year, the New Guinea sighting in 1955, the Betty and Barney Hill sighting in 1961, the Lakenheath-Bentwaters case in 1956—probably the best evidence of UFO activity ever recorded—and the Rendlesham Forest case in 1980, also highly impressive and compelling.

The famous Socorro sighting was probably a hoax, the Portage County police chase almost certainly a combination of Venus and a weather balloon being mistaken for a UFO, and the New Zealand film beyond any reasonable doubt the result of earthquake activity.

Since all these cases are relatively familiar and have been written about extensively elsewhere, it might be more interesting to focus upon sightings that have been observed during the early part of the twenty-first century.

THE LAKENHEATH-BENTWATERS CASE

This remarkable series of encounters involved two separate Royal Air Force stations. It included sightings by pilots flying two different planes, airborne radar sightings on one of the planes, three radar trackings by three separate ground control bases, and visual sightings by control tower staff at two bases. Such a wealth of documentation is almost unique in UFO phenomena. It is one of the most impressive UFO sighting cases of all time.

The affair began with a radar sighting at Bentwaters RAF station. This sighting was described as an object moving between 4,000 to 9,000 miles an hour and moving in a straight line from forty to fifty miles before vanishing from the screen. It was said to resemble an ordinary plane in all its characteristics, except its astonishing speed.

Half an hour later, another sighting appeared on the radar at Bentwaters. This time the object covered a distance of fifty-five miles in fifteen seconds, equivalent to a flight speed of 12,000 miles an hour. No terrestrial aircraft in 1956, military or civil, was capable of achieving such speeds. While the object was being tracked on radar, ground staff at Bentwaters saw a light hurrying above them. At the same moment, the pilot of a C-47 aircraft also saw a light scampering below his plane.

RAF Bentwaters passed an alert message to RAF Lakenheath, where a visual sighting and two radar trackings of the object had also been observed that night at approximately the same time as the Bentwaters sightings. Lakenheath Radar Traffic Control Center reported observing "an object seventeen miles east of the Station making sharp rectangular course in flight. This maneuver was not conducted by circular path, but on right angles at speeds of 600-800 mph. Object would stop and start with amazing rapidity."[12]

At midnight, the Chief Fighter Controller at RAF Station Neatishead was alerted. He scrambled a De Havilland Venom night-fighter interceptor from Waterbeach and sent it off in pursuit of the target, which was soon lost. A second target was also spotted by the Venom pilot, which his navigator described as "the clearest target I have ever seen on radar." It was also detected by the plane's own airborne-radar system.

At this moment, the UFO was being followed from the air, both visually and on radar, and by ground radar at Neatishead and Lakenheath. To the astonishment of the Venom pilot, within fifteen seconds, the object suddenly appeared behind him and he tried frantically to shake it off. For ten minutes, the UFO chased the Venom before standing still at last and allowing the fighter to return to base.

A second Venom was then scrambled to take its place, but an engine problem forced it to abort the mission. Not long after that, the UFO passed out of the range of ground radar, moving off at a speed around 600 miles an hour. Lakenheath continued to track odd sightings of it on their ground radar until 3:30 a.m. the following morning. This case, not surprisingly, was described by the Condon Report as "the most puzzling and unusual case in the radar-visual files."[13]

It is a baffling series of events and, although it is quite likely that more than one object was involved in the sighting, there is simply no way of accounting for the UFO that stalked the Venom fighter. The variation in speeds reported by Bentwaters and Lakenheath make it a likely possibility that Bentwaters saw a meteorite (although the speeds it records would be slow for that type of heavenly body), but that explanation simply cannot account for the behavior of the object that prevented the Venom aircraft from pursuing it. This case is perhaps the most indisputable evidence of piloted, purposive activity by a craft of a type that was completely unknown at the time. Even Condon could not explain it away.

MODERN UFO SIGHTINGS

UFOS OVER DOCKLANDS, LONDON, 2000-2001

In 2000 and 2001, the Woolwich UFO Research Group reported a number of unexplained sightings in the Docklands area to the Ministry of Defence. Their response was to dismiss them and say that there was no reason to be concerned about possible violations of airspace near London City Airport.

In December 2000, a triangular-shaped UFO was seen over the Millennium Dome, the sighting lasting for a few minutes. The following year, another UFO, described as being bright orange in color, was seen hovering, again directly over the Dome. The group reported the sightings to the MOD, claiming that they constituted a possible threat to planes taking off or landing at the London City Airport. The MOD did not agree and the group's sightings were not investigated further.[14]

TINLEY PARK SIGHTINGS, CHICAGO, 2004-7

Tinley Park, in Chicago, saw a number of UFO sightings between 2004 and 2007. They have generally taken the form of unidentified lights, almost always seen at night. The first UFO sighting in Tinley Park occurred on 21 August 2004. It was described by witnesses as being three red, slow-moving lights in the sky above the Park. On 31 October 2004, the lights were seen again, and further sightings of them were made on 1 October 2005. Following each of the sightings, the National UFO Reporting Center received dozens of reports about them. The director of the center spoke of the high quality of the testimony.

THE TINLEY PARK SIGHTINGS ARE AMONG THE MOST WELL-DOCUMENTED CASES THAT WE HAVE SEEN. YOU HAVE MULTIPLE WITNESSES,

MULTIPLE VIDEOTAPES, EYEWITNESS REPORTS, AND FEDERAL AVIATION ADMINISTRATION AND LAW ENFORCEMENT DOCUMENTATION."[15]

Three red lights appear to hang in the air in a number of different positions. The sheer volume of footage shot by residents makes these one of the best documented sightings of recent times.

A UFO expert has made a detailed study of the Tinley Park sightings and is convinced that they represent some of the best evidence ever recorded.

"WHAT WE ARE LOOKING AT ARE THREE, POSSIBLY FOUR, LIGHTS ACTING EITHER IN CONJUNCTION WITH EACH OTHER OR AS PART OF A FIELD OF SOME SORT," HE SAID. "THEY KEEP GEOMETRIC FORM, AND GENERALLY ACT AS OBJECTS THAT ARE IN SOME WAY CONNECTED TO EACH OTHER."[16]

PILOT SEES UFOS OVER ALDERNEY, CHANNEL ISLANDS, 2007

On 23 April 2007, a pilot was flying from Southampton on the south coast of England to Alderney in the Channel Islands. During the flight, he and his passengers saw two UFOs for a period of around fifteen minutes. Both the pilot and passengers described seeing two large, apparently stationary, craft that glowed with a brilliant yellow light.

Another pilot flying nearby also saw one of the unidentified objects. Radar detected an object in the same position and time as the pilot's sighting. The weather conditions were good and visibility excellent.

The initial sighting was of a bright yellow light. At first, the captain thought that it was a reflection, but he soon realized that it was an emission of light that had a clearly defined shape. It appeared to be pointed at each end and was a bright yellow color with a band of dark gray surrounding it.

A passenger on the flight not only confirmed the details of the captain's sighting, but also noticed a second shape behind the first one. Both objects were described as flat disks, bright yellow in color with a dark band surrounding them.

No satisfactory explanation for the sightings has been found, and the pilot is convinced that they did not represent any kind of aerial vehicle he had ever seen.[16] The objects were both detected on radar and the possibility of the lights being simple reflections is ruled out both by the careful tests the pilot undertook and the accounts of the other witnesses.

UFO CRASH IN ALASKA IN 2007

On 25 September 2007, over the island of Kodiak in Alaska, one of the strangest recent UFO events took place. A bright object, flowing with streamers and giving off considerable electrical discharge, was reported to have crashed. Many witnesses, including police, testified to the phenomenon, but the Coast Guard was unable to detect any evidence of a crash. Residents of a nearby village claimed that the object followed a course from east to west and was slowly descending before it vanished from sight behind the mountains. Other witnesses describe a clearly visible explosion, although what could have caused it remains a mystery.

Investigative units eliminated the possibility of meteors and the next step was to contact various space agencies, considering that the object might have been a crashed satellite. This possibility was also ruled out after all the various space bodies confirmed that none of their satellites had crashed. Whatever was observed that day remains an enigma.[17]

TURKEY UFO SIGHTINGS CAUGHT ON VIDEO, 2008

Between May and September 2008, a night guard in Turkey made a series of sightings of UFOs, which he captured on video. Around two and a half hours of video recordings were made and the footage was examined by the Sirius UFO Space Science Research Center in Turkey, who described it as "the most important UFO images ever."[18]

The footage was carefully analyzed frame by frame, and other witnesses to the sightings were interviewed. The Sirius Center concluded that: "This video footage is 100 per cent genuine," adding that the objects observed were not terrestrial craft, planets, or atmospheric phenomena. The chairman of Sirius said that "in the close-up of some footages of the objects, entities in them can be distinctly made out."[19]

COPS CHASE UFO IN WALES, 2008

On 8 June 2008, a police helicopter in South Wales was waiting to come in to refuel. The control tower at the airport gave them clearance, having received no reports of any other craft in the area, nor any sign of them on radar. While the helicopter was hovering and waiting to land, the crew noticed a bright object immediately above them, which they described as being "flying saucer shaped." As they observed it, the object flew down towards them at "great speed." The pilot banked the aircraft sharply to avoid a collision, after which the object flew away.[20]

The police officers decided to give chase to the UFO, following it across the Bristol Channel until, not far from the North Devon coast, their fuel ran low and they were forced to abandon the pursuit. The crew declared that the object was "clearly visible" to them.[20] A retired RAF glider pilot also observed the object, which he described as "peculiar with lots of flashing lights."[21]

South Wales police force, obviously embarrassed by the entire event, issued a statement which said: "We can confirm that the Air Support Unit sighted an unusual aircraft. This was reported to the relevant authorities for their investigation."[22] The Ministry of Defense, in flat contradiction to the statement by the police, declared that it had "heard nothing of the incident. But it is certainly not advisable for police helicopters to go chasing what they think are UFOs."[23]

In spite of the public testimony of the police officers and the initial response from the police authority, the official position of the South Wales force is now that the helicopter did not give chase to the object.[24] No explanation for the events has been put forward by either the Ministry of Defense or the police force.

UFO AT O'HARE AIRPORT, CHICAGO, 2008

On 7 November 2008, a group of United Airlines staff, including pilots, described seeing a strange craft hovering above O'Hare Airport in Chicago. They said that it was shaped like a saucer, did not have any lights, and remained poised above the airport before suddenly vanishing from view as it shot upwards through the clouds.

The Federal Aviation Administration admitted that the control tower at O'Hare had been contacted by a supervisor who asked if they had seen a disk-shaped object spinning in the skies above. The controllers claimed that they saw nothing and that nothing unusual was detected following a radar analysis. The FAA's explanation was that what had been seen by the witnesses was "a weather phenomenon." Their spokeswoman said: "That night was a perfect atmospheric condition in terms of low (cloud) ceiling and a lot of airport lights. When the lights shine up into the clouds, sometimes you can see funny things." She added that the FAA would not be conducting any kind of investigation into the reported sighting. A United Airlines spokeswoman claimed that the company did "not recall" discussing "any unusual incident" on 7 November.

Many of the witnesses were extremely angry that the authorities refused to investigate their sighting. One of them said firmly: "I know that what I saw and what a lot of other people saw stood out very clearly, and it definitely was not an [Earth] aircraft." The UFO flew through thick cloud and was difficult to see. As it approached the clouds, it seemed to form an open gap of clear air through the clouds before passing through them, the gap closing a few minutes after the UFO had vanished from sight.

The FAA initially denied there they had received any reports of a UFO sighting, but were later forced to "correct" their initial statement after the *Chicago Tribune* filed a request under the Freedom of Information Act. This showed that a United supervisor had contacted the FAA about the sighting.

So, what exactly did the staff of O'Hare see that day? A number of observers, including professional pilots, gave clear descriptions of the phenomenon. Both the FAA and United staff definitely gave erroneous statements to the public; and the explanation for what was seen was "a weather phenomenon," which seems extraordinarily lame when the level of competence of the observers reporting it is taken into account. The refusal of the FAA to investigate is bizarre, and unless it was an extraterrestrial craft, the only other logical explanation is that it was some kind of vehicle from an American secret military program.[25]

NORWEGIAN SPIRAL UFO, 2009

On 9 December 2009, a beam of blue light with a gray, spiral shape coming out of one end was observed at night over Norway. It could be seen from as far away as Sweden, and was photographed in both countries. The spiral light lasted only for some two to three minutes, but was intensely bright. The light looked as if it came from behind a mountain before stopping dramatically in mid-air and then spiraling outwards.[26]

Theories about exactly what was being observed soon began to be put forward. Meteors were quickly ruled out, as was the well-known phenomenon of the "Northern Lights."[27] Some people thought that it might be related to the recent scientific experiments with the Large Hadron Collider in Switzerland.[28] Others suggested that it might be a wormhole in space opening up.[29] Most people, though, were convinced that it was clear evidence of an extraterrestrial spacecraft.

Eventually, the truth emerged, following suggestions from a number of scientists who believed it was probably a failed Russian missile launch.[30] The Russians admitted that one of their missiles had failed and that this was responsible for the dazzling display of lights over Scandinavia.[31]

FLYING PYRAMID OVER MOSCOW 2009

In December 2009, a UFO was seen hovering above the Kremlin in Moscow. Witnesses described it as being a mile wide and as resembling a "hovering pyramid," or "Darth Vader's Imperial 'Cruiser'." Two different spectators filmed the event—one from a car at night and another while it was still daylight.

The UFO was described by Nick Pope, formerly in charge of UFO reports for the Ministry of Defense, as "one of the most extraordinary UFO clips I've ever seen. At first I thought this was a reflection, but it appears to move behind a power line, ruling out this theory."[32] No explanation has been offered by the authorities, and other than the usual claims that the sightings were "hoaxes," the obvious answer is that a real UFO was seen that day.

UFOS CLOSE AIRPORTS IN CHINA, 2010

The year 2010 saw two airports in China closed following UFO scares. The first took place at Xiaoshan Airport on 7 July, when a plane preparing to make its descent contacted the control tower to report having seen an object in the skies. Within minutes of the pilot's report, air traffic control grounded all outbound flights and re-routed incoming aircraft to airports in Wuxi and Ningbo. A total of eighteen flights were affected by the UFO and it was an hour before normal service was resumed.

Local residents added to the mystery by producing photographs taken earlier in the day before the flights had been grounded. They showed an object, glowing with golden light and hovering in the sky, having a tail similar to that of a comet. The object was also said to be emitting rays of red and white light.[33]

Theories immediately started to be put forward. Secret flights by America or Russia were a popular idea. Another was that it was some new Chinese secret military project. Most, though, preferred the theory that it was an extraterrestrial spaceship.[34]

Eventually, an official "explanation" was put forward. The photos taken by residents were claimed to be light reflecting off an aircraft. The night-time sightings were probably nothing more unusual than the strobe lights of a plane flashing.[35] It is possible that what the residents saw an hour before the air crew might have been an entirely different phenomenon, but it is hard to accept that experienced pilots would not recognize aircraft strobe lights. On the other hand, a conveniently anonymous source informed *China Daily* that the sighting had "a military connection."[36]

An airport in Bauotou, Inner Mongolia, was forced to shut down to avoid aircraft colliding with a UFO on 11 September 2010. Three planes had to keep circling the airport until it finally disappeared. Two other flights were diverted to alternative landing places and the airport was shut for an hour "to guarantee safety." A bright light was seen shining in the sky on September 11, about two and a half miles away from the airport. It vanished as suddenly as it had appeared.

Again, explanations for the event were offered, the most common being secret military tests and—a more bizarre theory—that the sighting was of local people flying illuminated kites at night.[37] Many locals, though, remain convinced that it was an extraterrestrial spacecraft.

JERUSALEM 2011—SIGNS OF THE SECOND COMING OF CHRIST?

In January 2011, stunned spectators in Jerusalem saw a ball of bright light coming down out of the sky and hovering above the Dome of the Rock in Jerusalem's Old City. For a moment it hung there, before disappearing at a tremendous speed. A light was also seen in the distance, seeming like a bright star that appeared to fall out of the sky and then hover above the shrine, before vanishing into the distance. The event was witnessed at one o'clock on Saturday morning and two separate videos of it were taken.[38]

The Dome of the Rock, also known as Temple Mount, is one of the holiest sites in the world, sacred to Jews, Christians, and Muslims. Religious believers immediately began to ask if it was a sign from heaven. Christians interpreted it as a possible indication that the Second Coming of Christ was imminent; Jews asked if it meant that the Messiah was at hand; and Muslims wondered if it meant the imminent arrival of the Mahdi.

All three groups, but particularly Christians and Muslims, have also speculated on whether the UFO over Jerusalem's Dome of the Rock was related to the sighting of a "rider on a white horse" seen by thousands of witnesses in Tahrir Square during the Egyptian uprising against former President Mubarak earlier that year. Skeptics have tried to explain it away as a lens flare, but it was observed by thousands of people at a most opportune moment in the Egyptian Revolution, and a figure riding on a white horse is, of course, one of the key figures in the Book of Revelation.[39]

At least three different people filmed the UFO as it hovered above the Dome of the Rock. Footage was shot from a number of different angles and all appear to be showing the same object. As flying above that location is strictly forbidden, the sighting could not have been of a plane or of light reflected from an aircraft.

Followers of Benjamin Creme's religious group immediately linked the UFO seen in Jerusalem with the sighting of a "rider on a white horse" observed in Tahrir Square, and claimed that they were signs of the imminent arrival of Maitreya, the World Teacher. Creme also declared that the rider on the white horse was a blessing from him on the work of liberation that the people of Egypt were attempting at that time.[40]

The video footage is highly impressive, and it is not surprising that so many religious believers have seized on it as confirming their hopes for some kind of return to Earth by Christ, the Messiah, or the Mahdi. The only answer from skeptics so far has been to claim that the videos are hoaxes. One person who took pictures of the UFO believes that the photos he took that day are actually of a ghost or spirit.[41]

UFO OVER SAO PAULO, BRAZIL 2011

In late February 2011, the Brazilian television station G1 showed a film of an object shaped like a disc that hovered among the clouds for a few minutes, before vanishing in a flash of bright light, leaving behind it a colorful trail.

Two witnesses saw the object above them as they were driving their car in the town of Agudos, near Sao Paulo. They left their car and shot video footage of the object with their camcorders. The men claimed the earth shook as the disc disappeared in a flash of light, and that other people had also reported the earth as having moved in the vicinity of their sighting. The U.S. Geological Survey said that there were no earthquakes in the region and the film has already been dismissed as a hoax by many UFO experts.[42]

UFO OVER THE BBC, LONDON 2011

On 26 June 2011, three white objects in the shape of discs were seen crossing the skies right above Yalding House, home of BBC Radio One. They were filmed on a mobile phone by a witness and, in the film, at least one other person is also busily taking pictures of the sighting. The footage is highly impressive and, so far, the only skeptical suggestion is that it might be an elaborate hoax created by the many special effects companies in the area.[43]

SIGHTINGS CAUGHT ON VIDEO IN NEW ZEALAND, 2011

In August 2011, two women from Rotorua in New Zealand saw and took videos of an unidentified object in the skies above them. One of the women said that she often saw planes and knew that the object she saw was not an aircraft.

Although she thought it might have been a comet, she said that it did not resemble any comet she had ever seen. The other woman who also videoed the encounter also contacted her about the sighting and said that she believed what she saw was "an angel."[44]

The video footage shot by the two women drew an international reaction. Even the vice president of the Rotorua Astronomical Society was unable to provide an explanation for the strange sightings.[45]

AUTHOR'S SIGHTING OF UFO IN SKY FROM BACK GARDEN

In September 2011, the author and his wife were sitting in the back garden of their house around midnight when they became aware of a bright light in the sky above. It radiated beams of light from it, always in the same direction.

On this particular September night, they took out their binoculars to observe it more closely. To their astonishment, it was not a star, but resembled a large spaceship. The front of the vessel had very powerful red and green lights that shone through the darkness. Its shape was elongated, with a well-lit upper chamber, and the brightness of its glow was dazzling.

Over the course of the next few nights, they went out once more into the garden. Sometimes the sky was so dark that not even the stars could be seen, but when visibility allowed they saw what seemed to be some sort of mothership with smaller scout ships associated. The object appeared to move very slowly from south to north. On successive nights it was once again found in the same position, hovering and emitting some kind of steadily pulsing light.

On one occasion, they saw an aircraft flying close by. The pilot must have seen the strange phenomenon. The object was seen at different times and in slightly different positions over a period of some hours during the course of about a week.

It appeared to be a mothership accompanied by other, smaller, scout ships. The object was seen over a period of some nights with good visibility and clearly appeared to be some kind of controlled, powered craft.[46]

THE PHYSICAL EVIDENCE

One of the most serious problems in Ufology is the relative scarcity of hard physical evidence of extraterrestrial activity. The scarcity of such physical trace evidence makes those cases where it has been detected all the more important.

One possible candidate for physical trace evidence is the sighting on 13 July 1969 in Garrison, Iowa, by two teenage girls, Patti Barr and her cousin, Kathy Mahr. Both saw a large, round object with a bright orange color and a double row of small lights across the middle. They watched it hovering over a soya bean field and it left a red glow where it had been observed. Next morning, Patti's father, Warren Barr, looked at the field and found wilted plants and a patch of bare ground in the shape of a circle that showed clear signs of burning.[47]

Perhaps the most impressive case involving physical traces is the UFO encounter reported over Falcon Lake, Canada. Steven Michalak was looking for minerals in the woods near the lake when he heard geese cackling in alarm. Looking up, he saw two reddish-colored, oval shapes in the sky descending rapidly to earth.

Michalak observed the strange objects for around thirty minutes. One of them took off soon after it had landed, but the other came to rest on a rock. In his own words, he saw the machine "changing in color, turning from red to gray-red, to light gray, and then to the color of hot stainless steel, with a golden glow around it." He added that the object "radiated heat."

As he gazed upon the vessel, he saw a door open with a purple light coming from it. Then he experienced "wafts of warm air that seemed to come out in waves from the craft, accompanied by a pungent odor of sulfur. I heard a soft murmur, like the whirl of a tiny electric motor running very fast."

Michalak decided to approach nearer to the vessel and heard voices coming from inside it. He tried talking to them in six different languages, but received no answer. Putting on some green lenses over his goggles he looked inside the opening. He later described what he saw:

> THE INSIDE WAS A MAZE OF LIGHTS. DIRECT BEAMS RUNNING IN HORIZONTAL AND DIAGONAL PATHS AND A SERIES OF FLASHING LIGHTS, IT SEEMED TO ME, WERE WORKING IN A RANDOM FASHION, WITH NO PARTICULAR ORDER OR SEQUENCE.

Michalak then examined the surface of the ship, which he found had neither rivets nor seams, as far as he could observe. While he was engaged in this activity, the vessel tilted and he felt a burning sensation around his chest. Then his rubber glove melted and his shirt caught fire, after which the ship rose up into the air and vanished into the distance.

He went at once to the hospital and was treated for chest burns. Michalak also informed the RCMP (Royal Canadian Mounted Police—the "Mounties"), who showed no interest in his story. Following the incident, he developed a number of strange medical conditions, including diarrhea, vomiting, and nausea, as well as losing twenty-eight pounds in weight. Even after his health returned to normal, he continued to experience some curious symptoms. Three weeks after his sighting, he developed blisters on his chest and a rash running from his chest to his ears. Five months after the event, he felt a burning sensation round his chest and neck, as well as developing red spots on his skin, swelling on his chest and hands, and he experienced dizzy spells.[48]

SUMMARY

What exactly do all these sightings over a period of more than sixty years mean? Some of them certainly are natural phenomena, especially ball lightning and earthquakes, which have been mistaken for UFOs. Others are clearly secret military projects, a tiny handful of them are hoaxes, and some are just poorly observed reports of planes, balloons, and similar objects.

A hard core of sightings remains, though, for which it seems impossible to find any other explanation than extraterrestrial visitations. Final proof of the existence of life on other planets would be one of the most exciting events in human history. Perhaps that fascinating prospect is drawing near at last.

ENDNOTES: CHAPTER FOUR

[1] Kenneth Arnold and Ray Palmer, *The Coming of the Saucers,* Amherst, 1952. It is, however, worth remembering that a farmer called John Martin, reporting a sighting in Texas from 1876, said that "the object was the size of a large saucer." Rowan Wilson, *UFOs*, Parragon, 1997.

[2] Army Air Force telex, 16 July 1947.

[3] A detailed study of the 1946 Scandinavian wave is given in Aimé Michel's, *UFOs: Anatomy of a Phenomenon*, Ballantine, 1987.

[4] Resistance, 19 July 1946.

[5] L'Aurore, 27 July 1946.

[6] Le Monde, 9 August 1946.

[7] La Depeche de Paris, 17 August 1946.

[8] Le Monde, 16 August 1946.

[9] Liberation Soir, 25 August 1946.

[10] Epoque, 28 August 1946.

[11] Ronald Story, *UFOs and the Limits of Science,* New English Library, 1981.

[12] *East London Advertiser*, 3 July 2011.

[13] "Lights in sky over Tinley Park have UFO believers looking up," *Chicago Sun Times*, 18 October 2006.

[14] Ibid; also Jeff Ruby, "Do You Believe?" *Chicago Magazine*, March 2007.

[15] Clarke, David, J. Baure, P. Fuller, M. Shough (2008), "Report on Aerial Phenomena observed near Channel Islands, UK, April 23, 2007," *Journal of Scientific Exploration* 22 (2): 291–308; Joel de Woolfson, "Pilot's UFO shock," *The Guernsey Press & Star,* 26 April 2007; Haines, Lester,. "UK airline pilots spot giant UFO, 'Mile wide' mystery object hovers off Channel Islands," *The Register.* 27 April 2007.

[16] Christiansen, Scott "UFO mystifies local officials". *Kodiak Daily Mirror*, 26 September 2007; "Red Fireball and Explosion Witnessed Over Alaska." *Skywatch Media.* 28 September 2007.

[17] Sebastian Lander, "Flying Saucer Filmed in Turkey," *The Sun*, 21 October 2008.

[18] "Video Shows UFO Aliens Flying Over Turkey," *The Herald Sun*, 22 October 2008.

[19] "UFO spotted by police helicopter," BBC News, 20 June 2008

[20] John Coles, "Cops chase a UFO over Cardiff," *The Sun*, 26 July 2008.

[21] BBC News, 20 June 2008.

[22] Ibid.

[23] Ibid.

[24] Agence France-Presse, "UFO alert: Welsh police spot 'unusual aircraft,'" Brietbart. com, 20 June 2008.

[25] CBS News, 11 February 2009.

[26] "Strange lights in Norwegian sky sparks mystery," *The Daily Telegraph*, 9 December 2009.

[27] .Virginia Wheeler, "Spiral UFO puts Norway in a spin," *The Sun*, 9 December 2009.

[28] "Norway wormhole is First Contact, claim UFO watchers," news.com.au, 10 December 2009.

[29] Will Stewart, "Mystery as spiral blue light display hovers above Norway," *Daily Mail*, 9 December 2009.

[30] "Strange 'Norway spiral' likely an out-of-control missile," *New Scientist*, 10 December 2009; "Norway spiral: A rocket scientist explains the mystery," *Christian Science Monitor*, 10 December 2009.

[31] Clara Moskowitz, "Russia admits missile caused UFO lights," MSNBC News, 10 December 2009.

[32] *Daily Mirror*, 18 December 2009.

[33] Mary Huang, "UFO in China's skies prompts investigation," ABC News, 14 July 2010.

[34] Ibid.

[35] Ibid.

[36] Ibid.

[37] ABC News, 5 October 2010.

[38] *Vancouver Sun*, 1 March 2011.

[39] *Sydney Morning Herald*, 4 February 2011.

[40] http://watcherslamp.blogspot.com, 8 February 2011.

[41] "Ghost Horse Caught on Tape During Egypt Protests Sparks Theories of Biblical Proportions," 4 February 2011, http://earthissues.com.

[42] Fox News, 1 March 2011.

[43] *West London Today*, 27 June 2011.

[44] *The Daily Post*, 6 August 2011.

[45] Ibid.

[46] Personal sighting by the author and his wife in September 2011.

[47] Jenny Randles ad Peter Warrington, UFOs: A British Viewpoint, Robert Hale, 1979.

[48] Story, "UFOs and the Limits of Science."

CHAPTER FIVE

SECRETS OF THE MOON

Poets and lovers have always praised the Moon. Her mild beams give light to the world when darkness reigns in the skies at night. The people of Schilda, "city of fools" in German legend, were once asked which was more important, the Sun or the Moon? Without even needing to think they answered at once: the Moon, of course. The Sun only shines by day—when we don't need it!

SCIENTIFIC MYSTERIES

The Moon has always been a source of magic and mystery. It holds many secrets, some of which remain unsolved to this day. One of the most baffling is its undoubted influence on the tides, the growth of crops, and the menstrual cycles of women. By all rational calculations, the Moon's distance from the Earth should be too great for the lunar gravitational pull to override the Earth's own gravity. Yet its influence upon all such things is a matter beyond dispute. How the Moon could possibly affect us as it does remains a mystery.

Scientists tell us the Moon is barren, lifeless, and inhospitable. They claim it was a planet formed when it spun off from Earth, going into an orbit of its own, partly circling Earth, partly orbiting around the Sun. These claims have been made since the seventeenth century, but in recent times, especially since the lunar expeditions, they have become more and more difficult to sustain. Though there is fierce controversy over the possibility of life, past or present, on the Moon, there seems overwhelming evidence now that the Moon is not, and never was, a body that spun off from the Earth. Indeed, it is increasingly doubtful if it was even a body formed within the solar system at all.

Even on inert matter, the Moon plays its part. Silver chloride for instance is crystallized by lunar influence. Radio reception can be affected by lunar interference, while the effect of the Moon, especially the full moon, on human behavior is well known. The very word "lunatic" comes from the Latin term for the Moon. How is that possible, given the relative distance of the two planets and the weakness of the gravitational pull of the Moon? Clearly, a whole series of fascinating questions about the way in which our satellite operates remain unanswered.

HOW OLD IS THE MOON?

Not surprisingly, people have always been fascinated by the Moon. Russian mystic Helena Blavatsky claimed, in 1888, that it was older than the Earth. She also claimed that the Lords of the Moon, our ancestors, pioneered and developed our planet.[1] The curious thing is that the NASA missions actually give strong support to her claim, based solely on messages that she claimed to have received from elemental Masters, dwelling in Tibet, that the Moon is older than the Earth. Although it has been suggested that Blavatsky's "Masters" were actually beings from outer space…

Another Russian, the Siberian magus Gurdjieff, had a very unusual theory about the Moon. He regarded it as a world that was still being born. The Moon, he claimed, was a living, breathing organism fed by Earth and slowly sucking away the vitality from the planet. As humanity advanced mentally and spiritually, it would escape from the malign influence of the Moon.[2]

MOON MADE OUT OF ICE?

Equally controversial is the Glacial Cosmogony put forward by the eccentric Austrian astronomer Hans Hörbiger. Because of the personal belief in his theory by both Hitler and Himmler, it became highly influential during the period of Nazi rule.[3] In essence, Hörbiger claimed that the birth of worlds in the universe came about as the result of a constant struggle between the elements of fire and ice. The Moon itself was a solid block of frozen ice. All the prior claims by Hörbiger have long since been conclusively refuted. The Moon is not made out of ice any more than it is out of green cheese; the origins of the universe were not the result of a cosmic battle between ice and fire, and almost everything that Hörbiger claimed about the Moon and the universe in general is clearly mistaken. There is, however, one surprising exception—a solitary grain of possible truth within his otherwise eccentric cosmology.

THE CAPTURE THEORY

The most interesting aspect of Hörbiger's cosmogony and the only one that seems to have gained in plausibility since the NASA spaceflights is his claim that the Moon is not a body formed out of Earth, but a planet that strayed into the solar system from outside and became trapped by the gravitational pull of Earth. This notion is known as "the capture theory."

In this simple form, the capture hypothesis has been gaining ground steadily since the 1970s. However, Hörbiger also claimed that the Moon that shines in our skies at present is not the only satellite to have circled our Earth. He believed in a whole series of lunar bodies, each, in turn, having first approached too closely and then becoming trapped by the gravity of Earth before gradually spiraling inwards until they crashed down upon the planet and caused widespread devastation.[4]

There is as yet no geological or archaeological evidence in support of Hörbiger's theory of more than one Moon. However, there is a considerable body of testimony in the form of myths and legends that speak of a time when there was no Moon at all in the sky.[5] There are also myths and legends of capture, collapse, and of their having been successive Moons.[6] There is additionally a very small amount of astronomical evidence in its favor, though it has always been hotly disputed.[7] Certainly, the calendar found at Tiahuanaco appears to refer to a time when the orbit of the Moon around the Earth was entirely different from its present rotation.[8]

NASA SAMPLES CONFIRM THE CAPTURE THEORY

What is beyond question is that the NASA expeditions have tended to confirm Hörbiger's claim that the Moon is not native to our solar system. To begin with, rock samples taken from the Moon are older than the oldest rocks found on Earth. That hardly makes sense if the Moon is the same age as our planet.[9]

Although the figures have been fiercely disputed, some lunar rocks appear to be older than the solar system.[10] This is quite inconceivable on the orthodox spin-off hypothesis, though it presents no problem at all if the capture theory is adopted. There is no reason at all why a body that came from outside the solar system should not be older than our system.

There are also problems with the composition of some of the material recovered from the Moon. As Urey pointed out, "moon rock has been shown to contain xenon isotopes from fission of plutonium-244 that are not found on Earth."[11]

The Apollo 12 and 14 missions brought back to our planet samples containing uranium 236 and neptunium 237, elements that have never been found on Earth in a natural form.[12] An entirely unique element named KREEP was also found on the Moon, having a high proportion of potassium, phosphorus, and rare earth elements. This new element was discovered by the astronauts of Apollo 12 and is dated at 4.5 billion years of age, even though the oldest known rocks on Earth go back no further than 3.6 billion years.[13] Once again, all the evidence points strongly to the probability of the capture hypothesis.

FOSSIL MAGNETIC FIELDS

A further problem is the presence of electromagnetic anomalies found within lunar rocks. The rocks brought back to Earth by the Apollo missions were found to contain "fossil magnetic fields."[14] This would only be possible if either the Moon had once possessed a huge core of molten iron or if it had passed through a global magnetic force field. Tests have shown conclusively that the Moon has never had a molten iron core. There is also no magnetic field of sufficient intensity anywhere within the solar system.[15]

The inescapable conclusion is that the Moon must be a body formed outside the solar system altogether, which at some time in its history passed through a strong magnetic field before coming into the solar system and being captured by Earth. This seems decisive evidence in favor of the capture hypothesis.

MORE MOONS THAN ONE?

Curiously, this magnetic anomaly also gives some support to Hörbiger's theory about a lunar capture and subsequent collapse upon Earth. As Ubell explained, "If the moon were once near the earth so that the earth's magnetic field could magnetize moon rocks, the two bodies would have been so close that the moon would break up under the gravitational pull of the earth."[16]

Such a close passage would indeed produce an effect of exactly this nature, which is, of course, what Hörbiger claimed to have happened with previous moons. This obviously offers no solution to the mystery of our present moon that must have been magnetized in outer space before being captured by earth's gravity. However, it may well be the correct explanation of previous moons and their demise.

While Hörbiger's theory as a whole is scientifically incredible, his notion of the Moon as a body captured by the Earth now seems highly probable. There is also good reason to suspect that his idea that the Earth has had more than one moon may also be correct.

MORE ELECTROMAGNETIC ANOMALIES

A change in the Earth's magnetic field from a reversed to a normal polarity took place around 10,000 B.C.[17] It is entirely possible that this may have been the occasion on which the Earth's previous moon approached too closely and collapsed upon the planet with catastrophic results. Certainly, there is abundant evidence from geology, archaeology, and legend that some kind of worldwide cataclysm took place around this date. The notion that it was caused by the collapse of a previous moon is, of course, just speculation. All the same, it does provide a rational explanation for an otherwise baffling series of events.

I have already mentioned the curious effect the Moon has on human beings, plants, and animals and, in particular, its power over the tides. It is not immediately obvious how a body so far away could have these effects.

It has been suggested that the mathematics involved make the whole idea of any lunar influence upon the tides impossible to explain. The only way in which it might make sense is if either the Moon were much closer to the Earth than we know it is, or, if some sort of electromagnetic phenomenon was involved. The case for just such a vortex system has been put forward by Last, for the following reasons:

THE PULL OF THE EARTH TO PREVENT THE WATERS FROM RISING INTO A HEAP AND MOVING IN THE DIRECTION OF THE MOON IS ABOUT 288,000 TIMES GREATER THAN THE PULL OF THE MOON. THE MOON COULD REGISTER NO ASCENDANCY OVER ANY PULL OF THE EARTH UNTIL A POINT WAS REACHED WITHIN 40,000 MILES OF THE MOON'S SURFACE COMPARED WITH ITS REAL DISTANCE OF 240,000 MILES. AS REGARDS THE TIDE ON THE OTHER SIDE OF

THE EARTH AWAY FROM THE MOON, THE POSITION IS STILL MORE IMPOSSIBLE.[18]

LAST GOES ON TO CLAIM THAT, CONTRARY TO WHAT ORTHODOX ASTRONOMERS BELIEVE, THE MOON DOES NOT REFLECT SUNLIGHT. INSTEAD, LUNAR LIGHT IS GENERATED BY THE INTERPLAY OF A ROTATING MAGNETIC FIELD BETWEEN THE EARTH AND THE MOON IN A VORTEX SYSTEM WITH THE EARTH REPRESENTING THE POSITIVE MAGNETIC POLE AND THE MOON THE NEGATIVE ONE.[19]

LIFE ON THE MOON

The most fascinating question of all, of course, is the oldest one: is the Moon inhabited? Or, if not now, was it ever a living world? The testimony of myth and legend is unanimous and unequivocal: the Moon, at least in earlier times, was alive and full of inhabitants.

In an almost forgotten fantasy, Cyrano de Bergerac wrote of how he had traveled successfully to the moon after being launched by eighteen rockets. Intriguingly, he correctly described the distance at which lunar gravity takes over from the earth's pull thirty years before Newton is said to have discovered the principles of gravity.[20]

ANOMALOUS LUNAR OBSERVATIONS

The first claim to have observed life on the Moon was made by the Restoration scholar Sir Paul Neal. Gazing through his telescope to scan the lunar landscape, to his amazement he saw a live elephant. Not surprisingly, this claim made him a laughing stock. The general consensus among his contemporaries was that a mouse had crept into his telescope. Clearly, ridiculous explanations of anomalous phenomena are not a purely modern device to avoid the challenge of change.[21]

The first anomalous lunar observations of stature were made by the great astronomer Herschel. In 1783, he saw star-like lights on the dark side of the Moon and viewed them again in 1787. On 2 October 1790, Herschel's most spectacular sighting took place. During a total eclipse of the Moon, he saw bright points of light, small and round, clearly visible.[22] Not surprisingly, in the fierce scientific debate that raged throughout the eighteenth and nineteenth centuries over the question of lunar habitation, Herschel was always confident that life did indeed exist on the Moon.[23]

Nor was Herschel the only person to see lights on the dark side of the Moon. Not only did he see them twice, but his observations were also confirmed with a further sighting by Wilkins in March 1794.[24]

The most spectacular of all the eighteenth century lunar observations were made by Schroeter. On 25 September 1789, he saw two lights around a circular shadow in the lunar Alps.[25] What is more, Schroeter was convinced that he had detected "a small twilight in the moon, such as would arise from an atmosphere capable of reflecting the rays at the height of about one mile."[26]

Nor was that the limits of Schroeter's astonishing claim. He added that he not only believed the Moon to be inhabited, but that he had observed "certain elevations which appear to him to be works of art rather than of nature." He also believed that there was some evidence of water vapor that could irrigate the planet.[27]

ANOMALOUS LUNAR OBSERVATIONS IN THE NINETEENTH CENTURY

Even more remarkable were the observations made by Gruithuisen in 1822. He described "great artificial works in the moon erected by the lunarians," adding that he believed them to be "a system of fortifications thrown up by the selenitic engineers."[28] He was even convinced that he had observed "a lunar city" on the borders of the Sinus Medii.[29]

Anomalous lunar observations continued throughout the nineteenth and twentieth centuries. On 16 October 1866, Schmidt observed Linné changing shape.[30] A truly remarkable event was observed on 13 May 1870, when a brilliant display of lights that appeared to be controlled was seen on Plato.[31] On 24 April 1874, Schafarik saw a brilliant white object cross the Moon slowly and pass on.[32] In March 1877, a dazzling light was seen in Proclus and another one near Picard.[33] On 23 November 1877, Klein saw a luminous triangle in Plato.[34] On 20 November 1878, an explosion was seen near Nicholi.[35] In 1894, Muller saw a round, black object crossing the Moon diagonally. The same object was also observed in 1895 by the director of the Smith Observatory.[36]

ANOMALOUS LUNAR OBSERVATIONS IN THE TWENTIETH CENTURY

The twentieth century continued to provide a series of bizarre lunar observations. In 1912, Harris saw a huge, dark disk gliding above the surface of the Moon. It was 250 miles long and 50 miles wide.[37] On 30 March 1950, Wilkins observed a strange glow in Aristarchus.[38] On 29 July 1953, O'Neill photographed an apparently artificial bridge in Mare Crisium with sunlight clearly streaming underneath it.[39]

Even more spectacularly, between 14 and 21 June 1959, Almor and other observers saw a dark, elliptical object maneuvering over 1,243 miles (2,000 kilometers) above the lunar surface, which made a complete transit of the Moon in 35 minutes, before reappearing once more as if it was a satellite. After the first few observations, it was found that the moment of its reappearance could be predicted exactly.[40]

LIFE ON THE MOON AND THE SPACE PROGRAM

Some of the most impressive evidence for the possibility of life on the Moon has come as a result of the space program. Very curious photographs have been released that are extraordinarily hard to explain away as natural phenomena.

There are also stories of UFO sightings and claims of contact by former astronauts and cosmonauts. Curiously, although NASA has been at pains to deny all the claims that their missions saw anomalies or made contact, the Russians have not taken the same view. A number of cosmonauts have been quite open about their sightings of UFOs while engaged in their space exploration.[41]

The earliest encounter appears to have been the strange photographs taken by astronaut James McDivitt on the Gemini 4 space mission.[42] He took a picture of an unidentified object through the capsule window. When NASA released the photos of the mission, McDivitt's shots were not among them. Instead, they offered the public a series of pictures of sun flares. Unusually, McDivitt broke ranks and protested that they were not the photos that he had taken. NASA hastily agreed and claimed that his pictures had not come out. Whether or not this is true, in those early days of space exploration their denial was enough to kill the story.

Film shot during the Gemini 12 mission in 1966 showed brilliant unidentified lights near the Moon.[43] No convincing explanation for these was ever offered. Instead, a strategy of denial and ever less credible attempts to portray them as purely natural phenomena began.

THE APOLLO 11 LUNAR MISSION AND UFOS

More unidentified flashing lights on the Moon were also filmed by Aldrin during the Apollo 11 lunar landing mission.[44] There have also always been rumors about what exactly it was that Armstrong and Aldrin saw when they landed on the Moon. Stories range from the lunar vehicle being pursued by an unidentified craft, of the astronauts finding huge spacecraft already parked upon the planet, and of the supposedly live broadcast of Apollo 11 being mysteriously censored as the crew reported seeing alien spaceships.

Ham radio operators allegedly picked up the "missing" transmissions from the spacecraft to NASA. However, the only evidence they have to offer is "transcripts." Slightly more compelling is the fact that the KGB also claim to have heard the "deleted" portions of the NASA broadcast. However, all intelligence agencies engage in disinformation and lies as everyday activities, so their statement cannot be taken simply at face value. The KGB, in particular, were past masters at peddling plausible untruths. What is a matter of public record is that the Apollo crew reported seeing a "light" on the rim of a crater. Immediately after this statement, transmission from the Moon suddenly and mysteriously shut down for two minutes. It is claimed that the transcripts picked up by ham radio operators and the KGB took place during the two-minute period when Apollo 11 was off the air.[45]

The following statement is alleged to have been made by Apollo 11 to NASA Mission Control:

THOSE BABIES ARE HUGE, SIR... ENORMOUS...OH, GOD! YOU WOULDN'T BELIEVE IT! I'M TELLING YOU THERE ARE OTHER SPACECRAFT OUT THERE, LINED UP ON THE FAR SIDE OF THE CRATER EDGE. THEY'RE ON THE MOON WATCHING US.[46]

Scientists working for the KGB add further lurid touches of their own. For example, Dr. Aleksandr Kazantsev claimed that Aldrin had actually filmed several extraterrestrial craft on the edge of the crater.

Armstrong is alleged to have admitted privately that Aldrin did shoot film of spaceships, but that the CIA seized it as soon as the Apollo crew returned to Earth. He is also supposed to have accused the CIA of being behind a sophisticated and wide-ranging cover-up operation about the NASA encounters with alien spaceships and even alien life.[47]

It is only fair to state that both Armstrong and Aldrin indignantly deny the claims made on their behalf. They are both adamant that no evidence of alien life or technology was found by them on their visit to the Moon. It is also only right to be wary of stories whose principal sources are radio hams and the KGB.

On the other hand, it was (and still is) highly suspicious that the mysterious two-minute break in transmission occurred when it did, just as the mention of a light in a crater had been made in full hearing of millions of people across the world. At the very least, it is probable that NASA panicked and switched off the public transmission facility in case anything out of the ordinary was about to be said.

PHOTOGRAPHIC ANOMALIES OF THE APOLLO 11 MISSION

There are a number of contradictions between the statements made by NASA about the physical state of the Moon and the photographs of the lunar mission released by them. The Lunar Rover, for instance, clearly throws up dust in what is supposed to be a planet without any atmosphere. Some of the photographs also show evidence of what appears to be some kind of artificial lighting. Most curious of all, a number of photos appear to show clear evidence of gigantic artificial structures on the surface of the supposedly lifeless Moon.[48]

There is also the curious "Chatelain affair." In April 1995, an article written by the former director of communications at NASA, Dr. Maurice Chatelain, made the astonishing claim that "several mysterious geometric structures of unnatural origin" had been both seen and photographed by the astronauts.

NASA's reaction to this statement was curious. Instead of asserting that the structures were simply natural features that had been mistaken for artificial ones, as was their normal procedure when claims of extraterrestrial life on the Moon were made, they denied that Chatelain had ever been connected with NASA in any way.

There is considerable disagreement about that particular question, with a number of other NASA employees flatly contradicting the testimony of their employer. Certainly, evidence from other former NASA staff backs up Chatelain's story. Donna Teitze, a photographic technician, Dr. Richard Bergrun, a scientist, Richard Hoagland, a consultant, Marvin Czarnik, an engineer, Ken Johnston, a data and photographic documentation supervisor, and Richard Nicks, a geologist, all support the essential claims made by Chatelain.[49]

WERE THE LUNAR LANDINGS FAKED?

The anomalies in many of the lunar photographs are among the key evidence offered by people who believe that the Apollo missions never took place at all and that the entire project was simply faked in a Hollywood studio. Curiously, some of these people believe both that the Apollo missions were faked and that astronauts met with extraterrestrial life on the Moon. Those who believe in both these incompatible ideas generally claim that Apollo missions 11-13 were genuine and that 14-17 were fictitious, as the aliens on the Moon warned the astronauts to stay away in the future.

The claims that the lunar landings were faked come in two forms. One theory is that it is impossible for astronauts to travel into space because of the intense solar radiation.[50] The second is that the missions never took place because of prohibitive costs and/or the existence of aliens, or at the very most, that the program was aborted early and the later missions shot in a studio. There is even alleged to be a "source" in NASA who has supplied details about the fake landings.[51]

The notion that solar radiation is so deadly that any kind of space travel would be impossible is obviously completely contradicted by the scientific evidence and it would rule out extraterrestrial visits by aliens to Earth as well, as journeys in the opposite direction. On the other hand, the suggestion that the lunar landings may have been at least partly faked is slightly more plausible.

The photo of Armstrong and Aldrin planting the American flag on the Moon, for example, is a genuine puzzle. Aldrin's shadow is clearly longer than Armstrong's and, yet, if the only available light on the Moon came from the Sun, such unequal shadows should not have been seen on the photographs.[52] The photo of the module from Apollo 14 resting on the lunar surface shows no crater beneath its metal feet. The words "United States" on the craft should be in shadow, yet they are clear and easily seen. Since there is no refracted light on the Moon, an observation confirmed by Aldrin, there must have been another source of light when this photo was taken.[53]

Photographs from both Apollo 15 and 16 show no stars in the sky above, yet, if there is no atmosphere on the Moon, as is constantly claimed, the stars would be clearly visible, more so than on Earth.[54]

In November 2002, astronomers used the Very Large Telescope (VLT), the most powerful telescope in the world, to try and detect proof of the Apollo landings. The photos they released subsequently have convinced all but the most hardened doubters, though some complain that they only appear to show the near side of the Moon, rather than its dark side.

EXPLANATIONS OF THE PHOTOGRAPHIC ANOMALIES

There are two credible explanations for the various curious anomalies in the NASA photos. Either the NASA missions were shot in a studio on Earth, or—surely a far more reasonable hypothesis—the photos were retouched when they reached NASA processing laboratories.

Photographs are edited for all kinds of reasons: to improve their quality, to improve their appearance and, which is probably what happened with the lunar shots, to iron out anomalies and make them disappear. It is far more credible that NASA decided to retouch photos to conceal evidence of alien life on the Moon, past or present, than that the lunar landing program itself was, partly or wholly, faked. Buzz Aldrin's indignation at the suggestion that he never went to the Moon at all is entirely understandable. Indeed, it is justified. There simply are not good enough reasons for believing that the lunar landings never took place.

What does seem entirely probable is that as soon as the material came back from the moon, and was received by NASA, they set to work on a cover-up program designed to suppress the overwhelming evidence of a lunar atmosphere and, in particular, of lunar inhabitation, past or present. The anomalies in the NASA photos represent an attempt to cover up the existence of some form of extraterrestrial civilization on the Moon, not that the Apollo program itself never took place.

EVIDENCE FOR LIFE ON THE MOON

It is doubtful if many people realize how strong the evidence in favor of lunar inhabitation, at least in the past, really is. Leaving aside the question of alleged contacts with Selenites, there is overwhelming evidence of apparently artificial structures of staggering size upon the planet.

The Shard, a one-and-a-half mile high spire of glass, has unfortunately been damaged by a meteorite. Its undamaged companion, the Spire, is a twenty-mile-high version of the Shard, located in the Mare Crisium, the very place where O'Neill photographed an artificial bridge in 1953. Why are there two versions of the same object, identical in every way but size, on different parts of the Moon?[55]

Other clearly artificial structures are "the Cube," a "megacube" on top of a tower seven miles high; the "Castle," a "geometric, glittering, glass object hanging more than nine miles above the surface of the Moon"; and the "City," a grid pattern resembling a city about the size of Los Angeles, and situated in the Ukari region, near a saucer-shaped crater.[56]

Photos from both the US and Soviet space programs also show "glass-like, highly complex domes" now clearly in ruins.[57] There is even a picture of Apollo 12 astronaut Alan Bean standing among "tiers of glass-like ruins."[58]

Other bizarre photographic anomalies include the "Bridge over the Sea of Crisis," a twelve-mile long structure; the "Blair Cuspids," seven 600-foot-high obelisks in the Sea of Tranquility; and the "Straight Wall," also known as "the Railway," a dead straight structure, 70 miles long and 12,000 feet high."[59] In fact, over 200 dome-like structures have also been photographed on the Moon. Even more curiously, some of them have vanished and then mysteriously reappeared in other areas of the planet.[60]

The notion of the absence of an atmosphere on the Moon is also becoming increasingly difficult to sustain. Apart from the photographic anomalies, most of which would disappear if the existence of a lunar atmosphere was admitted, there is also the fact that cloud formations above the Moon have been observed and photographed. A hundred-mile-wide cloud of vapor was also detected by NASA's instruments and explained away with one of the most ludicrous excuses ever used to support the increasingly fragile cover-up: it represented the urine ejected into space by NASA astronauts. Apollo 8 also sent back photos that showed lush, green vegetation on the supposedly arid and lifeless lunar hills. Other photos clearly indicate the presence of water on the planet.

In the light of all these facts, as Chatelain himself remarked, the existence of a cover-up is no longer a hypothesis, but a simple fact. For whatever reason, NASA undoubtedly has been concealing evidence of lunar habitation, past or present.

IS THE MOON A PLANET OR AN ARTIFICIAL SATELLITE?

Another extraordinary fact about the Moon is that it appears to be hollow. Strangely, H. G. Wells suggested this in his science fiction novel *The First Men in the Moon*.[61] Certainly, the Apollo 12 lunar module rang like a bell for an hour after it landed, and the Apollo 13 satellite produced a ringing sound that lasted for eighteen hours. NASA astronauts reported that meteorite impacts on the Moon also led to a prolonged ringing.[62] It is not easy to understand how this could happen unless the Moon itself was hollow.

This curious phenomenon has led some scientists to claim that perhaps the Moon is not really a planet at all, but a spaceship or artificial satellite launched into space by an advanced galactic civilization a long time ago.[63] The Soviet scientists who are the leading exponents of this theory believe that the Moon was abandoned countless eons past and that it is a dead world now. However, they imply that when it was a functioning satellite full of inhabitants, it may have sent out missions to Earth to explore and colonize our own planet. This would represent the real source of human civilization, an input from a superior culture whose base was the now-defunct satellite we call our moon. While the satellite theory does seem unlikely, the existence of an advanced civilization on the Moon, at least in the past, now seems virtually certain.

RECENT EVIDENCE OF LIFE ON THE MOON

In July 1999, two biologists from the Russian Academy of Sciences made a sensational announcement at an astrobiology conference in Denver, Colorado. The two scientists, Stanislav Zhmur and Lyumila Gerasimenko, told the delegates that they had examined microorganisms brought back to earth by Luna 16 and compared them with the Luna 20 mission core samples. During the course of this analysis, they had discovered what are known as "spiral filamentous microorganisms found on present-day Earth."[64]

Luna obtained its samples through drill cores controlled by robots that were also hermetically sealed while they were on the Moon. On their re-entry to Earth, they were immediately analyzed under controlled conditions in a laboratory. Zhmur declared that "the lithified remnants are tightly conjugated with the mineral matrix." There was no possibility that the samples had been contaminated.[65]

To put it in plain English, the microfossils were embedded within the lunar rock itself, frozen within the samples. This is clear evidence that life, at least at the microbial level, once existed upon the inhospitable surface of the Moon.

Astronaut Pete Conrad confirmed that bacteria could survive upon the planet. Apparently, an earlier lunar mission had left behind a piece of equipment and his own team brought it back to Earth for analysis. They discovered that the bacteria within it had not only survived, but actually managed to grow and develop. It is clear from Conrad's own account that at least some forms of life can live, thrive, and increase on the supposedly dead planet.[66]

The evidence of glass structures in Mare Crisium, rectangular structures in the Kepler crater, manufactured edifices in Hortensius, and the other strange artificial constructions we have already discussed, all show clear proof of former lunar civilization. The new evidence from Russian scientists simply gives a biological confirmation to the existing testimony of lunar archaeology.

We can now confidently say, yes, there once was life on the Moon, our nearest neighbor in space. From the evidence of the network of large artificial structures they built upon the planet, we can also state with certainty that it was intelligent life.

For all we know, there may still be aliens dwelling upon the planet. Our ancestors may well have come to Earth and brought civilization to humans. There may yet be distant cousins of ours living in the lunar landscape.

Even now they may still be visiting our planet.

ENDNOTES: CHAPTER FIVE

[1] Helena Blavatsky, *The Secret Doctrine,* Theosophical Publishing House, 1970 (first edition 1888).

[2] P. D. Ouspensky, Tertium Organum.

[3] Michael FitzGerald, *Hitler's Occult War*, Robert Hale, 2009.

[4] H S Bellamy, *Moon, Myth and Man*, Faber, 1938.

[5] Ibid.

[6] Ibid.

[7] H. S. Bellamy and Peter Allen, *The Great Idol of Tiahuanaco*, Faber, 1959.

[8] Ibid.

[9] Don Wilson, *Our Mysterious Spaceship Moon*, Sphere, 1976.

[10] Ibid.

[11] Dr. Harold Urey, *Chemistry*, February 1974.

[12] Report by the Argone National Laboratory to the Third Scientific Conference, Houston.

[13] *Science News*, June 1973.

[14] Earl Ubell, *New York Times* magazine, 15 April 1972.

[15] Dr. Charles Sonnett, Deputy Director of Astronautics, NASA Ames Research Center.

[16] Ubell, op. cit.

[17] *Science News*, 29 January 1972.

[18] C. E. Last, *Man in the Universe,* Werner Laurie, 1955.

[19] Ibid.

[20] Cyrano de Bergerac, *Voyages to the Sun and Moon*, Routledge.

[21] Timothy Harley, *Moon Lore,* Charles E. Tuttle, 1970.

[22] W. Raymond Drake, *Messengers from the Stars*, Sphere, 1978.

[23] Philosophical Transactions of the Royal Society, 1795.

[24] Drake, op. cit.

[25] Ibid.

[26] John Brinkley, *Elements of Astronomy*, Dublin, 1819.

[27] John Narrien, *An Historical Account of Astronomy*, London, 1833; also, Philosophical Transactions of the Royal Society, 1792.

[28] Gruithuisen, quoted in Harley, op. cit.

[29] Drake, op. cit.

[30] Ibid.

[31] Ibid.

[32] Ibid.

[33] Ibid.

[34] Ibid.

[35] Ibid.

[36] Ibid.

[37] Ibid.

[38] Ibid.

[39] Ibid.

[40] Ibid.

[41] *UFO Reality*, Issue 9, August-September 1999.

[42] Ibid.

[43] Ibid.

[44] Ibid.

[45] Ibid.

[46] Ibid.

[47] Ibid.

[48] Ibid.

[49] Ibid.

[50] *X-Files*, Issue 2, 1997.

[51] Ibid.

[52] Ibid.

[53] Ibid.

[54] Ibid.

[55] *Fortean Times*, Issue 90.

[56] Ibid.

[57] Ibid.

[58] Ibid.

[59] Wilson, *Aliens*.

[60] *Unexplained: Beyond Reality*, September 1997.

[61] H. G. Wells, *The First Men in the Moon*.

[62] Wilson, *Aliens*.

[63] This has been suggested by astronomer Andreas Kaiser. The Soviet scientists Mikhail and Alexandra Cherbakov also argued strongly in favor of it in *Komsomolskaya Pravda,* 10/1/1970. Don Wilson, op. cit., also suggests that the Moon may be an artificial satellite.

[64] Stanislav I. Zhmur and Lyudmila M. Gerasimenko. "Biomorphic forms in carbonaceous meteorite Alliende and possible ecological system—producer of organic matter hondrites" [abstract] in *Instruments, Methods and Missions for Astrobiology II,* Richard B. Hoover, Editor, *Proceedings of SPIE* Vol. 3755 p. 48-58 (1999).

[65] Ibid.

[66] Jane Goldman, *The X-Files Book of the Unexplained*, Volume 2, Simon and Schuster, 1996.

CHAPTER SIX

THE MYSTERIES
OF MARS

To the ancients, Mars was the bringer of war, a malevolent planet that glared down upon Earth with a fierce, red glow. Now, as our own planet sends out space probes to map and analyze the planet, we wonder if in olden days vast aerial armadas swept down to Earth from Mars to make war upon humans or bring them the benefits of a more advanced civilization than our own.

David Bowie famously asked the question in his song "Is There Life on Mars?" Of course, he was far from the first to raise that issue, but it remains a burning question even today. Over the course of the last 200 years, opinions on the subject have fluctuated wildly. At first, the consensus was that life probably did, at least in the past, exist there. Then the pendulum swung to complete rejection of the idea. In recent times, a growing body of evidence has made scientists cautiously optimistic about the prospects of at least some kind of life on the planet in the distant past and perhaps even life at the present time.

CANALS ON MARS

One fateful night, in 1877, when Mars was in opposition to Earth, Italian astronomer Giovanni Schiaparelli trained his telescope upon the "red planet." To his utter amazement, he saw a vast network of dark lines that criss-crossed Mars. Astronomers before him had often seen patches of light and darkness upon the planet. However, before Schiaparelli's observations, conducted with the very latest telescopic technology of his day, no one had seen these mysterious lines.

Schiaparelli referred to them by the Italian word "canali," which simply means "channels." By an unfortunate mistranslation into English from Italian this became "canals." At once, speculation ran riot, for canals, of course, are always the product of design by some kind of intelligent life.[1]

Schiaparelli's observations may have been the first recorded sighting of the Martian canals. They were not, however, to be the last. Other astronomers also began to report seeing the lines. As time went on, even maps of them were produced. Polar ice caps and clouds were also recorded.[2]

The most indefatigable researcher into the canals of Mars was the brilliant, but eccentric, astronomer Percival Lowell. Using telescopic, photographic, and spectrographic analysis, Lowell was able to "discover" over 700 canals about 300 miles long, intersecting at oases.[3] Rival astronomer Campbell, using exactly the same methods and equipment as Lowell, determined that none of these canals existed or could exist upon Mars.[4]

The Ufologist Aimé Michel has his own theory about the Martian canals. He claims that they do represent clear evidence of intelligent life, but not in the way that Lowell thought. Michel believes that the canals are actually green lines upon the planet that carry life. In support of his theory he cites the following extraordinary facts:

IN 1909, ANTONIADI REPORTED THE APPEARANCE ON MARS IN THE CENTER OF THE ELYSIUM DESERT (AT 240 DEGREES LONGITUDE AND 10 DEGREES LATITUDE NORTH) DUE NORTH OF MARE CIMMERUM, A SMALL GREEN PATCH—AN "OASIS." IN 1939, THAT IS THIRTY YEARS LATER, THE PATCH HAD VANISHED, BUT THE ASTRONOMERS FOUND THAT TOW OUTLINES OF CHANNELS HAD APPEARED AT THE NORTHERN AND SOUTHERN ENDS OF THE DESERT AT CYCLOPIA AND AMEATHEA. THE TWO CHANNELS GREW LONGER DURING SUBSEQUENT OPPOSITION. IN 1959, OBSERVERS WERE AMAZED TO DISCOVER THAT THEY HAD JOINED UP AFTER CROSSING 1,000 TO 1,500 MILES OF DESERT IN A STRAIGHT LINE. FURTHER, THEY HAD JOINED UP AT EXACTLY THE SAME POINT WHERE ANTONIADI HAD FOUND HIS "OASIS" FIFTY YEARS EARLIER, AS THOUGH THEY KNEW WHERE THEY WERE GOING.[5]

Michel suggests that this demonstrates "some mental activity, proof of brain power, or possibly, of some industrial development."[6]

ANCIENT KNOWLEDGE OF MARS

Another Martian anomaly concerns the knowledge of the two moons of Mars by ancient people. They were spoken of as early as the time of Homer's *Iliad*.[7] Virgil also mentioned them a few centuries later.[8] The French satirist Voltaire spoke of them in the eighteenth century along with much other astronomical information supposedly not discovered until long after his time.[9]

Most impressive of all the early references to the moons of Mars, however, is the detailed description given of them, in 1726, by Jonathan Swift. He gave a reasonably accurate account of the size of the moons, their distances, and their period of rotation.[10] When American astronomer Asaph Hall finally observed them through a telescope in 1877, he was so struck by the relative accuracy of Swift's account that in a moment of superstitious dread he named them "Phobos" and "Deimos," meaning "fear" and "terror."[11]

THE MYSTERY OF THE MOONS OF MARS

There are a number of anomalies connected with the Martian satellites. To begin, no other satellites known to us are so close to their own planet, nor so small in size. Even stranger, Phobos moves across Mars from west to east, quite unlike normal moons attending on planets. Both satellites also reflect far too much light for bodies made out of rock and earth.

These strange aspects of the behavior of the moons have led to the claim that perhaps they are artificial satellites made out of metal. The leading exponent of this theory was the Russian astrophysicist Shklovski.[12] In support of his claim, he pointed out that Phobos appeared to be gradually slowing down and that the thin atmosphere present on Mars meant that planetary action alone could not account for the satellite's retardation.

Phobos has also unquestionably deviated from its normal path by as much as two degrees. Shklovski went on to claim that both Phobos and Deimos were not moons, but artificial satellites launched centuries ago and gradually decaying.

Curiously, the scientist was not the first to make this suggestion. Nearly a hundred years earlier, Blavatsky had also claimed that the moons of Mars were artificial.[13] However, Mariner 9 photographs show clearly that Phobos and Deimos are in fact barren chunks of rock.[14]

MESSAGES FROM MARS

On 13 November 1897, a truly remarkable event took place, offering the best evidence up to that time for the possible existence of life on Mars. The *New York Times* wrote up the story as follows:

MESSAGE PERHAPS FROM MARS
STRANGE CHARACTERS FOUND IN AN AEROLITE WHICH STRUCK
THE EARTH NEAR BINGHAMPTON

BINGHAMPTON, NOV. 13. SCIENTISTS IN THIS CITY ARE PUZZLING OVER AN AERIAL VISITOR THAT DROPPED IN THIS VICINITY EARLY THIS MORNING. PROF. JEREMIAH MCDONALD, WHO RESIDES ON PARK AVENUE, WAS RETURNING HOME AT AN EARLY HOUR THIS MORNING WHEN THERE WAS A BLINDING FLASH OF LIGHT, AND AN OBJECT BURIED ITSELF IN THE GROUND A SHORT DISTANCE FROM HIS PREMISES. LATER IT WAS DUG UP AND FOUND TO BE A MASS OF SOME FOREIGN SUBSTANCE. IT WAS STILL HOT, AND WHEN COOLED OFF IN WATER WAS BROKEN OPEN. INSIDE WAS FOUND WHAT MIGHT HAVE BEEN A PIECE OF METAL ON WHICH WERE A NUMBER OF CURIOUS MARKS THAT SOME THINK TO BE CHARACTERS. WHEN OPENED THE STONE EMITTED A STRONG SULPHUROUS SMELL.

PROF. WHITNEY OF THE HIGH SCHOOL DECLARED IT TO BE AN AEROLITE, BUT DIFFERENT FROM ANYTHING HE HAD EVER SEEN. THE METAL HAD BEEN FUSED TO A WHITISH SUBSTANCE, AND IS OF UNKNOWN QUALITY TO THE SCIENTIFIC MEN WHO EXAMINED IT. THE AEROLITE IS NOW ON EXHIBITION, AND WILL BE PLACED IN THE GEOLOGICAL COLLECTION OF THE HIGH SCHOOL. SEVERAL PERSONS HAVE ADVANCED THE OPINION THAT THIS IS A MESSAGE FROM ANOTHER PLANET, PROBABLY MARS. THE MARKS BEAR SOME RESEMBLANCE TO EGYPTIAN WRITING, IN THE MINDS OF SOME. PROF. MCDONALD IS AMONG THOSE WHO BELIEVE THE MYSTERIOUS BALL WAS MEAN AS A MEANS OF COMMUNICATION FROM ANOTHER WORLD.[15]

One is immediately reminded that some of the witnesses to Roswell spoke of the markings on the wreckage found at Brazel's ranch as being like hieroglyphics. Perhaps this is not simple coincidence and there is a more dramatic explanation for these facts. At this distance of time and with the relatively unsophisticated methods of analysis available to the local scientific community in 1897, it is hard to state conclusively that this was a message from beyond Earth, still less to attribute its origin to Mars. All the same, it is a truly baffling mystery.

RADIO MESSAGES FROM MARS?

We come now to the claims for radio messages from Mars. The earliest such claim appears to have been made by that neglected genius Nikola Tesla. On 7 December 1900, a series of lights were observed by astronomers, apparently in the form of dots and dashes, the symbols of Morse code. Tesla also received the same signals on his experimental radio.[16]

In September 1921, while he was experimenting on board his yacht, Electra Marconi picked up some curious signals, apparently in code, on the astonishing wavelength of approximately 93 miles (150,000 meters). At that time, no terrestrial radio had a transmission range greater than approximately 8 miles (14,000 meters). This strange phenomenon led Marconi to suspect that he had somehow tuned in to radio broadcasts relayed from Mars.[17]

Between 22 and 23 August 1924, Professor David Todd, using a wavelength of approximately 3 miles (6,000 meters), set up a radio photograph transmission machine, hoping to capture photographic signals from Mars. His machine was in operation for a total of thirty hours. During that time, he was able to record a regular pattern of dashes and dots from his side of the instrument. Another observer working completely independently of Todd also picked up the same pattern of dots and dashes.

What was even more remarkable about Todd's observations are what was detected from the Martian end. "On the other side, at intervals of half-an-hour, appeared a group of signals which took the rough form of a human face. Experts in codes and intelligence of the United States Army and of other countries did not succeed in deciphering the signals of this cosmic emission."[18]

HAS THE MARTIAN LANGUAGE BEEN DECODED?

During the latter part of the nineteenth century, four different women, all mediums, gave detailed accounts of life on Mars through a process known as channeling.

The most impressive was Catherine Muller, better known by her pseudonym of Hèléne Smith. She not only declared that she had made many out-of-body trips to Mars by using astral projection, but also claimed to have learned the Martian language. Swiss psychologist Theodore Flournoy investigated her case and became fascinated by it.[19]

Her account of Martian dress, behavior, customs, and other aspects of their life was interesting, but what Flournoy found most impressive was the language that Smith spoke in her trance states. He analyzed it carefully and found that it had its own grammatical structure and, that while the words were apparent gibberish, they possessed consistent meaning. He concluded that she had invented an entirely new language and learned its "rules."[20]

Smith's accounts of Mars were the most detailed and consistent of all the "psychic" accounts from this period. Other channeled testimony from the period contradicts Smith on a number of points, particularly the Martian language. The Martian adventures recounted to psychologist Carl Jung are less detailed and impressive than Smith's version of life on Mars. Another woman was hypnotized in France and described floating up into space and visiting many planets. She claimed to have met a friend who had been dead for ten years on one of her visits to Mars. Not much of her testimony adds anything significant to the information communicated by Smith. Smith's testimony remains the most impressive "channeled" account of life on Mars.[21]

CONTACT WITH MARS

Many people claim to have made contact with Mars, including George Hunt Williamson, George Adamski, and George King. One of the most interesting contact reports was by the now almost-forgotten Cedric Allingham.

Allingham claimed that, on 10 February 1954, he was visited by aliens from Mars. His experience took place at Forres in Scotland and began when, to his amazement, he saw a saucer-shaped object descending from the sky above and landing. His astonishment grew still greater as a figure resembling a human being emerged out of the craft.

A mutual attempt at communication between the alien and Allingham through the use of sign language led to the conclusion that his visitor came from Mars. Unfortunately, though

Allingham produced a photograph as testimony to the truth of his encounter, it is unimpressive.[22]

Robert Dickhoff, another contactee, makes the astonishing claim to have gained access to the "Martian archives." According to these sources, human civilization was instituted by beings from Mars, who created the two lost worlds of Lemuria and Atlantis, as well as setting up seven cities in the Antarctic that are now buried beneath the polar ice. He adds that the Martians are the true overlords of Earth.[23]

MISSIONS TO MARS AND STRANGE ASTRONOMICAL OBSERVATIONS
Mars and the Scientists

Mars has always been thought of as the most likely planet in the solar system to support life. Not only does the testimony of myth and legend tend to support the idea that all the planets in our system are inhabited, but a whole series of observations using many different methods of discovery and analysis have given greater plausibility to this view.

Unfortunately, the scientific accounts of Mars have altered dramatically over the years. The evidence from telescopic observation led astronomers to believe that the atmosphere was 96.5% nitrogen, 1.2% argon, and the remainder being oxygen, carbon dioxide, and water vapor.[24]

This remained the orthodox view until the spectrographic analyses conducted since 1950, which painted a very different picture of the Martian atmosphere. Their findings were that no oxygen at all existed on the planet and almost no water vapor, the rest being carbon dioxide.[25] Somewhere along the line, the plentiful supply of nitrogen had disappeared, together with the argon.

In 1958, Sinton made a spectrographic analysis of Mars. He found evidence of the existence of seaweed, which would require the presence of water and the possibility of carbon-based life upon the planet.[26] In 1962, Russian scientist Kozyrev claimed that the red color on Mars was not the natural color of the surface, but the result of the presence of blue and violet rays in the atmosphere. He also believed that the Martian atmosphere was similar to that of Earth. Kozyrev, too, found evidence of vegetation upon the planet.[27]

None of the claims by either man survived the observations of Mariner and Viking, although subsequent observations have suggested that there might once have been water and vegetation on Mars.[28]

Astronomical anomalies of Mars

It remains a mystery how Galileo was able to see the four moons of Jupiter through his telescope in 1609, yet failed completely to detect the two moons of Mars, which are considerably closer. How could they have altered their positions so dramatically in 200 years? And how were Homer and Virgil able to write about them at a time when telescopes supposedly had not even been invented?

We have seen already that, in principle, Mars at least used to be a planet with the capability of supporting intelligent life. There is now considerable evidence to support this idea. Various anomalous astronomical observations from the nineteenth century onwards give strong support to the notion of life on the planet.

Charles Fort spent his life uncovering and recording strange facts and was particularly assiduous in gathering material that suggested the evidence of life on Mars. He describes two anomalous observations in October 1892: one by Lockyer, who detected the presence of clouds upon the planet, and one by Secchi, who observed a spot on Mars.[29]

Two years later, red lights were seen to "wink" on Mars, followed by apparently answering lights appearing on the Moon. On 8 May 1873, white spots were observed.[30] An extraordinary event took place on 7 June 1873, when a luminous object was observed emerging from the planet. Even more remarkably, it was later seen to explode in the air above what was then the Austro-Hungarian Empire.[31]

May 1877 saw yet more anomalous phenomena. That month light spots were observed during an opposition of Mars. At the same time, an unidentified object was seen visiting the Moon. Its journey was followed by curious unexplained changes in the lunar crater Linné.[32] On 10 June 1892, Mars was dotted with lights.[33] Pickering recorded a bright spot on the planet on 25 November 1898.[34]

More anomalous astronomical observations

20 May 1903 saw an object like a dust cloud observed on Mars by Lowell. New canals were also discovered that year spreading out from Lacus Solis. In addition, a huge yellowish cloud was seen covering Trivium Charontis. In December 1911, yet another yellow cloud hid Sytris Major from sight. Further formations of unusual cloud types were seen in 1924 and 1926.[35]

A brilliant flaming spot was seen on Sithinium Lacus on 4 June 1937, while April 1938 saw Slipher observe evidence of changes in the Martian canal system, which appeared as if they were the result of deliberate intelligent activity.[36]

In 1948, a sighting of a huge translucent cloud was seen, while in December 1951, a remarkable observation was made by the same astronomer. A brilliant glare was seen on Tithonius Lacus together with what looked exactly like a snowstorm over the South Pole of Mars. July 1954 saw another brilliant flare on the planet.[37]

The oppositions of Mars to Earth in 1954 and 1956 brought a whole cluster of reports of anomalous observations together with a vast increase in the number of UFO sightings. Both Fort[38] and Vallee[39] have demonstrated a statistically significant correlation between oppositions of Mars and UFO sightings.

Observations reported during this period included vast yellow-colored dust circles, lights on the planet, strange objects seen on or near the surface, a melting of the ice-cap on Mars, new canals, some sort of vegetation and, most intriguing of all, a cloud in the shape of the letter "W," 1,100 miles long, which remained visible for two whole months. It was pointed out that as the telescopic image was received upside down, the "W" might really have been an "M"—"M" for Mars, perhaps?[40]

MARINER TO VIKING

The Mariner space probe then gave yet another picture of the Martian atmosphere. Again, carbon dioxide was found to predominate, but argon was now said to constitute as much as 30% of the atmosphere. This time they also found evidence of oxygen, carbon monoxide, water vapor and hydrogen, though all in small quantities.[41]

The Viking probes then reduced the volume of argon dramatically to a mere 2%. Nitrogen was found in proportions of around 2%. Carbon dioxide now constituted 95% of the atmosphere. The remainder was made up of oxygen and water vapor. Once again we saw observations directly contradicting the earlier confident pronouncements about the atmosphere and life potential of Mars.

The images received from Viking's observations have led modern astronomers to conclude that the canals are an optical illusion resulting from the natural human tendency to see patterns in unrelated dots. As for the famous "dark spots," they are simply areas of desert and not as was once believed Martian seas.

On the other hand, Viking demonstrated that lakes and seas certainly were a feature of the Martian landscape at some point in the distant past. There was also evidence of rock erosion by rain. Beneath the polar ice-caps on Mars lies a vast quantity of frozen water. Viking also showed that the planet had enjoyed spells of quite temperate weather during which it would have been possible for the planet to have supported life. It has also sharply altered previous perceptions about the Martian atmosphere, making it appear a less hostile environment and one in which life could have developed.[42]

How is it that such utterly contrasting views of the Martian atmosphere and water possibilities could all be based upon the latest scientific equipment and methods available at the time? Is it really credible to believe that 96.5% nitrogen could simply disappear—or be mistaken for carbon dioxide? Both nitrogen and carbon dioxide are eminently familiar to us, and it seems at least curious that an error in this order of magnitude could have been made.

In the same way, it seems odd that the percentage of argon could be as high at 30% and in other observations not traced at all. Is it really as simple as an improvement in our technology—or have conditions on the red planet changed dramatically in fifty years? Or is it that the date released to the public earlier was deliberate disinformation to conceal evidence of life on Mars? Or, for that matter, the result of the more recent probes? Clearly such a wide variation of descriptions of the Martian atmosphere and life-bearing potential is at the very least surprising.

Even the material sent back by Mariner has not stood up to subsequent scrutiny. Mariner 4, for instance, reported in July 1965 that Mars had an atmosphere mainly of carbon dioxide and nitrogen, with some oxygen, argon, and water vapor. Mariner 5 reported, on 30 July 1969, that the planet had an atmosphere mainly of carbon dioxide with no nitrogen, but with methane gas and ammonia near the South Pole.[43]

What the Mariner missions also showed, however, quite unexpectedly, was that although the Martian canals appeared to be purely natural phenomena, they were amazingly wide and deep. Some canals were 700 miles long and 200 miles wide.[44]

VIKING

In 1976, Viking landed two vehicles on the surface of Mars. They found some evidence of inexplicable chemical activity in the Martian soil, but no evidence of life past or present. The effect of Viking I on the speculation about life on Mars was rather curious. On the one hand, it seemed to kill off the possibility that life existed on the planet. On the other, it left researchers with more anomalous data to explain.

Just as in 1954 and 1956 a cloud shaped with the letters "W" or "M" had been observed, so too Viking sent back photos to Earth of rocks with mysterious letters, "B" and "S" being the most prominent, and the number "2" clearly marked upon them.[45]

Viking's confident pronouncements that there was no life on Mars seemed to put an end to speculation. Then, many years later, scientists from the National Autonomous University of Mexico carried out more rigorous experiments. To their delight they found strong evidence that Viking appeared to have missed clear signs of life on Mars.[46]

The university found "low levels of organic compounds in these soils, but we cannot detect them by the same technologies used by the Viking mission." In other words, the methods of analysis and testing that Viking used were inadequate and, with the use of more sophisticated and modern technology, signs of life are definitely present. By 2011, further analysis reinforced the results of the previous tests and it was confirmed that Viking had discovered signs of life, but that the procedures used to evaluate them had been unable to detect them.[47]

Clearly, in spite of the initial negative findings, Viking did discover signs of life on the planet. It opens up a whole range of new possibilities about life in the solar system.

SURVEYOR

One of the functions of the Surveyor probe, launched on 15 September 1997, was specifically to examine the mysterious features of the red planet in detail and to attempt to determine whether or not they were natural or artificial in origin. It investigated every inch of Mars over a two-year period and its results were hoped to be able to furnish the basis for a projected map of the planet. At some unspecified date in the future it remained their goal, at least publicly, to send astronauts on a mission to Mars.[48]

One of the results of Surveyor was to confirm the existence of water on Mars—not only that, but fresh water that was flowing and that carried sediment. It also implied that the planet was capable of supporting life, not simply in the past, but even today. Between 1999 and 2005, it took thousands of pictures, including gullies and craters with fresh deposits that were clearly the result of the action of flowing water. An excited scientist from Arizona State University commented: "Five years ago, we were talking about water on Mars five million years ago. Today, we can honestly talk about water on Mars today."[49]

PATHFINDER

The Pathfinder unmanned probe monitoring Mars also threw up some curious anomalies. So bizarre are some of the data and photographs sent back from the planet that Hoagland and other researchers have openly accused NASA of attempting to cover up the existence of an ancient civilization on Mars. Certainly, some of the photos of what NASA claim are rocks look far more like mechanical objects. As the ENTERPRISE Mission, a research group, commented; these include:

> SEVERAL IDENTIFIABLE TRACKED VEHICLES, SEVERAL EXPOSED (THOUGH HIGHLY ERODED) MOTOR-LIKE DEVICES SOME WITH ASSOCIATED WINCHES); A VARIETY OF WHEELS; COUNTLESS CYLINDRICAL-LOOKING CANISTERS STREWN ACROSS THE LANDSCAPE, OR PROJECTING UPWARD FROM THE LANDSCAPE, MANY WITH EQUALLY GEOMETRIC, MACHINE-LIKE PROJECTIONS; AND COUNTLESS OTHERS, UNRECOGNIZABLE BUT HIGHLY GEOMETRIC (AND UNLIKELY GEOLOGICAL) SURFACE FEATURES, ON A WIDE VARIETY OF SCALES, ALL INTERMIXED WITH A VARIETY OF GLASS-LIKE, CLEARLY REFRACTING PANE-LIKE FEATURES EXTENDING (ALSO AS NO "ROCKS" COULD OR SHOULD) TRANSPARENTLY ABOVE THE DUSTY MARTIAN SURFACE.[50]

THE MARTIAN TRIANGLE

Another Martian anomaly is the so-called "Martian Triangle," a hypothetical force field analogous to those alleged to exist in the "Bermuda Triangle." The Martian Triangle, or, to give it its more technical name, "Square Co-ordinate XV," arose from various malfunctions that befell a number of probes in the region of Mars. By 1976, four American and four Soviet space probes had been damaged in one way or another while approaching the planet. The problems included burnt-out circuits, inexplicable failures in radio transmission, exploding batteries, failures of the steering system, and damage to modules on landing.

Considering the enormous technical difficulties that the space probes faced even reaching Mars, none of these problems are particularly surprising. Even on Earth electrical equipment malfunctions or breaks. How much more likely is it that, given the additional problems of deep-space operations, there should be additional complications for which it is almost impossible to plan in advance or to understand and rectify if discovered?

Even so, it has been suggested that cosmic life forms concealed on Mars are responsible, anxious to prevent humanity from landing upon their planet. A Viking technician added to the speculation by making the incautious remark "an unseen highwayman up there seems always to know when we are sending something up in his neighborhood."[51] No doubt this was said in a moment of understandable exasperation at yet another failure, but it led to wild speculation and a host of conspiracy theories that helped to hold back public support for further space exploration.

In August 1993, after yet another failure—this time to regain radio contact with the Mars Observer—the voices of the conspiracy theorists were raised again and the phrase the

"Martian Triangle" once more appeared in the news. They took a perverse pleasure in pointing out that of over twenty attempts at missions to Mars since the early sixties, nearly all of them had failed. In the majority of cases, the problem was a communications breakdown. When the Russians sent out a mission in 1989; it too lost contact, although in this case it was because the mission controllers sent the wrong signals to the craft. With the vast distances involved, the technical problems, and the underfunding of space budgets for many years, it is hardly surprising that most of the missions have failed. The idea of a Martian Triangle is, however, romantic and appealing, simply not borne out by the facts.[52]

THE FACE ON MARS

It was also the Viking probes, far more detailed and complex than any of the previous investigations into the planet, which first led to the amazing discovery of the "face on Mars." As NASA researcher Toby Owen studied the pictures of the Cydonia region, he blinked in astonishment to see what looked exactly like a pair of eyes. On a closer examination, he saw that not only eyes, but an entire face could be seen in the photos from the Plain of Cydonia. There were two eyes, a nose, and a mouth, clearly visible and obviously intentionally delineated.[53]

Further investigations by Vincent DiPietro and Gregory Molenaar began in 1979, when they discovered a second NASA photograph of the "face." They also found evidence of eyeballs, teeth, and hair. On comparing the geology, meteorology, and other factors of the Cydonia region, they found no natural explanation for the face. In fact, the harder they looked at Cydonia, the more they discovered other anomalous photos.

Ten miles south-southwest of the site of the face, the two researchers found another "mountain." This one was shaped like a pyramid, but with five triangular sides running straight from the base of the object to the point at the top. Each side had a V-shaped formation at the bottom, which appeared to be some sort of supporting system for the entire edifice. Unlike the results of normal weather erosion, the most worn areas were at the base, not in the middle section as they should have been.[54]

Erol Torun, who had worked as a cartographer for the US armed forces and was highly skilled in the analysis of photos taken by satellites, then set to work to examine the pyramid-shaped mountain. He found that there was "no known natural mechanism to account for the D & M Pyramid's formation."[55]

Even more surprisingly, a mathematical analysis of the shape of the object showed that it appeared to have been constructed in accordance with the principles of geometry. As he remarked, the chances of such an apparently artificial structure also happening to exemplify geometrical tenets by pure chance was extraordinarily remote.

Torun's findings were picked up by Richard Hoagland, whom we have already come across in the context of evidence for intelligent life on the moon.[56] Contemplating the possibility of final proof of life on Mars with some excitement, Hoagland compared the Martian monuments with similar ones on Earth. He realized that about two miles west-southwest of the Face there were a number of apparently artificial formations that looked like the nucleus of a city. They were ordered in geometrical shapes and clustered around a central region, rather like a city center. As Hoagland was quick to point out, the central focus of the square would enable a profile view of the face. He also confirmed DiPietro and Molenaar's finding that one of the sides of the Pyramid is directed straight at the Face. Struck by all the rapidly accumulating evidence, Hoagland described the monument as the "Martian Sphinx." He suggested that it might have been a focus of religious activity.[57]

It is not at all inappropriate to refer to the Face as a Sphinx. The details of the monument remind us irresistibly of Egyptian pictures, in particular the long sideburn-type section of the face being uncannily similar to the sort of head-dresses worn by the Pharaohs.

Hoagland and various scientific colleagues of his discovered that each planet appears to possess a curious energy vortex that occurs at exactly the same map reference in each case, 19.5 degrees latitude. The Cydonia region of Mars, the red spot of Jupiter, and Avebury in Somerset are all on this same degree of latitude.[58]

Later researches by an independent team of scientists and mathematicians showed beyond doubt the extraordinary correlation between Avebury and Cydonia. Did Martians supervise the building of Avebury in Britain? Is that why Britain was thought of in the ancient world as a sacred land?

David Percy took this data and formulated a highly original, if controversial, theory on the basis of it. He believes that the Martians used some kind of spinning saucer technology that enabled them to create an artificial atmosphere upon their planet.[59] Hoagland's researches are compelling; Percy's theory is purely speculative.

Many attempts have been made to debunk the anomalous structures found on Mars, particularly the Face. It has been explained away as a purely natural feature and the various other examples of unequivocal evidence for life on the planet as simply misperceptions of data. In spite of these denials, the Cydonia monuments represent some of the strongest evidence in favor of the existence of life on Mars.

FOSSILS FROM MARS

The year 1996 saw one of the most exciting and explosive discoveries by NASA scientists. That year researchers at the Johnson Space Center cut open a meteorite from Mars that had landed on Antarctica in 1984. Inside it they discovered fossils dating back at least 3.5 billion years. They may even be earlier, as the rock in which they were embedded was dated 4.5 billion years ago. The exciting fact is that NASA was forced by that latest anomalous find to at least consider the possibility of life on Mars at some indefinite period in the past.[60]

As usual, there were a cluster of people anxious to deny facts that conflicted with their fixed opinions, but the matter was resolved decisively in 2009 when more advanced and sophisticated testing methods demonstrated conclusively that the meteorite did indeed contain genuine fossils from Mars.[61]

LATEST EVIDENCE FOR LIFE ON MARS

In July 2011, yet more evidence for the existence of life on Mars was discovered. It has been established that the red rocks on the planet are heavily coated with iron oxide, and we know from conditions on Earth that life can and does flourish in exactly those circumstances.[62] Researches by NASA and the SETI (Search for Extraterrestrial Intelligence) Institute have produced sufficient incontrovertible evidence finally to persuade the space agency that the case for at least the past existence of life on Mars is no longer a speculative theory, but an established fact.[63]

In 2012, NASA'S Curiosity Rover discovered pebbles on Mars and also the existence in the past of a flowing stream. Curiosity discovered hundreds of the stones and, from the evidence it sent back to Earth, scientists estimate that the stream was probably waist-high. The pebbles have been dated to around two million years B.C. and constitute the strongest evidence to date in favor of the existence of life on Mars in the past.

Curiosity sampled the Martian atmosphere and an analysis of the results showed that the planet was formerly much warmer and wetter, with a strong possibility of liquid water having existed on the surface of the planet. This environment would have created a favorable situation for life. On the other hand, Curiosity detected only small amounts of methane, which led the scientists to conclude that although there may have been life on Mars in the past, it no longer exists there. The NASA MAVEN mission will investigate the causes of the apparent depletion of the Martian atmosphere.

In an unrelated but exciting development, French scientists have discovered a new virus, which they have named the Pandoravirus. It is ten times larger than any virus previously known and only 6% of its genes are similar to earthly viruses. The French researchers have concluded that the virus may have originated on Mars and somehow arrived on Earth. Once more, the body of evidence in favor of life on Mars in ancient times continues to accumulate.

WERE MARTIANS OUR ANCESTORS?

We know that Mars once had the capability of supporting life. At an earlier stage in its development, Mars actually presented more favorable conditions for life than Earth, and it is entirely possible that, as the environment on the planet changed, Martians came down to Earth in search of a new home in which to settle. Mars is further away from the Sun than the Earth and would, therefore, have cooled down earlier than our own planet. Perhaps, as their own world became too cold for them, the Martians sent out a fleet of spaceships to colonize Earth.

The Martians may have founded Atlantis and Mu or built the vast terrestrial monuments of the Sphinx, the Pyramids, Avebury, and Stonehenge. Human civilization might have been created by Martians and we ourselves, the human race, might not even be natives of Earth, but ultimately the descendants of pioneers from Mars.

We do not know and may never know, but the evidence is there and it is strong. One day, when our own spaceships land at last on Mars, we may find the faces of our own ancestors staring back at us in surprise.

ENDNOTES: CHAPTER SIX

[1] Drake, op. cit.

[2] Wilson, *Aliens.*

[3] Drake, op. cit.

[4] Ibid.

[5] *Flying Saucer Review*, March-April 1960.

[6] Ibid.

[7] Homer, *The Iliad.* Numerous editions.

[8] Virgil, *Georgics.*

[9] Voltaire, *Micromegas.*

[10] Jonathan Swift, *Gulliver's Travels.*

[11] *Planets*, Issue 16, May-June 1964.

[12] Iosif Shklovski and Carl Sagan, *Intelligent Life in the Universe,* Delta, 1967.

[13] Blavatsky, op. cit.

[14] John S. Lewis, *Physics and Chemistry of the Solar System,* Academic Press, 2004.

[15] *New York Times*, 14 November 1897.

[16] Drake, op. cit.

[17] Ibid.

[18] Ibid.

[19] Theodore Flournoy, *From India to the Planet Mars*, Harper, 1900.

[20] Ibid.

[21] *Fortean Times*, No 76.

[22] Cedric Allingham, *Flying Saucers from Mars*, Frederick Muller, 1954.

[23] Robert E. Dickhoff, *Homecoming of the Martians*, Health Research.

[24] Drake, op. cit.

[25] Ibid.

[26] Wilson, *Aliens.*

[27] *Izvestia*, 13 April 1962.

28 Drake, op. cit.
29 Charles Fort, *New Lands*, Mayflower, 1974.
30 Ibid.
31 Ibid.
32 Ibid.
33 Ibid.
34 Ibid.
35 Drake, op. cit.
36 Ibid.
37 Ibid.
38 Fort, op. cit.
39 Jacques Vallee, *Challenge to Science*, Neville Spearman, 1967.
40 Drake, op. cit.
41 *Scientific American*, September 1975.
42 Wilson, *Aliens.*
43 Drake, op. cit.
44 Ibid.
45 Wilson, *Aliens*
46 Brian Handwerk, "Viking Mission May Have Missed Mars Life, Study Finds," *National Geographic,* October 23, 2006.
47 *Journal of Geophysical Research*, 9 January 2011.
48 *The Sun*, 13 September 1997.
49 *The Times*, 7 December 2006.
50 *Aliens*, October 1997.
51 Wilson, *Aliens.*
52 Steve Connor, "Triumph of the Martian Triangle," *The Independent on Sunday*, 29 August 1993.
53 Wilson, *Aliens.*
54 Ibid.
55 Ibid.
56 Ibid.
57 Ibid.
58 Richard Hoagland, *The Terrestrial Connection* (DVD).
59 David Percy, *The Face on Mars: The Avebury Connection* (DVD).
60 Wilson, *Aliens.*
61 *Geochimica et Cosmochimica Acta*, November 2009.
62 David Perlman, "Possibility for life on Mars found by scientists," *San Francisco Chronicle,* 6 July 2011.
63 *International Journal of Astrobiology*, 1 July 2011.

CHAPTER SEVEN

OTHER WORLDS

W e have seen already that the evidence in favor of the past existence of life on the Moon and Mars is overwhelming and that even the possibility of continuing life there is now, at the very least, an open question. Could signs of life be found, past or present, within other planets in our own solar system?

THE SOLAR SYSTEM

VENUS

After Mars and the Moon, the most favored candidate for possible life within the solar system is Venus. Its much closer proximity to the Sun has always made doubters consider that unlikely, but the results slowly emerging from the Venus Express satellite data are changing the previous perspective on the planet. Once regarded as a flaming mass of poisonous gas, it now appears that the planet may actually be more similar to our own than was previously believed.

The evidence from Express suggests strongly that the gaseous planet was and perhaps still is full of fresh liquid water. Venus was not always a world of storms and gas clouds. Express discovered large quantities of oxygen and hydrogen, and in the exact chemical proportions on which water is formed upon Earth. Like water on our planet, the water on Venus would evaporate into a gaseous form if ultraviolet light from the Sun struck it.

As a result of the data collected by Express, it is now thought that not only did Venus once have an earth-like atmosphere, but probably possessed oceans. These conditions are ideal for the development of carbon-based forms of life such as we find on Earth.[1]

More evidence in support of life on Venus was found when scientists, in 2004, analyzed data and found that the clouds on the planet "could harbor life."[2] We know that life on Earth can exist within clouds, and there is no inherent reason why the same should not be equally true of Venus. The latest researches have shown that, at one time, Venus presented a more favorable environment for life than our own planet and that the changes in temperature and atmospheric pressure would have been gradual enough for life to have found ways of adapting to them—or, of course migrating to other planets such as Earth.[3]

Further support for the idea of possible life on Venus came in 2007. As scientists examined the data being fed back to Earth by Express, they realized that until a billion years ago, the climatic and environmental conditions on both planets were almost identical. Then Venus was hit by a greenhouse effect that made the surface temperature of the planet almost inconceivably hot, bombarding the planet with solar radiation and ultraviolet light.[4]

Even though the process was gradual and may have given time and opportunities for Venusians to adapt to the changing conditions on their world, it is also possible that they might have left and moved to our own relatively near planet. Professor David Grinspoon has gone as far as to state that "there is some reason to believe Venus may have been the best haven for life in the early solar system."[5] In July 2008, two scientists claimed that life from Venus could have come to earth, blown to our planet by strong winds. It would only take weeks, or even days, for microbial life to reach Earth from Venus.[6]

The most recent discovery has been that Venus possesses an ozone layer high up in the clouds above. Until this latest evidence, only Earth and Mars had atmospheres where ozone had been detected. Now that the Venus Express has found further evidence of the possibility of life on the planet, scientists are becoming excited about the future prospects.[7]

MERCURY

Mercury, the nearest planet to the Sun in our solar system, is a world of extremes. On the side facing the Sun, the temperature reaches 700 Kelvin, while the parts of the planet that never experience sunlight are as cold as deep space. On the face of it Mercury is a thoroughly uninviting environment, and yet curiously, it has all the conditions that scientists regard as essential for making life on other planets possible.

Mercury has oxygen, water, and methane—all necessary conditions for life. On the other hand, the oxygen levels are low, the temperature variations very extreme, no present sign of liquid water rather than simply water in the atmosphere or as ice, and the methane is thought to come from volcanic activity, rather than as a result of metabolic waste processes.[8]

Although the daytime surface temperature is fierce, it is possible that there might be life around the polar regions of the planet. Mercury has a magnetic field that protects it from solar storms and cosmic rays, as well as a large surface gravity that also holds out promise of life. In 2009, NASA made perhaps the most surprising of all its discoveries about Mercury—the planet had water. Even though it remains an extreme environment with fierce contrasts of heat and cold, the presence of water and of oxygen in the atmosphere means that the chance of life on the planet is higher than anyone expected.[9]

JUPITER

Jupiter, the largest planet in the solar system, has often been ignored when the possibility of life is considered. Its atmosphere is largely made up of ammonia and methane and it is believed that the planet also contains a layer of ice some 17,000 miles thick. Then, in 1961, astronomer Carl Sagan suggested that the huge cloud cover on Jupiter could protect and even nurture life upon the planet.

Sagan carried out experiments in the laboratory, creating a simulated Jupiter, recreating its atmosphere before bombarding it with ultraviolet rays. He found that the ultraviolet entering the atmosphere led to the production of simple organic molecules and that the penetration of the sun's rays onto the surface of the planet caused infra-red radiation. The heat created by this process was trapped by the cloud cover and formed oceans of ammonia or, crucially, water. The molecules dissolved into the oceans and Sagan remarked that the chemical processes created "would create the conditions necessary for complex pre-biological organic reactions." He also considered that the crust of Jupiter might not be the icy wilderness generally believed and that its temperature might be moderate enough to allow similar evolutionary development to the kind found upon Earth.[10]

Following the first Jupiter probe in 1976, Pioneer 10, Sagan speculated again on possible life upon the planet. Three years later, he and Edwin Saltpeter produced a paper on the subject. They speculated that there might be "abundant biota" in the atmosphere and also three different types of marine animals within the ocean. The presumption was that they might breathe helium—abundant on the planet—and that many organisms might be huge in size.[11]

In recent years, attention has shifted from Jupiter itself to its surrounding moons, particularly Europa and Ganymede, both of which are considered to be strong candidates for harboring life. From 1995, NASA space probes monitored the whole region of Jupiter and the data they transmitted back to Earth led to a growing view among scientists that life on the moons of Jupiter is now not simply possible, but probable. By 2009, the information received led one scientist to declare that: "I'd be shocked if no life existed on Europa."[12]

It was felt that the most probable form of life to inhabit Europa would be some kind of marine animal. Not only is there a vast ocean on the moon, but there is sufficient oxygen on the satellite to support a large population.[13]

SATURN

Saturn is felt to be one of the least promising candidates for life within our solar system. Its environment is one where there are fierce winds, high pressure, strong gravitational pull, and extreme temperatures, principally sub-zero, although in parts of the planet it is 80 degrees. The atmosphere contains ammonia and water, so there is the possibility of life, particularly some type of marine animal, but, overall, it is considered too hostile a place.

Saturn's moons Titan and Enceladus are much more promising candidates. In 2011, scientists speculated that both satellites might well harbor life, particularly Titan. Both planets have liquid water and Enceladus has hot springs that erupt from the volcanoes on the otherwise frozen surface. The NASA probe Cassini found exceptionally warm temperatures in the south polar region of Enceladus. There was also strong evidence of a salt-water ocean and of the presence of carbon, methane, ammonia, and nitrogen.[14]

Titan is thought be an even more promising candidate for life than Enceladus. It has abundant lakes and hydrocarbons and is considered extremely similar in its chemical state to Earth in its earlier days. On another of Saturn's moons, Hyperion, hydrocarbons have also been detected.

While the prospects for life on Saturn itself remain slim, the chances that it might well exist on at least one, and possibly three, of its satellites now appear strong.[15]

URANUS

Uranus is considered one of the least likely candidates for life within the solar system. The planet's surface is principally made up of ammonia, methane, water, and the solid part of its surface is ice. The atmosphere is overwhelmingly composed of hydrogen.

The temperature on the planet is exceptionally cold, and although there are warmer places within it, the atmospheric pressures are tremendously powerful and would make it hard for life to survive. Without sufficient sunlight to provide "power" or any evidence of volcanic activity that could generate heat, it would be difficult for life to survive there.[16]

On the other hand, given the high percentage of water on the planet, it is possible that marine life might be able to exist. The warmer parts of Uranus may also be more promising habitats than presently believed and the gas clouds that surround the planet may also have given birth to avian life forms. A long-shot perhaps, but not impossible.

NEPTUNE

Neptune is further out in space than Uranus, but water is abundant there. It too has large gas clouds, so as with Uranus, the possibility of marine or avian life cannot be dismissed out of hand. Life flourishes on some of the most inhospitable environments on Earth, and it seems equally possible that it may also do so on the remoter planets of the solar system. For the moment, only the presence of abundant water makes it a faint possibility, but it remains one of the least likely places to harbor life.

PLUTO

Pluto sadly has now had its status degraded from that of a full planet to a mere asteroid. As it has three attendant moons (Charon, the best known), this seems surprising. Again, the hypothetical prospects for life are not considered good, particularly in terms of the fierce cold that pervades the planetoid. On the other hand, the Hubble Space Telescope has shown that it has gravitational pull upon it from its satellites, which creates friction and, therefore, turns some of the frozen water ice into liquid water. As such, it has the basic elements for life to arise.

NASA has also discovered that the surface of Pluto, while cold by the standards of Earth, is nowhere near as cold as was previously believed. Methane has also been found on the planet, as well as water in the clouds and ice. It has even been discovered to have a relatively weak "greenhouse effect." All in all, taken together with the data about friction, Pluto is now perhaps a stronger candidate for life than has been the case in the past.

CERES, THE NEW PLANET

Having somewhat irrationally demoted Pluto from the status of a planet to an asteroid, the International Astronomical Union then chose to upgrade Ceres from asteroid rank to that of a "dwarf planet." The prospects for life on Ceres are considered to be surprisingly good. It is believed to have oceans, a more attractive atmosphere than Pluto, and, in general, to be the most likely of all the outer fringe bodies within the solar system to harbor life.

HYPOTHETICAL PLANETS

A number of hypothetical planets have been suggested as existing within the solar system. The best-known and most plausible is Vulcan, most famous as the home of Mr. Spock in *Star Trek*, but originally proposed to explain irregularities in the orbit of Mercury by the French astronomer Le Vérrier, co-discoverer of Neptune, in the nineteenth century.

Later researchers were able to explain the anomalies without the need for the existence of a planet between Mercury and Venus, the solution Le Vérrier proposed. The idea of Vulcan as a "real" planet is now generally dismissed, although a minority of astronomers continue to think that some celestial body may exist in the general area where Le Vérrier placed it. Generally, the view is that such worlds would be asteroids rather than whole planets, but it is not impossible that undetected planets may exist in that region.[17]

Other hypothetical planets within the solar system lack the benefit of a great scientific name like Le Vérrier's to buttress their claims. Truman Bethurum, on the basis of his dubious "contact" claims, declared that the planet Clarion existed on the dark side of the Moon.[18] Howard Menger just as questionably declared that he had visited this non-existent planet.[19]

PLANET X AND THE DOOMSDAY SCENARIO

In recent times, particularly by people who have been interested in the Mayan calendar, it has been suggested that a hypothetical body known variously as Planet X, Eris, Hercolubus, Sedna, Tyche, Nemesis, Comet Elenin, or Nibiru exists as a tenth planet within the solar system. This world is dangerous and will eventually cause another cosmic catastrophe that will lead to the end of life on Earth.[20]

The name Nibiru, which has come to be the most common name for the hypothetical planet, was used originally by Zecharia Sitchin, a science fiction writer and ancient astronaut theorist. It comes from ancient Mesopotamian mythology and Sitchin insisted that it had no connection with any kind of cosmic calamity. For what it is worth, he regarded it as being the twelfth planet of the solar system, not the tenth.[21]

According to Sitchin, Nibiru, also known as Marduk, passes by Earth every 3,600 years. During its passage, the planet's inhabitants visit Earth and teach humanity their higher wisdom. Sitchin identified these star travelers as being the same as the Annunaki mentioned in Sumerian mythology and claimed that they were the origin of religion on Earth, humans having wrongly identified the extraterrestrials as gods.[22]

In 1995, Nancy Lieder claimed she had been told by contacts from Zeta Reticuli that Planet X, as she referred to it, would collide with Earth sometime in the early part of the twenty-first century.[23] Her ideas spread slowly until, in 2001, they attracted the notice of a wider audience when a book about them was published.[24]

Lieder said that Planet X was around four times as large as Earth and that when its perigee occurred on 27 May 2003, the Earth would stop rotating for almost six days. This would lead to a massive polar shift and the displacement of the Earth's crust.[25]

When nothing happened in May 2003, Lieder immediately claimed that her statement had been deliberate disinformation to mislead the authorities who, she said, were planning to use the arrival of Planet X as an excuse for worldwide repression.[26]

In 1996, Lieder identified Planet X with Sitchin's Nibiru and agreed with him that it was the twelfth planet of the solar system,[27] Sitchin indignantly denied any relationship between her ideas on the subject and his own.[28]

The original idea for Planet X came from discrepancies that astronomers in the nineteenth century believed existed in the orbits of Uranus and Neptune. Percival Lowell, the man who launched the idea of Martian canals, thought that the orbits of the two planets were not as they should be and put forward the theory that both were being affected by the gravitational pull of another planet, which he referred to as Planet X. Other astronomers searched for this planet for over a century, but there is no evidence that it exists.[29]

After a while, Lieder's ideas were taken up by people interested in the Mayan calendar, who believed that Planet X was connected with it in some way. Since that will be discussed in the final chapter, those theories will be looked at there.

LIFE ON THE SUN

The idea that the Sun might be an inhabited world is very ancient. As well as the many myths and legends of sun gods, imaginative writers have explored the idea for 2,000 years. More surprisingly perhaps, many distinguished scientists regard it as at least theoretically possible.

In 1795, the great astronomer Herschel claimed that it was highly probable that life did exist upon the Sun. He believed that it was simply a large planet with a solid surface and an atmosphere that would make the existence of life upon it possible. Herschel wrote:

> THE SUN APPEARS TO BE NOTHING ELSE THAN A VERY EMINENT, LARGE, AND LUCID PLANET. ITS SIMILARITY TO THE OTHER GLOBES OF THE SOLAR SYSTEM LEADS US TO SUPPOSE THAT IT IS MOST PROBABLY INHABITED BY BEINGS WHOSE ORGANS ARE ADAPTED TO THE PECULIAR CIRCUMSTANCES OF THAT VAST GLOBE.[30]

Other astronomers agreed with Herschel and, as late as the 1860s, many supporters of the idea of life on the Sun continued to press the case for its existence. Then opinions began to change and the whole idea was dismissed as impossible, largely because of the fierce temperature on the planet.

In 1951, a German engineer put forward the theory that sunspots were holes that led to the interior of the Sun. In his opinion, it was possible that life might exist in the heart of the Sun. He made a very public bet that scientists would be unable to prove that life did not exist on the planet, but a German court ruled against him and forced him to pay the German Astronomische Gesellschaft the money he had wagered.[31]

Later, scientists began to revise their opinion on this subject. In the first place, two of them have estimated that, in around five billion years time, the Sun will become a red giant and the Earth will become part of a huge gas cloud as a result. However, the Earth will survive inside the Sun's nuclear furnace and, eventually, the Sun will expel it. Beneath the surface of the planet, microbial forms of life that are heat-resistant will be able to survive.[32]

Other scientists have gone further, claiming that life on other planets might be fundamentally different from life on Earth and that it might be possible for organisms to live inside the Sun. The idea of plasma-based life forms has attracted particular attention from scientists.[33]

FURTHER AFIELD

Given the present level of our technology and the current unwillingness of governments to deploy significant funding to space research, it is likely to be a considerable time before we are in a position to acquire the data to evaluate the chances of life on other worlds. There are a number of solar systems considered as possible candidates, but, at present, there is simply not enough evidence on which to make an informed judgment.

SETI AND CETI

SETI (the Search for Extraterrestrial Intelligence) and CETI (Communication with Extraterrestrial Intelligence) are projects that have been in and out of fashion since the nineteenth century. Greater technological development since those days has dramatically improved both the methods of detecting intelligent life elsewhere in the universe and the prospects of being able to communicate with it in the event of its discovery.

The twentieth century saw a surprisingly large number of signals from space picked up by radio receivers, which appeared to show evidence of order and intention. Particularly promising in terms of apparent evidence for extraterrestrial contact is what is known as long delayed echoes (LDEs). The study of LDEs, and, in particular, a remark made about them in the 1960s by Professor Ronald Bracewell, led to a breakthrough in SETI.

ALIEN MESSAGE DECODED?

In 1973, Duncan Lunan, a Scottish astronomer, declared that he had succeeded in decoding an LDE received at Eindhoven, Holland, in 1920.[34] He claimed that the signals were actually charts of constellations of stars and could plausibly be interpreted as signifying that the messages implied that their transmissions came from these constellations. He found that there were striking similarities to Boètis, Epsilon Boètis, and Arcturus, also known as Alpha Boètis. Lunan also discovered that Arcturus was in the position that it would have occupied around 11,000 B.C.[35]

Bracewell was delighted by Lunan's claims, regarding them as the best evidence yet for successful communication between Earth and other worlds, though others were less convinced. Apart from the inevitable accusations that Lunan had distorted his data to get the results he was seeking, there was also the suggestion that plasma clouds in space could have been responsible for slowing down the signal. Although serious criticisms have been made of both Lunan's methodology and conclusions, as yet they have not been disproved. The present balance of evidence is slightly in favor of Lunan's theory being correct.

ANOMALOUS RADIO SIGNALS

Anomalous radio signals were also detected by the Radio Institute at Gorki in the Soviet Union. Curiously, they were detected in 1973, the same year that Lunan claimed to have decoded the Eindhoven LDE. Both the Soviet astrophysicists who detected them were unequivocal in their belief that they originated from outer space. One of them, Dr. Nikolai Kordashev, said openly: "We have been receiving radio signals from outer space in bursts lasting from two to ten minutes. Their character, their consistent pattern, and their regular transmissions leave us in no doubt that they are of artificial origin—that is, they are not natural signals, but have been transmitted by civilized beings with sophisticated transmission equipment."[36]

His colleague, Dr. Vsevolod Troitsky, also stated that: "They are definitely call-signs from an extraterrestrial civilization."[37] However, as from time to time happened under the former Communist regime, exciting and challenging claims were soon being back-pedaled rather rapidly. Troitsky later suggested that they might be the result of solar activity. Other Soviet scientists blamed an American spy satellite orbiting in space. The truth may never be known, but it remains a fascinating enigma. Radio communication remains one of the most likely methods to produce clear proof of extraterrestrial life.

QUASARS AND PULSARS

Nobody really knows what the Russians detected in 1973, but the wisdom of caution where anomalous signals from space is concerned was shown by the pulsar fiasco. In 1965, regular periodic emissions were found in a radio source. At once, astronomers began to suggest that an extraterrestrial civilization was attempting to make contact. Two years later, a star that transmits radio frequencies at regular intervals was discovered. Its discoverers, half-seriously, named it LGM (little green men).

Further analysis and observations led to the discovery of two new and entirely unexpected natural phenomena. The 1965 signals came from what we now call a quasar; the 1967 ones came from what we now know as pulsars. The astronomers who had jumped too quickly to an extraterrestrial explanation looked extremely foolish as a result.[38]

LASER TECHNOLOGY

Carl Sagan, who devoted a considerable portion of his career to the investigation of SETI and CETI, believed that though radio transmissions may be a useful method of trying to communicate with intelligent life elsewhere in the universe, a more promising method might lie with the laser technology now available to us. In Sagan's view: "lasers offer optimal improvement, and will be entirely suitable for interstellar contact."[39]

Anthony Lawton believed that lasers already suggest that CETI transmissions have been beamed at Earth in recent years. He pointed out that lasers could be used to create anomalies in the solar spectrum, adding that fifteen stars had been discovered through its use, all within a hundred light years of Earth that possessed anomalous spectral radiation. He admitted that all were probably caused by purely natural phenomena. However, if any of those spectral anomalies had been deliberately engineered, that would and could only mean intelligent extraterrestrial life.[40] Lasers have not yet provided unequivocal proof of a directed origin from outer space, but are a major tool in the continuing SETI research.

THE WONDERFUL WIZARD OF OZMA

In 1960, Professor Frank Drake of Cornel University began an ongoing project involving radio monitoring stars. His objective was to see if any of the radio signals coming from them were artificial in origin. The two stars chosen for his original study were Tau Ceti and Epsilon Eridani, both about eleven light years away from Earth. Drake called his program "Project Ozma," implying that it was about as likely to succeed as the journey to find "the wonderful wizard of Oz."

In spite of his pessimism about the prospects of success, Drake tuned his eighty-five-foot dish to Tau Ceti and Epsilon Eridani for a period of six months. He chose to keep it tuned in to the twenty-one centimeter waveband, the frequency at which radiation is emitted by hydrogen atoms.

Almost as soon as Project Ozma began, Drake and his team got the shock of their lives. They detected an obviously artificial signal from Epsilon Eridani. No apparent source for the signal, other than a transmission from the star, could be found at first. Drake, though, was far too cautious to make a premature announcement of a successful SETI experiment. After a few weeks of careful investigation, he discovered that the true source of the signals was radar equipment from military aircraft. His caution preserved his project from the ridicule that a false claim would have caused.

In 1971, Drake became involved in an altogether more extensive program known as Project Cyclops. This made use of a massive observatory with a series of radio telescopes having a ten-mile diameter. Cyclops was designed to listen in to literally millions of transmissions from stars as far away as several hundred light years. The Cyclops program unfortunately would have been so expensive to institute and maintain that it never progressed beyond the drawing board. However, it remains one of the great enduring monuments to the human imagination.[41]

HOW PROBABLE IS EXTRATERRESTRIAL LIFE?

If life exists, how common is it? Harlow Shapley, using a highly conservative model, came up with a figure of a minimum number of around ten thousand million inhabited worlds.[42] Drake, working on a more optimistic projection, estimated over one hundred thousand million planets capable of supporting life in our galaxy alone.[43]

If either figure is even approximately correct, in spite of the obvious technical difficulties that still persist, we can look forward confidently to the eventual successful discovery of and communication with extraterrestrial intelligence.

ACTIVE SETI: THE RISKS

Professor Stephen Hawking was unenthusiastic about the prospects of "active SETI"—the deliberate transmission from Earth to other stars in order to alert them to our own existence. His view was that it posed considerable danger and warned scientists against pursuing the project any further. Hawking declared: "If aliens ever visit us, I think the outcome would be much as when Christopher Columbus first landed in America, which didn't turn out very well for the Native Americans."[44]

In 2010, SETI celebrated its fiftieth anniversary with a conference. One or two delegates shared Hawking's concerns. Others, though, pointed out that there were already enough radio and television transmissions into space that were not even directed consciously towards contact with extraterrestrials and that active SETI posed no additional risk.[45]

ORBITAL ASTRONOMICAL OBSERVATORY

One of the most promising attempts to detect alien life came about as a result of the space program. The date 8 April 1966 saw the launch into space of the world's first OAO (orbital astronomical observatory). Unfortunately, it suffered a power failure after only two days that put it out of action completely.[46]

Two years later, OAO-2 was launched. It failed to achieve a stable orbit in space. The Copernicus satellite, launched in 1972, also failed to fulfill the high hopes that had been placed upon it.[47]

A sufficiently large orbiting space telescope could, at least in theory, both detect and transmit back to Earth any evidence of anomalous and possible extraterrestrial phenomena. However, the unwillingness of governments to fund such programs adequately has made it extremely difficult for SETI researchers.

The Space Shuttle and Space Station Mir showed that placing sophisticated hardware into space really does result in a more accurate record of the universe. Hopefully, future projects that are able to build upon their expertise and achievements will be even more successful in transmitting data of vital astronomical importance back to Earth.

NEW PLANETS DISCOVERED

The year 1994 saw a major breakthrough in SETI research. Aleksandr Wolszczan of Pennsylvania State University discovered three new planets outside the solar system orbiting a sun. Unfortunately, it was a dead star, a pulsar.[48]

The year 1995 saw a more promising discovery. Two astronomers in Switzerland found that 51 Pegasi, a star extremely similar to our own sun, had a planet accompanying it. However, the distance of the planet from the sun was so close that they doubted if any life could flourish with the intense heat to which the planet would be exposed.

Later that year, the most dramatic of these new planetary discoveries was made. Geoffrey Marcy and Paul Butler of San Francisco State University located two planets well outside the solar system. These were observed in orbit around the stars 47 Ursae Majoris and 70 Virginis. This time, the stars gave the appearance of being alive and the planets were at a sufficient distance from the sun for the presence of water and rain to be possible. The temperature was also more similar to our own world than those of any other planet that has been currently discovered. Although somewhat hotter than Earth, it would not be sufficiently so as to inhibit the possibility of life.[49]

COMMUNICATION WITH EXTRATERRESTRIAL INTELLIGENCE

On the communications side, a number of ambitious projects were set up in the 1970s. The *Voyager I* and *II* spacecraft were launched from the Kennedy Space Center in Florida in 1977. Each craft carried within it a selection of items designed to demonstrate to any discoverers that there is intelligent life on Earth. It included maps, charts, and photographs of our planet and solar system, the DNA structure on our planet, cultural achievements, sporting activities, and the life cycle of humans from conception to death. The craft had the capacity to transmit information back to Earth as they went on their long journey into space.[50]

The year 1992 saw the inception of NASA's High Resolution Microwave Survey (HRMS) program. It would have been the most ambitious SETI monitoring exercise ever mounted. A thousand stars would have been scanned by the most powerful telescopes in the world and tens of millions of radio frequencies investigated.

In the brief time that it was allowed to function, HRMS was an outstanding success. Then, sadly, Congressional "pork barrelers" passed a bill that specifically forbade NASA to search for signs of extraterrestrial life. From now on, government funding for SETI programs was effectively ended.[51]

The passing of this measure by Congress was one of the darkest days in twentieth century history. Seth Shostak of the California SETI Institute compared it to allowing Columbus to build and equip his ships, but telling him he would not be allowed to sail.

Fortunately, the generosity of private individuals and companies resulted in a scaled-down version of HRMS being created. The SETI Institute and other private institutions gave generous funding to what became known as Project Phoenix. Although it was on a far smaller scale than its predecessor's, it was still able to continue with targeted searching for signs of extraterrestrial life.[52]

MUSIC FOR THE STARS

One of the most recent and possibly unusual attempts to communicate with extraterrestrials is a project created by Doug Vakoch of the SETI Institute in collaboration with composer Andrew Kaiser of Carnegie Mellon University. The two men have written music that they hope might be sent out into outer space to identify aspects of human culture. The music they have composed is similar to previous musical attempts at communication with the universe, such as "The First Theremin Concert for Aliens" and the *Voyager* Golden Record, both of them previously released into the infinite expanses of deep space.[53]

ALTERNATIVE APPROACHES TO SETI

As well as the use of radio signals and lasers, other approaches have been suggested. Most, such as the use of gravity waves or neutrinos, are simply too costly to be practical. On the other hand, as Shostak suggested, there are still some methods that might pay dividends and would not be prohibitively expensive. For example, he felt that attempting to detect stars that showed excessive infrared emission might be a sign of "waste heat" generated by some kind of mechanical process.

Drake himself has proposed searching for stars that have spectral lines that have been created by compounds that do not occur naturally. He gave chlorofluorocarbons as an example of something that never occur in nature and that create strong spectral lines even in small quantities. It would be relatively easy for such tests to be carried out. Shostak added that "the assumption is that there's something more interesting to be found now that you're going to be spending a lot of time looking at that spot in the sky."[54]

SEARCH FOR PLANETS OUTSIDE THE SOLAR SYSTEM

One of the key questions that remain unanswered is how typical a model is our own solar system, with a central sun around which planets orbit. A computer simulation from the University of Washington attempted to show the process of planetary formation. Its results found that planets are formed around a "young" star and they develop regular orbits.

In the early twenty-first century, one of the principal focuses of astronomers has been the search for planets orbiting other stars. To date, over 100 such worlds have been found. The majority of those discovered so far have been huge gas giants, similar in size and chemical composition to Jupiter, but with continuing improvements in technology smaller planets are confidently expected to be found that may be brighter prospects for discovering life.[55]

SCEPTICAL ARGUMENTS

Before the 1960s, the majority of scientists were broadly hostile to the very idea of life on other planets. Even though the mood shifted with the development of the space program, and a gradual realization of the improbability of such a vast area as the universe possessing only a single inhabited world within its borders, the continuing failure of SETI to produce any tangible results led to a return to the earlier skeptical approach towards the prospects. SETI research became known as a "science without a subject." Not until the late 1990s did the scientific community slowly change its mind about SETI. From the 1980s onwards, the majority scientific opinion shifted once more and the consensus became that life on other planets, however remote, was virtually certain.

THE ARGUMENT FROM DNA

Among biologists, there is considerable confusion as to how they would be able to fit in the existence of life on other planets with the prevailing ideas about DNA. Stephen Jay Gould is quite willing to entertain the possibility. He argues that it is more improbable to believe in the uniqueness of Earth than in the general diffusion of life throughout the universe. Others take a different view, and deny the very possibility of extraterrestrial life.

For a long time, the biologist Richard Dawkins adopted that attitude. He argued that the likelihood of the DNA code arising in more than one place by chance was so remote that there could not possibly be life on other planets. Although he finally abandoned that position, it continued to govern the underlying assumptions of his later theory on alien life.

Jacques Monod, the poet among the neo-Darwinians, wrote: "Before life did appear, its chances of doing so were almost nonexistent. The universe was not pregnant with life nor the biosphere with man. Our number came up on the Monte Carlo game. Is it surprising that, just like the person who has just made a million at the casino, we should feel strange and a little unreal?"[56]

Apart from the fact that this is simply a series of personal opinions rather than a scientific statement, it also begs the question. Monod's claims rest upon two assumptions, the first that DNA is unique to Earth and the second that no principle of self-organization exists in the natural world. Many scientists believe that he is entirely wrong on both issues.

Paul Davies commented on the ideas of Monod and scientists who share his views on these subjects:

SELF-ORGANIZATION ABOUNDS IN PHYSICS AND CHEMISTRY: IN SUPERCONDUCTORS, LASERS, ELECTRONIC NETWORKS, TURBULENT FLUID EDDIES; NON-EQUILIBRIUM CHEMICAL REACTIONS, THE FORMATION OF SNOWFLAKES. WE EVEN SEE IT OCCURRING IN ECONOMIC SYSTEMS. IT WOULD BE ASTONISHING IF SELF-ORGANIZATION DID NOT OCCUR IN BIOLOGY TOO. YET ANY SUGGESTION THAT BIOLOGICAL ORDER MIGHT ARISE SPONTANEOUSLY—I.E., THAT COMPLEX BIOLOGICAL SYSTEMS MAY ALREADY POSSESS AN INHERENT ORDERING CAPABILITY—IS CONSIDERED A DANGEROUS HERESY."[57]

THE ARGUMENT FROM ABSENCE

Eric Jones and Frank Tipler both calculated that indisputable proof of extraterrestrial life and direct contact with aliens ought to have been shown a long time ago. They argued that the "great silence" means that Earth really is the only habitable world, or at least the only planet where intelligent life exists.[58]

The essential idea behind these views is the maxim known as Occam's Razor, the notion that if there is no need to suggest the existence of a hypothetical entity, then it probably does not exist. On the other hand, Occam's Razor is only a methodological principle, rather than a law of nature. Quantum physicists, in particular, have been forced to suggest all kinds of purely hypothetical entities to explain gaps in the sub-atomic world, some of which, such as tachyons, have never been observed and probably never could be observed, even in principle. As such, science has been compelled more and more to allow for the existence of a range of entities that violate Occam's Razor.[59]

It is also worth remembering another logical principle, that absence of evidence is not necessarily evidence of absence.

THE "VOLUME OF TRAFFIC"

One of the principal problems for many scientists about accepting the reality of alien contact is what is known as the "volume of traffic" argument. Jacques Vallée, for instance, after some years of research into the UFO phenomenon and into contact stories in particular, worked out that there must have been somewhere in the region of fourteen million extraterrestrial visits to Earth. Surely, he said, it is hard to accept such a high number of visits, many of them apparently purposeless. Why would advanced civilizations send out so many vehicles to our planet and why is so much of their behavior seemingly so irrational? His researches led him to believe that it was incredible that such a high volume of traffic would be so focused upon Earth and he proposed a new explanation for UFOs as a result of his investigations.[60]

INTELLIGENT ALIEN DESIGN

WAS GOD AN ASTRONAUT?

Although the idea that the human race was "intelligently designed" by aliens was put forward earlier by other writers, it was Erich von Däniken who first popularized the concept, in a series of sensational best-selling books. His formulation of the basic idea was far cruder than the sophisticated formulations of scientists, but it struck a chord with the public.[61]

THE ORIGINS OF LIFE?

The biologist Francis Crick is best known as the co-discoverer of DNA, but during the sixties and seventies he became troubled by the question of the origins of life. Attempting to reconcile the orthodox Darwinian theories with the complexity of the DNA structure, Crick became convinced that natural selection and random adaptations by chance alone simply could not account for the rich tapestry of life. Instead, he began to think in terms of some kind of purposive, intelligently designed mechanism.

Crick and Leslie Orgel then investigated possible ways in which that could take place and, in 1973, they jointly proposed what they called the theory of "directed panspermia" to account for the problems of complexity and the apparent necessity for some kind of design rather than chance alone. Orgel and Crick suggested that life on Earth was designed and "seeded" on our planet by intelligent aliens.[62]

Crick and Orgel's radical new theory was immediately greeted with howls of protest and derision. The irony of an avowed atheist like Crick putting forward what was seen as a "naturalistic" version of the idea of intelligent design led to all manner of personal attacks. It was suggested that his failure to account for the origins of life had led him to abandon scientific principles in favor of wild speculations. Crick, embarrassed by the hostile response from his fellow scientists, retreated from his challenging hypothesis. He later claimed that he might have been mistaken about the difficulties of the spontaneous appearance of DNA upon Earth.

Dawkins, having formerly believed in the impossibility of extraterrestrial life altogether, later shifted his position dramatically to a characteristically unusual form of the intelligent design hypothesis. What marks him out as different from the creationists is that he places intelligent aliens, rather than God, as the mechanism behind the development of civilization. In some respects, Dawkins' theory is an atheist version of the Garden of Eden story.[63]

Like Crick, Dawkins has faced considerable criticism and ridicule for his theory of "intelligent alien design." There are certainly problems in the way he has presented it. For instance, he made the throwaway remark: "I suppose it's possible that you might find evidence for that [Intelligent Design] if you look at the details of biochemistry, molecular biology, you might find a signature of some sort of designer." Yet when philosopher Anthony Flew remarked: "It seems to me that Richard Dawkins constantly overlooks the fact that the findings of more than fifty years of DNA research have provided materials for a new and enormously powerful argument to design," Dawkins condemned Flew's opinion as "senile." What, though, does his statement mean, other than that there is some evidence of purpose and design within the framework of life?[64] As Paul Davies pointed out some years ago, accepting the existence of purpose and design does not commit you to belief in a supernatural god.[65]

In an interview in 2010 with Matt Ridley, Dawkins declared: "It could be that at some earlier time, somewhere in the universe, a civilization evolved, probably by some kind of Darwinian means, probably to a very high level of technology, and designed a form of life that they seeded onto perhaps this planet."[66] Apart from the lack of clarity as to exactly what Dawkins means by words like "designed" and "seeded," during the interview he spoke about creating artificial bacteria. Then, making a huge and completely unjustified leap, Dawkins declared that, because we have been able to sequence the genome of Neanderthal man, it would be possible to "create" a Neanderthal human, if a modern woman could be found to give birth to the baby.

The difference both in kind and degree of the two operations is so vast that they are almost beyond comparison. To create bacteria is one thing (and a relatively simple task); to form an artificial cell that can develop into a human being is quite another matter. The size of the genomes in bacteria compared with that of a mammal, let alone a human, is hugely different in range; and how would it be possible, even if it were feasible to create the DNA, to arrange it in a structure that would form a nucleus? Dawkins' statement that it would be possible to "create" a Neanderthal, upon which Ridley failed to challenge him, is simply false.[67]

As a final point, it is only necessary to say that Neanderthals, in spite of their bad "press" over the last two centuries, were not "ape men," but fully human. It is as unnecessary for us to "create" a Neanderthal as to "create," for instance, an Italian. We might justifiably add that the hypothesis of "genetically designed humans" faces serious problems if we assume that only our own species was "created" or "seeded" by aliens. How do we explain the virtual identity of DNA between ourselves and apes, to say nothing of other mammals? How do we explain the near identity of DNA between all species living upon the planet?

Unless we are prepared to accept an alien race "designing" or at least "seeding" every single species on Earth, the whole theory falls to the ground. The difficulties with the whole notion of "alien intelligent design" make the idea that God created everything in the universe look simple and unproblematic in comparison. If Dawkins claims that the existence of God violates Occam's Razor, so too does his own hypothesis of "alien intelligent design."

THE PANSPERMIA HYPOTHESIS

This theory was originally proposed by Fred Hoyle, and he and Chandra Wickramasinghe have developed it over the years. It suggests that life began in outer space and was blown to Earth by winds or similar mechanisms, taking root on our planet and slowly evolving over the course of time.

It is still not generally accepted by the majority of scientists, although that is less true now than when it was first put forward in the 1960s. One great advantage it has over the idea of "directed panspermia" is that it still employs the process of evolution, but simply makes the arrival of life on Earth the result of a chance bacterial contact that developed under the particular conditions of our planet.[68]

The Future?

PROOF OF ALIEN LIFE BY 2030

On 27 June 2011, Russian astronomer Andrei Finkelstein made a bold claim. He declared that aliens undoubtedly existed and predicted that they would be found within two decades. Speaking at an international conference on SETI in the Russian city of St. Petersburg, Finkelstein said: "The genesis of life is as inevitable as the formation of atoms."[69] He claimed that life obeyed the same principles throughout the universe and followed the same processes of development.

Perhaps the most exciting and challenging part of Finkelstein's statement was his claim that we would have definite proof of the existence of alien life within twenty-five years. He did not go as far as saying that we would be able to communicate with extraterrestrial life, but that we would be able to detect their signals.

A number of astronomers agree that Finkelstein's time scale for discovering ET is a reasonable one. Five years before Finkelstein's statement, Seth Shostak of the SETI Institute produced a paper in which he estimated that intelligent alien life would be discovered within twenty-five years. He firmly agreed with Finkelstein's suggestion that the 2030s would see the final proof of extraterrestrial contact with humans.[70]

WHAT WILL ALIEN LIFE BE LIKE?

Most people still seem to expect that intelligent life on other planets, or any extraterrestrials that make contact with us on Earth, will almost certainly be humanoid. This is perhaps a rather arrogant assumption on our part. Sometimes we forget that the way in which life developed on our own planet and, in particular, the fact that humans ended up becoming the dominant species, might just be an accident caused by our greater ability to adapt to the specific conditions present on Earth. Given an entirely different environment, who knows what types of intelligent life might exist upon other planets?

What we regard as one of the defining features of an advanced civilization and a superior intelligence, the ability to design and use tools, might simply be an aspect of the way our own species evolved and adapted to the environment on Earth. Even on our own planet it is arguable how powerful human beings really are. We have not yet found a way to prevent natural disasters such as earthquakes, volcanoes, or tsunamis from overwhelming our lands, nor can we prevent the growing incursions of the sea from taking away ever increasing amounts of fertile land. For all our advanced technology, humans appear to be a species in gradual retreat. Perhaps, just as the dinosaurs had their day and vanished, so too will the human race.

It is always worth remembering that species, even on Earth, can survive under the most extreme and unpromising conditions. For instance, in Idaho a new form of life has been discovered known as the Methanogens, living in the earth's crust 600 feet below the surface. They eat hydrogen, breathe in carbon dioxide, and exhale methane. In spite of possessing neither sunlight nor oxygen, they not only survive, but flourish.[71] For all we know, they may be far more typical than our own proud species of what life on other planets might be like.

Finklestein believes that if we discover intelligent extraterrestrial life, it is likely to be human or humanoid in form. Shostak is less convinced, pointing to the rich diversity of life upon Earth as a counter-example. On the other hand, he believes that hands and arms are essential aspects of any life form that is able to create a technically advanced society.[72]

Whatever the future holds, it seems that the day of indisputable contact between humans and extraterrestrials might be here sooner than we imagined. It is an exciting prospect.

ENDNOTES: CHAPTER SEVEN

[1] Vdamico, "Was there once life on Venus?" www.environmentalgraffit.com/space/news.

[2] Martin Redfern, "Venus clouds 'might harbour life,'" BBC News, 25 May 2004.

[3] Ibid.

[4] Roger Highfield, "Did life once thrive on evil twin Venus?" *Daily Telegraph*, 28 November 2007.

[5] Grinspoon, quoted by Sean Henahan, www,accessexcellence.org

[6] BBC News, 25 July 2008.

[7] "Scientists discover ozone layer on Venus," SPACE.com staff, 11 October 2011, www.space.com/13244-venus-atmosphere-ozone-layer.html.

[8] www.universetoday.com/82772/planets.

[9] Luke McKinney, "If There's Water on Mercury, Can Fish be Far Behind?" www.dailygalaxy.com, 26 March 2009.

[10] "Life on Jupiter?" *Time Magazine*, 25 August 1961.

[11] Carl Sagan and Edwin E Saltpeter, "Particles, Environments and Possible Ecologies in the Jovian Atmosphere," *Astrophysical Journal Supplement*, 32, 737, 1976.

[12] Victoria Jaggard, "Could Jupiter Moon Harbor Fish-Size Life?" *National Geographic News*, 16 November 2009.

[13] Ibid.

[14] Ray Villard, "Could Saturn's Moon Enceladus Nurture Alien Life?" *Discovery News*, 8 June 2011.

[15] David Foss, "Titan: Oasis For Life As We Don't Know It," www.universetoday.com, 11 June 2011.

[16] Fraser Cain, "Could There Be Life on Uranus?" www.universetoday.com, 7 October 2008.

[17] Richard Baum and William Sheehan, *In Search of Planet Vulcan, The Ghost in Newton's Clockwork Machine*. New York: Plenum Press, 1997.

[18] Truman Bethurum, *Aboard a Flying Saucer*, De Vorss, 1953.

[19] Howard Menger, *From Outer Space to You*, Saucerian Books, 1959.

[20] Phil Platt, "The Planet X Saga: Nancy Lieder," http://badastronomy.com.

[21] Zecharia Sitchin, *The 12th Planet*, Harper, 1976.

[22] Ibid.

[23] www.zetatalk.com.

[24] Mark Hazlewood, Blindsided: *Planet Earth Passes in 2003, Earthchanges!* First Publish, 2001.

25 Nancy Lieder, "Pole Shift Date of May 27, 2003," www.zetatalk.com.

26 Nancy Lieder, "Zeta Talk: White Lie," www.zetatalk.com.

27 Nancy Lieder, "Planet X," www,zetatalk.com.

28 Zecharia Sitchin, *The End of Days: Armageddon and Prophecies of the Return*, William Morrow, 2007.

29 Myles Standish, "Planet X—No dynamical evidence in the optical observations," *Astronomical Journal*, 105 (5)

30 William Herschel, Philosophical Transactions of the Royal Society of London, 1795.

31 E. J. Öpik, "Is the Sun Habitable? An Astronomical Law-suit, a prize and a tragedy," *Irish Astronomical Journal*, 7 (No. 1), 1965.

32 K. R. Rybicki and C. Denis, "On the final destiny of the Earth and the solar system." *Icarus* 151, 2001.

33 A. D. Maude, A. D. "Life in the Sun," in I. J. Good, (ed.), *The Scientist Speculates*, Basic Books, 1963.

34 Duncan Lunan, *Man and the Stars*, Souvenir Press, 1974.

35 Ibid.

36 Stuart Holroyd, *Alien Intelligence*.

37 Ibid.

38 Ibid.

39 Carl Sagan (editor), *Communication with Extraterrestrial Intelligence,* MIT Press, 1973

40 Holroyd, op. cit.

41 Ibid.

42 Harlow Shapley, *Of Stars and Men*, Elek, 1978.

43 Holroyd, op. cit.

44 Stephen Hawking speaking on a Discovery Channel program 2010.

45 Jeff Foust, "SETI at 50," *The Space Review*, 23 August 2010

46 Robert M. Powers, *The World's First Spaceship Shuttle*, Stackpole Books, 1981.

47 Ibid.

48 Goldman, *X-Files 2.*

49-52 Ibid.

53 Michael Schirber, "Extraterrestrial DJs," www.alienlife.com/.

54 Foust, op. cit.

55 www.astrocentral.co.uk/.

56 Jacques Monod, *Chance and Necessity*, Fount, 1979.

57 Paul Davies, *Are We Alone? Philosophical Implications of the Discovery of Extraterrestrial Life*, Penguin, 1995.

58 Eric Jones, *Where is everybody?* An account of Fermi's question. Los Alamos National Laboratory, 1985; Frank Tipler, "Extraterrestrial Intelligent Beings Do Not Exist," *Quarterly Journal of the Royal Astronomical Society*, vol. 24, no 267, 1981.

59 Not least the "many worlds" or "parallel universe" model put forward by Everett, Graham, and Wheeler, in which, essentially, everything is possible in an infinite series of possible worlds.

60 Jacques Vallée, *Passport to Magonia: On UFOs, Folklore and Parallel Worlds*, Contemporary Books, 1993 (first edition 1969).

61 Von Däniken, *Chariots.*

62 Francis Crick and Leslie Orgel, "Directed Panspermia," Icarus, vol., 19, pp. 341-346.

63 Matt Ridley interviewing Richard Dawkins at the Centre for Life, Newcastle upon Tyne, England, 10 June 2010.

64 William Hooper, "Richard Dawkins on Intelligent Alien Design," http://www.theoligarch.com/, May 2008, ommenting on Dawkins' statement in his interview with Matt Ridley.

65 Paul Davies, *The Accidental Universe*, Cambridge University Press, 1982.

66 Dawkins-Ridley interview.

67 Ian Kaplan, commenting on the Dawkins-Ridley interview. www/3quarks.com/.

68 Fred Hoyle and Chandra Wickramasinghe, *Lifecloud—The Origin of Life in the Universe,* J. M. Dent and Sons, 1978

69 Natalie Wolchover, "Will We Really Find Alien Life Within 20 Years?" www.space.com, 20 June 2011.

70 www.astrocentral.co.uk/.

71 Kelly Young and David L Chandler, "Extreme bugs back idea of life on Mars," New Scientist, 7 December 2005.

72 Natalie Wolchover, "Will We Really Find Alien Life Within 20 Years?" www.livescience.com/ 28 June 2011.

CHAPTER EIGHT

FIRST CONTACT

WHEN THE STAR TRAVELERS WALKED AMONG US

All over the earth, from every color, race, and creed, come legends of the time when the Earth was young. Every culture, however advanced or fallen from the position of its ancestors, tells the same story of a lost golden age.

In those times, the Gods walked the Earth along with ordinary men and women. Humanity watched the stars and listened to the wise words of the gods. They brought life to the Earth and raised people up out of savagery. On the high places, the hills and mountains, in the depths of the lakes and seas and rivers, and on the lush green valleys of the earth, our ancestors built their temples to the gods and served them.

Two million years or more ago, human beings lived and walked upon this Earth of ours. In the dizzyingly rapid space of sixty-five years, humans went from making an aeroplane flight lasting seconds to landing a manned spacecraft on the Moon. Given two million years of existence, what wonders might not have been achieved in that time frame?

Under the debris of rocks and sand and rubble, on the beds of the ocean, and in forgotten hills, we have found relics of civilizations long since forgotten, or even dismissed as myths and fairy tales. Troy was no more than an imaginative poem by Homer till Schliemann rediscovered it in the nineteenth century. The very existence of the Hittite Empire—to which Troy was allied—was not even suspected until archaeologists, purely by chance, uncovered the remnants of a once-mighty civilization.

Our ancestors kept their faces turned towards the stars and planets, where they believed that the gods lived. In their eyes, the gods came down to Earth regularly and watched over the people of the planet. Legend even speaks of how the races of humanity were different in those days, and how the seed of the gods from the sky mingled at times with the native dwellers on the Earth. The offspring of these unions between the Earthfolk and the Star People led to a race of heroes being born.

In Egypt, one of the oldest known human civilizations, the time of the kingdoms was reckoned by four eras. The oldest was the Age of the Gods, when they walked on our planet and ruled the world. Then came the Age of Heroes, the demigods, those who descended from the marriage of gods and humans. Then came the Age of Manes, the spirits who watched over the Earth before humanity was ready to assume the burden of leadership itself. Finally came the Age of Kings, during which purely human rulers took up the task of steering the people of the planet into the paths of wisdom and justice.

When the gods walked upon Earth, there was justice and harmony among the peoples of the world. There was no war or hunger, nor did the Earth cry out in pain as her flesh was cut and her mineral treasures extracted. The gods took no more than they needed from Earth, and harvested her bounty in a spirit of infinite love.

THE FALL OF THE STAR TRAVELERS

Then times changed; greed, exploitation, oppression, and war flourished among the people of the planet. Even among the gods themselves, factions began to spring up. Humans sided with one party or another, and terrible destruction fell upon the planet. The Earth, which had been a living Paradise, became a place of terror and hardship.

Just as every race and religion has a tale about a lost Golden Age, so too they all have a legend of the Fall. Human beings stopped walking in the ways of the gods, and even some of the gods themselves fell from grace and became demons. Soon, the reign of the gods was over for good, and the world they left behind was smashed into ruins, broken beyond repair.

In some remote parts of the world, scattered remnants of seedbearers carried on in the best way they could. Rituals continued to be carried out, even after the reasons for them had long since been forgotten. For a while, the wisdom and knowledge handed down by the gods continued in a weaker form. The philosophy behind it had been lost, though, and, soon, even the mechanics of how to use the knowledge became a forgotten art.

Only old traditions, gradually dismissed over the course of time as fairy stories, still spoke of the old ways of the gods who had come down from the sky and taught the people of Earth. Those who still follow the gods in their heart, even though their days passed long ago, also speak of a time when they will return once more to help their people again.

WAR IN THE HEAVENS

One of the most intriguing questions about the advanced civilization brought to earth by the Star Travelers is how and why their societies fell. There are various theories, but one of the most remarkable is the idea that they possessed nuclear weapons and destroyed the world they had built in an atomic war.

Both geology and tradition make this idea a lot more plausible than it might seem at first glance. Ancient Indian writings not only describe events and their consequences that sound uncannily like nuclear war, but they also use some extremely unusual units of measurement of time. Two particularly relevant time measurements mentioned are the Day of Brahma, which covers a period of 4.32 billion years, and the Kashta, which is equal to 0.00000003 of a second. The only thing in nature that is measured in billions of years or millionths of a second is the rate at which isotopes decay. Uranium has a half-life of 4.51 billion years, K mesons millionths of a second or even less. It does seem an extraordinary coincidence that legends speak of events strikingly resembling nuclear war and ancient writings in Sanskrit divide time into periods that coincide so closely with the disintegration rates of isotopes.

There is also considerable evidence from archaeology and geology that strongly supports the idea of nuclear warfare on earth in ancient times. In the region of the Upper Ganges, the very part of India where the legends describe battles that sound very much like a conflict involving nuclear weapons, countless ruins have been discovered showing clear signs of charring.

Mysteriously, they do not appear to have been burnt in the normal way. The appearance is often of huge masses that look as if they have been soldered together and have been described as "looking like tin struck by a stream of molten steel."[1]

In the south of India, buildings have been found with walls that are corroded, glazed, and split, as if by some enormously powerful force. The stone furniture found there had been vitrified. Even a volcano, still less a natural fire, could not have produced such a phenomenon. The only explanation that accounts for this particular type of destruction is a nuclear explosion. It is worth adding, at this point, that a Russian researcher found, in this very area, a human skeleton showing a level of radiation fifty times the normal rate.[2] Similar discoveries have also been made in the region of Babylon.[3]

In 1952, archaeologists in Israel found a layer of green glass that had been fused to a thickness of a quarter of an inch, covering an area of several hundred square feet. Its appearance was remarkably similar to the vitrified sand produced by the atomic tests undertaken in Nevada, USA, during the 1950s.[4]

Similar finds have been made in Arabia, the Sahara Desert, and the Gobi Desert. Most strikingly of all, near the present Chinese nuclear test site, fused quartz has been found dating back thousands of years, almost identical with those produced by the modern Chinese nuclear tests.[5] In Britain, too, there is clear evidence of vitrified fortresses and towers.[6]

Both North and South America not only offer legends of some kind of holocaust, but also archaeological evidence that nuclear conflagration may have occurred. In Peru, near the ancient and mysterious fortress of Sacsahuaman, no less than 18,000 square yards of mountain rock has been vitrified. The stone blocks of the fortress itself also show clear signs of vitrification.[7] Similar discoveries have been made in Brazil.[8]

The Southwest and West of the United States contain the most extensive series of vitrified ruins on the American continent. Death Valley is particularly rich in these remains. Both the rocks in the area and an ancient city with streets have been affected by the process of vitrification.[9] Similar remains have been found in Arizona, Colorado, and the Mojave Desert, as well as in other parts of California.[10] The whole area is full of fused stones, fused glass, and liquefied metal.

There are various legends testifying to something that sounds exactly like nuclear war. The First Nation Peoples of Canada report that "demons came and made slaves of our people and sent the young to die among the rocks and below the ground. But then arrived the thunderbird, and our people were freed. We learned about the marvelous cities of the thunderbird, which were beyond the big lakes and rivers to the south. Many of our people left and saw these shining cities and witnessed the grand homes and the mystery of men who flew upon the skies. But then the demons returned, and there was terrible destruction. Those of our people who had gone southward returned to declare that all life in the cities was gone—nothing but silence remained."[11]

This account clearly describes people in some kind of aerial craft engaged in a war with others who lived further north. The nature of the terrible destruction is not specified and it is possible that it might have been a natural catastrophe, such as an earthquake or a volcanic eruption. Given the sketchiness of the legend, it is perhaps wise to regard it as valuable supporting testimony rather than material of primary importance.

The Native American Hopi in the Southwest of the United States have a slightly more enlightening account of the catastrophe. Their account declares that various nations "made a patuwvota and with their magical powers made it soar through the sky. On this many of them flew to a great city, attacked it, and returned so quickly that the inhabitants did not know where their attackers came from. Soon others from many nations were making patuwvotas, and flew to attack one another. So corruption and destruction came to the Third World people, as it had come to those who were before."[12]

This account, too, speaks of aerial warfare, but there is nothing specifically atomic about the destruction it mentions. Possibly some sort of flying machine, even a hot air balloon, carrying a kind of bomb or other projectile might have caused sufficient devastation to strike terror into the minds of a primitive people. Suggestive though the Hopi legends are, we cannot state on the basis of them that they constitute evidence for a nuclear catastrophe in ancient America.

Rather more specific are the accounts given by the ancient Indian epic known as *The Mahabharata*. This dates back to 500 B.C., but internal evidence within the poem suggests that the events it describes took place at least 2,000 years previously. The poem speaks of gods and kings riding about in "aerial chariots with sides of iron clad with wings," which certainly reminds us of the aircraft-like vehicles described by the Hopi and the Canadian native tribes.

The Mahabharata also describes an eighteen-day war in the region of the Upper Ganges, which involved these vimanas (aerial chariots) being used to launch some kind of devastatingly powerful weapon. It tells how a warrior called Adwattan "unleashed his Agnaya weapon, incapable of being resisted by the very gods." The result was that "dense arrows of flame, like a great shower, issued forth from creation, encompassing the enemy. A thick gloom swiftly settled upon the Pandava hosts. All points of the compass were lost in darkness. Fierce winds began to blow. Clouds roared upward, showering dust and gravel. Birds croaked madly, and beasts shuddered from the destruction. The waters boiled, and the creatures residing therein also died."[13]

It is difficult to explain this description in any other way than as a record of a nuclear attack and, though attempts have been made to suggest that it was either a form of natural disaster accompanying a war or simply a poetic fantasy, the details are so unusual, so specific, and have such a resonance for our world that has known the power of nuclear energy since 1945, that surely the only correct way of reading it is as a description of a nuclear war.

Another passage in *The Mahabharata* is even harder to dismiss when it speaks of "an incandescent column of smoke and fire, as brilliant as ten thousand suns" being launched against the enemy. The results are also astonishingly detailed and utterly familiar to an age that knows only too well the destruction that nuclear power is capable. The poem tells us that "the corpses were so burnt that they were no longer recognizable. Hair and nails fell out. Pottery broke without cause. Birds, disturbed, circled in the air and were turned white. Foodstuffs were poisoned. To escape, the warriors threw themselves into streams to wash themselves and their equipment."[14]

Pre-atomic scholars could make nothing of passages like this, but with our greater knowledge of nuclear energy, we can read them in a different light. The description of the brilliant fiery column, intense heat, shock waves, poisoning of foodstuffs, the appearance of the corpses, the loss of hair and nails, all sound uncannily like the effects of an atomic bomb.

Nobel Prize-winning scientist Professor Frederick Soddy commented on the ancient legends of *The Mahabharata* in 1909 and felt moved to speculate. "Can we read into this," he wrote, "some justification for the belief that some former forgotten race of men attained not only to the knowledge we have so recently won, but also to the power that is not yet ours?"[15]

The power of which Soddy spoke was, of course, the power of atomic energy. He felt that the only reasonable scientific explanation of these passages was that, at some point in the distant past there had been a civilization on earth that had discovered the use of nuclear power. No other explanation covers all the available facts and, when the testimony of tradition is confirmed and supported by the results of geology and archaeology, it seems certain that nuclear war on our planet took place at some as yet undetermined time in the remote past.

BRINGERS OF WISDOM

These legends of bringers of wisdom are generally referred to by anthropologists as culture bearers. One of the many stories about them, found particularly in the Americas, speaks of a white prophet who wandered from land to land. He is always spoken of as using the cycles of Venus to predict the future and even told the people that Venus was "his" star. He used to pray facing the planet, and said that its sacred number was thirteen, which was also his number. In some versions of the myth he is even referred to as the God from Venus. He is said to have made the people build a stone calendar including the cycles of Venus, the precession of the equinoxes, and the transit of planets.[16]

A number of important truths are hidden behind this strange story. Three key motifs feature in the legend: one, the curious figure of the white prophet himself; another, the reference to him as being a God from Venus; and third, the importance of the number thirteen. Throughout history, certain numbers have been looked upon as special, lucky, or unlucky. Seven and thirteen are the most common numbers to attract those reputations.

It may be simple coincidence, but Venus makes thirteen revolutions around the Sun to every eight of the Earth. One hundred and four years is a complete cycle of Venus and fifty-two years a half-cycle. Both cycles were studied and used, especially the half-cycle of fifty-two years. Thirteen is the number of Venus among the Native Americans and eight the number of Earth. It is surprising that they possessed such detailed astronomical knowledge of the periods of rotation of Earth and Venus.

Archaeological discoveries also support the idea of early knowledge of highly complex astronomical discoveries. In the city of Teotihuacan, for instance, situated near Mexico City, the lost Toltec city of Tula was found when excavations were carried out during the Second World War. The archaeologists found that it had been the center of an advanced civilization. They discovered a number of pyramids, one representing the Sun, one the Moon, and a strange but particularly fascinating one, the Pyramid of the Serpent. This structure was built up in a series of layers, comprised of eight shells, with a further shell being added to the pyramid every fifty-two years.[17]

THE BAFFLING RIDDLE OF THE PREHISTORIC CITY OF TIAHUANACO

Even more impressive than the remains of Teotihuacan are the ruins of the ancient city of Tiahuanaco in Bolivia. These are truly awe-inspiring, the city itself being situated at the astonishing height of 15,000 feet above sea level. There are no settlements nearby, and the atmospheric pressure is almost half that found at sea level. The air is so thin that it burns the nose and throat, and visitors to the site almost invariably suffer from mountain sickness.

The whole area is simply too high up to have supported the enormous number of people that would have been needed to create the vast stone ruins found on the site. No seeds can grow on the high, rocky mountain crags. How could the people who lived there have even managed to feed themselves, still less create the giant ruins of Tiahuanaco? How was it possible for the laborers on the site to have toiled in such extreme conditions and built this vast city complex?

Even from the ruins, it is immediately obvious that Tiahuanaco was once a vibrant, flourishing metropolis. It had water conduits, stonework fastened together with copper clamps, menhirs, temples, and other highly skilled works of construction. The stone walls of the temple were set on stone foundation blocks weighing up to 100 tons each, held in place with silver tenons.

As was their way when they conquered the Americas, the conquistadors simply looted the precious metal and as much of the stone as they could carry away easily. The only reason that Tiahuanaco survived was because its remains were too heavy for them to move. Even so, they destroyed who knows what priceless treasures in the course of their greed. In addition to the man-made destruction, earthquakes also played a part in collapsing the walls. For all the twin ravages of the assaults of nature and human activity, what remains of the city is profoundly impressive.[18]

Perhaps the most astonishing single sight in Tiahuanaco is a twenty-ton block of sandstone over twenty-four feet long. This massive block, known as the Great Idol of Tiahuanaco, was actually a calendar. It gave the precession of the equinoxes and the position of the Moon and its movements, together with the astronomical seasons. Perhaps most remarkable of all, it showed clearly that it was based upon the notion of a round Earth rotating in space.[19]

Another extraordinary creation is the Gate of the Sun in the same city. This is a solid ten-ton block, cut from a single piece of stone, and with a doorway through it leading...

nowhere. Carved on this massive gate is a series of signs and symbols, all representing the precession of the equinoxes and solstices, the position and movements of the Moon, both real and apparent, and a clear awareness of the rotation of the Earth. When the native Aymara tribe was asked by their Spanish conquerors who had built the ruins, they simply shrugged and admitted that they had no idea. The gods themselves must have been its builders, the Aymara told them.[20]

Incredibly elaborate carvings are also found on the stone, and the stone itself has been perfectly cut, in exact geometrical measurement. How could hard stone be cut and carved so exactly, so exquisitely, so intricately, with nothing more than simple tools of stone?

There is considerable dispute over the age of Tiahuanaco. The generally accepted date for its construction is 500 A.D. The furthest back in time that prehistorians are willing to consider as a possibility is 1000 B.C. However, there are serious problems that make even the earlier dating difficult to accept.

In the first place, bones of long extinct animals have been found on the site. That is not a major objection to the proposed dates, since the animals might well have been alive earlier and their remains simply found in the region.

A far more devastating criticism of the hypothesis of a relatively late date for Tiahuanaco is that drawings of extinct animals, some supposedly extinct as long ago as a million years B.C., have been found depicted on local pottery from the site. The only possible explanations are that either the animals survived in the inhospitable climate and conditions of Tiahuanaco until a far more recent period than was thought possible, or the site itself dates back to a time when the animals still lived upon the Earth.[21]

Even more conclusive evidence of the vast antiquity of Tiahuanaco is shown clearly from the testimony of the calendar. This unambiguously describes a time when the rotation of the Moon around the Earth was entirely different from its present cycle. It also refers to a specific and significant date in the history of Tiahuanaco.[22]

Nor is it possible, even at the earlier date of 1000 B.C., to account for the foundation of the city at such a high altitude and with insufficient vegetation to feed the population, still less to sustain an army of building workers. There was, however, a time when the site of Tiahuanaco not only stood above sea level, but was actually a port. At that period, building the city would have been entirely possible. As this earlier time, a date of earlier than 10,000 B.C. also corresponds with the evidence from the calendar; it is clear that the site must go back at least as far as that.[23] The evidence of the drawings suggests an even greater antiquity for this historic and extraordinary site.[24]

There are also rumors of sunken ruins hidden beneath the deep waters of Lake Titicaca, the body of water that abuts the city. Though Titicaca is an inland lake, it contains animals that are only found elsewhere within the ocean. It too must once have stood at sea level. Jacques Cousteau, explorer of the depths of the ocean, made a submarine descent to Titicaca, but did not discover any ruins. Whether or not there remain secrets hidden at the bottom of the lake is yet to be fully determined.[25]

Knowing that an advanced civilization existed on the site perhaps a million or more years ago is only the beginning of the mysteries of Tiahuanaco. Not only does its high culture long predate the empires of Egypt or Mesopotamia, but how on earth could such triumphant examples of perfect geometry and engineering have been accomplished so long ago? And what are we to make of the local legends that speak of the Gods from the Sky—the builders of Tiahuanaco? Do they really refer to extraterrestrial beings that designed and built the city with the aid of advanced technology from outer space? Was Tiahuanaco the headquarters of Mars Base One?

DISASTER STRIKES THE EARTH

A worldwide catastrophe hit the Earth at around 10,000 B.C. A cosmic disaster, whose origins and extent are still unknown, destroyed the high civilizations that had flourished on the planet for millennia. With its coming, the greatness of Tiahuanaco and other thriving centers of culture and advanced knowledge ended. Humanity plunged back abruptly into a more primitive state than its forbears.

A thousand years later saw the beginnings of agriculture upon the planet, though it would be more accurate to speak of the rediscovery of farming. As well as that development, and the slow rebuilding of cities—Jericho, Chatal Hüyuk, Hacilar, all built around 8000 B.C.— we have nothing but a long period of darkness in human history. Not until the great kingdoms of Egypt and Sumeria sprang up, literally overnight, already fully-formed, around 5000 B.C., did humans finally begin the long re-ascent to civilization. Two thousand years or so later, the cities of Mohenjo-Dara and Harappa in India followed suit, again with no obvious precursors.

How is it that these nations came into being as already fully developed civilizations? There was no intermediate period of slow growth from a more primitive state to a higher one, as is normal throughout human history. Could it be that the gods from the sky, having abandoned Earth at around 10,000 B.C., created Egypt and Sumeria on their return as new centers of wisdom?

THE RETURN OF THE STAR TRAVELERS

This brings us to consider the question of the Sphinx. The general consensus has been that this remarkable monument was built around 2500 B.C. However, the research of Schoch has proven that the Sphinx was actually weathered by water, not wind, and that a more likely date for its construction is around 10,000 B.C.[26]

There also, curiously, seem to be links between the Sphinx and the planet Mars. Additionally, there are links between the Cydonia region of Mars and Avebury. A monument on the planet is strikingly similar to figures found in Egypt, including the Sphinx. Did travelers from Mars come back to Earth, after the great cataclysm that hit the planet around 10,000 B.C., and build the Sphinx in Egypt as a way of preserving some of the knowledge that had been lost in the catastrophe?

THE MYSTERY OF EASTER ISLAND

Another baffling mystery is the secret story of the great lava stone statues found on Easter Island. This tiny place, adrift in the Pacific Ocean, the nearest substantial land-mass being Chile some 2,350 miles away, houses 800 massive statues of stone. The heads and torsos on the statues are strange figures, built upon the top of volcanic rock. They rise to a height of 70 feet and weigh as much as 50 pounds each.

Originally, they stood upon platforms of stone, further massive red stones being placed on their heads. The stone itself had been cut and transported from a distant quarry. When it was finally rediscovered in 1722, the entire population of the island numbered no more than a few thousand. Devastating slave raids had reduced the population to a hundred by the nineteenth century, before it slowly began to recover.

Thanks to the investigations of Thor Heyerdahl, we now know how the statues were moved into position. What we still do not know is how they were cut originally, nor, most important of all the unanswered questions: Why? Heyerdahl could only discover fragmentary legends about the construction, stories of civil war, cannibalism, and a sudden, dramatic descent into barbarism.[27]

The astonishing volume, scale, and sophistication of building in prehistoric times is another remarkable mystery. The huge standing stones, menhirs, dolmens, and other examples of ancient architecture are often on a monumental level. One standing stone in Brittany, for instance, is 85 feet high and weighs 342 tons. There are so many huge prehistoric structures that it is hard not to wonder if there may be more than myth in the ancient claims that such structures were built by giants, or the gods.

PREHISTORIC ASTRONOMY

The evidence of extremely advanced astronomical knowledge in ancient times is also overwhelming. As early as Homer, the existence of the two moons of Mars, invisible to the naked eye and supposedly not even discovered by telescopes until over 200 years after its invention, was known. Supposedly, primitive South American tribes knew that the Earth was a sphere, and the correct period of rotation for both the Earth and Venus. The ancient Egyptians and the Dogon tribe of Mali in North Africa knew not only of the existence of the star Sirius, but also of its two invisible companions. The Dogon still perform a centuries-old dance portraying the fifty-year orbit of Sirius B around Sirius A. Yet it was supposedly not even known until the second half of the twentieth century that Sirius even possessed another star associated with it. How is such astonishingly accurate astronomical information possible?[28]

A huge stone calendar at Glastonbury, measuring thirty miles in circumference and clearly intended to be visible from above, has been carbon dated to 18,000 B.C.[29] The Calendar of Tiahuanaco, of course, is outstanding, one of the great astronomical recording devices. Equally impressive are those used by the mysterious Maya.[30]

Numerous other anomalous evidence of astronomical knowledge that could not have been known to ancient and primitive people and yet clearly was possessed by them, also at present defies rational explanation.

Something is clearly very wrong with the orthodox account of prehistory. Shambling, apelike barbarians who were barely human were able to create works of genius. And, of course, the traditions and testimony of the people is that their knowledge was brought to them by culture bearers, often gods who came down from the sky above and taught them what they knew. When they went away at last, humans relapsed into the barbarism from which the gods had raised them up.

THE RIDDLE OF THE NAZCA LINES IN THE DESERTS OF PERU

The curious markings in the deserts of Peru known as the Nazca Lines are another baffling mystery. They date back at least as far as the first century A.D., and are massive designs drawn in the sand of the desert. Animals and birds are drawn in correct proportion, something that European artists were unable to achieve before the Renaissance. Some extremely complex geometrical designs are traced upon the sand. Straight lines, running on for many miles, are also depicted. All of these feats were carried out supposedly without knowledge of the principles of trigonometry and geometry, nor with the assistance of modern surveying techniques and equipment. The vast network of lines and figures was designed and created with an exactness and precision that are truly remarkable.

Even more baffling than the sheer size and scale of the project is the fact that the lines drawn so carefully in the sands of the desert are all but invisible when observed from the ground. Only when viewed from the air do they stand fully revealed in all their awe-inspiring beauty and complexity. Who created these lines in the desert, and why? And why is it that the lines are almost invisible except when seen from an aerial vantage?

Essentially, there are five basic explanations in the field. The earliest theory, and the one most easily disproved, is the idea that the lines were prehistoric roads. The second is that they served an astronomical purpose, acting as a calendar and even an observatory. The third is that they were sacred trackways for religious pilgrimages. The fourth is that they were prehistoric airstrips. The fifth is that they were either landing strips or navigational aids for prehistoric spacecraft.

The theory that the lines were roads built by the Incas or their predecessors has been demolished by the extensive research of Paul Kosok, Maria Reiche, and John Hyslop.[31] The essential points are that the trackways are thoroughly impractical if viewed as roads; that roads were built to take account of natural features rather than being rigidly straight; and that it seems highly improbable that prehistoric people would have built roads which are almost invisible on the ground but highly visible from the air. The road theory has now been abandoned by all serious researchers of the Nazca mystery.

The astronomical theory has been championed particularly by Maria Reiche. This remarkable woman spent years surveying, researching, and evaluating the lines, and her work in the field demands respect. Nevertheless, her theory does not stand up as a complete explanation of the Nazca Lines.

In the first place, the astronomer Gerald Hawkins calculated possible astronomical and calendar uses. He found that although there was an above average correspondence of markings to possible astronomical correlations, the majority of lines showed no such relationship.[32]

Secondly, because heavenly bodies change their positions, it is impossible to determine exact alignments without knowing the age of the Nazca Lines themselves. Although these have been dated within the approximate margins of 100 B.C to 100 A.D., this dating is largely guesswork. They might be much older than that or much later. There simply is not enough evidence to support Reiche's calendar theory, and such evidence that does exist suggests that a purely astronomical use for Nazca is unlikely.[33]

On the other hand, that some kind of astronomical observations were indeed part of the functions of the Nazca Lines seems highly probable. South American astronomy was highly developed and inextricably linked with the religious beliefs of the people. It employed intricate and sophisticated methods of calculation and displayed a more advanced knowledge of the heavens than that of the Europeans who conquered their country. Though Reiche and Kosok were wrong to claim that the lines were purely or even primarily astronomical in intention, they were absolutely correct in their contention that one of the many aspects of Nazca was indeed as an astronomical calendar.[34]

The main protagonists of the theory that the Nazca Lines were sacred pathways are Tony Morrison and Johan Reinhard.[35] When he began investigating the markings, Morrison considered Reiche's calendar theory the most plausible explanation. His mind was changed when, five years after his visit to Nazca, he was making a film about wild life in the Andes. As he climbed up a hill beside a lake in Bolivia, to his astonishment he saw a perfectly straight line leading away from it, down the hillside and right out into the barren, inhospitable desert area. What was more, an animal sacrifice had been made there recently, and it seemed as if the worshiper had used the straight line path up the hill to bring his offering to the gods.[36]

It was ten years before Morrison was able to mount an expedition to investigate his new theory. He began by surveying a large area of Bolivia, seeing a vast network of straight lines extending more than twenty miles around the slopes of Sajama, the second highest mountain in the country.[37] At the village of Sajama itself, lines were running in every direction, seeming to be linked either to local churches or to small shrines placed carefully on top of the mountain.[38]

His local informants told him they related to the spirits of the mountains, who were responsible for bringing hail, frost, and rain to the people. The shrines were meant as offerings to invoke the protection of the powerful mountain spirits.

Morrison found no evidence that there was any astronomical significance to the placing of the lines. He came instead to the conclusion that the lines were simply paths used by particular worshipers or groups of worshipers as they followed the shrines up along the mountains. In his opinion, the lines were simply sacred roads connecting one holy place with another.[39]

Morrison's theory has a great deal of plausibility, but fails to answer a number of questions. A network of straight lines leading to clearly marked shrines along a mountain is one thing. It is not so easy to understand why worshipers at Nazca went to the trouble of drawing elaborate figures and geometrical shapes in the desert sand.

Reinhardt, by contrast, claimed that he did know why these strange and apparently unnecessary markings were made. In his opinion, they were designed to persuade the spirits of the mountain to send down water to irrigate the deserts. He did, however, admit that there remained many mysteries about the Nazca Lines that required further investigation.[40]

Neither Morrison nor Reinhardt can offer any convincing explanation as to why the lines are only visible from the air. It seems incredible that the people of Nazca would have gone to so much trouble to placate the mountain gods when no other culture in the world has ever adopted such an elaborate and complicated way of trying to invoke them. Why has no other known culture attempted anything similar to the Nazca markings for this purpose? There are many other monuments to mountain gods and spirits of the air around the world, yet not one of them resembles Nazca. Though an interesting hypothesis, the sacred pathways idea is clearly false.

The prehistoric airstrip theory has been put forward by Jim Woodman.[41] Woodman points out, rightly, that the technology to build a hot air balloon has been available to the human race almost since the beginning of time. In November 1975, he tested his theory by successfully flying a hot-air balloon across the pampas. Ground investigation also found evidence of "burn pits" and "charred rocks."[42] Woodman's theory is the most plausible of all the explanations put forward for the Nazca markings. The biggest argument against it is the absence of much in the way of positive evidence in its favor. The fact that balloon flights could have taken place does not mean that they did. In addition, it only explains the how of their construction, not the far more interesting question—why?

The idea that the lines were designed as landing strips for aircraft was put forward by Harold Wilkins and George Hunt Williamson before being popularized by von Däniken.[43] It is only necessary to point out that any spaceship would become stuck in the pampas as soon as it landed, and that no evidence of any UFO landings in the region has ever come to light. As Peter White remarked:

> SURELY THIS WAS THE CLEANEST AIRPORT IN THE WORLD'S HISTORY? WHERE ARE THE FOUNDATIONS OF THE CONTROL CENTRE? WHERE THE DROPPED BOLTS, SPANNERS, ODD BITS OF JUNK, THROWN AWAY FOOD WRAPPINGS, AND ALL THE OTHER LITTER THAT INDUSTRIAL TECHNOLOGIES PRODUCE?[44]

Although a remarkable achievement, the Nazca Lines clearly were not intended to be used as airstrips or airports for spacecraft. It is, however, entirely possible that the original designers of the lines were extraterrestrial themselves, or that humans constructed it under the supervision of extraterrestrials.

There is already sufficient evidence to suggest that contact between extraterrestrials and humans during prehistoric times is highly probable. It is also highly likely that the input from the Star Travelers explains the otherwise baffling evidence of early knowledge of advanced mathematics, science, and technology.

WHERE DID THE STAR TRAVELERS COME FROM?

Where did the Sky Gods come from? Were they all from one planet or have there been visitors from other worlds? As mentioned, both Mars and the Moon were once inhabited planets. Other worlds spoken of as harboring life are Venus, Mercury, and Jupiter. The possibilities of life on Saturn, Uranus, Neptune, and Pluto are considerably more remote, although recent discoveries by NASA have made Saturn and Uranus far more likely candidates for planets with inhabitants than was once believed. As for the notion of life on the Sun, while an intriguing possibility, it is highly improbable.

Maybe there have been several waves of visitors to our planet. Perhaps the Moon dwellers came to our world and set up home upon it, probably around 10,000 B.C. Maybe the Martians came later, bringing civilization to Egypt and Sumeria. Some of the evidence from myth and legend suggests that the Venusians came later still, around 1500 B.C.

Mars and the Moon, our two nearest neighbors, seem, perhaps not surprisingly, to have played the most important role in our affairs. Perhaps the different ethnic types on Earth represent the successive waves of alien landings and subsequent interbreeding with humans. Were the ancient Egyptians, for instance, the offspring of Martians? We shall see later that this is a distinct possibility.

We do not know, and perhaps never will know, the whole truth about the prehistory of the human race. What seems highly probable, though, is that at various times in the history of our planet, the development of humanity, particularly in terms of technology, culture, and civilization, perhaps even genetically, has helped along by space travelers. We, who think of ourselves as a unique special creation of God, or alternatively as a vastly improbable cosmic accident, should now begin thinking of ourselves as one among many life forms in the universe. Life in the universe is abundant; it is extraordinarily unlikely that we are the only intelligent beings living within it.

The men and women of Mars and the Moon are our own sisters and brothers, whom we meet on the street every day. Their pioneer ancestors helped to build our planet and bring it to the dawn of civilization. Maybe even now their descendants are helping us still. As we progress in our turn, reaching out on our own magical journeys towards distant planets and far away stars, our human spaceships, too, may one day touch down on worlds already inhabited. In years to come, perhaps their descendants will tell stories of the strange gods who came from a distant planet called Earth, bringing with them the gifts of civilization to the dwellers on their world.

ENDNOTES: CHAPTER EIGHT

[1] Rene Noorbergen, *Secrets of the Lost Races*, New English Library, 1980.
[2] Ibid.
[3] A Gorbovski, cited in Noorbergen, op. cit.
[4] Noorbergen, op. cit.
[5] Ibid.
[6] Ibid.
[7] Ibid.
[8] Ibid.
[9] Ibid.
[10] Ibid.

[11] Ethnologist R. Baker, quoted by Noorbergen, op. cit.

[12] Frank Waters, *Book of the Hopi*, Penguin, 1977.

[13] *The Mahabharat*a.

[14] Ibid.

[15] Frederick Soddy, *The Interpretation of Radium*, John Murray, 1909.

[16] L. Taylor Hansen, *He Walked the Americas*, Spearman, 1963.

[17] Ibid.

[18] Charles Berlitz, *Mysteries from Forgotten Worlds*, Corgi, 1974.

[19] H. S. Bellamy, *Built Before the Flood*, Faber, 1943.

[20] H. S. Bellamy and Peter Allen, *The Calendar of Tiahuanaco*, Faber, 1950.

[21] Ibid.

[22] Ibid.

[23] Ibid.

[24] Berlitz, op. cit.

[25] Ibid.

[26] Graham Hancock, *Fingerprints of the Gods*, Heinemann, 1995.

[27] Thor Heyerdahl, Aku-Aku, Allen and Unwin, 1956.

[28] Murray Hope, *Ancient Egypt and the Sirius Connection*, Element, 1990.

[29] Berlitz, op. cit.

[30] Adrian C. Gilbert and Maurice M. Cotterell, *The Mayan Prophecies*, Element, 1990.

[31] a) Paul Kosok and Maria Reiche, "The Mysterious Markings of Nazca," Natural History, vol. 56, 1947; b) John Hyslop, *The Inca Road System*, Academic Press, 1954.

[32] Gerald Hawkins, *Ancient Lines in the Peruvian Jungle*, Smithsonian Astrophysical Observatory, 1969.

[33] R. A. Williamson (editor), *Archaeoastronomy in the Americas*, Bullens Press, 1981.

[34] a) Tony Morrison, *Pathways to the Gods*, Paladin, 1978; b) Johan Reinhardt, *The Nazca Lines: A New Perspective on their Origins and Meaning*, Editorial Los Pinos, 1985.

[35] Morrison, op. cit.

[36] Ibid.

[37] Ibid.

[38] Ibid.

[39] Ibid.

[40] Reinhardt, op.cit.

[41] Jim Woodman, *Nazca: Journey to the Sun*, John Murray, 1977.

[42] Ibid.

[43] a) Harold T Wilkins, *Flying Saucers from the Moon*, London, 1994; b) George Hunt Williamson, *Road in the Sky*, Neville Spearman, 1960; c) Erich von Däniken, *Chariots of the Gods?* Souvenir Press, 1970.

[44] Peter White, *The Past is Human*, Taplinger, 1976.

CHAPTER NINE

THE WEB OF CONSPIRACY

Over the years, since Arnold's sighting launched the modern explosion of flying saucers, Ufologists have put forward a range of different conspiracy theories. Most are incompatible with one another, but that does not seem to stop their supporters from arguing in favor of two mutually exclusive theories.

On the other hand, there undoubtedly have been conspiracies, cover-ups, and disinformation coming from the authorities with regard to many UFO cases. The case of Roswell is so well known that it will not be dealt with in this chapter. Instead, readers should consult the three excellent books on the subject (Michael Hesemann and Phillip Mantte, *Beyond Roswell*; Stanton Friedman and Don Berliner, *Crash at Corona*; and Tim Shawcross, *The Roswell File*). The question of possible suppression of data regarding life on the Moon and Mars has been dealt with in the chapters on those planets.

UFO COVER-UPS

There is little doubt that governments and intelligence agencies have lied about UFO cases and tried to suppress and cover up information. It is difficult to understand why they would bother if there truly was nothing to hide.

What would the purpose of such a cover-up be? One theory is that they are trying to hide the fact that UFOs are from outer space and that governments are powerless to check their activities. Another is that they are hiding the fact that human governments are actively cooperating with aliens. The third is that they are hiding secret weapons projects for which democratic approval has not been secured. The fourth is that the whole UFO program is a deliberate exercise in mind control by organizations such as the CIA.

We need not waste much time on the last suggestion. If intelligence agencies really possessed the ability to control people's minds at will, they would hardly need to resort to more conventional methods of repression, intelligence gathering, and national defense. The mind control methods would make them invincible. Yes, intelligence agencies have been involved in mind control programs, but the results have never been particularly impressive. They have achieved some success, but certainly not remotely to the extent that would make the hypothesis that intelligence services were behind the UFO phenomenon a credible idea.

The suggestion of the omnipotence of the aliens also makes little sense. It is hard to understand why governments would try to hide the fact that extraterrestrials are so all-powerful that we are unable to stop them from invading our airspace, abducting and raping our men and women, abducting and mutilating our cattle, and even allegedly warning off our astronauts when they go to the Moon. If this was really how governments felt about the UFO phenomenon, they would behave entirely differently. They would go public and appeal for world cooperation in the face of a common danger. Both Reagan and Gorbachev agreed that a threat from outer space would unite the human race as nothing else could.[1]

One could also look at the problem from the other point of view. If the aliens are so all-powerful, why are they simply carrying out Viking-style raids upon Earth, rather than trying to conquer at last some of the weaker countries, if not the whole world?

ALIEN LIAISON

This is the claim that governments, particularly the US, are actively engaged in a program of cooperation with extraterrestrials and are developing alien technology in return for allowing them to carry out sinister projects of their own, such as genetic experiments and similarly unpleasant activities.[2]

There is no doubt that government secret projects and hidden bases exist in almost every country of the world. It is also fair to say that more advanced research, such as the Stealth bombers and the Star Wars programs, was principally carried out in secret.

On the other hand, the extreme difficulty of a secret of this kind, involving so many thousands of people—to give a conservative estimate of the numbers that would be involved in such an extensive and elaborate cover-up operation—makes it highly implausible that it could or would remain secret for very long. There is some tantalizing evidence to suggest that "black projects" have been centered on some kind of "saucer-type" experiments, but the overwhelming probability is that those involved are entirely human. Nor is it easy to see what the aliens would gain from such a cooperation. If they were so much in advance of our own level of technical development, what would be their motivation for assisting us to develop weapons that might possibly threaten them over the course of time?

SECRET WEAPONS

Of all the conspiracy theories in the field, the notion that UFOs are at least in part some sort of secret military experimental program is by far the most likely. There is considerable evidence that suggests it is the true explanation for many of the various UFO cases. It is also clearly applicable to many of the abduction testimonies. The following facts are strongly supportive of the theory.

1. UFO sightings first began to be seen following the arrival in the United States of German scientists who had been working on German secret weapons and, in particular, on rocket technology
2. From 1941 onwards, the Germans were working on, among other secret projects, variants on the Schriever-Habermohl "flying disk."[3]
3. In 1945, the aeronautical engineer Sir Roy Fedden declared that the Nazis had been working on advanced propulsion craft that were well ahead of any other aerospace technology in the world. A few years later, he confirmed that the UFO sightings resembled some of the Nazi technology.
4. In 1956, Captain Edward Ruppelt, leader of the UFO investigative program "Project Blue Book," commented that "the only known craft that could even approach the performance of the objects reported by UFO observers" were Nazi secret weapons.[4]
5. Daniel Fry, a former employee at White Sands, reveals that many secret projects were carried out at the US air base under the supervision of Wernher von Braun and other former Nazi rocket scientists from exactly the same period of time that UFO sightings first began to be observed on a widespread scale.[5]
6. Secret military projects with advanced aerospace technology represent an entirely rational explanation for government cover-ups. It is entirely logical for them to deny the existence of, or to suppress information about, such activities, just as it is for intelligence agencies to substitute disinformation for genuine facts.

101

7. The CIA eventually admitted that the majority of genuine UFO sightings over the United States (as opposed to misidentifications of natural objects, hallucinations, and hoaxes) were in fact sightings of secret military projects by the military.[6]

On balance, the notion that the US and other governments are trying to cover-up secret projects is far and away the most probable explanation for their behavior.

MAJESTIC-12

Researchers into the Maj-12 conspiracy (as it is generally known) appear to find it exceptionally difficult to agree among themselves. Some of them have also changed their minds about either the status of the project itself over the years or of the documents that have been produced in support of the claims made about Maj-12.[7]

The Maj-12 documents describe a meeting between President Truman and various VIPs concerning UFO activity. Their status remains hotly disputed.[8]

The most careful and thorough analysis of the documents shows that they are almost certainly forgeries. As for the contents, there are problems with the reports of the meetings in terms of the times they are alleged to have taken place. The most likely explanation is that they are either a conscious hoax or else deliberate disinformation on the part of the CIA and similar government agencies. It is highly likely that Truman sat down to discuss the UFO phenomenon with senior advisers in an attempt to ensure exactly what it was and whether or not it constituted a threat to national security. More than that, we cannot reasonably say.

THE CATTLE KILLINGS

A series of mysterious killings of livestock have occurred, particularly in the Midwest and Western regions of the United States. The first case took place in Colorado in 1967, and a three-year old horse named Lady was the victim. Her head was stripped clean of flesh and muscle, even her brain, spine, and internal organs were missing. There were no signs of blood or tire tracks anywhere near the dead animal. Various circular marks were found on the ground, described as "exhaust" marks. A circle of holes was also found nearby and a Forest Ranger also checked both the body and the area around for radiation with a Geiger counter. He found some evidence of radioactivity in the area of the exhaust marks, but the closer he came to the horse's body the lower the radiation readings became.[9]

Ten days later, Dr. John Altshuler investigated the case. What he found both shocked and puzzled him. He saw at once that the animal had been killed cleanly, almost surgically, and that no predator would have been capable of such precision. There was clear evidence of "a vertical, clean incision" and he felt that the "flesh had been opened and cauterized with a surgical cauterizing blade. The outer edges of the cut skin were firm, almost as if they had been cauterized with a laser."[10]

What baffled the doctor most of all was the complete absence of blood. As he said in bewilderment, "You can't cut into a body without getting some blood. Whoever did the cutting took the horse's heart, lungs, and thyroid. How do you get the heart out without blood?"[11]

Since the unfortunate Lady met her death, literally thousands of similar killings have been reported. Most cases involve cattle, but horses, sheep, goats, and even cats and dogs have been the victims of this barbaric practice.[12]

Officer Gabriel Valdez of the New Mexico State Police carried out a number of investigations into mutilation cases in his own area. His reports noted clear evidence that aircraft had landed in the vicinity, leaving clear marks on the ground beneath them. They also noted the increased level of radiation found in the region where the dead animals were found. Valdez concluded that, as a result of his investigations, he believed that the mutilations were being carried out for some sort of genetic research or possibly germ warfare testing.[13]

Clearly these experiments require sophisticated and expensive equipment in order to carry them out. The main question is, of course, who is responsible for these killings? Ufologist Paul Bennewitz claimed that aliens were abducting the animals in order to make humanoids out of "specific cattle parts." He added that the US Government was in league with the extraterrestrials and "agreed to the cattle mutilations" in return "for the atomic ship and technology."[14]

By contrast, George Erianne, who spent seven years investigating the phenomenon, came to the conclusion that the cattle mutilation killings were part of a secret germ warfare program by the US Government. The animals were first tranquilized and then taken by helicopter to another location, where they were drained of blood and had various organs removed from their bodies through laser surgery.[15]

Numerous witnesses and physical evidence confirm the presence of helicopters and aircraft in the vicinity of the cattle mutilations. There is also clear forensic evidence that a pesticide that acts as a tranquilizer was also found in the same area.[16]

Erianne's theory, after which he began to receive death threats—a possible confirmation of its truth?—seems the most plausible explanation of the whole distasteful phenomenon of the cattle mutilations. Extraterrestrial? It seems unlikely.

SECRET EXPERIMENTS

The Second World War was over at last; the Germans and their dreams of a world empire of Nazi Supermen had been crushed by the Allied forces. Already, though, the minds of the military and intelligence community within both the United States and the Soviet Union were turning towards the next war—the Cold War. From wartime friends and allies, the Americans and Russians were about to become bitter enemies. This hostility lasted until the arrival in power of Gorbachev, which led to the total transformation of relations between the two countries.

The Nazi scientists, who had conducted experiments of horrific barbarity upon human victims, were nevertheless wanted men in another sense of the expression. From 1946, a project named "Operation Paperclip" was launched by the Americans to spirit these very scientists out of Germany and employ them on secret projects within the US. The Russians also hastened to make use of their services in secret operations of their own. Even the British recruited a few scientists who became involved in developing the country's nuclear capability.

Soon, former Nazi war criminals began working at the Air Force School of Aviation Medicine in Texas. They soon showed that they had not changed their spots by commencing a series of radiation experiments on human beings. Most had no idea that they were being subjected to this treatment. By 1951, the AFSAM was so pleased with the results of this program that they asked for more German scientists to join the project, adding that their work had been "of real value to the Air Force."[17]

Nor was it only the Germans who benefited from this sudden amnesia. Japanese scientists from the notorious Unit 731 had engaged extensively in chemical and biological warfare. They had operated on people without anesthetic, practiced experimental surgery on healthy victims, and deliberately infected people with deadly diseases. At the end of the war, General McArthur specifically requested immunity from prosecution for these people. The US Government was happy to comply. Before long, the Americans were using techniques derived from Japanese war criminals on their own people.[18]

Is it possible that many of the supposedly alien abductions, medical procedures, and genetic experiments are actually being carried out by entirely human intelligence agencies, rather than extraterrestrial ones? There are several cases where that appears distinctly possible, particularly Christa Tilton's strange visit to an underground base and Leah Haley's treatment at the hands of government authorities.

On the other hand, the majority of abduction cases do not fit into that scenario and, however strange they may appear, the behavior and appearance of the entities involved in the procedures are too decidedly non-human for that to be an overall explanation.

AREA 51

In the deserts of Nevada there are massive buildings, bunkers, and a runway. None of these things appear on any official map and all unauthorized visitors are warned that "deadly force" may be used against them. People who have disregarded these warnings have been fined and imprisoned, though, as yet, no one appears actually to have been killed for trespassing there.

The area in question is the Nellis Air Base and Nuclear Test Site. One particularly secret area is in the region of Groom Lake. Unofficially, the base is known as Area 51 or Dreamland. "Dreamland" is the radio call sign for the Nellis Air Traffic Control staff. The very existence of Area 51 was denied by the US Air Force until 1994.

The secret base was founded in 1954 as a site for Lockheed Aircraft to develop new advanced spy planes for the CIA. Perhaps the most famous aircraft flown there over the years is the Stealth bomber. Other projects included RPVs (remotely piloted vehicles), cruise missiles, and hypersonic spy planes.[19]

Ever since the 1950s, UFO sightings have been reported in the area. Mike Hunt, working on radio maintenance at the time, claimed to have seen a saucer-shaped craft in Area 51. He described it as looking like "a small private aircraft," but with "no wings or tail."[20] Hunt also claimed to have heard about take-offs and landings of the craft, though he was never allowed to witness these events. He refers to a top secret program known as Project Red Light, which was in operation during his time at the base and that was in some way connected with flying disks.

An unidentified medical expert also referred independently to Project Red Light. He claimed that it moved into the base in the early 1950s and was connected with "flying disks." He additionally referred to UFO research and test flights as having been carried out at the base.[21]

Captain Nunnallee of the US Air Force claimed that a security guard told him that "on one occasion he saw the [hangar] door open during the night and saw an unusual object come out and take off straight up."[22] This object was described as being "disk-shaped with dull tone lights."[23]

Journalist Robert Dorr, a former USAF veteran, also claimed that a crashed saucer was recovered on the East Coast of America and transferred to Area 51. Dorr's source for this story was supposedly a member of an Air Technical Intelligence Team. He also told Dorr that the craft was collected and transferred to the Nellis Air base in April 1953. Dorr's informant told him that there was considerable debate when it arrived at the base over whether or not the spaceship could actually be flown.[24]

Colonel Robert Gammon, a US Army historian, described a joint Army and Air Force project to develop a flying saucer, which he claims was initiated around 1955. There is no doubt that both services were extremely interested in the Avro Canada VZ-9, a flying disk that first flew in 1959, but was canceled a few years later. It is highly significant that a CIA memorandum from 1955 includes the following extremely interesting statement that John Frost, who designed the VZ-9, "obtained his original idea for the flying machine from a group of Germans just after World War II."[25]

In spite of these various claims for early involvement with the Area 51 and Groom Lake projects, it was not until 1989 that the public became aware of the existence of the area in question. This came about as the result of a series of sensational claims by Bob Lazar. Lazar began by declaring that he had actually worked on UFOs in Area 51 and that they used what he called "a gravity propulsion system" powered by "an antimatter reactor."[26]

At first, Lazar thought he was working on a secret military project, but once he had actually entered one of the disks, he became convinced that their origin was extraterrestrial. He claimed that subsequent briefing projects that he was ordered to read included autopsies of entities resembling "Grays," who apparently originated from the Zeta Reticuli star system. Lazar also declared that "aliens had killed guards and scientists at the base in 1979."[27]

The Groom Lake region is particularly secretive about its various projects, so much so that a journal hardly known for its friendliness towards extraterrestrialists described numerous cases of both top secret, but conventional, aircraft and flights of vehicles using "unconventional propulsion systems."[28]

Aviation writer Jim Goodall claims: "There are at least eight Black Programs flying out of Area 51." He believes these include both secret military projects and alien craft.[29]

We may never know the truth about Area 51 and the strange activities that take place inside the mysterious base in Nevada, but that a range of mysterious and secret projects are being carried out in the region is certain.[30]

AREAS 19 AND 20

These much less well known sites are part of the same complex in Nevada as Area 51. They were used as nuclear test sites for a number of years, although it is not clear what purpose they serve currently. The land on which they stand appears uninhabited and desolate, its emptiness strangely pierced by an electric power cable that appears to go nowhere and be connected to nothing at all. Perhaps the facilities at this part of Dreamland are located entirely under the ground, rather than on the surface, as is the case with most of Area 51.[31]

MEN IN BLACK

One of the most intriguing aspects of Ufology is the frequent association of sightings of UFOs, reports of abductions, and even monsters and demons with a curious group of people known as "the Men in Black," often shortened to MIB. To date, there have been few reports of Women in Black, although the hugely entertaining film starring Tommy Lee Jones and Will Smith called *Men in Black* ended with the recruitment of a "woman in black" to the team. That, however, is Hollywood, and reports of female MIBs are rare indeed.

EARLY MIB EXPERIENCES

The MIB have been described as "the most secret organization in the world," the anti-alien CIA" and "Brothers of the Shadow."[32] The first example of the phenomenon occurred in 1947, the same year that Kenneth Arnold launched the modern wave of UFO sightings. Two men from the US Coast Guard, Harold A. Dahl and Frederick I. Crisman, saw a UFO above the waters of Puget Sound, Washington. Not long after their sighting, Dahl reported being visited by a man dressed entirely in black who warned him not to talk about his experience.

The next example of the appearance of the MIB did not take place until five years later. On 25 July 1952, an Italian fisherman, Carlo Rossi, was angling in the River Serchio near San Pietro a Vico, when he saw a circular object seeming to hover above the river. He concealed himself and watched the UFO passing overhead and, as soon as it had vanished, left the scene. Even though he did not speak about his sighting to anyone, when he returned to the river on 15 September to fish, he suddenly found a man dressed in a dark blue suit by the river, evidently waiting for his arrival.

Rossi said that the MIB spoke Italian, but with such a strong accent that he thought he was probably Scandinavian. He also remarked on his "extremely angular features." The man asked Rossi if he had seen any strange objects in the sky recently, but the fisherman, feeling intimidated by the man's somewhat aggressive attitude, pretended that he had seen nothing. He then offered Rossi a cigarette, which the fisherman claimed had a gold mark upon it. Rossi began smoking it and immediately felt extremely sick, whereupon the stranger snatched it from him, tore it up, and threw it away. Then he left the baffled fisherman standing by the bank of the river.[33]

ALBERT BENDER, FIRST FAMOUS MIB VICTIM

The Albert Bender case in 1953, although not the first MIB experience, was the event that first brought the MIB phenomenon into public awareness. Bender had been researching UFOs for some time and was the head of an organization known as the International Flying Saucer Bureau. He had also written to a friend, telling him that he had now discovered the true explanation for flying saucers. His letter included the details of what he felt to be the correct solution.[34]

Soon, Bender began to receive telepathic instructions to stop studying and releasing information on UFOs. He also began to suffer from headaches and found himself tormented by strange smells and "bluish flashes."[35]

One evening, as he was sitting in a cinema, a man suddenly appeared out of nowhere in the seat next to Bender's. His face was dark and his eyes, which glowed, were described by Bender as being "diabolical."[36] Soon after this eerie encounter, he began to suffer from poltergeist phenomena.

Bender's reaction was to try to establish telepathic contact with the entity. After two unsuccessful attempts, he finally made contact. His account is as follows:

I FELT A TERRIBLE COLD CHILL HIT MY WHOLE BODY. THEN MY HEAD BEGAN TO ACHE AS IF SEVERAL HEADACHES HAD SAVED UP THEIR ANGUISH AND HEAPED IT UPON ME AT ONE TIME. A STRANGE ODOR REACHED MY NOSTRILS—LIKE THAT OF BURNING SULPHUR OR BADLY DECOMPOSED EGGS. THEN I PARTLY LOST CONSCIOUSNESS, AS THE ROOM AROUND ME BEGAN TO FADE AWAY."[37]

He then had an out-of-body experience in which he heard a voice that he said "permeated me, but in some way did not seem to be an audible sound. The voice seemed to come from the room in front of me, which remained pitch dark."[38]

Before long, this psychic experience was followed by a direct visitation from three "men in black." Bender had been away on holiday for two weeks and, on his return, he noticed a number of strange events. The most marked were the smell of sulphur and the fact that his radio was switched on and burning hot to the touch. After experiencing blue lights, dizziness, and an icy coldness in his body, he dimly saw his tormentors appear.

THE ROOM SEEMED TO GROW DARK, YET I COULD STILL SEE. I NOTED THREE SHADOWY FIGURES IN THE ROOM. THEY FLOATED ABOUT A FOOT OFF THE FLOOR. THE THREE FIGURES BECAME CLEARER. ALL OF THEM WERE DRESSED IN BLACK CLOTHES. THEY LOOKED LIKE CLERGYMEN, BUT WORE HATS SIMILAR TO HOMBURG STYLE. THE FACES WERE NOT CLEARLY DISCERNIBLE, FOR THE HATS PARTLY HIT AND SHADED THEM. THE EYES OF ALL THREE FIGURES SUDDENLY LIT UP LIKE FLASHLIGHT BULBS, AND ALL THREE WERE FOCUSED UPON ME. THEY SEEMED TO BURN INTO MY VERY SOUL AS THE PAINS ABOVE MY EYES BECAME ALMOST UNBEARABLE. IT WAS THEN THAT I SENSED THAT THEY WERE CONVEYING A MESSAGE TO ME BY TELEPATHY.[39]

The three men in black told Bender that nobody would believe his story, but gave him a shining disk, which he could use if he wished to contact them. After a while, they took him to an underground base in Antarctica where he found three humanoids engaged in the process of extracting seawater for some kind of chemical process, which they told him had a purpose on their own planet. He also met some beautiful alien women and a supposedly wise being that nevertheless made a number of elementary blunders about astronomy.[40]

Bender was then warned off any further research into UFOs. He followed this advice and found that his curious physical symptoms stopped as soon as he did so. A few years later, he eventually published a guarded and heavily expurgated account of his experiences. In spite of the obvious omissions and rewriting, it still makes compelling reading. One of the most remarkable aspects of the case is that the three visitors showed him a copy of the letter that Bender had sent to his friend.[41]

MIBS AFTER BENDER'S CASE

Bender's visit from the three MIBs took place in September 1953. A few months later, two other Ufologists, Harold H. Fulton, head of the Civilian Saucer Investigation of New Zealand, and Edgar R. Jarrold, head of the Australian Flying Saucer Bureau, both received visits from strangers who threatened them and who decided, as a result of this intimidation, to close down their organizations.[42]

In February 1955, John Stuart in New Zealand saw a UFO and then, when some kind of metal fell from the object, picked it up and took it home. The following evening, he was visited by a man dressed in black who told Stuart that he had no right to the fragment of metal that he had found and that he should give it to him instead. He then gave Stuart a considerable amount of information about UFOs and he felt thoroughly intimidated and even terrified after the man's visit. Stuart commented: "I have a feeling that someday there will come a slow knocking at my own door."[43]

On 18 May 1968, a particularly surreal MIB encounter took place following a UFO sighting in Elizabeth, New Jersey. George Smyth, one of the people who had seen the UFO, found himself receiving telephone calls that warned him to avoid speaking to anyone about the UFO phenomenon or attending conferences on the subject. Strangely, Smyth described the three visitors as resembling closely the men he had been specifically warned not to contact – Gray Barker, John Keel, and James Moseley. Even more bizarre, all three men were miles away from Smyth's home at the time of the MIB visitations, as attested to by a number of independent witnesses.[44]

By the 1960s, the MIB phenomenon had become such a frequent accompaniment of UFO sightings that researcher John Keel investigated it in some detail. He came across numerous cases of abusive behavior, attempted intimidation, kidnapping, and even the apparent use of brainwashing techniques to leave people disorientated, physically ill, dazed, mentally ill, or suffering from memory loss. Keel made inquiries and found that the FBI, NSA, CIA, the military, and other government agencies all denied either knowledge of or involvement in MIB activities.[45]

WHO ARE THE MEN IN BLACK?

So, who exactly are the Men in Black? The first and most obvious theory, in spite of the official denials, is that the MIB actually are government representatives, particularly of intelligence agencies. This certainly seems a possible explanation in terms of the experiences of some contactees and quite a few abductees. Christa Tilton, Leah Haley, and Mrs. Verona are three obvious "fits" with this explanation.[46]

Another theory is that the MIB represent a hidden civilization in an inaccessible region of Earth, such as Antarctica, the Gobi Desert, the Himalayas, or the Amazon.[47]

Some are undoubtedly hoaxes or practical jokes. Others are equally clear cases of hallucination or mental disturbance. However, the MIB phenomenon is sufficiently common and widespread for these explanations to cover only a small minority of cases.

The other possible tries are that the MIB really are aliens, visitors from other dimensions, ghosts, or psychic projections. All of the theories face considerable problems, but some of the cases seem to fit each one of them.

The biggest difficulty with accepting the notion that MIB experiences representing genuine extraterrestrial visitors is the frequent ignorance that they demonstrate about elementary facts of astronomy. That an advanced civilization, traveling the stars and sending spaceships to Earth from other systems, could possibly make such simple mistakes defies belief.

The interdimensional theory relies on the possibility that travel between different "dimensions" of the universe is a practical reality. Although it is supported by many of the most illustrious names in quantum physics, it remains a hypothesis, rather than an established scientific fact.[48]

The ghost theory is supported by the curiously old-fashioned clothes, cars, behavior, and even ways of speaking displayed by the MIBs. On the other hand, it is hard to see why so many ghosts would feel the need to intimidate and threaten UFO witnesses or researchers.[49]

The psychic projection theory is supported by the fact that often there are multiple witnesses to an event, but only one experiences an MIB phenomenon, even though they are in the presence of others.[50] The best argument in favor of the psychic projection theory is put by Randles, although (as her two articles in *Fortean Times* show) she also believes that many MIB encounters are the work of genuine government agents.

Probably no single theory of the reports gives the complete explanation. That some MIBs are genuine extraterrestrials seems highly probable, just as the idea that some really are government agents. The ghost, interdimensional, and psychic theories are less likely, but do seem to fit a minority of cases.

We may never know the truth about this strange phenomenon, but it clearly has a strong and direct link with UFOs, and only with UFOs. All we can do is wait and hope that the mystery will soon be solved.

ENDNOTES: CHAPTER NINE

[1] Speech by Gorbachev at the Kremlin, 18 February 1987.

[2] Timothy Good, *Alien Liaison: The Ultimate Secret*, Arrow, 1992.

[3] Frank E. Stranges, *Nazi UFO Secrets and Bases*, IEC, 1982.

[4] Peter Brookesmith, *The Age of the UFO*, Orbis, 1984.

[5] Daniel Fry, *The White Sands Incident*, Best Books, 1966.

[6] Gerald A. Haines, "CIA's Role in the Study of UFOs, 1947-1990," Studies in Intelligence, Spring 1996.

[7] Most notably, Good, who has shifted from his original belief in the genuineness of the documents to his current position that, although the documents themselves are fakes, possibly deliberate disinformation put out by the CIA, the Maj-12 project, and committee did exist and the documents represent at least some sort of account of their workings. For the ways in which his views have changed, compare Good's *Above Top Secret*, Sidgwick and Jackson, 1987, where he subscribes to the genuineness of the documents, to *Alien Liaison*, 1992, where he suggests that the documents were forged, but that the contents are essentially a truthful account of secret UFO projects and a cover-up authorised by Truman.

[8] The most plausible case for the genuineness of the Maj-12 program and the supporting documents is found in: Stanton Friedman, *Top Secret/MAJIC*, Marlowe, 1997.

[9] Gene Duplantier, *The Night Mutilators*, SS and S Publications, 1979.

[10] Linda Moulton Howe, *An Alien Harvest*, Linda Moulton Howe Productions, 1989.

[11] Ibid.

[12] Duplantier, op. cit.

[13] New Mexico State Police Report, 15 December 1976.

[14] Letter from Bennewitz to Good, in Good's *Alien Liaison.*

[15] *Arizona Wildcat*, University of Arizona, 14 September 1982.

[16] Ibid.

[17] Letter from General O. O. Benson, Commandant of SAM, to the Surgeon General, March 1951.

[18] Communication between McArthur and the Committee for the Far East.

[19] *The X-Factor*, No 1, 1997.

[20] Letter from Mike Hunt to UFO researcher David Dobbs, 20 April 1980.

[21] William S. Steinamn and Wendelle C. Stevens, *UFO Crash at Aztec: A Well-Kept Secret*, UFO Photo Archives, 1986.

[22] Nunnallee's report to UFO researcher Tom Adams.

[23] Ibid.

[24] *Ideal's Home Magazine*, No 3, 1978.

[25] Ibid.

[26] Interview with Lazar, KLAS-TV, Channel 8, Las Vegas, March 1989.

[27] Ibid.

[28] *Aviation Week* and *Space Technology*, October 1990.

[29] *Gung-Ho*, February 1988.

[30] Mark Piesing, "The (very) secret history of Area 51," *The Independent*, 5 July 2011.

[31] David Darlington, *Area 51: The Dreamland Chronicles*, Henry Hall, 1998.

[32] *Secret Wisdom*, No 1, July 1997.

[33] Jenny Randles, *MIB: Investigating the Men in Black Phenomenon*, Piatkus, 1997.

[34] Details of this case were first made public in 1956. The principal accounts of it are: a) Gray Barker, *They Knew Too Much About Flying Saucers*, Werner Laurie, 1956; b) Albert Bender, *Flying Saucers and the Three Men*, Saucerian Books, 1962.

[35] Bender, op. cit.

[36] Ibid.

[37] Ibid.

[38] Ibid.

[39] Ibid.

[40] Ibid.

[41] Ibid.

[42] R. W. Boeche, "UFOs: Caught in a Web of Deception," Gulf Breeze UFO Conference, 12 February 1994.

[43] Ibid.

[44] Timothy Green-Beckley, *Mystery of the Men in Black: The UFO Silencers,* Inner Light, 1990.

[45] John A. Keel, *Our Haunted Planet*, Galde Press, 1999 (first published 1971).

[46] Jenny Randles, "Who Were the Men in Black?" *Fortean Times*, June 2009; and "Government Heavies or Alien Agents?" *Fortean Times*, July 2009.

[47] Examples of this type of theory are found in the following books: a) Alec McLellan, *The Lost World of Agharti*, Souvenir Press, 1982; b) Andrew Tomas, *Shamballah: Oasis of Light*, Sphere, 1977; c) Jim Marrs, *Alien Agenda: Investigating the Alien Presence Among Us*, Harper Torch, 1998. Donald Worsley, alien abduction researcher, is the leading champion of the Amazon Rainforest as a UFO/MIB base of operations.

[48] Jacques Vallee, *Messengers of Deception: UFO Contacts and Cults*, Daily Grail, 2008 (first published 1975).

[49] Keel, *Our Haunted Planet.*

[50] The best argument in favor of the psychic projection theory is put by Randles, MIB, although (as her two articles in Fortean Times show) she also believes that many MIB encounters are the work of genuine government agents.

CHAPTER TEN

THE CHANGING EARTH

REVELATIONS

On 4 January 2011, the Chinese television station Xinhua made the sensational claim that President Obama was preparing to tell the world that extraterrestrial civilizations existed and some of them were living on Earth.[1] This extraordinary statement hardly attracted the notice of the world's media—why not? Surely such a news item would be one of the most significant events in human history?

Around the same period, the US State Department sent a telegram to their embassy in Ukraine instructing its employees that: "It is critical all embassy staff understand that they are not to discuss under any circumstance concerns DOD [US Department of Defense] has with UFOs entering orbit; once again, the seriousness of this matter cannot be overstated."[2]

The announcement, first expected in January, was then delayed until 4 July 2011. Then a further delay occurred, 11 September 2011 being given as the expected date for Obama to make his revelation to the world.[3] Since that date also passed without any announcement by the President, no further predictions have yet been made.

LIVING IN THE END TIMES

NATURAL DISASTERS

In recent years, the Earth has been through natural disasters on a huge scale and more frequently than ever before. Earthquakes, volcanic eruptions, tsunamis, flooding, coastal erosion, hurricanes, and tornadoes have swept across the world in a destructive frenzy. The year 2010 was the worst year for natural disasters in recorded history and the new phenomenon of "superstorms" has continued and is increasing.

There have been scientists who have issued dire warnings that the magnetic poles of the Earth are moving more rapidly. A geologist claims that the continent of Africa is literally splitting apart, saying: "The earth is in upheaval in northeastern Africa, and the region is changing quickly. The desert floor is quaking and splitting open, volcanoes are boiling over, and seawaters are encroaching upon the land. Africa, researchers are certain, is splitting apart at a rate rarely seen in geology."[4]

In the Yellowstone National Park area of the United States, land is rapidly being lifted up by tectonic pressure from the earth below. A leading American scientist warned that earthquakes will become more common and their destructive power even greater, leading to the destruction of entire cities.[5]

TWO SUNS IN THE SKY

An Australian physicist predicted that, by 2012, there would be a second sun in the sky above our planet. He explained that Betelgeuse was losing mass and collapsing and would turn into a supernova in the very near future. When that event occurred, for a little while, we would see two suns in the sky and there would be no night during that period.[6]

Although the physicist himself denied this, many people believed that this supernova was yet another sign of the end of the world.

MASS EXTINCTION

Throughout human history, as the geological record testifies eloquently, our planet has been assaulted by natural disasters that have all but wiped out life on Earth. There have been a number of "mass extinction" events, most famously the sudden disappearance of the dinosaurs, which were literally caught unawares by some as yet not fully understood or explained cosmic catastrophe.[7]

Myths and legends speak of the earlier times within human memory when disaster overtook our planet. Noah's Flood is a tradition found among every people of the globe and there is abundant evidence that it represents some real historic event in the infancy of the human race.

We know that meteors and comets do occasionally hit the Earth and have caused major devastation in the distant past. It is anything but implausible to assume that the same type of event could occur in the future. Obviously, the equipment in our observatories and the technical knowledge of our astronomers is far greater than thousands of years ago, but we are still exposed to possible near misses from celestial bodies and it is always possible that some of these objects might impact upon the earth with catastrophic consequences.

How realistic is the prospect that the human race might be about to face yet another mass extinction event? So many things can go wrong and we have so little control over nature that the confident predictions by scientists that we have nothing to fear might be complacent.

DAMAGE TO THE RINGS OF JUPITER AND SATURN

During the 1980s, a series of comet strikes hit Jupiter and Saturn and left ripples in the rings of both planets. The rings have now become tilted and twisted into a "spiral pattern of ripples within the rings." The Saturn impacts occurred in 1983 and the Jupiter ones in 1994.[8]

It may be that these cosmic impacts and the changes to the rings of the two planets are a sign of a future problem and represent something we should worry about. They might be forces that will play a part in fundamental alterations to Earth and perhaps signs of a forthcoming destruction of our own planet. The human race might be standing on the brink of doom and destruction or the Star Travelers may be about to come to our rescue. Only time will tell which of those theories is the correct one.

PLANETARY IMPLOSION

The experiments at the Large Hadron Collider in Switzerland are designed to replicate the "Big Bang" believed to have started the universe, but have alarmed many people. Their creation of a highly dangerous form of material known as quark-gluon plasma was achieved by speeding up lead particles at the speed of light. Even the Hadron scientists admit the process has the potential to destroy Earth. The amount of the particle formed is huge, far greater than the heart of the Sun, and almost at the level of mass of a black hole. It is one hundred thousand times hotter than the Sun and the densest known object in the cosmos other than, of course, a black hole.[9]

If one of the thousands of particles that Hadron has created sank to the center of the Earth, it would begin pulling in mass towards it, leading eventually to the sucking inside itself of the whole planet and its implosion. As the most scientifically impressive advocate of this theory puts it, the LHC experiments could create black holes that might fall into the center of the planet and "eat the Earth from the inside out in a few years time."[10] A fascinating possibility and one of the more plausible of the various doomsday scenarios, but generally thought to be extremely unlikely.

THE MILKY WAY EQUILATERAL PLANE ALIGNMENT—MAP OF DISASTER

Another disaster scenario was the idea that the Earth, some time round about 2012, would enter the part of the Milky Way known as the "equilateral plane." Scientists more or less agreed that it would happen, but not on what its effects on the planet would be.

On the winter solstice in 2012, the Sun was aligned with the very center of the Milky Way for the first time in some 26,000 years. This event was predicted to bring about widespread disruption owing to the interference with the normal transmission of energy from the rest of the Milky Way to Earth.[11] An astronomer claimed that there was nothing exceptional about the alignment and that it happens twice a year on a regular basis already.[12]

It was during the 1990s that a number of people noticed that a comparatively rare astronomical alignment would occur. It involved the Earth's winter solstice and the equatorial plane of the Milky Way. Before long, some people began associating this alignment with the forthcoming end of the "long cycle" of the Mayan Calendar. A precise date of 21 December 2012 was arrived at and the coincidence of this particular astronomical alignment with the end of the Mayan Calendar led to an outpouring of theories that the two events were both connected and represented the imminent end of life on Earth, at least as we know it.

The alignment of the Earth and Sun within the Milky Way was something that many people feared. The Sun and the solar system are some considerable way from the equatorial plane of the Milky Way. As the Earth rotates around the Sun periodically, it traverses the equator of the galaxy at an angle of approximately 60 degrees. Twice a year the Sun, the Earth, and the galactic equator are aligned together. This is normal, but the special feature of the 2012 alignment was that it occurred when the Earth was experiencing its winter solstice period and that particular combination of alignments only occurs every 25,800 years, not twice a year as with the ordinary equatorial traverse.

This rare alignment could have foreshadowed a major change in the destiny of our planet, but not necessarily in a negative way. Certainly, so far its effects on the Earth have been negligible. We will consider this question further when we give a more detailed assessment of the Mayan Calendar hypothesis. The evidence from history is that unusual astronomical phenomena always appear to be associated with life-changing events in the story of our planet, so perhaps it does represent just such a defining moment in Earth's existence.

SOLAR FLARES – AN END TO LIFE ON EARTH

Another "end time" possibility is the well-known phenomenon of solar flares. These are drastic, rapid, and intense displays of exceptional brightness. Within the atmosphere of the Sun a build-up of magnetic energy occurs, which, when released, results in a solar flare. An intense and unusually high amount of radiation is emitted throughout the electromagnetic spectrum when this happens.

Although the phenomenon of solar flares is not in itself unusual, NASA confirmed that the year 2012 saw a particularly intense and prolific period of solar flare activity. In itself that would not perhaps be a major cause for concern, but taken in conjunction with the other unusual astronomical phenomena accompanying that time, perhaps it was yet another sign of imminent transformation or annihilation.

As usual, the scientists disagreed. They conceded that 2012 saw what is known as Solar Maximum Cycle 24 and that solar activity and, in particular, solar flares increased dramatically, producing what one scientist has described as "a huge firework display."[13]

Every decade the Sun's magnetic field undergoes a change in its polarity. It is highly probable that ancient people knew of this solar cycle and that they used it to forecast events and organize their lives around it. Earth as a whole is bathed in constant radioactivity and the Sun's rays have been striking our planet for millions of years. During the period of a solar maximum, the Sun emits energy equivalent to 100 billion atomic bombs. This is what causes solar flares, and the fact that the latest solar cycle is predicted to be the most intense and powerful for many years is a cause for alarm to many people.

X-ray solar flares are a particular worry as they travel at the speed of light and can reach Earth in only eight minutes. As soon as they hit the planet's atmosphere they are absorbed into the ionosphere, itself a highly charged atomic environment. They disrupt communications, except at very low frequencies, and can cause serious problems when they occur.

Another possible problem with solar flares is known as "coronal mass ejections." Sometimes these are produced when a flare takes place. These ejections are much slower than X-rays, but can cause more problems if they hit Earth. They travel rapidly enough to reach our planet within a matter of hours.

If a coronal mass ejection (CME) hits Earth, generally, it will be repelled by the planet's own magnetosphere. That would force it to bypass the Earth and no serious problems would be caused. If the magnetic polarities were at opposite poles, magnetic reconnection might occur and this would connect our own magnetic field with that of the Sun. When that happens, we experience the aurora.

High energy particles would also be emitted into the magnetosphere of Earth. The magnetic field lines of the Sun would fold around our planet. The Van Allen radiation belt would also become "super-charged," which could lead to radiation sickness, damage to cells and long-term higher risks of cancer. However, these effects would only be experienced by astronauts rather than impacting directly upon our own planet. There would be an adverse effect on power lines and electrical equipment, but only enough to cause disruption and certainly not enough to threaten the existence of life on Earth. So, solar flares are not likely to be a serious problem and actually another doomsday scenario seems more probable: the return of the Ice Age.

A NEW ICE AGE

Far from solar flares being likely to trigger a superheating of the planet, the start of the latest solar cycle has surprised physicists by the low level of activity on the Sun. If anything, the relative lack of sunspots has led many scientists to believe that we might be about to enter a new Ice Age on Earth.

For many years, the hypothesis of global warming has been in fashion. Since the beginning of the new millennium, in particular, that view has been challenged with increasing frequency. The data from NASA in particular is showing the opposite, that we are becoming colder and that the Sun's activity is less powerful and generating a smaller amount of heat than previously.[14]

There is a lot of evidence in favor of the theory of "global cooling." Sunspot activity for instance is predicted to disappear completely after 2022. This is expected to produce a rapid and sharp decline in temperature, and, the last time that happened, Earth entered its most recent "Little Ice Age" between 1645 and 1715. Glaciers, though not uniformly, are growing over the face of the Earth, winters are becoming colder and arriving earlier, and the growing strain on energy resources is making it more difficult to maintain supply on a regular basis. Of all the doomsday scenarios, the prospect of a new Ice Age seems the most likely.

COSMIC COLLISIONS

There have been many times in the past when Earth has been hit by other celestial bodies. The majority of them have been relatively small meteorites, but some, such as the strange object that crashed down on Tunguska in Siberia at the beginning of the twentieth century, were far more powerful. There is now a consensus among scientists that an asteroid or a body of similar type and size was responsible for the extinction of the dinosaurs and many theories have also attributed the death of other civilizations to the impact of various cosmic bodies impacting upon the Earth.

According to astronomers, no planetary body of any appreciable size is likely to come into collision with the Earth in the foreseeable future, nor even to approach closely enough for its presence to be dangerous. The Planet X/Nibiru advocates disagree and, at the moment, all we can do is wait on events. Even the scientists grant a one-in-a-thousand chance of such a giant celestial body impacting upon our planet, which is comparatively low odds against its occurrence. The testimony of history, geology, myth, and legend strongly supports the claim that such events have taken place in the past and may well do so again.

PLANETARY INFERNO COMBUSTION

This is a kind of nuclear reaction with the power to set the whole Earth on fire and wipe out every trace of life upon it within fifty seconds of its initiation. Many planets are already huge gas giants with inflammable atmospheres that make the prospect of any meaningful form of life inconceivable. However, it is not easily apparent that this is either likely to happen to Earth or that we would not receive clear signals of its imminent occurrence.

DEATH OF THE EARTH'S CORE

A scientist has suggested that a black hole may have breached the core of the Earth. He suggests that it is reversing the magnetic polarity of our planet, causing its core to spin and will eventually swallow up the bulk of the planet.[15]

If, as the scientist thinks may be possible, the black hole is not stationary, that raises a very alarming prospect. If it were to move, it would be pulled back towards the center and as it gathered speed would go straight through the center to the other side of the Earth. Once enough matter had been accumulated, the black hole would swallow up the Earth in a matter of hours.

MAGMA CRUST

Another doomsday scenario is the idea that the Earth's axis will spin out of control as a result of the magma on which its crust sits becoming more active. The Earth's increasingly erratic rotation will lead to the crust of the planet shifting violently, and volcanoes, earthquakes, and tsunamis will destroy it.

Because the magma is unstable, these processes will increase and accelerate. In the end, the effects will become so marked and cataclysmic that civilization upon Earth will be wiped out and human life on the planet may be destroyed completely.[16]

WILL EARTH BECOME A GAS GIANT?

According to one theory, the Earth's core is a natural nuclear reactor that is slowly heating up the planet and will eventually turn it into another gas giant like Jupiter. Tremendous amounts of energy would be released and the Earth would begin to counteract gravity, also heating up the atmosphere. Even if this scenario is possible—which would require a number of factors to be operating simultaneously—it is not generally considered likely.[17]

MICROBES FROM OUTER SPACE

One of the by-products of space exploration has been the arrival on Earth of deadly types of bacteria to which humans have little or no resistance. In zero-gravity, environments, such as deep space microbes, become more virulent and dangerous than they are in the atmosphere of our own planet. Since space exploration began in the 1960s, more and more bacteria have been brought back to Earth and may be at least partly responsible for the growing number of strains of microbial infection that are resistant to antibiotics.[18] Experiments on mice showed that mortality rates were three times as high as resulted from normal terrestrial bacteria. One of the less welcome side-effects of the space program might be deadly bacterial infections.

ALIEN INVASION

Many people believe that extraterrestrials have been steadily building up their strength and are planning an invasion of Earth in the very near future. Some see them as wise and benevolent beings who will come to our planet to save us from the consequences of our own actions. Others regard them as being evil and bent upon our subjugation.

THE MAYAN CALENDAR

The Mayan calendar was devised thousands of years ago and the current "long cycle" was due to end on 21 December 2012. That set alarm bells ringing among all kinds of people and it was increasingly claimed that the end of the calendar cycle might coincide with some kind of intervention on Earth by aliens as well as the end of our present life on the planet.

The Mayans used a variety of calendars which were primarily concerned with varying agricultural cycles. However, most of them were "short." One lasted for 260 days and another for 365 and both were combined to form a "Calendar Round" of about 52 years. Each of the Calendar Rounds also contained other cycles, one of thirteen days and another of twenty. They additionally had a calendar based upon the position of the planet Venus in the sky at night, however, these particular calendars were only useful up to fifty-two years previously. To describe or record events in the more distant past they devised a new system known as the "Long Count," covering a period of 5,126 years. Because of the complicated decimal system they used, many people believed that the latest Long Count would end on 21 December 2012. Others disputed this and suggested dates ranging from as far ahead as 2020 for the projected end of the Long Count cycle of the Mayan Calendar. Mayan myths are contradictory on the subject, but most seem to predict some kind of religious transformation rather than an apocalyptic end to the world. It is not even certain that the Mayans did regard the end of this particular cycle as representing anything of particular significance.

As one expert on the subject wrote:

"WHEN A CALENDAR COMES TO THE END OF A CYCLE, IT JUST ROLLS OVER INTO THE NEXT CYCLE. IN OUR WESTERN SOCIETY, EVERY YEAR 31 DECEMBER IS FOLLOWED, NOT BY THE END OF THE WORLD, BUT BY 1 JANUARY. SO 13.0.0.0.0 IN THE MAYAN CALENDAR WILL BE FOLLOWED BY 0.0.0.0.1 – OR GOOD-OL' 22 DECEMBER 2012, WITH ONLY A FEW SHOPPING DAYS LEFT TO CHRISTMAS."[19]

One of the more bizarre aspects of the Mayan Calendar 2012 theorists was the claim by some of them that a small French village would survive the coming universal cataclysm. It was besieged by thousands of Ufologists as a result of this idea. The village of Bugarach has a permanent population of 189 people, but they believed that it, along with perhaps some other sacred mountains, would be spared and those who dwelt there would be taken away in alien craft and would avoid the devastation awaiting Earth.[20]

When the predicted end of the world or mass alien arrival failed to materialize, the alternative view, that the calendar might represent a new spiritual awakening and the growing awareness that we are not alone in the universe, remained popular and was obviously not affected by the failure of the Doomsday scenario.

THE POSITIVE SLANT ON 2012

Most of the talk about the Mayan calendar and the impending arrival of 2012 focused on a negative outcome. The general trend was towards a doomsday scenario. There were plenty of good reasons to be concerned about the future but perhaps there were also good reasons to doubt that we were facing the imminent demise of the world, or at least the end of human life on Earth.

Many people, particularly among the contactees, believed the opposite. They thought that we were in line for a new phase of life on Earth and that extraterrestrials would be a huge force in the growing development of the planet. We were instead going to be entering a higher cycle of evolution and our lives would be transformed utterly.

THE NEXT STAGE OF EVOLUTION

We have seen the development from amoeba to fish, fish to amphibians, amphibians to reptiles, reptiles to mammals, mammals to humans. Now we will see the next phase of evolution, the progression of humanity. It will not be simply on the physical, but also the mental and spiritual developments that we will make our next astounding conquests of the universe. The discovery and use of the powers of the mind will be the next step forward. Our coming voyages into "inner space" will be every bit as exciting as our continuing exploration of outer space.

How are we to take this next step in our evolutionary journey and what part will the Star Travelers play in our future development? We look up at the sky and see our Sun, the planets, and stars glowing brightly in the vast canopy of space. We are on Earth and the Earth itself a planet within the solar system—our own humanity linked with that of the world in which we live as an inextricable part of a great invisible chain of being.

With every breath we draw in, we take a part of the universe inside ourselves. With every exhalation of breath, we return a part of ourselves to the universe. This process of a continual drawing in and expelling out, of transforming what to us is essential for life and for other life forms poisonous, is one of the great mysteries of existence. Everything seems to interact together harmoniously. We breathe in what we need and breathe out what the plants require. They breathe in what we do not need and breathe out what they do not need. A wonderful balance of life is preserved simply through the simple act of breathing. Every breath taken on this planet affects every other life form upon it, perhaps even every living creature throughout the universe.

As we must draw in breath to continue to live, so too we must constantly expel it also. This unchanging cycle of breathing is broken only by death. Each breath is unique, individual to ourselves alone, and yet also rises from and is diffused among the atmosphere of the entire planet.

In the same way, without the Sun to give us light and heat, we would perish in a cold so extreme that not even dwellers at the poles of the Earth would be able to imagine it. The Sun gives life to our world and the Sun is the center of the life force without which there could be no life within it. As the rays of the Sun strike the Earth, they give life to the planet, to ourselves, and all other life forms that dwell within and upon it. In the same way, each planet within the solar system receives the beams of sunlight directed upon it. The energy from the Sun is received by each planet, absorbed by it, and transformed, in turn, to energy appropriate for the conditions of the world itself. Then each planet in its turn also "breathes out" the solar rays which it has received, transmitting out that primal, but retuned, energy along with its own individual essence.

We know the power of the Sun to govern our lives. Without its light and heat nothing would grow on Earth, nor could there be any life to make the planet fertile. We also know the power of the Moon. Her inexplicable pull upon the tides, the seasons of the Earth, and the changes within a woman's body are all well known to us.

EVOLUTION

Electricity, magnetism, plasma, nuclear power, and gas are simply different forms of the energy transmitted to our planet by the Sun. Floods, tidal waves, hydro-electric power and earthquakes are equally different manifestations of the power exerted over our planet by the Moon. Every day, at the bidding of the mysterious power of the Moon, cities rise and fall several times.

When sunspots and magnetic disturbances resulting from the action of the Sun appear in space, all of our communication systems, compasses, and even our power stations are affected by its activity. The growth and decay of plants and trees is governed by the monthly procession of the Moon around the Earth. She makes the sap rise and fall within the trees, the leaves and flowers flourish and wither.

As the Sun and Moon affect and influence every aspect of life upon the Earth, so, too, the other planets within our solar system also have a part to play. In the Golden Age such knowledge was handed down as part of the Ancient Wisdom brought to us by the Star Travelers. One of their most important teachings was that the ring of planet, up to and including Saturn, governed involution and those beyond it evolution. It is surely no accident that Uranus, Neptune, and Pluto all rotate in the opposite direction from the "inner planets" of the solar system.

In the tradition of Ancient Wisdom, the Sun is spoken of as the bringer of life. Mercury is the bestower of fertility and Venus the bringer of love and the principle of creativity. Mars symbolizes desire, power, and the quest for progress. Jupiter represents organization, analysis, discovery, and the thirst for knowledge. Saturn's task is to allow the individual self to emerge from the group consciousness into its own self-awareness. Uranus represents the mental, Neptune the emotional, and Pluto the spiritual aspects of our development.

THE LAW OF CONTINUITY AND THE LAW OF CHANGE

Ancient Wisdom teaches us that, like ourselves, the planets are constantly evolving into higher, more perfected worlds. As the full potential of the solar system unfolds, so the rays or vibrations of the system transmit themselves more fully throughout the system and help the evolution of the universe on its way.

In the same way, Ancient Wisdom also teaches us that there are two great principles in nature that govern everything. The first is that of Force and the second of Form. Force without Form is an undifferentiated cosmic sea of loose energy, but Form cannot act without Force to provide the motive power for its design. Force and Form are inseparable, each the twin engines that drive the evolution of the universe and life within it.

Scientists have been trying for centuries to put together a complete, coherent philosophy that expresses all the knowledge at their disposal. This ambitious enterprise is known as Grand Unification Theory (GUT for short). Ancient Wisdom tells us that all laws, whether scientific, human, or spiritual, are ultimately reducible to two: the Law of Continuity and the Law of Change. Without motion there could be no change; without change there could be no life, only a waxwork museum of dummies. It is only through motion, the force of change, that life comes into being.

In the same way, the Law of Continuity governs the regularities we perceive. Gravity, relativity, all the principles of mechanics and structure depend upon it. Without change there could be no creation; without continuity there could be no form through which the creative principle could express itself.

The laws of continuity and change work together to create a continual process of transformation throughout every aspect of the universe. From the primeval "soup" to cellular life, from the cell to the inorganic world, from the inorganic to the world of plants, from plants to animals, animals to humans, we see the working out of this transformative process.

We are evolved beings, like everything else within the universe. It is the constant operation of the laws of change and continuity upon form through which alone force is able to manifest itself that birth, growth, development, decay and rebirth take place.[21]

We, as humans, know our birth, development, and decay. With our death the existence of ourselves as entities within a physical body comes to an end. Some claim that at death we are reincarnated into the bodies of others; still others claim that at death we pass into a new state of spiritual being in which we achieve immortality.

All these claims are difficult to prove or disprove. The law of transformation provides a possible solution to the paradox of death. All that lives within the universe is subject to death, yet death involves a gross violation of the Law of Continuity, known in physics as the Principle of the Conservation of Energy. Only the law of transformation can account for the paradox. Through its operation, though the form of manifestation changes, the fundamental energy of force through which the form manifests itself remains constant. There is neither less nor more than enough energy in the universe at any given time. What alters are the forms within it and their continual adaptations to the force that relentlessly drives the law of change.

INNER AND OUTER SPACE

We still have to learn the workings of inner space. The kingdom of the mind is one of the least understood aspects of our being. Ancient Wisdom speaks much about the power of thought. As we gaze out upon the world around us, the world of objects and people and animals, the world of our everyday consciousness that we take for granted, we do not pause to think that what we see is not the world as it is, but the world as it is mediated and interpreted by our mind.

Ancient Wisdom has known this fact throughout countless eons. The great philosophers have known it for two and a half thousand years. In the twentieth century, the scientists began to catch up at last. The development of quantum physics overthrew the established certainties in classical science, introducing a range of concepts entirely familiar to Ancient Wisdom, but previously unknown to scientists.

Perhaps the most striking are those of the observer-created universe, where the reality of what is observed is dependent on the individual observer; the notion of many worlds, also known as other dimensions or parallel universes; the relativity of time and space; the overthrow of the principles of causality and causation, since at the quantum level, events can precede their causes; and the notion of the universe as a hologram on a gigantic scale. All these theories challenge fundamentally the old certainties and make us recognize how much our conception of the world around us is dependent upon our own interaction with it. The idea of separation is old-fashioned; we and the universe are one.

THE LIVING UNIVERSE

Recent years have seen the realization that the Earth itself is a living organism. This awareness, known as the Gaia hypothesis, has at last provided a metaphysical basis acceptable to scientists for environmental concern. We live; the Earth lives; the planets live; the universe lives.[22] We are minds functioning inside a physical body; the Earth's mind functions within the structure of a physical planetary mass; the planets also have their own minds, and the universe itself is both the sum of the individual minds of its constituents and an organic system, a Universal Mind for want of a more suitable expression.

Just as the planets rotate in curves, as space-time is curved, so too the universe itself is curved. As the Earth is part of the solar system, the solar system part of the Galaxy, and the Galaxy part of the universe, so the universe itself is a system made up of other systems. We are part of a universe that is a whole system of interlocking energy fields, from the microcosm to the macrocosm.

As each energy field within the universe is co-extensive with the others so too other living beings are co-extensive with us. Matter is easily converted into energy; the process of the conversion of energy into matter has not yet been so easily accomplished. However, as we live, so we grow, drawing energy from the sun and soil. This achieves in a slow process the conversion of energy into matter. Nuclear physics has amply demonstrated the results of speedier conversions in the field of atomic energy.

The living universe is a gigantic organism with rich, complex laws and systems that appear to hold true throughout the cosmos. It is now almost doubtful whether there is any difference between organic and inorganic matter.

THEORIES

JINN

At this point, the Eastern doctrine of the elementals known as "jinn," "djinn," and "genies" becomes relevant. Jinn are said to be co-extensive with our world and to have appeared earlier than human beings. They are described as beings of light and fire rather than water and clay like humans. As they are created from light energy, the process of converting energy into matter would take far less time to accomplish in such beings. It could even involve conversion at a speed approaching the velocity of light. Being formed of light they would be capable of penetrating solid matter, appearing and vanishing instantaneously and also condensing light into a super-concentrated form.

All this is speculation and the notion of jinn has tended to be regarded in the West as no more than a charming fancy. In the East, it is different, and jinn are looked upon as real beings with a more ethereal dimension than our own material make-up. Sonia, the abductee whose disappearance was caught on CCTV, firmly believes that jinn were responsible for her ordeal. Nor is the notion of jinn significantly different from the ultraterrestrial theories put forward by Keel, Vallée, and other researchers in the field. It is not a hypothesis to be dismissed as lightly as is often done. Jinn are simply a particular form of a long tradition of elementals. The importance of such encounters is becoming more and more widely recognized by UFO researchers.

Nuclear physics demonstrates that such beings would be at least, in principle, possible. All atoms are stable; light particles are easily affected by solar rays and similar types of cosmic radiation; and some atomic elements are so inherently influenced by natural forces that they can form new elements by a process of radiation.

If we condense light into a beam, a high-energy form of light known as lasers is the result. The curious and frequent association of highly concentrated beams of light with UFO sightings could be the result of some kind of laser process. Lasers are also often involved with the mysterious cattle mutilations and killings. Electromagnetic anomalies and curious fogs also accompany many UFO sightings particularly those in which time distortion elements occur. It is perhaps at least worth considering whether or not they may be somehow connected with the activities of beings such as jinn.[23]

ELEMENTALS

What exactly are elementals? The most obvious theory is that they are creatures from other dimensions. Another plausible suggestion is that they are spirits. The most likely explanation, however, is that they are thought-forms.

Tibet is full of stories about an entity described as a tulpa, a form created by the mind of an adept and projected outwards until, unless its creator dissolves it, it takes on a life of its own and roams the world at will. There is considerable evidence that Tibetan monks were involved in the deliberate projection of a tulpa in the form of a flying saucer in 1926. There is also evidence that they launched more than one of these tulpas in the same form during the late 1920s.[24]

Matter has been described with some justification as crystallized thought. The creation of a tulpa is a deliberate attempt to operate in a material medium through the use of a thought form taking the aspect of a projected visualization. Even the CIA has successfully managed the creation of tulpas to the embarrassment of some of its bosses!

We have also seen how, to a considerable extent, each of us partly creates the universe we observe through the act of perception itself. Jinn or similar beings would then be another example of just such an act of creation on the part of the human mind. Once created, unless dissolved, such elementals operate within our own world and can cause havoc. Poltergeists are a classic example of the problems that such subjective entities may cause.

THE PSYCHIC HYPOTHESIS

It is clear, particularly on examination of some of the abduction cases, that a psychic component appears to be involved in many instances. There is little doubt that humans subjected to traumatic experiences often give a particular "gloss" to them and it is not at all easy to distinguish between a "subjective" and "objective" experience.

Vallée, and others who broadly share his views, claim that UFO bases may not necessarily be on other planets or stars, but here on Earth. Jinn or related elementals could be hiding themselves away by making use of their inherent powers of transformation. As such, they would be the true alchemists, the masters of the secret of the transmutation of matter that still eludes us, except at the level of sub-atomic physics.[25]

Vallée, Keel, and others of their school believe that some at least of the UFO phenomena can be explained by what they call an "interdimensional" or "ultraterrestrial" hypothesis. Jinn, elementals, and aliens are, in their view, creatures partly psychic in origin and partly inhabitants of another dimension. In some forms of the theory, the idea that these creatures have bases on Earth is put forward.

Even though the existence of bases upon Earth is very likely, it is not possible to use hypotheses such as jinn and tulpas, psychic disturbances, or other dimensions, to account for the staggering volume of sightings and contacts reported by hundreds of thousands of credible witnesses with no reason to lie about their experiences. Jinn, psychic phenomena, and interdimensional beings would certainly help to explain some of the more bizarre cases, but the "bread and butter" sightings require a more mechanical solution.

PHYSICAL EXPLANATIONS

There are many physical explanations other than the extraterrestrial hypothesis that attempt to solve the UFO mystery. We have seen already that there is much truth in the secret weapon theory, particularly in terms of the "ghost rockets" seen after the end of the Second World War. Even the CIA has admitted that many UFO sightings in the United States were actually caused by American secret projects.

Perfectly natural phenomena, both commonplace and unusual, undoubtedly also play a part in mistaken UFO sightings. Planets, particularly Mars, Venus, and Jupiter, have often been mistaken for UFOs when they are particularly bright in the night sky. Atmospheric anomalies, especially ball lightning, have been misidentified as flying saucers. It is also true that gaseous and particularly earthquake activity frequently produce effects that are described by witnesses as taking the form of a classical UFO shape.

All these things undoubtedly play a part and the psychic and elemental theories have made valuable contributions to the solution of the UFO problem. Even so, there already exists more than enough evidence that Earth really is being visited by extraterrestrials. We must always remember that there may be more than one answer to any particular problem.

WE HAVE CONTACT

Once again, we come back to the fact that from ancient times our planet has been visited by Star Travelers. In the olden days, they shared their wisdom with us and perhaps their more recent comings have also been to turn us away from the paths of folly and into a new way of looking at the universe and a new pattern of behavior.

What level of civilization are they likely to have achieved? It is obvious that they cannot be at a lower state of development than Earth or they would be unable to make their celestial visits to our planet. They must, therefore, be at a more advanced state than we are. If they turned out to be as far ahead of us as we are of animals, they would be entirely beyond our comprehension and it is unlikely that they would bother to contact us at all. The most likely answer, therefore, is that they are more advanced than humanity, but not to such a great extent that contact between our two civilizations would destroy or at least overwhelm us.

Professor Stephen Hawking's fears about the impact of extraterrestrial contact would, therefore, seem to be unfounded. The prospects of our interaction seem more likely to be positive and beneficial.

Nor is it clear that the influence would be entirely one way. There might be many areas and subjects on which they are ignorant and where the people of Earth could offer the aliens our wisdom, learning, and skills.

IMPLICATIONS

What are the implications for science, religion, and philosophy if it could be demonstrated definitively that life exists upon other planets? It is not too strong to suggest that it might be the most important discovery in human history. Both religious leaders and scientists would have to radically rethink some of the most basic principles of their philosophy of life.

There are many religious fundamentalists who believe that the existence of life on other planets conflicts directly with their own views. They firmly believe that the Earth is a specially favored planet within the universe and that God chose it alone to demonstrate his wisdom, goodness, and power.

Others, perhaps the majority of religious believers, think differently. Why should God not choose to spread His creative power throughout the universe? Human parents may have many children, so why should we assume that God would behave any differently?

Many scientists, particularly biologists, are also unhappy at the thought of alien life. We have already seen Monod's passionate defense of the privileged status of humans as the only form of life within the universe. Others have more flexible ideas on the subject.

If life is somehow an incredibly lucky accident, even more improbable than picking the winning lottery ticket, then the odds against it happening by chance more than once in the universe are infinitesimal. Conclusive proof of the existence of intelligent life upon other planets would certainly pose serious problems for the current neo-Darwinian orthodoxy, which remains committed firmly to the notion of a purposeless, random universe.

The existence of other forms of life, particularly if several worlds could be shown to possess intelligent living beings, would seriously challenge many of the existing preconceptions.

At present, as Monod has eloquently explained, the process of evolution is believed to be entirely the result of "chance," "necessity," and "random adaptations," rather than the result of any kind of purposive behavior. If life were abundant within the universe, or even if it was simply more widely distributed than is presently known, that would argue strongly in favor of some kind of replicating mechanism, to put it no stronger, which in turn implies at least an inbuilt principle of design. To Monod and those who share his views this is almost as unpalatable as the notion of the creation of the universe by an act of God.

It is not easy to see why the neo-Darwinians cling so desperately to the dogma of a purposeless universe. They believe in physical laws that apply throughout the cosmos, even ones whose very validity is increasingly coming under attack; they observe purposive actions in humans, animals, and even plant and mineral life. Yet they refuse to entertain the idea that this clear and unequivocal evidence of purpose, of an existence in which certain goals are pursued, exists in the natural world, in spite of the incontrovertible proof that it does.

The irony is that they genuinely believe that they are being cool, rational, hard-headed, and scientific by adopting this approach. The sad reality is that they are behaving exactly like those people who refused to look through Galileo's telescope and gave him the choice of denying his theories about the universe or being burnt at the stake. Such attitudes hardly represent a truly scientific approach to the discovery of knowledge and establishing the truth of what is and is not real within the universe.

INTELLIGENT DESIGN AGAIN

We have already seen that Dawkins is prepared to entertain the notion of "intelligent alien design." This idea strikes right at the heart of orthodox biological thinking. Apart from the other objections that have been raised against it the idea runs the risk of falling foul of what is known as an "infinite regress."

Basically, the infinite regress is like the child's question: If "x" caused "y," what was the cause of "x"? The infinite regress is that ultimately, however far back in the chain we go when seeking to establish a "first cause," nothing corresponding to such a principle ever seems to be discovered. This is one of the biggest logical arguments against what is known as the "cosmological argument" for the existence of God.

The cosmological argument claims that every event has a cause and, therefore, there must have been a first cause, God. For many centuries, that view was put forward by many fine minds, but it has long since been shown to be logically invalid. Apart from the fact that quantum physics has demonstrated that it is not the case that every event is preceded by its cause, the infinite regress proves logically that if every event has a cause then the idea of an "uncaused" first cause is a contradiction in terms. If every event does not have a cause then the whole basis of the claim that a "first cause" is necessary falls to the ground. Either way, the cosmological argument is logically invalid.

If, as Dawkins for instance now seems willing to accept, aliens from other worlds "seeded" and even "designed" life on our planet, that notion also has to face the challenge of the infinite regress. Perhaps life on earth did develop elsewhere and was then planted on our planet by extraterrestrials. If so, from where did they receive their DNA? Was it a case that life arose spontaneously elsewhere by pure chance and that aliens saw to it that it sprang up on our own planet?

Surely this is a redundant hypothesis. If Occam's Razor is sufficient reason for Dawkins to rule out the existence of God, why do we need to assume that DNA arose on another world by pure chance and was then "seeded" and "designed" upon Earth? If alien life exists, as seems virtually certain, that surely points to a different explanation, that the DNA code and life itself is distributed throughout the universe, rather than being unique to simply one planet. That is surely the most logical explanation.

Whatever its source, it seems virtually certain that DNA and life must exist on a large scale throughout the universe. Why should we assume it is only found on Earth?

CHANCE AND NECESSITY

Chance and necessity, according to the neo-Darwinians, are the two principles that govern the operation of the universe. The most exact and invariable physical laws that apply throughout the cosmos are nothing more than pure chance. So, too, is the intricate structure of DNA, the atmosphere of our planet, and every aspect of any activity throughout the universe. It is all pure luck and there is nothing but random fortune in the whole history of the universe.

How necessity, the physical laws governing the behavior of planets, the laws that control the functioning of the body and brain of humans, the laws on the basis of which our products are designed and upon which they operate, all these and other aspects of life could be so apparently determined and invariable and yet be the accidental result of pure luck, is never coherently explained. Even Monod, whose defense of necessity is more rigorous than perhaps any of his fellow disciples, does not satisfactorily explain the existence of order within the universe. His "explanation" is that we are simply uniquely fortunate.

How is it that if nothing but chance has led to such an intricate and complex balance and pattern of forces and forms, do we find any sort of order rather than utter randomness and chaos wherever we turn? Perhaps the question should rather be how such apparent order and complexity could arise out of sheer good fortune. Some scientists have attempted to provide answers to that challenging obstacle.

CATASTROPHE THEORY

René Thom is the founder of this branch of science.[26] It is one of the most exciting new areas of research and contains some of the most radical breaks with established scientific thinking since the arrival of quantum physics and relativity. Catastrophe theory deals with sudden changes of state or form of organisms and shows how these rapid alterations in state or form, that are apparently random in nature, actually obey clear and defined physical laws and seem to show evidence of purposive activity rather than being purely chance occurrences.

CHAOS THEORY

Every bit as radical and challenging as catastrophe theory, chaos science displays how phenomena that appear to be random and chaotic actually display underlying principles of order. It shows that the very concept of chaotic activity is a contradiction in terms and that all activity appears to display purposive behavior.[27]

LIFE FIELDS

Biochemist Rupert Sheldrake created such a stir with his first publication that the scientific journal *Nature* was sufficiently outraged to denounce it as "a book for burning."[28] Such an extraordinary response from scientists to a radically new theory is almost unprecedented. It is difficult to find any parallel in the scientific world other than the Nazis denunciation of relativity as being "Jewish physics" and the attempts by those scientists who distrusted the theory to have it banned under the Nazis.

Sheldrake found that "life fields" appeared to exist within nature that showed clear evidence of organization and purposive, directed development and evolution. His theories remain controversial, in spite of the fact that, so far, every single scientific experiment that has been carried out to test his hypothesis has vindicated his theories.

THE HOLOGRAPHIC UNIVERSE

This theory, which arose out of the discovery of holography in the 1960s, was put forward independently by David Bohm[29] and Karl Pribram.[30] Both men spent a considerable amount of time studying a number of problems in physics and came to the conclusion that the majority of them could be solved, or at least explained, more satisfactorily if the notion of the universe as a giant hologram was adopted.

This theory is strikingly similar to some of the accounts given by contactees. Many of the strange environments described by them are specifically compared with holograms. As further research is conducted on the human brain, the extent to which in many ways it seems to resemble holographic processes is striking.

Once again, the extent to which purpose, organization, and direction exist within the universe is demonstrated clearly. Wherever we look, in every aspect and area of life, clear and indisputable evidence of purpose striving towards an end, of design, exists. The fear that the preferred Gods of chance and necessity may not be able to fulfill the tasks assigned to them leads some neo-Darwinians to show hostility toward the abundant evidence, suggesting that their dogmas are seriously in need of revision.

PURPOSE-DRIVEN EVOLUTION

What all these researches seem to point to is a cycle of evolution that is driven and directed by an internal purpose, a seeking after some kind of result. The technical term for this is "teleology" and it is increasingly being believed that a teleologically-driven evolutionary mechanism is at work throughout the universe whereby organisms (and human/alien life among them) reach out towards a goal.

This idea is currently coming back into favor after being rejected for the last hundred years or so. Perhaps the most complex, breath-taking, and compelling presentation of the teleological viewpoint was put forward by Samuel Alexander. He spoke of the universe as having "a nisus towards Deity," a tendency to evolve to ever greater complexity and to a higher level of development and intelligence. In Alexander's theories, life is a continuous evolutionary process, its ultimate goal being to bring God to birth. Alexander sees God as the ultimate goal of the universe, the end towards which it strives and the purpose of everything that happens within it. Rather than being the creator of the universe, Alexander sees God as its final realization.[31]

Although they approach the question from very different perspectives, both Alexander and scientists like Paul Davies, David Bohm, and Karl Pribram, find the whole notion of a universe without purpose, design, and the principle of teleology underpinning the whole basis of life inconceivable, even incomprehensible.

ANCIENT WISDOM

It is now time to take stock of our discoveries. We have seen ample evidence that in days long gone the Star Dwellers walked upon our own Earth. That time is still remembered among humans as the Golden Age.

When the Gods walked among us, they shared their knowledge with humans. When we lost sight of them, all that remained were myths, legends, and curious customs that spoke of a tradition now lost to us. We called it the Ancient Wisdom.

Though only fragments of the lost learning remain, enough pieces exist for us to be able to put together some parts of the jigsaw. We know it involved complex mathematical, astronomical, and engineering knowledge. It also involved the use of certain types of energy that are still unknown to us. It was additionally bound up with concepts of harmony and holism. When the Gods walked the Earth, and humans still held the key to ancient wisdom in their hands, the world was at peace with itself.

The Fall, which also saw the departure of the Gods, left humanity groping in the darkness for wisdom. Only the dimly remembered fragments of the lost learning were able to carry them through this time of confusion and uncertainty. Even though the Gods from the Sky had gone, there remained the promise that they would return. Throughout history, there are many signs that, from time to time, they did. Since the explosion of the wave of UFOs following the dark days of the Second World War, they have visited Earth frequently.

THE AGE OF AQUARIUS AND THE RETURN OF THE STAR TRAVELERS

We are now in the Age of Aquarius and many ancient prophecies tell us that during this era the lost keys to Ancient Wisdom will be finally rediscovered. With the forgotten knowledge joined to our own, we will be able to go forward and build a civilization greater than any seen before.

It is also prophesied that, during that period, we will see the triumphant return of the Star Travelers. For centuries, they have sent us signs of their care and concern for the planet. The wave of UFOs that surfaced after the end of the Second World War marked a new era in human existence. We are waking up slowly to find ourselves in a New Age.

The new concern for the fate of the environment, the rise of new ideas, new therapies, new technology, new systems of social and economic organization, a new awareness of ourselves as dwellers upon Spaceship Earth: all these things are part of a growing awareness of our imminent future. We are becoming more conscious of the profound emptiness of our present lives and seeking desperately for a meaning and sense of purpose in our existence that seems forever to elude us when we try to find it.

Many turn their gaze inwards, seeking answers in yoga, meditation, new religions, and new quasi-religious therapies. Others fix their gaze steadily upon the stars, hoping or fearing intervention from outer space. Not through either the inner or outer way alone will we find the answers we seek. To recover the lost truths of the Ancient Wisdom and integrate them into our own personal and social lives, we must follow both an interior and exterior road. Both are necessary and neither is sufficient on their own. The Star Travelers are coming back to us at last and will help us make our voyages of discovery. They will guide us through the maze of inner and outer space and lead us towards a glorious and enlightened future.

SPACE SHUTTLE

For many years, the Space Shuttle was one of the most exciting ventures in the exploration of outer space. Its original concept was as a base from which further missions could be sent out and perhaps also to establish the possibility of permanent colonies in space.

The Space Shuttle program began on 12 April 1981, and continued until 21 July 2011. The first shuttle was *Columbia*, followed by *Challenger, Discovery, Atlantis* and *Endeavor*. It placed crews in orbit, launched satellites, and built the International Space Station. For many years, it was one of the most exciting and vibrant aspects of the space program, opening up at least the possibility of permanent human inhabitation of space.

The Shuttle arose at least partly out of the dreams of pioneering thinkers, such as Gerard O'Neill. He dreamed of establishing permanent colonies in space from which we could go on to explore and colonize planets and universes step by painstaking step.[32]

The Shuttle never realized O'Neill's dream of space colonization and it does not seem likely that it will be realized in the foreseeable future. The Shuttle also had more than its fair share of tragedy during its operation, claiming the lives of some of its astronauts. On 28 January 1986, all seven crew members were killed when *Challenger* disintegrated not long after its launch. On 1 February 2003, it disintegrated during its re-entry and once again all seven crew members on board were killed. This second tragedy, together with the rising economic costs of maintaining the program, led to the whole basis of the Shuttle being questioned by politicians anxious to cut spending. Eventually, their views prevailed and the Shuttle program ended.

An unmanned version of the Shuttle was considered during the 1980s, known as the Shuttle C. It was proposed to carry cargo into space, but the plans never came to fruition. Another idea was to make it carry paying passengers at a cost of 1.5 million dollars a seat, but that idea also fell by the wayside.

Shuttle, in particular, the Spacelab part of its program, made the collection of scientific data in space far simpler than previously. It brought much valuable data back to Earth where it was processed and ana lysed in laboratories. The Shuttle represented a huge contribution to extending our knowledge of space and of the origins of the universe. It was a sad day when *Atlantis* made its final landing at the Kennedy Space Center in Florida and brought to an end thirty years of cutting-edge research and space exploration.

THE SHUTTLE REPLACEMENT

The *X-378* is a reconnaissance vehicle described as being a replacement for the Shuttle. It is a military spy craft that carries out aerial surveys over regions of the world in which the US military and intelligence agencies are interested. In 22 April 2010, it was blasted into space by the Atlas rocket, which itself then went into orbit around the Sun.[33]

Boeing has also become involved in developing a successor to the Shuttle that will be capable of flying people to the International Space Station. At the moment, it is designed only for that purpose, but who knows what the future might bring?[34]

THE JUPITER PROBE

On 5 August 2011, NASA launched its most ambitious unmanned mission to date. The probe Juno left Earth on a voyage to discover at least some of the secrets of Jupiter.[35] Juno was planned to arrive on Jupiter by 2016 and its mission was to study the planet's atmosphere, its magnetic field, the core of the planet, and its auroras. NASA believes that Juno will teach us about the formation and development of the solar system and provide the answers to many unanswered scientific questions.

According to Scott Bolton of NASA:

> JUPITER HOLDS SECRETS ABOUT HOW THE SOLAR SYSTEM FORMED. IF WE WANT TO GO BACK IN TIME AND UNDERSTAND WHERE WE CAME FROM AND HOW THE PLANETS WERE MADE, JUPITER HOLDS THIS SECRET. JUPITER WAS LIKELY THE FIRST PLANET TO FORM, AND BY LEARNING MORE ABOUT THE EARLIEST STEPS IN THE HISTORY OF THE SOLAR SYSTEM, WE LEARN ABOUT OUR HISTORY, TOO. BY GOING BACK TO SQUARE ONE WITH JUPITER, WE GET TO UNDERSTAND HOW WE GOT HERE.[36]

Juno will investigate how much water exists on the planet, why it has such large magnetic fields, and whether or not there is a solid core beneath its atmosphere. It will also try to measure how deep the famous "red spot" on Jupiter is. We know already that it is over 15,000 miles wide. Whatever secrets the planet holds, NASA is hopeful that Juno will uncover them. This latest mission to one of the remotest planets in the solar system represents perhaps the most ambitious space project since the lunar landings.

SUMMARY

We have now come to the end of our research. In a short summary, we will draw together all that we have learned and establish what the true meaning is of the many visitations by the Star Travelers to our planet. What do they mean? Why are they coming among us? And do they bring any kind of message with them from a more advanced civilization? These and other questions will be briefly examined in the Conclusion.

ENDNOTES: CHAPTER TEN

[1] "Millions of Chinese stunned after government makes Obama UFO statement," *EU Times*, 23 January 2011.

[2] Ibid.

[3] Axel Bojanowski, "High Speed Geology: Violent Seismic Activity Tearing Africa in Two," *Der Spiegel*, 20 January 2011.

[4] "Obama ET UFO Disclosure Announcement Rescheduled for September 11/11," www.youtube.com/watch?v=IgDEOd2sc08.

[5] Dr. Michio Kaku, "Kaku Says Virginia Earthquake Should Be A Wake-Up Call," *Washington Post*, 23 August 2008.

[6] David Gardner, "Earth to get 'second sun' as supernova turns night into day," *Daily Mail*, 10 March 2011.

[7] Paul Rincon, "Dinosaur extinction link to crater confirmed," BBC News, 4 March 2010.

[8] "A New Wrinkle: Comet Strikes in the 1980s and 1990s Left Ripples in Jupiter's and Saturn's Rings," John Matson, *Scientific American*, 31 March 2011.

[9] "The LHC will implode the Moon or PUT OUT THE SUN," Lewis Page, www.theregister.co.uk/ 3 March 2010.

[10] Ibid.

[11] "2012 AD—Mayan Calendar Galactic Alignment," by Keith Hunter, www.ancient-mysteries-com/ 2008.

[12] "Will Earth pass through the galactic plane in 2012?" by Bruce McClure, http://earthsky.org/astronomy-essentials ,25 January 2011.

[13] "2012: No Killer Solar Flare," Ian O'Neill, www.universetoday.com/, June 21, 2008.

[14] "The New Ice Age: Climate change could slow as sun simmers down," David Derbyshire, *Daily Mail*, 17 June 2011.

[15] "Scientist: Black Hole Has Breached Earth's Core," http://beforeitsnews.com, 6 June 2011.

[16] "Earth Changes and the Pole Shift," Gerard Zwaan, http://poleshift.ning.com/, 30 October 2010.

[17] "Earth as a Gas Giant," Adam, http://crowlspace.com/, 29 March 2011.

[18] "Deadly Microbes from Outer Space," Barry E DeGregorio, *Discover Magazine*, February 2008.

[19] "Great Moments in Science," Dr. Karl, www,abc.net.au, 15 April 2008.

[20] "French village which will 'survive 2012 Armageddon' plagued by visitors," Henry Samuel, *Daily Telegraph*, 21 December 2010.

[21] Tom Mawby Cole and Vera Carson Reid, *Gods in the Making: Man and the Law of Continuity*, Andrew Dakers, 1939.

[22] James Lovelock, *Gaia: A New Look at Life on Earth*, OUP, 2000.

[23] Sabri Iskender, *Mysteries of the Universe*.

[24] Michael FitzGerald, *Hitler's Occult War*, Robert Hale, 2009; Nicholas Roerich, *Altai-Himalaya*, Jarrolds, 1930; Nicholas Roerich, *Himalayas: Abode of Light*, David Marlowe, 1947 ; Alexandra David-Neal, *With Mystics and Magicians in Tibet*, Bodley Head, 1931.

[25] Vallée, Magonia.

[26] David Aubin, "Forms of Explanations in the Catastrophe Theory of René Thom: Topology, Morphogenesis, and Structuralism," in *Growing Explanations: Historical Perspective on the Sciences of Complexity*, ed. M. N. Wise, Durham: Duke University Press, 2004, 95-130.

[27] Alligood, K. T., Sauer, T., and Yorke, J.A., *Chaos: an introduction to dynamical systems*, Springer-Verlag New York, LLC, 1997.

[28] Rupert Sheldrake, *A New Science of Life*, J. P. Tarcher, 1981.

[29] David Bohm, *Wholeness and the Implicate Order*, Routledge, 1980.

[30] Karl Pribram, (ed.), *Origins: brain and self organization*, Lawrence Erlbaum, 1994.

[31] Samuel Alexander, *Space, Time and Deity*, Macmillan, 1920

[32] Gerard O'Neill, *The High Frontier: Human Colonies in Space,* William Morrow, 1977.

[33] William J. Broad, "Surveillance Suspected as Spacecraft's Main Role," *New York Times*, 22 May 2010.

[34] Fox News, 28 June 2010.

[35] Andrew Hough, "Juno: NASA's $1.1bn probe heads to Jupiter to unlock solar system secrets," *Daily Telegraph*, 5 August 2011.

[36] Ibid.

CONCLUSION

The mystery of UFOs has fascinated humans since the end of the Second World War. Even ancient people appear to have seen and experienced extraterrestrial contact or sightings of one sort of another. Perhaps now as our own capacity to explore and communicate with world beyond our own grows and development we may be standing on the brink of one of the most momentous events in all human history: definite proof of the existence of life on other planets.

With increasingly violent natural disasters, a growing inability to cope with the effects of often reckless technological development, economic problems, new bacterial infections from outer space, perhaps the enormous wave of sightings and contacts between humans and extraterrestrials in recent years is now pointing the way towards a possible intervention in the affairs of our planet by aliens to rescue us from the consequences of our present actions.

Why are increasing numbers of Star Travelers coming to Earth? It could be to rescue us from imminent danger, to conquer our planet, or to bring us some kind of message, perhaps a deeply spiritual one.

It is possible that more of them are coming because their own technology may have advanced considerably since the early days of their visits. On the other hand, it could simply be that we have become more aware of their presence, and that in the past their visits were overlooked or misrepresented as being angels or similar types of beings.

Their motives for coming to Earth remain unclear. If they were simply coming to our planet in order to enslave us or destroy our world, surely, as a more advanced species than our own, they would already possess the capability to take over the planet as easily as, say, Europeans were able to subdue the inhabitants of Australia, North America, or Africa, which makes the idea of conquest or destruction at the hands of alien invaders seem unlikely.

If they have come to bring us some kind of message, what could that be? The claims of contactees seem fairly consistent in that respect. The aliens appear to be deeply troubled by our warlike behavior and our lack of care and stewardship towards natural resources upon the planet. They also appear to be anxious to push us in a more "spiritual" direction, but not necessarily in terms of established religion. Their desire appears to be for us to look at the world and the universe around us in a new spirit and with a different attitude.

Perhaps they have come to Earth to remind us of the forgotten truths of Ancient Wisdom, the laws of continuity and change, the Earth itself, and the wider universe as all part of a living organism. Perhaps they want to save us from ourselves and the consequences of our own greed, folly, short-sightedness, and lack of care for the planet we inhabit.

The year 2012 was not the end of the world, but perhaps it really was the end of an age. If so, it may just be that what is to come will be the beginning of a new and higher phase, not simply of human civilization, but of evolution on the planet and maybe even throughout the universe. Even if the proposed date for this event may be exact, it seems increasingly certain that at some time in the very distant future, the Earth really will be entering a new and unimaginable era. The existence of extraterrestrial life will be established beyond a doubt and direct human-alien contact at every level will make the world we know at present utterly transformed.